MORE PRAISE FOR ASIAN ECLIPSE: EXPOSING THE DARK SIDE OF BUSINESS IN ASIA (1st Edition)

"This book uncovers a great deal which Asian companies and governments would like to remain underwraps."

Steve Vines
Author of *The Year of Living Dangerous–Asia: From Financial Crisis to the New Millennium*

"Backman has uncovered a vast amount of hard-to-find information. On top of that, he has brought these characters to life and provides a crucial missing link in the coverage of business in Asia."

Justin Doebele
Forbes Global

"This book gathers together, like no other volume I've seen, a stupendous catalogue of business shortcomings and outright commercial mischief occurring in Asia during the long years of unparalleled prosperity."

James Clad
Professor of Asian Studies
Georgetown University
Author of *Behind the Myth: Business, Money and Power in Southeast Asia*

"*Asian Eclipse* helps to put Asian risks into their proper perspective. The region still offers great potential, but realizing that potential will not be nearly as easy as many were assuming. This book shows with numerous examples the major obstacles that stand in the way."

Robert C Broadfoot
Founder and Managing Director
Political and Economic Risk Consultancy, Ltd (PERC)

"Michael Backman's book offers some penetrating insights into the seamier side of Asian business...The work also offers a rare glimpse into the highly successful though often secretive, overseas Chinese business networks worldwide."

Rosalie L Tung
Professor of International Business
Simon Fraser University

D0035053

ASIAN ECLIPSE

Exposing the Dark Side of Business in Asia

Revised edition

ASIAN ECLIPSE

Exposing the Dark Side of Business in Asia

Michael Backman

Revised edition

John Wiley & Sons (Asia) Pte Ltd

Singapore • New York • Chichester • Brisbane • Toronto • Weinheim

This publication is designed to provide accurate and authoritative information in
regard to the subject matter covered. It is sold with the understanding that the publisher
is not engaged in rendering professional services. If professional advice or other expert
assistance is required, the services of a competent professional person should be sought.

Other Wiley Editorial Offices

John Wiley & Sons, Inc., 605 Third Avenue, New York, NY 10158-0012, USA
John Wiley & Sons Ltd, Baffins Lane, Chichester, West Sussex PO19 1UD, England
John Wiley & Sons (Canada) Ltd, 22 Worcester Road, Rexdale, Ontario M9W 1L1, Canada
John Wiley & Sons Australia Ltd, 33 Park Road (PO Box 1226), Milton, Queensland 4046,
Australia
Wiley-VCH, Pappelallee 3, 69469 Weinheim, Germany

Library of Congress Cataloging-in-Publication Data:

Backman, Michael, 1967–
    Asian Eclipse: Exposing the Dark Side of Business in Asia/Michael Backman—Rev.
    and updated ed.
        p.   cm.
     Includes bibliographical references and index.
     ISBN 0-471-47912-8
        1. Corporate culture — Asia.   2. Industrial management — Asia.   3. Business
    enterprises — Asia.   I. Title.

    HD58.7.B342   2001
    338.095—dc21   00-052866

Typeset in 10/12 point, Palatino by Linographic Services Pte Ltd
Printed in Singapore by Craft Print Pte Ltd
10 9 8 7 6 5 4 3 2 1

For Lance and Betty Chinner

Contents

Introduction

Planet Hollywood is an American icon. But one of the major owners of the worldwide restaurant chain lives in South-East Asia. In fact, given all the hype, it might come as a surprise to learn that Arnold Schwarzenegger, Bruce Willis, and Demi Moore don't control the company. The real force behind Planet Hollywood — the man who bankrolled it in its early days and who until late 1998 controlled around a quarter of its stock — is Ong Beng Seng of Singapore.

The Stars and Stripes have become synonymous with the perfume and jeans empire of designer Tommy Hilfiger, but Hilfiger owns very little of the company that bears his name. Silas Chou of Hong Kong is the main force behind Tommy Hilfiger.

Nothing could be more American than the wood-fired, oven-roasted chicken and honey-baked beans of the restaurant chain Kenny Rogers' Roasters. But country music star Kenny Rogers doesn't own the chain of almost 200 stores worldwide that bears his name either. Vincent Tan of Malaysia does.

Laura Ashley and Crabtree & Evelyn, two names that are synonymous with English style, aren't controlled from England but from Malaysia. The first by Khoo Kay Peng and the second by Lee Oi Hian.[1]

When super-models Naomi Campbell, Claudia Schiffer, and Elle Macpherson ventured to Jakarta in late 1996 to open Asia's first Fashion Café, they chose several locals to be their partners. But one of them has since turned out to be distinctly unfashionable — Titiek Prabowo — the middle daughter of Indonesia's then-president, Soeharto.

Western icons, Asian owners — such are the fruits of the global marketplace. And these days, the Asian owners are from South-East Asia as much as they are from Japan. Economic meltdown or not, Asia is important to the West. It's been that way for centuries. 'Whoever is lord of Malacca has his hand on the throat of Venice,' dramatically intoned Tomé Pires in 1515, the leader of the first official European mission to China, after visiting Malacca in what is now Malaysia.[2]

GETTING RICH AND STAYING THAT WAY

What does an economy need for sustained prosperity? These are some basic rules that hold around the world. There must be:

1

- effective standards of corporate governance to ensure that managers and the controlling shareholders do the right thing by other investors;
- a high degree of corporate transparency and adequate external auditing;
- efficient stock exchanges;
- markets that are either competitive or under the constant threat that they might face real competition;
- legal frameworks that are efficient and transparent, with judicial systems to enforce the rules credibly and without favor;
- a clear distinction between regulators and the regulated;
- banking systems that are independent, transparent, and competitive; and
- a well-resourced, inquisitive, and independent media.

With perhaps the notable exception of Singapore, Hong Kong, and to a lesser degree, Taiwan, these principles aren't generally adhered to in Asia. In fact, many Asian political and business leaders have gone out of their way to eschew them. Asia, somehow, is 'different' and, therefore, doesn't need the checks and balances, and accountability that the rest of the world needs; these aren't compatible with the consensual 'Asian way' — or at least, that's the argument.

BUSINESS THE ASIAN WAY

Corporate Asia can be a full frontal assault on one's senses, especially if one is used to orderly markets, transparency, and the rule of law. The first shock is Asia's companies — not so much their size, but their scope. Many have grown into conglomerates because the owners seized opportunities that were there, rather than those that matched their fields of expertise. Asia's big business groups may be large but they are rarely integrated; their tentacles reach out randomly rather than in a complementary manner. Standards of corporate governance and transparency are poor in some Asian countries, as are management and the level of disclosure. Auditing and accounting practices may be of low quality and may not be comparable to those in the West. Laws in several countries are rendered inoperable by petty bribery and favoritism. Bankruptcy codes aren't enforced in many countries, so that sick companies don't die, they just spread their disease.

The appalling state of the legal framework across much of Asia means that commerce has yet to rise above economic tribalism. The most prominent 'tribe' is the region's overseas Chinese. Asia's leaders might talk about the importance of community, but in reality, Asia is dominated

2

by communalism. If one doesn't belong to a commercially powerful tribe, the best way to get a piece of the action is to forge links with the political elite and leverage on these connections. So, in much of Asia, the mixture of business and politics has not so much given rise to the lobbyist as it has to the crony capitalist.

Abuses meted out to minority shareholders in much of Asia (those shareholders that don't have a connection with the controlling shareholder) mean that the underlying value of a company's assets isn't the best way to value its shares. Instead, the quality of its management, the actions of its controlling shareholder, and its level of disclosure are more relevant criteria. Strong cash flow is one thing, but if it flows into the controlling shareholder's back-pocket at the expense of other shareholders, then it's quite another. And all of this is against a cultural backdrop that eschews accountability and checks and balances, but trumpets the benefits of consensus and collectivism. The lack of accountability allows too many of Asia's entrepreneurs to keep their profits and pass on their losses — to a bank, and ultimately its depositors, through bad loans, their minority shareholders, or the government for those with the right connections. Corporate Asia isn't a place for the foolhardy. Nor is it a place for the ill-informed.

GLOBALIZATION AND THE ASIAN WAY

In the age of globalization, the world is reduced to a single marketplace, which means there is just one set of rules. Asia can no longer afford to indulge in an 'Asian way' when it comes to business. The world's economies (even Asian ones) and the companies in them must march to the same tune. Asia may have its unique cultures and values, but at the end of the day, a crony is a crony, poor disclosure is poor disclosure, and a shonky bank is a shonky bank. Sound corporate governance, like 'virginity,' is a condition that is under constant threat from temptation. And in the age of global competition, sound corporate governance, like 'virginity,' refers to only one condition, whereas cronyism, poor corporate practice, and corruption each cover a multitude of sins. This book is an investigation into Asia's sins of cronyism, corporate malpractice, and corruption, and not the conditions of a fall from grace.[3] John Naisbitt, in his book, *Megatrends Asia*, describes the world's tallest towers, the 88-story twin Petronas Towers in Malaysia, as symbols of Asia's modernization. He couldn't have been more wrong. Composed mostly of elevator shafts because of their height, the towers are symbols of excess and inefficiency. The real Asian 'miracle' is that the region-wide economic crisis of 1997–98 didn't happen earlier. The problem for Asia now is just how many of the bad old ways remain.

3

SECTION 1

THE FRAMEWORK

CHAPTER 1

Bureaucrats, Bribery, and Bankruptcy

High-level corruption is present in many Asian countries, but a far greater threat is petty corruption. From China to Indonesia, even the best-drafted laws are rendered useless by low-level bribery. At fault is low pay in the civil service — from the judges down — and insufficient penalties for the culprits.

orruption exists everywhere. It's how it is treated that counts. It is no accident that in South-East Asia the two countries with the highest standards of living — Singapore and Malaysia — also have the best legal systems. (Brunei, with its oil reserves and 'Shellfare' state, is an aberration.) The country with the lowest living standards — Indonesia — also has the most corrupt, inefficient, and poorly enforced legal system. There is a clear message in this, but much of Asia has been slow to catch on. Good laws mean good living — although good laws alone aren't enough. They must be enforced. Business environments that aren't governed by sound legal codes and that offer investors little protection tend to be those where personal connections and relationships (*guanxi*, as the Chinese call them) are most important. Personal connections with local politicians or local big business players can offer a measure of security that is otherwise denied by the legal system in such environments. Once the local legal system becomes more watertight, the need to establish personal relationships to cover one's investments is less necessary. The trouble with economies where laws are inadequate and the need for connections is high, is that, usually, only the locals have the connections; this constitutes a high barrier to entry for foreign investors. Investing in such countries without legal protection and strong local connections is a bit like walking into a strange room at night without turning on the lights. Steps must be tentatively taken to soften the blow of an almost inevitable impact.

Economies cannot maintain their high growth if the only way to invest in them is through personal connections. Eventually, all the connections become satiated and the investment dries up. Sound laws don't exhaust themselves; connections do. Thailand and Indonesia discovered this after several years of record investment. They reacted to Asia's 1997–98 economic crisis by drawing up new business laws and codes. Often, there was little wrong with the old ones — they simply weren't enforced. The new laws seemed to be drawn up to appease foreign institutions such as the International Monetary Fund (IMF) than to achieve any practical purpose. Having seen the new laws enacted, the IMF then ticked the box and handed over the next installment of emergency loans, without considering if these new laws would be effective. In most cases they will not be, because it is the culture of corruption that is the problem, not the laws. The well-worn Asian ruse of form over content had paid off yet again.

THE LAW OF THE JUNGLE

Asia's legal systems are various and complex — a legacy of different cultural and historical backgrounds. It isn't possible to provide a definitive account of the region's legal systems in this book; instead, what follows is a sample.

As far as business litigation is concerned, the legal systems of Singapore and Malaysia are about as good as they can be, given both countries' economic positions. Like Hong Kong's legal codes, both are modeled on the British case law system, although both have done away with jury trials; instead, judges make decisions. Whether trial by judge or by jury is preferable is the subject of ongoing debate. However, both have something that most other legal systems in Asia don't have: speedy and transparent legal processes — and speed is of essence when it comes to business. Malaysia's legal system isn't overly resourced, but it is relatively open and free of corruption.

That's the good news. The legal systems of the rest of South-East Asia offer little encouragement to foreign investors or anyone else. Thailand's legal system is a mess and Indonesia's, a complete mess. In both countries, business people don't usually bother to take matters to court; it simply isn't worth it. Legal processes are archaic, marked by arbitrariness; and once hearings have concluded, there is no certainty as to when a decision might be delivered. Moreover, due legal process in both countries, very often, offers more — not less — uncertainty. Furthermore, judges are paid notoriously low, which not only makes them more susceptible to corruption but also implies that their average quality isn't particularly high. In Indonesia, when a decision is finally delivered, it may comprise little more than the decision. Sometimes it is accompanied by some legal or logical reasoning, but often it isn't. Judgments might well be based on public opinion as much as on anything else — and sometimes they are.[1] Also, judicial independence is barely aspired to, let alone the reality. If you are a foreign investor in Indonesia and have been defrauded by your local partner who happens to be a son or daughter of the president or someone else of note, you can certainly forget about redress through the court system. In fact, you can forget about redress at all. Usually, foreign and local partners are able to coexist if it is to their long-term mutual benefit. Knowledge of future payoffs is a good enforcer of current agreements. But when circumstances change and the foreign partner has outlived its usefulness, written contacts begin to be worth less and less. Grievances are solved best by arbitration and, failing that, they are best forgotten. Leveraging on personal connections is the best method of enforcing contracts and avoiding problems. But these connections usually must have true depth and must go beyond simply 'knowing' someone. In Asia, having someone's business card doesn't constitute having a connection with them; having been in the same class at university often does.

The Philippines is at the other end of the scale in terms of the willingness to go to court. Liberal gun laws aren't the only thing that the Philippines inherited from the United States, its former de facto ruler. A fondness for litigation is another. The Philippine legal system is modeled on that of the United States; it even uses U.S. legal precedence. However, like much of Asia, the Philippines doesn't have a jury system for criminal cases; judges make decisions alone. Nuisance and harassment cases are common. A 1996 study of 74 multinationals found that, collectively, they had 1,200 legal cases pending — an average of 16.2 per company — only 35% of which had been initiated by the company. Almost half of these cases had been pending for more than five years and some for as long as 12 years.[2] Initiating legal action in the Philippines is easy compared to, say, Thailand or Indonesia, where it is a chore. However, in terms of outcome, the Philippine system can be almost as frustrating and ineffectual.

But perhaps the last word on attempting to enforce contracts in the face of inadequate legal structures should come from a senior business manager of the Shan State Army whom I met in Rangoon, Burma (Myanmar), in late 1998. For decades, the army has been fighting for independence of Shan State from Rangoon, so it cannot exactly rely on the country's courts and the legal system. Over black tea and betel nut, I asked the manager how, then, does he deal with aberrant business partners. His method although very effective, leaves little room for appeal: he invites them to Shan State and then waits for their car to pass through a mountain ravine, where he can blast it with a rocket launcher. This is no idle threat. In the early 1990s, the Shan State Army captured much of the arsenal of the infamous drug lord, Khun Sa. Also in the haul were about a dozen Stinger missiles.

COPYRIGHT AND TRADEMARK PROTECTION

The lack of protection of intellectual property is one of the more mundane consequences of an unsound legal system. China is routinely presented in the world's media as a habitual abuser of copyright protection, but it is far from alone. Copyright is a perennial problematic issue for many Asian governments. It is a complex issue, but very often there is a lack of will on the part of many Asian governments to enforce international copyright protection. Form over content is as important as ever: many Asian governments, when challenged on the issue in the international arena, hold up as their defense their first-class copyright laws but conveniently forget their record on enforcement.

Services are undervalued in Asia. Tangible items are valued; intangibles less so. This is partly cultural. Legal advice, marketing, and accounting are all under-acquired by many Asian companies. Intellectual property is no different. Why pay for it when it can be had for free? Royalty payments and licensing fees just make no sense to many Asian entrepreneurs, especially those from the old school. Also, observing copyright means paying due deference to the owners of the copyright — but very often they are anonymous and have no connection with the potential copyright abuser. So, it isn't surprising that copyright owners receive the treatment they do in Asia. Anonymity is tantamount to irrelevance.

Industrial producers in Asia often use pirated software, chemicals, production designs, and pharmaceuticals — often without even realizing that they are doing anything wrong. The proportion of unlicensed software in use in China is estimated to be no less than 96%. The estimate for Indonesia is 93%, Thailand 84%, the Philippines 83%, and Malaysia 70%.[3]

Counterfeit merchandise is rampant in Asia despite high-profile international efforts to stamp it out. Even in Singapore, one is occasionally offered fake Rolex watches while strolling down Orchard Road, the city's main shopping boulevard. The night markets of Kuala Lumpur, Penang, Chiang Mai, Jakarta, Bali, Guangzhou, Saigon, and elsewhere in Asia are still filled with watches, lighters, clothing, and perfumes that sport unlicensed brand names. Pirated versions of newly released videos, compact discs, and software such as *Microsoft Windows* and *Office* can all be easily had for the asking. Rather than break trademark laws outright, manufacturers sometimes circumvent them by slightly modifying existing brand names. And it isn't only U.S. and European brand names that are targeted. Executives from Hitachi of Japan once found that their competition in Indonesia included electronic products marked 'Hitachin' and 'Mitachi.'[4]

In 1991, Indonesia introduced changes that it said would help guard against copyright and trademark abuse in response to rising concerns around the world about Asia's performance in the matter. But it didn't try very hard. Three years later, it played host to one of the most bizarre cases of trademark infringement probably ever seen. An Indonesian company that had produced fake Pierre Cardin leather goods successfully sued the French designer himself in an Indonesian court for breaching *its* trademark. The company had registered Cardin's name and logo in Indonesia as its own and claimed that the designer, by selling genuine Pierre Cardin articles in Indonesia, was infringing on its rights. The French designer, understandably, was incredulous and incensed. He flew personally to Jakarta to make his case. The same Indonesian company also successfully sued Dunhill and Levi-Strauss on the same basis. It turned out that the company, one of Indonesia's biggest leather goods manufacturers, had taken local trademarks on at least 100 famous overseas brand names.[5] Not all Indonesian companies accrued brands for their own manufacturing. Many simply registered foreign names and logos locally and then waited for the products to be sold in Indonesia. As soon as they were sold, the local trademark owner would threaten the foreign company with legal action. Rather than face the hassle and uncertainties of a case that might take years to wind its way through Indonesia's courts, the foreign companies invariably settled out of court — which was precisely what the locals were after. Infringements as gross as this have now largely ceased — some credit is due to Indonesia for the advances it has made in trademark protection in recent years, but there is still some way to go.

PETTY CORRUPTION

Confucianism is sometimes accused of promoting corruption in East Asia. Individuals are morally expected to improve the welfare of their relatives and friends through their influence and contacts.[6] The Confucian preoccupation with reciprocity also plays a role. If one does another a favor, it is incumbent on the recipient to return it. Rules and laws are expressed in the vaguest terms in many East Asian countries, thus allowing for a fair degree of discretion on the part of civil servants. The selectivity forced on civil servants by vaguely worded laws means that every time they grant a license or approval, they are in effect giving a favor. If Confucianism has any relevance, it then confers on the recipient the obligation to return the favor, perhaps by way of a payment. To the idealized Confucian robot mercilessly thrust into a tangled web of reciprocity, such a payment is a gift. To the cynical Westerner, it is of course a bribe.

A bribe is a bribe, and whatever its cultural underpinnings, its effects are the same. Low-grade corruption is one of the biggest threats to law enforcement on Asia's streets and commercial sectors. It features in both the public and private sectors. In private companies, purchasing managers in many parts of Asia are given kickbacks for what they buy, secretaries are given 'presents' by airlines to ensure that they book their bosses on these airlines, and pension funds cut personnel managers in on commissions for signing up staff to these funds' financial planning programs. In the government sector, much of the petty corruption is borne from absurdly low levels of pay and involves small payments to officials to complete paperwork, provide information, and so on. Usually, it means paying the officials simply to do their job and not to break the rules. A government employee might, for example, process an investment approval application within two days or two months depending on the inducements offered for diligent work.

In some respects, this is an informal 'user pays' mechanism, where the users of government services top up government workers' salaries — those who use the service, pay for it. In theory, this sort of low-grade criminality might lead to greater economic efficiency. The payments are like a price that serves to ration demand. However, it also means that small payments can be used to jump queues, and time and resources are spent on negotiating precisely what 'fees' should be offered. Worse still, even the pettiest of bribes can add significantly to business costs occasionally, particularly if the cost of the delay or damage inflicted on business by government officials is out of proportion to the payments that the officials might hope to receive. In Thailand, the Philippines, China, Vietnam, and Indonesia in particular, the practice of paying government employees for their services is endemic. The following is a description of how rife the culture of petty corruption has become in Indonesia. Indonesia has been chosen simply because it is regularly assessed by business people in surveys to be the most, or close to being the most, corrupt country on earth.[7] And for most business people, it isn't the sometimes spectacular corruption of senior political figures that impinges most on their daily business, but the low-grade, petty corruption of the bureaucracy.

The 'Franchising' of the Government in Indonesia

There are almost 100 million people on the central Indonesian island of Java, most of whom are ethnically Javanese. Javanese culture has a very long history imbued with a mix of mystical, animist, and Islamic traditions. This cultural center also happens to be Java's geographic center where a number of important palaces (the *kratons*) survive. The *kratons* were the center of several sultanates. Polygamy ensured that the sultans had large families so that, today, a significant proportion of the Javanese people can claim some sort of link to a royal house. These are the *priyayi* — the noble — who historically didn't work. Their main function was to lord over the commoners and be the font of Javanese culture. Not only did they not work, but they had to be seen to avoid physical labor. Work was considered demeaning and coarse (*kasar*, as the Javanese say.) The *priyayi* survived by collecting rent from the property they owned and 'taxes' (disguised rent) on the monopolies and other privileges they granted. Commerce was seen as a 'lowly' occupation — something that was undertaken by the heathen (that is, the non-Moslem) Chinese. This can be seen in the location the Javanese chose to build their principal *kratons* — right in the middle of Java, i.e. as far away from the coast as possible, with all its unpleasant associations with trade and commerce.

There is an element of the *priyayi* culture, and those who aspire to it, that survives on Java to this day. Indeed, Javanese culture has evolved to be one of the most rent-seeking on earth. Today, the Javanese (and those imbued with Javanese culture) struggle not so much over production but over opportunities to make money that don't involve work. There is no equivalent of a Protestant work ethic, but more a Javanese rent-seeking ethic. Almost everyone seems to be at it — trying to get their 10% here, their gratuity there. One cannot park on the side of any public road in Jakarta without some self-appointed 'parking attendant' running over to extract Rp 2000 (about US$0.25 as at mid-2000) as one attempts to drive away. Any visit to a government office for information will almost certainly be met with a demand for 'photocopy' or 'cigarette' money. And when haggling over a price in a shop, shop attendants will regularly conspire with the customer against their employer and whisper to the customer the minimum price that they know their employer will accept if the customer is prepared to give them some 'commission' on the side.

Indonesia is also prone to rioting and looting — looting, after all, isn't about high-minded ideals such as political reform and 'people power'; it simply is about getting something for nothing. In May 1998, when Jakarta was the scene of the country's worst riots and looting in about 30 years, many expatriates and minority ethnic Chinese were desperate to make their way to Jakarta's international airport to flee the country. For the locals in the slums that surround the toll-road, the mass exodus represented one final opportunity to extract some 'commission.' They set up as many as six roadblocks on the way to the airport, stopping cars and demanding money from the occupants before allowing them to pass through. Fleeing Western expatriates simply had to pay up. Fleeing Indonesian-Chinese also had to endure taunts and threats of violence.

This endemic petty corruption forms the cultural backdrop to Indonesia's bureaucracy today. It also serves to explain the extraordinary corruption of Indonesia's political leaders.

There is a saying in Indonesia that if you call the police when you have a problem, you will only end up with more problems. It is no exaggeration to say that the Indonesian public have no confidence whatsoever in the police or in many other public officials. Most of the corruption is petty, and is more irritating than anything else. Being stopped by Jakarta's traffic police and asked for money is so commonplace, that it is soon forgotten. Relatively few people bother to insure the contents of their home. One reason for this is that insurance companies usually require a police statement if you are burgled, and that often means having to pay the police to turn up and then to file a report. The police might even choose to help themselves to your possessions for their trouble. Laws in Indonesia are, at best, arbitrary, and the local police take full advantage of this fact.

Sometimes, the corruption isn't so petty but is usually just as unsophisticated. In late 1995, the Jakarta branch of the Hongkong and Shanghai Banking Corporation (HSBC) received fake transfer orders by telex supposedly from several European banks. The branch duly transferred the money — US$34 million — to accounts at several local banks. The fraudsters then went to those banks and withdrew the money. By the time HSBC realized that it had been bilked, only US$7.7 million remained uncollected in one of the local banks, Unibank. HSBC contacted the authorities and instructed Unibank to hang on to the cash. The police took an immediate interest and demanded the impounding of the US$7.7 million as 'evidence.' The bank offered to provide a notarized copy of the transfer order instead. But no, only the cash would do. With uncustomary zeal at crime-solving, the police even threatened to arrest bank staff unless the cash was handed over.[8] The bank held out and eventually the police backed down — this time.

Many positions in Indonesia's bureaucracy are effectively 'auctioned.' These include the more desirable positions within the traffic police, customs and immigration departments, and court clerks. Junior officials must pay their superiors a quota from their earnings to secure these spots. They keep any money over and above the agreed quota raised from accepting bribes from members of the public. Those who fail to meet their quota are moved on in favor of those who can. Even Indonesia's embassies aren't immune to this. Some consular staff 'purchase' their positions around the world and use them to raise cash from members of the public who, for example, need to renew a visa to return to Indonesia. In order to avoid deliberate slow processing, many applicants have learned that they must pay an additional 'fee.' Most diplomats' postings are for three or four years, but it isn't uncommon for Indonesian diplomats to stay in a post for much longer than that. Sometimes, it is because they are exceptionally good at their jobs and are serving their country well. At other times, it is because they have 'purchased' the right to stay there, and use it to haul in cash.

Immigration officials at any of Indonesia's international airports frequently and brazenly ask for bribes from members of the public as they present their passports for stamping. Adjacent to the row of immigration counters at Jakarta's Soekarno-Hatta International Airport is a small room to which any foreigner or Indonesian national whose papers aren't in order is directed and where entry to Indonesia can routinely be purchased for as little as US$50. Indonesia's Chinese face enormous troubles here. Many still have uncertain citizenship and thus face great difficulty in obtaining the correct travel documents. Mostly, they are wealthy, have little political protection, and thus are easy picking for poorly paid immigration officials. Many don't even bother with the formality of lining up at the immigration counters — they matter-of-factly march straight over to the interrogation room, passport in one hand and wallet in the other.

Jail wardens too are well placed to collect lucrative, unofficial payments. On the rare occasion that important business people are jailed in Indonesia, they are often able to bribe themselves out on regular day release so that they can attend to work at their office during the day and return to jail at night. All of this is unofficial, of course, and relies on the prisoner returning to jail for the head count.

In May 1996, Eddie Tansil, Indonesia's highest-profile corporate convict at the time, escaped from jail. Tansil, an Indonesian-Chinese businessman, was convicted in 1994 of bribing Indonesian state bank officials to obtain US$430 million in unsecured loans. He later defaulted on almost all of them and was found guilty of effectively stealing US$620 million in loans and interest from the Indonesian government. Bribing state bank officials is nothing new in Indonesia; it happens with monotonous regularity. What was different about Eddie Tansil was that not only was he arrested for it, but he also actually went to jail. His imprisonment was something of a national atonement for the country's collective sins. So when it was revealed that his brush with what passes as the law in Indonesia had ended with his escape, the effect was cathartic. But how did Eddie Tansil, a convicted briber, escape from jail? Naturally, he bribed his way out! It took prison authorities a good number of days to raise the alarm that Tansil was missing. Why? For a fee, they had regularly allowed him out of jail to pursue his business activities, and on all the other occasions, he had returned. This time, they thought he must have been delayed and became concerned only after several days had elapsed. Rumors of Eddie Tansil sightings around Jakarta were frequent during his time in jail, and one businessman even swore that he had played a round of golf with the convict on the resort island of Bali. He had Tansil's business card to prove it. Tansil has since vanished altogether, and is rumored to be in either Taiwan, China, or the United States.

The guardians of Indonesia's national treasures are as susceptible as the country's guardians of prisoners when it comes to corrupt behavior. In 1996, several employees of the National Museum in Jakarta stole five paintings from the national collection. Among them was an important work by the Dutch-trained Javanese artist Raden Saleh (1807–80).[9] No one realized that they were missing until the donor of several of the paintings happened to flick through a catalog for a Christie's International auction of South-East Asian art in Singapore and recognized several of the lots as his donations. Understandably appalled, the donor raised the alarm and the culprits at the museum were identified and later put on trial. Christie's in Singapore withdrew the lots and admitted that it had made almost no check on the provenance of these paintings that would have ascertained whether they were stolen property.[10] The Indonesian media embarked on a self-indulgent orgy of blaming the rich foreign collectors for buying up Indonesia's heritage. But the real question is: Why are such poorly paid and thus potentially corrupt officials charged with guarding the National Museum's holdings? I, too, had a first-hand encounter with the willingness of some of the National Museum's staff to leverage the nation's treasures for the sake of private gain. When I arrived at the museum one day, only to find it unexpectedly closed, a guard at the entrance offered a 'special' tour of the museum, presumably for a 'special' price. I declined.

But what about the judiciary in Indonesia? The monthly salary of a judge with ten years of experience in a first-instance court in Jakarta was Rp 1.5 million, or about US$380, in mid-1997. By the end of that year, with the rupiah's depreciation, that monthly salary had shrunk to the equivalent of just US$160. I paid my driver more than that when I lived in Jakarta. Are judges corrupt? With salaries like that, they have little choice. Place two warring but wealthy companies in court with a judge who is paid so pitifully and you don't end up with a court case; you end up with an auction.

This much was acknowledged by a retiring Supreme Court judge, Asikin Kusumaatmadja, when he claimed that half of Indonesia's judges were corrupt. This figure was disputed by the chairman of the Indonesian Barristers Association who claimed that the real proportion was at least 90%.[11] The Supreme Court — Indonesia's highest court — has itself been riddled with corruption. One of its members, Adi Andojo Soetjipto, was forced out when he revealed that several Supreme Court judges had colluded with plaintiffs over a Jakarta land case that involved a bribe of at least US$500,000 in December 1995.

Just how endemically corrupt Indonesia's bureaucracy has become was made very clear in the following letter that was published in the Indonesian-language daily *Kompas* and again in the English-language *Jakarta Post*. It is worth repeating in its entirety and original form despite the writer's initial, typically Indonesian obliqueness:

Dear Sir

The law certainty can only find expression in the courts. It is advisable that law practitioners be involved in any workshop or hearing with the House of Representatives to determine, as far as possible, that law certainty can still serve its purpose.

It is absurd that judges should be subject to 'tour of duty' programs, while court clerks, who manage the administration of lawsuits, stay in the same positions for years and years, if necessary until retirement.

The Jakarta courts that are lucrative have been most desired by court clerks. Some court clerks in Jakarta may have worked for about 20 years in these courts, while their colleagues in the provinces must do with only their salaries. The former can live quite affluent lives because they have the opportunity to distribute law cases, arrange execution schedules and so forth.

To use plain, everyday language, they are referred to as rich clerks of the court.

It is high time the minister of justice took corrective action on the matter and gave a fair chance to court clerks in the provinces.

O.C. Kalgis
Jakarta

Yes, the writer was complaining about Jakarta-based court clerks having more bribe-taking opportunities than their provincial counterparts. And yes, rather than question the acceptance of bribes, the writer was really appealing to the justice minister to arrange things better so that provincial clerks could earn more through bribe-taking. The culture of petty corruption in Indonesia has reached the point where the allocation of bribe-taking opportunities has become a legitimate topic for public debate rather than the bribery itself!

THE BANKRUPTCY OF BANKRUPTCY IN ASIA

During the Asian economic crisis of 1997–98, the flood of assets for sale that many in the West had expected did not occur. There were not the fire sales and corporate bargains to be had. Why not? Because the most-affected parts of South-East Asia lacked well-enforced bankruptcy laws to prise insolvent assets from the hands of their owners.

The almost total inability in some countries of creditors to force delinquent borrowers into bankruptcy was in part both the cause of the crisis and then the savior of many of Asia's founding families. With this fundamental recourse denied to them, lenders have very little way of recovering what is rightfully theirs. Locals might resort to having their bad debtors beaten up, maimed, and sometimes killed. But that isn't the normal preferred recourse of legitimate Western lenders to Asia.

Filial piety and ancestor worship are very important in Chinese culture, and more broadly, although to a lesser degree, in most other Asian cultures. They present a cultural blockage to the introduction of decent bankruptcy laws. Going bankrupt is a loss of 'face' anywhere in the world, but if one is Asian, and especially if one is Chinese, it might well be an insult to one's ancestors. This tends to compound the personal devastation — after all, most firms in Asia are family-run and represent the cumulative efforts of not just the present generation, but that generation's ancestors as well.

Cultural nuances and other difficulties aside, bankruptcy laws exist in Asia and have existed for quite some time. The problem, as ever, is enforcement. The bankruptcy code that was in force in Indonesia until mid-1998 when new codes were rushed in to please the International Monetary Fund (IMF) were modeled on the Dutch Bankruptcy Act of 1896. It was old, but that didn't mean it was bad. It allowed for not just the liquidation of a defaulting company, but also for a court-supervised restructuring, somewhat akin to the Chapter 11 process of the United States where independent trustees manage insolvent companies while they are restructured under court supervision. As two Singapore-based lawyers, Emalia Achmadi and Jaap Trommel, have pointed out, relatively complex and large bankruptcies have been satisfactorily handled by the Act in Holland, including the recent bankruptcies of Dutch aircraft manufacturer Fokker and truck manufacturer DAF. The Act has been amended a number of times, but essentially has remained unchanged. It is seen as one of the best-drafted Acts in Dutch legislative history.[12] It, therefore, follows that Indonesia's bankruptcy code was also of relatively high quality. And indeed it was. One comparative study of insolvency codes even ranked Indonesia's code as 'pro-creditor,' behind Singapore's and Hong Kong's but ahead of Japan and the United States.[13]

So, obviously, the problem with Indonesia's bankruptcy law wasn't the law itself. The problem was, as ever, its enforcement and this was so poor that the law was almost never used. In the ten years to 1994, bankruptcy procedures were used in a pitiful 13 cases, and only four were in relation to insolvent companies.[14] In Indonesia, companies simply never (or almost never) go bankrupt. And this means creditors very often don't get their money back. Companies have been allowed to limp along indefinitely after having been subjected to the most atrocious internal fraud, theft, and mismanagement, leaving a trail of bruised bankers and other creditors in their wake.

In Thailand, creditors didn't even have the luxury of a decent bankruptcy law. The only option for defaulting companies was liquidation. (A supervised restructuring wasn't available.) Even when wind-up procedures were under way, the process took almost a year and only if there were no legal problems. Often there were, so the procedure sometimes took as long as five years.[15] The lack of a restructuring option meant that defaulting companies and their owners (usually founding families) would resist at all costs. And, of course, a complex, under-resourced, and often corrupt court system meant that resistance wasn't too difficult. On top of that, official court fees can be quite steep and these must be paid by the litigant.

Both Thailand and Indonesia introduced new bankruptcy laws in mid-1998. Both sets of new laws were arguably improvements on the previous ones. The new Thai law allowed for a restructuring option, although a senior Thai Justice Ministry official conceded that bankruptcy procedures under the new law might still take as long as seven years.[16] At least the Indonesian law allows for the much speedier processing of cases. But neither of the new laws is accompanied by the introduction of salary increases for judges and other court staff to make them less susceptible to bribe-taking. The changes have plenty of form but, as usual, are sorely lacking in genuine content.

The commencement of Indonesia's new bankruptcy court was predictable enough. The court threw out its first case to have the diversified Ometraco Corporation wound up. The bankruptcy suit with around US$125 million at stake was rejected on the bizarre basis that a similar suit had been filed against one of Ometraco's subsidiaries.[17] A month later, it did indeed declare its first bankruptcy. It was in relation to a local property company, Modernland Realty. At stake was an unpaid debt worth a paltry US$10,000.[18] Why an action involving only US$10,000 should succeed, but one relating to US$125 million should fail, left bankers mystified.

Loans and Gifts: Lending in Indonesia

The threat of being forced into bankruptcy is a powerful one that banks and other creditors can use to force borrowers to repay loans. But what happens if the option effectively isn't available? This and easy state bank credit for the well-connected has induced a culture of loan repayment avoidance in Indonesia. So, often, borrowers don't pay back loans from banks and other creditors even when they have the ability to do so. It is almost as if many of Indonesia's elite are no longer able to discern between loans and gifts. This was most evident when, after having accepted the IMF's emergency loans in late 1997, then-president Soeharto proceeded to vacillate on the terms, with news of this backdown or that backtracking trickling out of Indonesia on an almost daily basis. The president and his government behaved as if loans were a unilateral gift. Seemingly, the money was in the bag and was theirs to do with as they pleased. Indonesia is a significant destination of multilateral aid — and the IMF's loans were being treated as if they were part of that.

What happened at the national level was highly symbolic of what occurs within Indonesia on a regular basis. Well-connected Indonesians routinely borrowed millions of dollars from state-owned banks without the slightest intention of paying them back. If they did, it was often on a concessional basis. One very senior Indonesian private-sector banker once told me that in Indonesia, if you borrow from a state bank and you bother to return it, then you are 'stupid.' Consequently, Indonesia's state banks became riddled with non-performing loans and were left standing only because of their sovereign guarantee.

Asia's economic crisis provided some Indonesian corporate borrowers with a very good excuse to attempt to avoid their debt obligations. Without any doubt, the rupiah's crash made it practically impossible for most Indonesian companies with U.S. dollar and yen loans to continue servicing their debts. But what was rather disturbing and also quite telling was the degree to which the claimed inability to repay loans was spread across almost the entire business sector. Yes, the rupiah had crashed, but many Indonesian companies are export-oriented and have strong U.S. dollar earnings. Many of these were actually *helped* by the rupiah's fall, but they joined their cash-strapped compatriots aboard the debt moratorium bandwagon by claiming that they too couldn't repay their debts, in the hope that they might be forgiven.[19] This shameful ruse was entirely consistent with an attitude to debt that had become all too typical in Indonesia over the last decade or so: a debt is only an obligation if there is no alternative but to pay it back.

Bankruptcy has not been a penalty for not repaying a loan in Indonesia. The same can be said for Thailand. So, in the aftermath of the Asian economic crisis, many Western business people traveled to either country to look for companies that were distressed and on the verge of liquidation that could be acquired. But almost none were found. Why? Because, distressed as most local companies were, none had the slightest intention of going bankrupt. Perhaps then, the local companies might have been willing to offer part of their equity so that the proceeds could be used to repay borrowings? But this wasn't an option either, for relatively few had any intention of repaying their debts either. Why should they?

CHAPTER 2
Auditing Asia

*A*sia's corporate sphere is more like something from the 'Wild West' than the 'tranquil East,' and yet international accounting firms have been active in Asia for decades. Have they been doing their job or have they been set an impossible task?

Accounting firms today wear many hats. No longer do they simply help companies prepare their books for taxation purposes. They now act as auditors, tax advisors, legal advisors, and management consultants. But it is auditing that has become one of their most important roles. Auditing is absolutely crucial to commerce and is an essential component of the framework of any modern economy. Without the reports of independent auditors, the public has no way of verifying companies' claims of their financial health. Without them, few investors would want to buy shares on the world's stock markets. Nor would banks want to lend money to companies. And, if companies were unable to raise funds for their expansion, the economies of the world would contract and ultimately collapse. Good auditing promotes strong, healthy economies. Poor auditing and inadequate disclosure do not. So, if money makes the world go round, it is the auditors who play an important role in oiling the cogs. It isn't every day that accountants are portrayed as the mainstays of society as we know it, but to a degree, they are.

The five biggest accounting firms in the world today are Arthur Andersen, Deloitte Touche Tohmatsu, Ernst & Young, KPMG Peat Marwick, and PricewaterhouseCoopers, which was created in 1998 by the merger of Coopers & Lybrand with Price Waterhouse. Each has set up shop in Asia. They now generate almost 10% of their worldwide revenue from the Asia-Pacific region, which in turn accounts for almost 20% of their total employees. There are dozens of local firms that offer all or some of the services that the big international firms do.

The auditing mosaic across Asia is complex, if not occasionally cracked, not least because of inadequate regulatory regimes and a business culture that rues disclosure. It is through this minefield that the accounting firms must tread, something they do with varying degrees of success.

AUDITING IS NOT AN ASIAN VALUE

Auditing is a sensitive matter at the best of times. And nowhere more so than in Asia, where firms — usually family-run and operating under legal codes that can often be described as embryonic at best — choose to list on the local stock exchange. When they do this, they are generally compelled to avail themselves of the services of a public accountant — often they choose a big-name international firm, particularly if they wish to attract the interest of American and European mutual funds and international banks.

Auditing is a process that doesn't lend itself particularly well to Asian culture. Out of necessity, it proceeds on the basis of double-checking, which is suggestive of distrust and is confrontational by implication. It also runs against a tendency in Asia's corporate world for secrecy and its dislike of transparency. In a society where management is patriarchal and the boss can do no wrong, it is an uncomfortable process to have the company's books assessed by outsiders. It is in this environment that Western accounting firms must operate.

Foreign accounting firms are sometimes required to take local partners. The big international accounting firms have a local partner each in Indonesia, for example. Arthur Andersen teamed up with what is now Prasetio, Utomo and Co; Deloitte Touche Tohmatsu with local firm Hans, Tuanakota and Mustofo; Ernst & Young with Santoso, Harsokusumo and Co; KPMG with Hanadi, Sudjendro and Co; Coopers & Lybrand, as it was then, with Sidharta and Sidharta; and Price Waterhouse with Hadi, Sutanto and Co.

Similarly, in Thailand, KPMG is known as KPMG Peat Marwick Suthee, Deloitte Touche Tohmatsu as Deloitte Touche Tohmatsu Jaiyos, and Arthur Andersen has paired up with SGV-Na Thalang and Co. In South Korea, KPMG is known as KPMG San Tong Corp and Arthur Andersen is known as Anjin and Co Arthur Andersen.

In some respects, such pairings help remove the angst that local businesses might have about exposing their inner workings to outsiders and having their affairs audited. But the degree to which the local version mirrors the international version in terms of service and independence varies from company to company and country to country. The international firms aim for the pairings to be seamless, but this can't always be assumed.

PAYING THE PIPER

One of the great problems for auditors in Asia is the tendency for many local listed firms to shop around for an auditor that is most likely to do their bidding. This problem tends to be obviated in more mature markets such as the United States, where a listed company's decision to replace its auditor usually attracts controversy and criticism. Analysts are left wondering if there is something that the company wants to hide. Shareholders become worried and may even desert the stock, the risk of which is a powerful incentive for public companies not to change their auditor flippantly. Replacing auditors is much more commonplace in Asia. Firms that do this don't attract the same odium as they do in, say, the United States — Asian markets are generally not yet mature enough for this. If companies don't get the result they want from their auditor, they may threaten to take their business elsewhere — a threat that is often carried out.

So, in Asia, the power balance between the auditor and its client is the opposite of that in the West. Hence, auditors face a great deal of pressure to be sympathetic toward the companies they audit or face losing their business. To be pure or to be profitable is the stark question that many accounting firms must face.

A particularly overt example of how this process can work occurred in early 1999 in relation to the Hong Kong electronics company, Wing Lee Holdings.[1] At that time, the company had been listed on the local stock exchange for only two years, but it decided to dump its auditor. The accounting firm had claimed that there was insufficient explanation to account for US$2.8 million of Wing Lee's turnover. On the basis of the information Wing Lee had presented, the auditor also felt that it was unable to determine whether 'proper books of account had been kept.' Since the auditor refused to budge, Wing Lee's chairman responded by claiming that the accounting firm had been 'unfair,' and fired it in favor of a competitor.

Accounting and auditing are not easy when companies tend to 'shop around.' The line dividing professionalism in auditing from an untrammelled race for the buck can be a difficult one to maintain, and nowhere is this more so than in Asia. In one or two Asian countries, some accounting firms have earned the reputation of massaging companies' financial statements and signing off on them, for an appropriate fee. Mutual funds, other investors, and stockbrokers are thus wise not to accept audited accounts at face value.

BEGINNINGS

Washington SyCip is to accounting in South-East Asia what the fabled Thai-Chinese Chin Sophonpanich was to banking. Chin used his connections throughout Asia's overseas Chinese community to lend to the region's budding entrepreneurs who were unable to get loans from Western banks. As they grew, so did Chin's Bangkok Bank, until it was the biggest bank in South-East Asia. SyCip set up SyCip, Gorres, Velayo, and Co (SGV) in Manila in 1946, not long after Chin set up Bangkok Bank in Thailand. His father, Albino, had been a prominent banker and SyCip was able to leverage the family's connections to support his fledgling accounting practice. SGV grew to dominate the accounting industry in the Philippines. It also set up branches in Taiwan, Thailand, Vietnam, and Indonesia. Many of SGV's clients were personal contacts of SyCip. He did a great deal to professionalize management and accounting practices in South-East Asia and is greatly respected around the world.

When the international accounting firms decided to move into Asia, and particularly into South-East Asia, they found that SGV had already sewn up much of the business. Several countries in the region required that foreign accountants pair up with local firms, out of fear that they would swamp the many fledgling local accounting practices. This strategy of pairing international accountants with regional auditors has since become standard practice.

CONNECTIONS

The constellation of politics and commerce in much of Asia means that to survive and thrive, businesses must forge good connections, and in this regard, international accounting firms are no different. As an example, one leading international accounting firm has established close relations with important cadres in China. In December 1997, it even hired the daughter of the State Administration of Taxation deputy commissioner, Xiang Huaicheng, as the tax manager for its Beijing office.[2] It proved a wise appointment, for in March 1998, after Zhu Rongji was elected China's premier, Xiang was appointed to Zhu's Cabinet as finance minister. The firm's deputy country managing partner for China, Nellie Fong Ku-man, also has close ties with the Chinese government. It appointed her in 1992 as one of its Hong Kong Affairs Advisors. In 1997, she was appointed to the Hong Kong Special Administrative Region Executive Council. This networking and relationship building in China has paid off. The firm is now the biggest foreign accounting firm in China, earning more fee income than any of its competitors.

It also does well in Indonesia, where good relations with government figures are also essential. Prior to the Asian economic crisis, it audited around 55% of the companies listed on the Jakarta Stock Exchange —

65% by market capitalization and 80% of Indonesia's top ten private banks. (Several have since succumbed to mismanagement and the Asia economic crisis in general.) Its professional staff in Indonesia total more than 800, or more than twice the number of its nearest rival.

KPMG's local partner in Thailand is Suthee Singhasaneh, a former finance minister and later, an advisor to General Chavalit Yongchaiyudh while Chavalit served as prime minister in 1996 and 1997.[3] Suthee sat on Thailand's Securities and Exchange Commission and spoke out regularly on taxation reform and other business issues. His position with the government and KPMG provides a good example of the enmeshment of politics, the civil service, and business in Thailand. Only, on this occasion, instead of senior executives of one of Thailand's big banks or industrial conglomerates being seated at the table, it was a senior figure associated with an accounting firm. It serves to underscore once again the dual nature of accountants: they are both businessmen in their own right and professional watchdogs. It is a duality that can be filled with contradictions.

AUDITING THE AUDITORS

The regulatory regimes that cover all aspects of corporate life in many Asian countries are lax, and auditing is no different. Asia's professional accountants often bemoan the fact that the regulations under which they operate are either inadequate or not enforced, which allows their competitors to cut corners. Alternatively, government bodies riddled with conflicts of interest determine them. Accounting standards in Japan are determined by a council in the powerful and interventionist Ministry of Finance, for example. The standards are weak and often subordinate to the Ministry's wider, corporatist agenda. The government-controlled Chinese Institute of Certified Public Accountants determines accounting standards in China. Not only is China's economy dominated by large state-owned enterprises, but the locally owned accounting firms are government-owned as well. It is a nefarious conflict of interest circle.

Some accounting firms in Asia have inordinately close relationships with their clients. During the worst days of the rioting in Jakarta in 1998, one local tycoon fled the city in his private helicopter, which was loaded with cash, his wife, and the wife of the public accountant of his listed companies — a generous, if not a rather symbolic, gesture. It is not uncommon for auditing staff to have private commercial relationships with the companies that they audit, to be related either by birth or by marriage to the owners of such companies, or to trade in the shares of the companies they audit. Indeed, insider trading is generally rife, and in some Asian countries, it is barely illegal. There are many instances of public companies giving their auditors office accommodation and other business-related input either for free or at greatly reduced rentals. There is one public accountant who has installed his wife as the local silent partner in a major European stockbroking firm; others are not without some related-party transactions of their own and contract out some of their client-related services to firms set up by members of their families. These practices can be something of a culture shock to Western expatriates who come to Asia to work in such firms. It is for this reason that they are often kept well away from the auditing divisions and instead tend to be restricted to the taxation or consulting divisions.

Practices such as these go unchecked, as ever, by inappropriate regulatory regimes. The United States, for one, has strict rules to protect auditor independence that are applied by the Securities and Exchange Commission. Of late, public accountants have tested these rules as they seek to branch out beyond their traditional areas of expertise. But in much of Asia, no such testing of the rules is necessary. Usually, they either don't exist or are barely applied. It is worth repeating that in Asia, it pays for stockbroking analysts and investors to check not only a listed company's audited results, but also who conducted the audit.

A STEEP LEARNING CURVE

Asia has been home to some spectacular corporate crashes. All too often, the companies involved are publicly listed and thus audited by a public accountant. Apportioning blame is often difficult, but the climate of poor disclosure and the management of local companies being either ignorant of their fiduciary responsibilities or disinterested in them represents an enormous challenge to the accounting profession.

This is not to say that the accountants themselves are always blameless. The collapse of the Carrian Group in Hong Kong in 1982 is a case in point. Carrian's auditors not only faced a massive negligence action but also the prosecution of members of its staff. The 1991 collapse of British tycoon Robert Maxwell's empire, in which fingers were also pointed at Maxwell's auditors, served to show that this need not be a peculiarly Asian phenomenon.

Nonetheless, what is peculiarly Asian is the mix of lax regulatory enforcement and compliance, family control of listed firms, patriarchal management, and an intense desire to avoid corporate scrutiny. Auditing in these circumstances is difficult and there are plenty of examples that provide testament to this.

Indonesia's Bank Summa collapsed in late 1992. The collapse wasn't just the result of bad luck but of systematic and blatant mismanagement that had been ongoing almost from the date of the bank's inception. Throughout much of that time, the bank was audited by an accounting firm that had routinely given the bank a clean bill of health. Presumably, much information had been hidden from the auditors. Absurdly excessive loans had been made to companies associated with the bank's principal shareholder and there was over-exuberant expansion offshore. It turned out, in fact, that more than half of the bank's total loans were made to affiliated companies, mostly for real estate speculation. The loan portfolio was a mess, with big loans collateralized against small assets and small loans against big assets. The bank was part of the Summa Group, which had expanded in little more than ten years from almost nothing to become a billion-dollar conglomerate that spanned real estate, banking, insurance, oil exploration, and telecommunications. It had operations in Indonesia, Singapore, the United States, Malaysia, and Vietnam, and even a small bank, Summa Handelsbank, in Germany. Summa was a house of cards — but it took its collapse with US$600 million in debts to demonstrate that.[4] Presumably when it did collapse, no one was more surprised than the bank's auditors.

In mid-1997, Singapore-based CAM International Holdings, a listed precision components maker, had a brush with bankruptcy after its independent auditor found irregularities in the company's accounts. The auditor compiled a report on what it found and forwarded it to the office of Singapore's finance minister. A new board was appointed at CAM and it commissioned another accounting firm to go over the company's accounts. Several weeks later, it presented the board with a 142-page report. The new auditors found systematic fraud through the creation of fictitious transactions, and a further four categories of questionable transactions. The irregularities went at least as far back as 1994 and possibly earlier. The new auditor was unable to ascertain what had happened in 1993 because the accounting books and records for that year were 'missing' and hadn't been seen for six months.[5] There is no doubt that the initial auditor had played a key role in exposing the irregularities at CAM once it had found them, and this led to several of CAM's executives being arrested. Nonetheless, it had signed off on CAM's accounts in previous years when many of the questionable transactions had occurred. The executives' activities and the time that elapsed before the company's auditors uncovered them took CAM to the brink of collapse at great cost to the company's minority shareholders and its creditors.

Another example on the Summa and CAM theme is the debacle that engulfed Thailand's Alphatec Electronics. Charn Uswachoke was the whiz kid of Thailand's stock exchange. 'A man of vision,' exclaimed

Asian Business magazine in 1995.[6] 'Mr Chips,' screamed a 1996 gee-whiz article in *Asiaweek*.[7] His ambition was to turn Alphatec, a basic assembler of integrated circuits, into a high-end manufacturer. Not content with owning one part of the circuit board process, Charn wanted to move both upstream and downstream and own all of it. He was also an auditor's worst nightmare.

Charn founded Alphatec in 1988. It swiftly became Thailand's biggest integrated circuit producer. But its growth was largely funded through debt. In 1993, the company listed on the Stock Exchange of Thailand and a new source of funds was tapped. In 1995, Alphatec secured a US$768 million loan to set up a new company, Submicron Technology, which was to build Thailand's first wafer chip fabrication plant. In no time, the Alphatec Group had grown to more than 30 companies.

Signs of trouble first emerged when Submicron got behind on almost US$190 million of its bills to U.S. and European suppliers.[8] Not long after, Submicron's parent, Alphatec, missed US$45 million in payments that were due on US$450 million of its convertible bonds, and a month later, it missed a US$34 million debt repayment. All was looking far from well.

Concern from Alphatec's international creditors was met with obfuscation and stonewalling by the board until it finally yielded to the creditors' demands and commissioned an independent audit of the books by a new accounting firm. The new auditor uncovered some terrible truths. Behind Alphatec's slick marketing and high-tech pretensions was a ramshackle corporate structure that was just perfect for hiding improper transactions. And hide is what the company did. There was much that hadn't been disclosed to the former auditor. Big losses were concealed with big borrowings: at least two sets of books had been kept; false profits of US$164 million had been reported between 1995 and April 1997, when in fact the company's true results were losses; US$127 million had been lent to 'related persons' — companies privately held by Charn — without the permission of the board; recorded revenues were between six and ten times higher than they actually were; funds had been shifted between companies to bolster accounts to attract loans and orders; and invoices had been faked to support fictitious transactions. Several actually misspelled the names of well-known Western companies. 'Philips' — as in Philips the Dutch electronics giant — had been misspelled 'Phiilip,' for example. Remarkably, previous audits had failed to pick this up.

Other suspicious trades between Alphatec and companies wholly owned by Charn were also detected.[9] One subsidiary had generated US$50 million in its first year, but struggled to remain profitable thereafter under the weight of more than US$40 million in loans that it had obtained in less than a year to support the Uswachoke family's private companies.[10] South-East Asia's answer to Silicon Valley was a total mess. The auditor's report had uncovered serious mismanagement and at least US$314 million in 'improper' transactions. It was about as much disclosure as some senior Alphatec managers could take. A group of them was soon discovered at the company's head office shredding documents.[11]

Charn resigned as CEO but the gesture lacked the personal touch we are told is very important in Asia — he failed to show up at work and he finally sent in his resignation via e-mail.[12] Other revelations followed. The names of employees had been used as nominees to set up margin share trading accounts to trade in Alphatec's shares. One secretary reportedly agreed to allow her name to be used by Charn's brother, Somkuan, for his Alphatec share trading. After Alphatec's troubles emerged, she was shocked to discover that the account was in debt to the tune of US$1.6 million and the brokerage house was pursuing her for repayment.[13]

But what was the board doing all the while when the spurious trades, transactions, and frauds were occurring? 'We trusted Khun [Mr] Charn, so the board never questioned what he had invested in,' explained one director.[14] It was an interesting interpretation of fiduciary duty.

Efforts to reorganize Alphatec's debts and restructure the company stalled because, under the absurd bankruptcy laws operating in Thailand at the time, the major shareholders — in this case, Charn and members of his family — effectively had the right to veto restructuring plans. Creditors were unable to have their preferred plans put in place because the very individual who had been responsible for the company's collapse — Charn — objected to them. Not only that, Charn's representatives on the board were able to vote down the proposal that the accounting firm that uncovered many of Alphatec's problems be retained, and instead had the initial auditor reinstated. Charn was later charged with falsifying his companies' accounts and barred from holding any executive positions or directorships with listed companies.[15] Charn was one fish that didn't get away. But Asia is a big sea and the auditing net is not all it could be.

AFTER THE WAKE-UP CALL

For a long time, the audits by international firms amounted to little more than substantiating companies' year-end records and the preparation of financial statements. Auditing is not continuous but a one-off process. It is passive and not predictive. Activities that might greatly affect a company's financial health, such as share, foreign exchange and derivatives trading, and mergers and acquisitions, are not usually reflected in a company's accounts until after they have occurred and the consequences are known. Although Asia's companies have full use of the array of modern financial instruments such as derivatives and options trading, many don't operate in legal and regulatory environments that have caught up with these new financial management developments. Perhaps in Asia more than anywhere else, listed companies need more — much more — assistance with their management of contingencies that might arise from such activities.

To this end, some accounting firms have begun to upgrade their auditing services offered to clients so that it occurs on a more continuous basis. This involves the auditor identifying events and actions that add to a company's business risks and continually assessing its ability to control them. In a sense, continuous auditing is equivalent to the auditor taking its clients by the hand and leading them away from the edge, rather than waiting for them to fall off the edge and then substantiating the fact. It's the sort of thing that many might have reasonably assumed had been going on anyway. But it wasn't. Arthur Andersen introduced to Asia what it calls 'The Business Audit,' Ernst & Young has introduced its 'Audit Innovation,' and KPMG its 'Business Management Process.' Each of these involves continuous auditing; the monitoring and assessment of risks as they arise. Possibly as a result, the next time an economic meltdown threatens Asia, it will be less severe than the 1997–98 crisis. Better and more continuous auditing should ensure that companies are more adequately prepared. It is, however, but a small step down a long road.

THE PARTY'S OVER

Due diligence, financial jurisprudence, and corporate governance are enormous challenges in Asia today. Much must change in Asia to prevent the next period of rapid growth being followed by another spectacular bust.

The pace of business in Asia was fast and furious throughout the 1980s and most of the 1990s. The rates of growth that companies could achieve were astonishing, and these included the growth that many accounting firms experienced. The auditing divisions of the many public accountants in Asia were too preoccupied with capturing their share of the boom and too little concerned with substantiating it. Coupled with poor regulatory requirements and supervision and an anti-disclosure culture, Asia's independent auditors have their work cut out. It is true that external auditors in Asia have been instrumental in identifying major cover-ups and attempted frauds. But much has been missed as well. There are many areas in need of reform in Asia, and auditing is one of them.

CHAPTER 3

Asia's Corrupted Business Media

There is an inextricable link between the free flow of information and the soundness and viability of an economy. The media must be free not only of government, but also of other business interests. Rarely in Asia is the business media genuinely independent and unfettered in its ability to report corporate misdemeanors.

Every business traveler knows the virtues of flicking through a local newspaper after arriving in a new country. When all else is strange, it is comforting to be able to pick up something as familiar as a newspaper and with relatively little effort be able to learn which issues are considered important locally, whether in politics or business. With a little local knowledge — a bit of the local color — and in no time, one begins to feel less of an outsider and less estranged from the new surroundings. The local media of a country is useful for something else as well. The media, and more particularly, good business journalism, is absolutely critical for exposing the fraud and cheating that can occur in business. The media doesn't keep just politicians honest, but business people as well.

In Western countries, one of the main reasons why companies don't rip off their partners, shareholders, customers, or even the wider community is that they are terrified their actions might be exposed. Media organizations usually have media as their core, and often, only business activity. They are well-endowed, pay their journalists well, and are genuinely competitive; their journalists usually subscribe to a formal code of ethics and conduct. None of this means that the Western media is perfect when it comes to business reporting, but it certainly helps.

The *Wall Street Journal* and *60 Minutes* undoubtedly do as much for corporate governance as do regular shareholder meetings and the actions of regulators. In this sense, the media, together with sound and enforced business laws and independent and thorough auditing, are part of a triumvirate that is essential for a well-functioning business environment.

So, how well does Asia's local media perform this role? The results are patchy. Censorship, low wages for journalists, poor distribution of foreign newspapers and books, and the lack of independence of local media outlets from big businesses all see to that. In many respects, the media in some parts of Asia is more part of the problem than the solution and is as much in need of reform as any other sector.

ON OFFICIAL SERVICE

In August 1994, the Indonesian government closed down three media outlets: a current affairs and business magazine called *Tempo* that was modeled after America's *Time* magazine, a popular tabloid called *Detik*, and a newspaper called *Editor*. The closures shocked observers in and outside Indonesia. Many thought the days of such blunt control of the media were over, but they were wrong. Two days before the closures, I visited the Jakarta offices of *Detik*. The atmosphere was celebratory. A few hours before my arrival, *Detik* had received a 'final' warning from Indonesia's powerful Ministry of Information. *Detik's* staff clearly enjoyed baiting the government and they weren't too worried. This, after all, was about the fourth 'final' warning in several months. *Detik* staff didn't take it too seriously and certainly didn't imagine that the paper's closure was imminent. *Detik* had attracted the ire of the government because it was licensed to report only on crime — it was supposed to be a crime tabloid. But the editorial team had adopted a somewhat more liberal interpretation of what constituted 'crime' and had taken to reporting the activities of then-president Soeharto and his ministers. Formally, this was a technical breach of its license. Less formally, it was sedition, and *Detik* paid the price.

Soeharto's government was very effective at controlling the media. The local media was cowered into practicing self-censorship, and the foreign media was controlled by delaying and sometimes banning outright those editions of newspapers and magazines that were deemed to be 'damaging.' Hard-hitting, investigative business reporting is one thing, but distributing it is quite another.

Vested interest might not be able to prevent revealing articles from being written and published but it might be able to stop them from being distributed. So, distribution is another point in the chain where the media's scrutiny can be stifled. The most extreme case of this is to be found in Indonesia, where a local company called Indoprom NV had managed to secure the local distribution rights for all major foreign newspapers and magazines. It achieved this by having a near monopoly of all the bookstores and newsagents in Jakarta's five-star hotels. Any foreign publication for which local distribution rights weren't awarded to Indoprom wasn't made available in those hotels — for foreign-language publications, this was tantamount to them not being distributed at all, since there were few other outlets for such publications in Indonesia. This monopoly might well have been as detrimental to Indonesia's economy as several other monopolies that were targeted by the IMF in its series of reforms forced on Indonesia as part of its 1998 emergency loan program for the country. It strikes at the heart of the free flow of information to Indonesia's business sector, and when it comes to doing business in a country such as Indonesia, information is like gold.

Indoprom's position has been enormously beneficial to the Indonesian government. Instead of having to deal with a myriad of distributors when it wants to control the flow of print media information into Indonesia, it need only deal with one company. The company's monopoly is very lucrative so it is only too happy to play along. During the Soeharto years, anything that Indoprom felt might be troubling for the government, be it an article on the Soeharto family's corporate empire in the *Asian Wall Street Journal* or a piece on the riots in East Timor in the *Far Eastern Economic Review*, was submitted to the Ministry of Information for perusal. Contracting out of government services is now commonplace in the West, but in Indonesia the government had effectively found a way to contract out censorship. A symbiotic relationship indeed!

In September 1996, I wrote an essay for the *Asian Wall Street Journal's* editorial pages on corruption in Asia. While I made it very clear that corruption was morally repugnant, I did argue that in limited circumstances corruption and nepotism might actually benefit an economy such as Indonesia's. The fact that Soeharto's eldest daughter was the biggest private developer of toll-roads in the country actually meant that toll-roads were built. If anyone else tried to build them, their attempts were likely to be defeated by Indonesia's obstructionist bureaucracy and other vested interests. The Soeharto family had the power to bulldoze their proposals through. And if it came to a choice between a Soeharto toll-road with no tender and a public tender but no toll-road, then really the choice for an infrastructure-starved country is an easy one. My article was relatively neutral and even made some points in favor of the Soeharto family's business interests, given Indonesia's other complexities. But the result was that Tuesday's edition of the *Journal* didn't hit the streets of Jakarta until the following Friday evening — the edition was held up in the Ministry of Information and passed up the line until some Ministry official felt able to release it for circulation.

Censorship by governments has decreased with time in Asia, certainly with regard to business reporting, although political coverage remains a touchy issue. But censorship by governments isn't all that prevents much of Asia's media from effectively exposing unfair business practices and safeguarding the interests of outside investors. One of the biggest problems is that too little of Asia's media is independent of other corporate interests.

THE FOURTH ESTATE AS REAL ESTATE

The *Sin Chiew Jit Poh* newspaper was founded in Singapore in 1929 by Aw Boon Haw, the Tiger Balm 'king,' who saw that a newspaper could be a good way of advertising his lines of medicated ointments. Aw was one of Asia's most prominent businessmen to establish media interests — not because of an intrinsic interest in the news but, rather, to support and promote other business interests. In the West, the media is or was central to the business interests of the great media proprietors — the Hearsts, the Beaverbrooks, and even the Murdochs of today. But in Asia, all too often, media outlets are not the core business activity of their major shareholder but are adjuncts — they are there to serve the interests of the rest of the business empire. News stories, for example, might be used to promote the products produced by a sister company. But that really is an aspect of the least concern. What is more troubling is that the newspaper is unlikely to expose the more controversial aspects of affiliated companies.

The opportunity for the business media to be compromised by affiliated non-media interests is great in Asia — too few media organizations concentrate on just the media.

One of the biggest conglomerates in Malaysia is the Malaysian Resources Group. It has interests in infrastructure development, engineering, power generation, and property. It also has a media arm through which it controls Malaysia's leading English-language daily, the *New Straits Times*, as well as the *Business Times* and the *Malay Mail*. It also controls TV3, a national television channel. Clearly, there is some potential for a conflict of interest between the media and non-media arms of a conglomerate such as Malaysian Resources when it comes to independent reporting.

Another big conglomerate is the Hong Leong Group, controlled by Quek Leng Chan. It is enormously wealthy, with interests in banking, finance, hotels, and property. It also controls the Nanyang Press Group, which publishes two of the larger Chinese-language newspapers in Malaysia, *Nanyang Siang Pau* and *China Press*, as well as at least 12 Chinese-language magazines. There is also a book printer and Channel KTV, a regional cable and satellite television company.

An important shareholder in *Ming Pao* is the Hong Kong-based Indonesian-Chinese businessman, Oei Hong Leong. In the early 1990s, Oei was one of the most spectacular investors in mainland China. He specialized in acquiring ailing state-owned enterprises, knocking them into shape, and then listing them on an overseas stock exchange so that he could recoup his investment. Maintaining good relations with Communist Party officials in China was obviously essential for this sort of business. Part of Oei's strategy was to buy, in 1993, the pro-Beijing Hong Kong business weekly, *Wide Angle*, in which Oei pushed the need for economic reform in China but also took to personally interviewing senior Chinese leaders, giving them an opportunity to showcase their views.[1]

Hong Kong's biggest selling English-language daily is the *South China Morning Post*. It is controlled by Robert Kuok, who has hotel, shipping, trading, real estate, and other interests in Hong Kong, China, and the rest of Asia. Despite Kuok having bought into the newspaper, there has been no perceptible change in its editorial policies and, fortunately, it remains one of the best newspapers in Asia.

The influence of Kuok's *South China Morning Post* extends beyond Hong Kong. It owns 15% of Bangkok's English-language daily, the *Bangkok Post*, which incidentally has Chartsiri Sophonpanich, the current president of Bangkok Bank — Thailand's biggest bank — sitting on its board.[2] The link in Thailand between big businesses and the media doesn't end there. The Crown Property Bureau, the private investment vehicle of the Thai Royal Family, owns a big slice of Thailand's ITV television station as does the diversified telecommunications group, Shin Corp, which bought a big stake in June 2000. The bureau is also one of the major shareholders in the Thai English-language business daily, *Business Day*. The newspaper doesn't exactly operate without fear or favor, at least where its major shareholders are concerned. In 1997, the *Bangkok Post* ran almost 100 stories that mentioned the bureau, whereas *Business Day* ran only one. 'It is the tall tree that catches the wind,' goes the Chinese saying. Sometimes Asian investors prefer no wind at all.

In South Korea, the leading daily, the *Chosun Ilbo*, is owned by Bang Woo Young and his family. The Bang family has big hotel interests, as well as publishing interests. The major *Joongang Ilbo* daily newspaper is owned by the giant Samsung Group. Its current publisher is Hong Seok Hyun, whose father founded the newspaper with Lee Byong Chul, the late chairman of Samsung. Hong is married to the sister of Lee's son, Lee Kun Hee, the current chairman of Samsung. What sort of coverage does the *Joongang Ilbo* give Samsung? When Kun Hee was indicted on bribery charges in 1995, it covered the event but only in relatively little detail despite it being corporate South Korea's biggest story in years. Another South Korean daily, the *Munhwa Ilbo*, is owned by the Chung family who owns the Hyundai Group.[3] The daily relied on Hyundai for more than 60% of its advertising revenue, at least until 1998 when economic pressures forced much cost-cutting in Hyundai. Yet another paper, the *Kyunghyang Shinmun*, was part of the Hanhwa Group, South Korea's ninth-largest *chaebol* (family-owned conglomerate), until late 1997. Press freedom has improved greatly in South Korea since the advent of popular elections in 1988, but there is still some way to go before it is independent of the *chaebol* — and it is the *chaebol* after all, with their overlapping ownerships, disregard of minority shareholders' interests, conspiratorial wheeling and dealing, and labyrinthine webs of interests that are so deserving of close and impartial scrutiny.

Media ownership in Indonesia is predictable enough. At the start of 1998, the biggest selling newspaper in Jakarta, the tabloid *Pos Kota*, was owned by Indonesia's Parliamentary Speaker, chairman of the then-ruling Golkar Party, and former Minister of Information, Harmoko. Harmoko owned stakes in many other Indonesian media outlets — stakes that were built up before and during his time as Minister for Information.[4] The English-language daily, the *Indonesian Observer*, was owned by Peter Gontha, a senior executive and part-owner of Soeharto's son, Bambang Trihatmodjo's Bimantara Group. Owner of the Alatief Group and former Minister for Manpower, Abdul Latief, owned the *Tiras*, *Harian Neraca*, and *Belanja* newspapers and magazines. Other major titles were owned by similarly well-connected businessmen.

The concentration of ownership of Indonesia's five privately owned commercial television stations is even greater. When President Soeharto stepped down in May 1998, two stations were owned outright by companies controlled by his children. Another was partly owned by one of his daughter-in-laws together with the head of the diversified Napan conglomerate. Yet another was majority owned by Indonesia's largest conglomerate, the highly diversified Salim Group. A Soeharto son also had a minority share in it. And the fifth private television station was owned by the diversified Bakrie Group.[5] Those television interests not directly owned by the Soehartos were influenced by them. The Napan, Bakrie, and Salim Groups all separately had joint ventures with members of the Soeharto family. The television stations were used openly to support their owners' other business interests, not just for favorable advertising, but also to push their strategic business interests. When, in late 1997, for example, the Indonesian government closed down a poorly run bank partly owned by Bambang and Gontha as part of the IMF's conditions for its emergency loans to Indonesia, Gontha appeared in a lengthy broadcast by the pair's RCTI television station to defend the bank and their management of it.[6]

The independence of the Philippine press from government influence has improved considerably since President Marcos was in power when all three major national dailies were owned by Marcos cronies. Much of the media has been reshaped since the Marcos days. Political comment is relatively free, although business comment may still be compromised by the new proprietors' other business interests.

During the dying days of the dictator's regime, several newspapers were established to satisfy the demand from the country's emerging middle class for more independent news coverage. One such newspaper was the *Philippine Daily Inquirer*, although a large part of its shares were bought in 1994 by a consortium led by Eduardo Espiritu, a former president of the large Philippine National Bank and, as of 1998, the country's finance minister. Other newspapers and media outlets too are linked to big non-media business interests. The daily *Manila Chronicle*, the *Manila Times*, the *Manila Bulletin*, the *Manila Standard*, and ABS-CBN Broadcasting are all parts of diversified industrial conglomerates.

Singapore's print media is dominated by the government-linked Singapore Press Holdings, which has near-monopoly ownership of all local newspapers and owns Times Publishing as well, the local book publisher and distributor. At first, this might appear potentially repressive, but in so far as business reporting is concerned, it has actually served Singapore relatively well. Importantly, the core activity of Singapore Press Holdings is media, so its newspapers are not beholden to other business interests as are many media outlets in other Asian countries. In addition, its journalists are very well qualified, relatively well paid, and drawn from countries around the world. Singapore's business newspapers have given prominent and detailed coverage to the misdeeds of some prominent local business identities and companies with little apparent fear or favor. In this respect at least, Singapore's media leads the rest of South-East Asia.

The Singapore government announced in June 2000 plans to issue new print media and broadcasting licenses but it was made clear that these would go to existing players.

AND NOW A WORD FROM THE SPONSORS

In many parts of Asia, local journalists are remarkably lowly paid. In fact, they are generally only slightly better paid than civil servants. Most journalists in Indonesia, for example, receive less than US$400 a month. The consequence of this is precisely the same as with civil servants: they are susceptible to bribes. In Indonesia, Thailand, and China, journalists are routinely paid by the organizers to attend press conferences. At the end of the conference, envelopes that contain money ('white envelopes,' as they are called in Thailand) are passed out to journalists, ostensibly for transport to get to and from the conference venue or for meals. The attendance money has become such an ingrained part of local journalists' culture in these countries that it is now scarcely possible to conduct a media conference without the promise to journalists of money or gifts, unless what is to be discussed at the conference is so newsworthy that journalists will attend anyway.

One problem with the practice in Indonesia at least, is that many local journalists have taken to bringing along their relatives to pose as journalists so that they too can collect an envelope. One large newsworthy company based in Jakarta manages to avoid paying local journalists to attend its media conferences by timing them with lunch and then providing a large quantity of free food. With the addition of journalists' friends and relatives, such media conferences have the tendency to degenerate into something that is more akin to a family banquet.

The practice of giving cash and gifts interferes with legitimate journalistic practice as well. 'Show-up' money is so entrenched in Indonesia that many local companies presume it is an accepted practice around the world. One Western journalist in Jakarta told me that on those occasions when he hadn't been told by local companies that they were about to hold a media briefing, it was because it was assumed that being a foreigner, his appearance money would be so great that it would be unaffordable.

This practice creates a dilemma for organizations connected with foreign governments that wish to hold media briefings. In 1996, the Australian embassy in Jakarta held a function to publicize the launch of preparations for the 2000 Olympics to be held in Sydney. The embassy wasn't in a position to pay journalists to turn up to cover the event. So the promotions agency that managed the event organized for an Australian airline to donate a return ticket to Sydney for a competition that only journalists who showed up on the night were permitted to enter. When the winner was announced, it turned out to be an Australian journalist. Fully aware of what the competition was all about, he refused the prize and had it redrawn. An Indonesian photographer for a local newspaper duly won the prize and was on his way to Sydney.

Appearance money paid to journalists is one thing, but much larger and more insidious payments have become commonplace as well. In Indonesia, there is a perpetual debate about where the true allegiances of the country's tiny but very wealthy Chinese minority lie. Investments in China by corporations owned by Indonesian-Chinese regularly draw accusations from some sections of the non-Chinese community that the local Chinese community has divided loyalties. There might be an element of truth in this, but undoubtedly most of the investment is made for purely commercial reasons. It certainly is substantial. They own shoe factories, industrial parks, pulp and paper plants, and office towers in Shanghai and elsewhere — and yet these investments almost invariably are not reported in the Indonesian media. How can this be? The reason is that local journalists are often paid not to write such stories. Similarly, it is remarkable how often a potentially big story appears in the Indonesian media in relation to alleged wrongdoings by a particular businessman or company — a story that would generate days of coverage anywhere else — only to disappear without any follow-up. Almost invariably, the silence of journalists has been bought. High principles can only be maintained for so long when one is paid so poorly. It is said that in Indonesia, journalists can earn more by *not* writing than by writing.

The problem appears just as rife in Thailand, although there is probably greater emphasis on paying for favorable reporting and positioning of products in the newspaper articles than in simply seeking to stifle investigative business reporting. Payment need not always be in money. Mobile telephones, gold necklaces, television sets, air-conditioners, stocks and stock options, and overseas travel have all been cited as having been given by companies to Thai journalists in Bangkok to ensure friendly coverage. Journalists aren't the only ones to benefit. Press photographers also get a cut, and sometimes allocate a share of their bounty to sub-editors to ensure that a particular photograph makes it into print.[7] Niceties such as alerting the reader that they are about to wade into an advertorial are of course dispensed with.

IF ALL ELSE FAILS ...

If government censorship, distribution controls, paying off journalists, and pressuring the owners of a news publication all fail to kill off an unwelcome story, then there might still be one last avenue for Asia's more sensitive corporate high-flyers. In May 1997, the Indonesian fortnightly magazine, *Swasembada*, published a series of articles on the business activities of Indonesian businesswoman, Endang Utari Mokodompit. She had pushed a bank she owned to insolvency by having it guarantee hundreds of millions of dollars in loans that she later couldn't repay. (Precisely how she did this is explained toward the end of Chapter 5.) The articles were courageous as Endang was politically well connected and a part of Jakarta's business establishment. Unfortunately for readers, a single buyer — widely believed to be Endang's bank — snapped up almost the entire print run of the edition — more than 30,000 copies. With a cover price of around US$3.30, it meant an outlay of around US$100,000. The buyer reportedly went to the factory where the magazine had just been printed and used its vehicles to block access to the building until the printers agreed to hand over their entire stock of the magazine. The vehicles were loaded up and the magazine was taken away before it could hit the streets. Indonesia's printing laws prevented *Swasembada* from printing additional copies because it had already exhausted its licensed print run.[8] What the articles detailed was how Endang had obtained the money, what she did with it, and how she had failed to pay it back. Other activities were also detailed, including failed investments in Singapore and involvement in an export financing scam. It was the sort of reporting whose threat forces business people to do the right thing — a wholly unwelcome development among local players in Jakarta's business scene.

The media is essential for ensuring good governance in business. Hamper, compromise, or starve its operations, and corporate managers and majority shareholders face one less constraint that helps to ensure that they do the right thing. In much of Asia, the constraint of the local media is simply yet another that is woefully inadequate. If the media in the West isn't perfect in its coverage of business, then in much of Asia, it is highly defective. The relative lack of constraints on corporate Asia leaves it a law unto itself. The results of this are the subject of the following chapters.

SECTION 2

FAMILIES, FIRMS, AND FORTUNES

CHAPTER 4

Merchants of Menace? Conglomerates Asian-style

Asia's conglomerates are too big, too unfocused, too poorly managed and structured, lack transparency, and are devoid of internal checks and accountability. There is no such thing as an 'Asian' way in the global age — just a right way and a wrong way, and the Asian way is the wrong way.

What does it take to make a conglomerate in Asia? There is a fairly standard recipe. Take a bank, add some trading interests, some manufacturing interests, a stockbroking firm, lots of real estate holdings, and perhaps a hotel, mix it all around to form a loose structure, but one in which lots of internal transactions take place, list some but not all of the companies on the local stock exchange, and put the lot under the control of one family. And there you have it, made to order: one Asian conglomerate. Trite though this may seem, it isn't too far from the truth.

It is difficult to find major companies — or even medium-sized ones— in Asia that are not part of a conglomerate. In Asia, most conglomerates are owned and ruled by families. The ethnic Chinese businessman in Asia who really has made it, is the one who either doesn't know which of his several business cards to give you or has solved the problem by combining his chairmanship and directorships on one card. With some considerable pride, he will sink back into his chair and savor your expression of disbelief as you turn over, open out, or unfold his business card to reveal his many positions and affiliations. In Asia, he is the envy of his competitors and colleagues alike. In the West, he is a management consultant's worst nightmare. In Asia, perhaps more than anywhere else, diversification is a way for companies' owners to build empires. It isn't a way to create value, and certainly not shareholder value.

STRUCTURES

Indonesia, the Philippines, Thailand, and South Korea are home to some of Asia's most unwieldy conglomerates. Rarely do they have one core area of activity — many simply jump into businesses every which way as opportunities arise and without giving much thought to overall synergies. Typically, a conglomerate comprises dozens of companies, sometimes hundreds. In South-East Asia in particular, conglomerates have tended to expand by adding lots of little companies rather than simply working on expanding several core companies; rarely do they focus on just one industry. Indonesia's Gemala Group typifies this problem. It is comprised of about 50 companies in interests that stretch from pharmaceuticals, to car batteries, hotels, and insurance. I once asked Sofyan Wanandi, the head of Gemala, if he, like his brother Jusuf, collects paintings. 'No,' replied Sofyan, 'I collect factories.' And that is the problem in Asia. Founding families have put great effort into assembling impressive arrays of companies, but almost no effort into putting them in any order.

The structure of many of Asia's largest conglomerates are, at best, chaotic. To refer to them as trading 'houses' is to give them undue credit; 'rubble' is perhaps more apt. Very often, the boundaries between the members of a group are blurred at best. Assets, inventory, and funds are passed among them without due regard to accepted principles of book-keeping. Holding companies — shell companies that are set up to own other companies so that the profits and revenues of the group can be centralized in the one place — might not be used at all, thus leaving many groups without any real structure. These groups are defined more by their disparate parts sharing a common owner than by anything else. They often have no legal standing as a group — the individual companies might be registered, but not the group itself. Its senior executives will normally have a formal position in one or more of the registered companies — perhaps as managing director of one, director of another, and so on. But, paradoxically, the one position they may have where real power resides — director at the group level — also happens to be the one that may well have no legal basis.

Sitting atop all of this is the chairman of the group, a figure who controls everything but who may well have no formal or legally recognized position in *any* part of the empire he controls. Robert Kuok (one of the wealthiest businessmen in Asia) is but one example. He resigned from his last formal position in his many publicly listed companies — chairman of his Hong Kong-based South China Morning Post (Holdings) — at the end of 1997. Despite an empire of hundreds of companies, of which at least 14 are listed on stock exchanges around Asia, no one has any doubts about who calls the shots, particularly on the big decisions.

CORPORATE OMELETTES AND SQUAT PYRAMIDS

Groups that keep expanding but don't modernize their structures ultimately lose their competitive edge. Poor structure leaves them with little transparency, either for outsiders or even for their owners. The lack of a coherent structure makes it difficult for groups to consolidate their results. This leaves many founding families with little idea of how their businesses are performing overall. Cash flow may be mistaken for profits, for example. Sometimes, they believe all is well when it actually isn't. Many Asian conglomerates that appear healthy suddenly collapse, and often no one is more surprised than the founding family.

In their quest to seek a structure, some founding families have their individual companies take equity stakes in each other. A web of cross-shareholdings might make a group more cohesive, but this still gives rise to little structure. The result is akin to a corporate omelette — quite flat and with each constituent part intermingled with others. But this may still do little for transparency. Some groups may also seek to list some — but never all — of their companies on the local stock exchange. This helps to give an appearance of modernity, but that's about all.

The Thai-Chinese conglomerate, Charoen Pokphand (CP), provides a good example of the omelette structure. Its structure is quite flat; there is no holding company, just a group of about four public companies in Thailand and several others elsewhere in the region; these are all linked to a myriad of private companies through cross-shareholdings. This structure also allows profit, inventory, and revenue to be moved from one unit to another, and with little transparency. It leaves potential foreign partners wondering what exactly they are dealing with and just how focused CP really is on their particular joint venture. Just when they think they understand CP, a new business pops up, and with it, another set of potential conflicts of interest. Practically every South Korean *chaebol* follows the omelette structure, which also extends to much of the economy with the *chaebol* themselves being linked to one another through cross-shareholdings and guarantees of each other's borrowings.[1] Omelette conglomerates have led to an omelette economy.

When Asian conglomerates do decide to adopt a more modern corporate structure, they generally opt for the squat pyramid model. A private holding company sits at the apex, a second tier holds the most-prized assets that are usually privately held, and a third tier comprises the group's publicly listed companies.[2] Such a structure makes it easier for the families to implement the maxim: What is profitable is 100% mine; what is less so can be shared with others. The publicly traded companies at the base of the pyramid often serve as stalking horses for cash. They sell their shares to the public and then pass the proceeds up the pyramid through a myriad of internal transactions. In return, other assets — those that are less profitable and, therefore, less desired by the controlling family — are passed down the pyramid.

PYRAMIDS, MAYBE, BUT WHERE ARE THE WINDOWS?

Asia's business groups present enormous problems for external stock analysts and auditors. Group results are rarely consolidated, and when they are, they are usually not disclosed to outsiders. When group holding companies are listed on a stock exchange, they are required to issue annual reports, which provide information on precisely what comprises the group and the group's overall performance. But holding companies that control all of a particular group are almost never listed in Asia. Usually only one or several subsidiaries will be listed, making it difficult and usually impossible for outsiders to gain an overall picture of the group and its performance, which of course is precisely the objective. So, while structuring a conglomerate into a pyramid assists the founding family in obtaining a clearer picture of their business interests, it does little for enhancing transparency for others. Consequently, it is virtually impossible to get a fix on how large most of Asia's groups are, and what their total assets and liabilities are.

Indonesia's Lippo Group provides an example of this. It has companies in Indonesia, Hong Kong, China, the United States, Singapore, and Australia. In all, it has more than 100 companies, of which fewer than 20 are listed. Its most profitable assets are held privately, whereas its publicly traded companies raise cash for the group. The more profitable any subsidiary happens to be, the more equity the controlling family is likely to have retained. All of the group's assets are held by a series of private holding companies. Groups like Lippo are more the rule than the exception when it comes to seeking internal transparency without compromising external opaqueness.

Ratings agencies face enormous difficulties in generating risk ratings for Asia's conglomerates and their subsidiaries. For example, should the rating of the bonds issued by a group member be assessed at the company or the group level? Ideally, a mixture of both. But how is it possible to assess risk for the group when its precise composition, let alone its overall performance, is kept secret? Similarly, groups' creditors can never be really sure if they have been given the full picture, and neither can prospective joint-venture partners. Of course, for the group, a lack of transparency has its virtues. Tax avoidance is one. Taxes cannot be levied effectively when so much is kept hidden. Not alerting competitors to commercially useful information is another virtue. As is keeping the founding family and its assets as small a target for social jealousy and unrest as possible, particularly if they belong to an ethnic Chinese minority.

ONE'S BANK: THE ESSENTIAL BUSINESS TOOL OF THE 1980s

A bank or an equivalent finance arm is an integral part of many Asian conglomerates. As we shall see in the following chapter, borrowing from one's bank is the best defense against poorly enforced business laws that make doing business with a competitor's bank inherently risky. Borrowing from the group's bank also means keeping interest rate margins in-house — another benefit. Yet another is that these banks need not be convinced to lend, they can simply be ordered to do so. In this way, banks that collected deposits from the public and then recycled the funds to their principal shareholders as loans, fed the growth of many Asian conglomerates in their formative years, particularly in the 1980s. The most overt example of this, as usual, is in Indonesia, where today there are approximately 200 private banks still in operation, all of which are attached to conglomerates. And these are just the licensed banks. It is likely that there are dozens — perhaps hundreds — of banks that are not licensed and, therefore, operate illegally and outside the Indonesian government's regulatory net, such as it is. Licensed or unlicensed, Asia's banks have been integral in providing easy credit to their affiliated groups and thus vital to the groups' growth.

ONE'S STOCKBROKING FIRM: THE ESSENTIAL BUSINESS TOOL OF THE 1990s

At first, Asia's founding families were suspicious of listing their companies on the stock market. Listing means disclosure, and disclosure means tax and accountability — not the most popular items on their agenda. Another problem was that many Asian companies couldn't list even if they wanted to. Their internal structure was so poor that they couldn't hope to meet minimum listing requirements. But it didn't take too long before the founding families realized what a boon listing on a stock exchange could be. Banks require that loans be repaid, but minority shareholders require no such thing of the cash that they hand over. Many founding families soon readied one or two of their subsidiaries for an initial public offering (IPO) and were away. Before long, the share market augmented the conglomerates' banks as an important source of capital. Owning a stockbroking firm, which meant keeping the brokerage fees in-house, became the 1990s' equivalent of borrowing from one's bank, which meant keeping the interest rate spread in-house. Indonesia's large number of private banks is now complemented by an equally large number of stockbroking firms. By end-1997, the country had 197 of them, or almost one for each of the 259 companies traded on the Jakarta Stock Exchange. Many were affiliated to local conglomerates. It is no secret that most of these stockbroking firms engage in proprietary trading, that is, they use their own capital to play the stock market, as well as act as the broker for the rest of the group, just as the conglomerates' banks act as the bankers to the group. This Indonesian example is replicated throughout Asia in varying degrees.

ONE'S COMPANY ONE'S CASTLE IN ASIA

Well, so much for how Asia's corporations look like from the outside. But what are they like on the inside? What is it like to be an employee in a typically Asian company? It all depends on what you are used to. After the Roman Empire crumbled, the rule of law was lost and the peoples of Europe were subjected to marauding bands of barbarians. To counteract the uncertainties of poor security and to fill the hiatus left by the Romans, a new system of social order emerged: the feudal system. It lasted in Europe from AD500 to AD1800 — a period of 1,300 years — and involved simple peasant folk being organized under an aristocrat or lord. The peasants worked their lord's lands in exchange for the security he provided and a small portion of what they produced. The mutual obligations between the lord and his peasants created a system of 'vassalage' — the owing of loyalty — where the peasants remained loyal to the lord and the lord to the king. The lord was omniscient, and all chains of command, leadership, and direction radiated from him. Peasants whose loyalty was held in question lived on the periphery of the village, where they could never be quite sure of the degree of the lord's umbrella of protection. The lords would form and re-form coalitions, alternating between fighting each other and forming alliances, as expediency demanded.

To the vast majority of peasants in Europe during this time, the village was their whole world. They could expect to live and die in it without ever having cause to move much beyond it. Outsiders weren't trusted, and with good reason. There was no social agreement or contract across feudal localities. Trust extended little further than the village boundary. External relations were the strict preserve of the lord; certainly it wasn't an area in which the common folk were expected or encouraged to indulge.

Feudalism died in Europe around AD1800. But that didn't mean it disappeared from the face of the earth. Variations exist in any low-trust society that operates without the benefit of sound legal structures — and that means in much of Asia today, and practically in all of it in the recent past.

Today, many Asian companies operate as little more than feudal bastions. In South-East Asia, particularly, the business environment can be as fraught with danger and devoid of the rule of law as life was in feudal Europe. Trust isn't broadly extended, and corporate structures have emerged to reflect this. Many Asian companies are like feudal villages — their employees are like the villagers and the founding patriarch like a lord. Like the villages of the Middle Ages, South-East Asia's conglomerates are relatively isolationist and attempt to provide as much of their own needs as possible. Many are highly vertically integrated. This means that the output of one group member is often the input of another. Very little is contracted out or sourced externally. After all, legal systems often are not available to enforce trust, so it is better not to trust outsiders at all.

THE LOYALTY LADDER: PROMOTIONS BY PERSONALITY

With trust in short supply outside the conglomerate, absolute loyalty is demanded from within it. Staff follow orders — management is rarely participative. Promotions often are not linked to merit as they are to the personal relationships junior staff may have with their superiors. Scaling the corporate ladder is a sign of one's trustworthiness, and not necessarily of one's inherent productivity. Subservience and sycophancy are rewarded; initiative, which by definition demonstrates a lack of dependence on senior staff, is not. Initiative, after all, carries with it the risk of showing up more senior staff, causing them to lose 'face'; therefore, it is disloyal and not encouraged. After all, feudal lords can only stay feudal if their underlings remain dependent on them. Senior managers are always right even when they are wrong, and junior employees should not express their opinions before their seniors do because it means their superiors have no room to move should their view be contrary. Superiors cannot be seen to be contradicted by junior staff, as this would imply a loss of authority. The best course of action for an employee is to say only what is expected and to keep one's real feelings private.

All this is a recipe for personalized networks and patronage within the firm, just as much as outside it. The result isn't the harmonious Asian workplace so often and so erroneously depicted in the West, but one that is highly political. Vertical trust is essential, but horizontal trust is selective. Middle managers fight it out for their bosses' attentions and notice; after all, promotion tends to be on the basis of personality and trust. Teamwork is replaced by strategic behavior, and middle managers array themselves like pieces in a chess game whose next move is contingent on everyone else's. Of course, any organization anywhere that promotes and rewards on the basis of personality and where procedures for advancement lack transparency will exhibit some of these characteristics. It is just that in Asia; companies such as this are the rule rather than the exception.

Staff, and especially senior staff, who leave a company to join another may well be seen as treacherous. Their departure implies a rejection of, and therefore, a loss of 'face' to, senior management. Often, there will be a great deal of demonizing of departed staff after they leave; or they are never mentioned again, as if they had never worked there at all. Remaining employees would certainly not want to openly canvas the true reasons for their former colleague's departure — the conclusions might be an affront to management. Outcomes aren't nearly as important as the process. Pleasing the boss is a far greater priority than, say, meeting targets — after all, everyone knows that numbers can be easily manipulated. A situation will be judged as a success if it is handled 'correctly,' even if the results aren't what was desired. Staff remuneration is heavily patriarchal in that it usually contains a high proportion of payments in kind or payments earmarked for certain types of expenditure. There might be a separate allowance for transport to and from work, employer-sponsored healthcare, and even rice allowances. These emphasize that the employer knows best. Staff expect their employer to look after them as a parent would a child; and to promote this mutual dependence, employers usually oblige. The culture of harmony, dependence, and community rather than individualism underscores the village nature of many Asian firms.

Obviously, the unwritten rules within a typically Asian company are utterly alien to the average Westerner. They are both complex and absolutely at odds with how workers are expected to behave in the West. And they are a significant barrier to entry for anyone who is not prepared to follow the rules of the game.

DWELLERS AT THE VILLAGE PERIPHERY: WESTERN EXPATRIATES

Management feudalism is most clearly observed in South-East Asia, where the lords are mostly ethnic Chinese conglomerate heads, the peasants their workers, and the king takes the form of the country's political leader. But who across Asia are the peasants kept on the periphery of the village because their loyalty is never quite beyond reproach? Western expatriates often unwittingly take this role.

Sometimes Western expatriates are employed in locally owned firms because they do *not* fit in with the structure of 'vassalage' and will toil on unaware of and unencumbered by the cultural baggage of loyalty over productivity. This makes them short-term but highly productive employees, ideal for troubleshooting, after which they can be eased out. At other times, they are hired by local firms simply to add prestige to the group, or so that it can present a Western face when it seeks loans from Western banks or wishes to appeal to Western fund managers. In this regard, Western expatriates are little more than corporate window-dressing — they are there to lend an air of modernity and perceived sophistication. But should they attempt to exert their role beyond this or question the prevailing ethics and practices, then they are often rebuffed.

Whatever the case, rarely are Western expatriates prepared for the mental maze and psychological maneuvering of their new workplaces. Unlike Western firms, Asian firms often don't have formal internal codes of conduct and written rules; everything depends on the whim of senior management and the founding family. As highlighted in Chapter 1, rules mean inflexibility and a ceding of control — and Asian corporate patriarchs (and their pretenders) simply have no desire to share power with a rule book. But just as in any economy that isn't governed by sound laws, companies that are similarly governed become riddled with personality networks and cliques. In such an environment, most Western expatriates who, as far as the local employees are concerned, have seemingly dropped in from nowhere, almost always will remain on the periphery. Entry to the firm is based on skill, but advancement and relevance within it proceed on the basis of patronage. Many Western expatriates who work for locally owned firms in Asia, leave them feeling that their skills and time have been largely wasted. Often, they are right. Life at the village periphery is like that.

KNOW-WHO BUSINESS

Connections and relationships are critically important when it comes to business in much of Asia. This is repeated so often that it has become something of a cliché. But it is true. In Asia, know-who is as important as know-how. Many in Asia claim that the importance of personal connections is central to their 'Asianness'; an integral part of 'Asian values.' But this really is more a sign of a culture that has evolved in the absence of the rule of law. When legal systems offer traders little protection, it is only reasonable that they should want to trade with just those they know and trust. Naturally, this is somewhat limiting; Asian business people are generally habitual networkers — extending the range of one's personal contacts means extending the range of one's scope for business. This has become so ingrained in many Asian cultures that it survives for some time after legal structures are in place and business can be safely pursued on an impersonal basis. The importance of contacts means that companies tend to be subsumed by personalities. Ask a senior Thai-Chinese businessman what he thinks of Malaysia's Lion Group and the questioner is likely to draw a blank. But ask him what he thinks of William Cheng (Lion's owner) and his face will light up with recognition. When Asia's more prominent entrepreneurs want to do business with the Lion Group, they don't so much call Lion as they do Cheng. This is precisely the opposite of the case in, say, the United States or Europe, where, for example, almost everyone has heard of Mattel, but almost no one would be able to name its CEO or principal shareholder. In Asia, personalities count. Companies serve senior management; rarely is it the other way round.

KEEPING IT WITHIN THE FAMILY

An important distinction is often made in Asia between 'insiders' and 'outsiders.' Outsiders must work hard to earn trust, and very rarely achieve it fully; whereas almost unconditional trust is automatically awarded to insiders, particularly family members. But a problem with family control is that the family is stuck if none of its immediate members is interested in business. What then is one to do: entrust management to insiders who are disinterested or entrust it to good managers who are outsiders? Some of Asia's business patriarchs have solved the problem by trawling the outer reaches of their families to look for those who have the right skills to take senior management positions in the family firm. Sometimes the links to the family can be tenuous, but as long as they can somehow be defined as 'family,' they can be deemed to fit the bill. Robert Kuok, who is perhaps the richest overseas Chinese businessman in the world, entrusts much of the day-to-day operations of his multi-billion-dollar Kerry Group to the husband of a niece. At least six other relatives hold senior management positions in the group. The late Sir Pao Yue Kong, the founder of the Hong Kong-based shipping group, World International, had only daughters, none of whom wanted to assume management roles in the family business, so each of Sir Pao's four sons-in-law did instead.

Many Asian business families are acutely aware of the need to have new skills injected into their companies, but at the same time are unable to cede management control to outsiders. What many have done is to send their children overseas for a Western education, and particularly to study for an MBA. They then return to the company and assume management positions. In this way, management can be both family and professional; in a sense, the family is able to have its cake and eat it too.

Even so, there may be only so many family members to go around. Not so long ago, many overseas Chinese firms recruited only managers from the same Chinese dialect group as the founding family when they had to look outside the family. Some firms still do this. When Thailand's enormous Charoen Pokphand Group expanded to Indonesia, the group's Chearavanont family entrusted the management of its new Indonesia branch only to Teochiu speakers — the same Chinese dialect group as themselves. However, the vast majority of Indonesia's Chinese population ancestrally are not Teochiu but Hokkien speakers. The Chearavanonts looked all over Indonesia for Teochius. One of the few significant pockets of them exists in Pontianak, a city in the Indonesian province of West Kalimantan on the island of Borneo. This was a rather obscure place to source for senior management, but that is exactly what the Chearavanonts did. Not surprisingly, selecting from such a small pool put a significant constraint on the management talent available to the company, and its fortunes in Indonesia suffered accordingly. Such practices put Asian companies at a clear competitive disadvantage when they grow, and when markets open up to competition from outside companies that are not similarly culturally constrained. These days, being so traditionally Asian is a luxury few companies in Asia can afford.

SERVICES

Family members are the most trusted in Asian firms, and beyond the family circle are concentric circles of others — the further away from the center, the less they are trusted. In one of the outer circles resides consultants, just beyond where Western expatriate employees might well be found. In Asia's heyday, when its economies were booming, many American and European consulting companies set up shop in Asia hoping to land enormous contracts with local firms. Many were to be disappointed. Rather than service the local firms, they often found themselves surviving on work from other American and European companies that had also set up shop in Asia. For many Western consultants, business was good, but the boom never really came. They did all right, but given Asia's economic growth, the potential size of the market, and the obvious need for their services, many Western legal, accounting, and other service-oriented firms should have done much better. Not only were the contracts not nearly as large as many had expected, but the fees achieved were often way below comparable work performed in, say, the United States. This isn't just a South-East Asian problem. Even in Japan, consulting fees are often far below what they are in the United States and Europe. Where the auditing fee for a major Japanese corporate might be US$600,000, the fee for a similar-sized company in the United States would be around US$5 million. Why is this? It certainly isn't because the business services sector in Asia is much more competitive than it is in the United States.

Put simply, services are undervalued as business inputs in Asia. Partly, the problem is that the conglomerates simply don't trust outsiders, which is what, by definition, consultants are. When loyalty is valued above all else, the concept of hiring consultants whose loyalty is at best only temporary and never really guaranteed is a complete anathema. Having them on the premises at all is perplexing enough, but then to actually pay for the privilege is revolutionary. There is a significant cultural bias in favor of tangible items in Asia, to say the least. Seemingly, if something doesn't have physical form, and form that isn't commensurate with its price, then it isn't worth having, and certainly not worth paying for. The Western manager might well commission a worldwide management consulting firm to review his firm's production processes and then marvel at the recommendations in the 100-page final report even though it cost him US$200,000. The ethnic Chinese founder, on the other hand, is more likely to hold up the report and wonder how a 'book' could possibly cost so much.

Formal staff training, technology, public relations, marketing and branding, legal advice, and auditing are all in this genre and all tend to be under-acquired by Asian companies. One way around the technology cost barrier for Asian firms is to form a joint venture with a Western partner in which the terms include technology transfer. Once technology has been transferred, the Western firm may well find that it has outlived its usefulness and the joint venture begins to unravel. Other services, if they can't be provided in-house, may simply be done without.

Market research is one such service. Typically, a Western company sets up in a new country after first commissioning market research to demonstrate a market gap and the potential for profits. But an Asian company (particularly those that aren't Japanese — the Japanese have become extraordinarily thorough in their market entry research) will typically invest in a new market based not on research but on local connections. A Thai businessman may choose to begin trading in Singapore because his son has moved there and he can act as the local agent, for example. This is one of the reasons why so many Asian companies have got it so wrong when they have attempted to invest in the West. They invest without doing their research first, and often without having the required personal connections on the ground. It is also why, when they do, they generally stick to real estate, which is relatively risk-free and doesn't require a great deal of research or supervision. Asia's dislike of service inputs is an attribute that sorely needs to change. A healthy demand for services is the sign of a wealthy and maturing economy. The migrant mentality of many of Asia's overseas Chinese and Indian entrepreneurs might have served them well in the past. But in a global economy where services have never been more important, a suspicion of intangibles and those who purvey them will simply see Asia being left behind.

CORPORATE MANAGEMENT AND STRUCTURE IN ASIA AND THE WEST

How best to summarize Asian business structures and management? The best way is to compare them with what is typical in the United States, the United Kingdom, and Australia. Typically, Asian firms differ greatly in their structure and their management style from what is the norm in the West. Table 5.1 summarizes 25 major areas of difference between the two styles, many of which have already been alluded to.

The structure and management practices of the corporations based in New York, London, Bonn, and Sydney are not perfect. Perfection in management and corporate structuring is one of those things that all companies would like to achieve but, because of definitional problems and a constantly shifting target, probably will never attain. But one thing is clear. What is typical practice in the West makes Western companies more agile and adept at handling crises than what is typical in Asia. We know this after the Asian economic crisis of 1997–98. Imperfect though they may be, Western business practices have triumphed and are to be aspired to. This is not to say that cultural differences are neither valuable nor to be celebrated. They are. But in the era of the global marketplace, cultural idiosyncrasies belong anywhere but in the boardroom. Ramshackle corporate structures and patriarchal management may be quaint, but they come at an enormous cost.

Table 5.1   Management and Corporate Structure in Asia
and the West — 25 Key Differences

Large Western firm	Large Asian firm
1. Short time horizons in decision making	Long time horizons in decision making
2. Driven by profit and/or market share	Driven by growth
3. Corporate direction is determined by overall corporate 'vision' and strategy	Corporate direction is determined by opportunity
4. Highly structured	Often poorly structured
5. Wide ownership (institutions)	Narrow ownership (family)
6. Professionally managed	Family managed
7. More focused on core businesses	Highly diversified
8. Invests on the basis of research	Invests on the basis of connections
9. Minority shareholders are well treated	Minority shareholders are abused
10. Dispersed decision making	Centralized decision making
11. Relatively small number of units/companies	Large number of units/companies
12. Prefers accrual accounting	Prefers cash accounting
13. Lots of contracting out and buying in	High degree of vertical integration and lots of internal transactions
14. Reliant on external funding	Prefers internal funding
15. Services are very important	Dislikes services
16. R&D-intensive	Little or no R&D
17. Participative management	Patriarchal management
18. Senior management is relatively aloof	Senior management is hands-on
19. Well-defined career ladder for staff	Vague career ladder for staff
20. High priority given to transparency, auditing, and disclosure	Low priority given to transparency, auditing, and disclosure
21. Fringe benefits are generally a small part of total remuneration	Fringe benefits are a high component of salary (remuneration is paternalistic)
22. Staff training is formal and structured	Staff are trained informally and on the job
23. Employees tend to be promoted on the basis of their inherent productivity	Employees tend to be promoted on the basis of their connections and perceived loyalty
24. Job descriptions are precise and employees are encouraged to use initiative	Job descriptions are vague and employees work as directed
25. Staff initiative expected and rewarded	Staff initiative discouraged

CHAPTER 5

Asia's Conglomerates and their Banks

The previous chapter examined why Asian conglomerates set up their own banks. This chapter looks at what they do to them. Much of Asia's banking system is a mess. Here's why.

If credit is the blood of an economy, then the banking system is its heart. And a strong banking system is essential to keep credit pumping through the economy. This means that banks must be prudently managed, carefully regulated (though not stifled), transparent in their operations and balance sheets, and, perhaps most importantly, independent of non-financial sector interests. In Asia, most local banks simply do not meet any of these criteria. Of course, the West has its own banking scandals, and the savings and loan institution (S&L) debacle in the United States in the early 1990s best epitomizes this. But even with the S&L fiasco, the US banking system still maintains its overall integrity. Sure, the S&Ls were a mess, but they were an embarrassing carbuncle on an otherwise solid system. And arguably, the single most important reason why the system remains solid is the major banks that underpin it are owned not by prominent business families with extensive external non-bank interests, but by pension funds and small individual stockholders, thus permitting a separation of ownership from management. The redeeming aspect of the S&L mess was that problematic institutions didn't constitute the entirety of its banking system. In much of Asia, they effectively do.

The abuses that are described in the following paragraphs are endemic across much of Asia; in the 'frontier' economies of Thailand and Indonesia, they are chronic. Banks have been poorly regulated — in some instances, staff of the central banks, which are responsible for banking supervision, are prepared to accept bribes to give private banks a clean bill of health when nothing could be further from the truth. Asia's banks are sinking under bad loans, and it's not only because of falling property prices. Poor management, poor supervision, and corruption are some of the other causes.

ASIA'S BANKS: AWASH IN A SEA OF VESTED INTERESTS

Borrowers must place a great deal of trust in a bank when seeking a loan. Usually, they must reveal to the bank their innermost commercial-in-confidence secrets — their business plans and their financial data. They are entitled to expect that such information will remain with the bank and that the bank will lend on the basis of the merits of what is being proposed. An ideal banking system is one in which banks are not compromised in their lending decisions by their other business activities or by the other business interests of their principal shareholders. They should be standalone institutions that are driven in their decision making by commercial considerations alone.

It is difficult to imagine how Asia's private banks could be more compromised. The major banks of almost every Asian country are attached to wider conglomerates that have a range of non-financial businesses. (Mainland China, Taiwan, and Japan differ from this basic model and are dealt with in later chapters. South Korea's major banks are not in the hands of the *chaebol*, but government intervention in their lending means that they might as well be. They are examined in more detail at the end of this chapter.) The majority shareholders of most of the banks also happen to be families, and each family member often has his or her own business interests, apart from whatever the family might collectively own. And in environments that lack even basic prudential supervision, it's not too difficult to see what these banks really are: piggy banks used by their controlling shareholders for private purposes while collecting funds from members of the public. This means that depositors' funds are lent out on a less than fully commercial basis and when the risks have not been independently assessed. There is one word to describe this sort of arrangement: dangerous.

Hong Kong's banks are generally quite robust. The role played by Hong Kong's banking regulators is all the more remarkable when it is considered that these days, the biggest game in town is property speculation. This, coupled with banking, normally makes an explosive cocktail. But not all of Hong Kong's banks are independent of non-financial interests. The Hongkong Chinese Bank is jointly owned by China Resources (Holdings), a business arm of China's Ministry of Foreign Trade and Economic Cooperation (Moftec), and the Lippo Group. Hence, the bank sits amid a web of overlapping interests in Hong Kong and China that include property, food distribution, power plants, industrial parks, breweries, port facilities, supermarkets, and department stores. Hong Kong's fourth-largest bank, Dao Heng Bank, is controlled by the Malaysian-Chinese billionaire, Quek Leng Chan. He has enormous holdings in Malaysia and elsewhere, but in Hong Kong, his non-financial interests include property developments that are held by the same holding company as his bank. The First Pacific Bank is controlled by the Hong Kong-based First Pacific Group, a conglomerate of interests that include property and telecommunications in Hong Kong and elsewhere in Asia. The group is controlled by Indonesian-Chinese billionaire, Liem Sioe Liong, and his associates. Dah Sing Bank, Wing On Bank, and Jian Sing Bank are all controlled by David Wong Shou-yeh and his family. The Wong family also has significant property developments in China and Hong Kong. These banks, while not among Hong Kong's major banks, share something with most of their South-East Asian counterparts — their majority owners have significant interests outside the financial services sector, heightening the potential for conflicts of interest between the banks' lending operations and their major shareholders' other businesses.

Much of **Taiwan's** banking system remains in state hands, although this is changing. Political interference in the banking system is being replaced by the conflicts of interest of the growing private-sector banks given their links to non-financial affiliates. Chinatrust Commercial Bank is among the largest of the new private banks. It is owned by one of Taiwan's wealthiest families, the Koo family. But banking isn't the Koos' only interest. They also control Far East Textiles, which is Taiwan's biggest cement producer, Taiwan Cement, as well as Taiwan Polypropylene, Grand Pacific Petrochemical, and a myriad of other interests. Another bank, the Far East Bank, is controlled by the Hsu family and is part of its Far East Textiles Group. The bank's sister companies include Taiwan's biggest textile exporter, Asia Cement, Far East Department Store, and Ju Ming Shipping. With such diverse affiliates, Taiwan's banks are not immune from the scandals that regularly engulf many of their South-East Asian counterparts. For example, the Bao Dao Commercial Bank was enmeshed in controversy in 1994 for buying land from its affiliates at an enormous premium over the payment the affiliates had made for it just one month before.[1]

Singapore is home to some of the largest private banks in South-East Asia. As prudently run as they may be today, they are not as independent from non-financial interests (in terms of their ownership or their subsidiaries) as might be expected in a city-state that has become famous for doing the 'right' thing. United Overseas Bank (UOB) directly owns more than a third of United Overseas Land (UOL), a large commercial property investor, and in turn, UOL owns a swag of UOB shares. In any case, both are controlled by local entrepreneur Wee Cho Yaw. Also, UOL owns most of the shares in the listed Hotel Plaza, which owns three hotels in Singapore and other properties worldwide. Wee has other interests as well. He is the chairman and part-owner of United Industrial Corporation (UIC), which is controlled by Indonesian-Chinese Liem Sioe Liong. UIC manufactures household detergents, is involved in printing and packaging, and controls Singapore Land, the owner of many prime office towers in Singapore. Wee also controls Haw Par Brothers International and Tiger Medicals, which hold the rights to the universal cure-all ointment, Tiger Balm. Clearly, UOB sits amid a complex web of non-banking corporate interests.

In **Thailand**, most major private banks are dominated by a single shareholder, and these shareholders usually have significant other non-bank interests. The country's biggest bank is Bangkok Bank, which is controlled by the Thai-Chinese Sophonpanich family. The family's core business is banking, but it also has important stakes in other major companies such as Bangkok Expressway (the publicly listed company that is building major toll-roads throughout Bangkok) and City Realty (a property arm). The family also has important rice-trading interests. Bangkok Bank itself has significant interests in companies that operate in non-financial sectors. There are more than 30 companies in which the family has a precise 10% stake and which operate in anything from textiles to food trading to chemicals.

One of the more spectacular bank failures in Thailand in recent years was the collapse of the Bangkok Bank of Commerce. Its demise provides a textbook example of all that is wrong with Thailand's banking system. The two senior managers at the bank, Kirkkiat Jalichandra and Rakesh Saxena, lent about a third of the bank's total loan portfolio to themselves. They also lent to senior politicians, embezzled the bank's funds, and fabricated its accounts. When the bank was on the verge of collapse with around US$3 billion in bad debts, rather than allow it to close, Thailand's central bank spent large sums of public money in attempts to bail it out. The rewards for imprudence can be high in Thailand, so it should be of surprise to no one that there is a lot of it.

Entrepreneurs for whom banking is just one activity own each of the **Philippines'** private banks. Metropolitan Bank and Trust (Metrobank) is one of the largest. It is controlled by the Filipino-Chinese George Ty. Banking is Ty's main interest, but it's not his only interest. He has a flour mill, a car assembly plant, a plastic factory, and large landholding in the Philippines and Taiwan.

The Spanish-descended Ayala family has its Bank of the Philippines Islands, which is the country's largest universal bank. The family's flagship company, though, is Ayala Land, which has enormous landholding. The family also controls local telecommunications firm, Globe Telecom, as well as a myriad of food, agri-business, and industrial interests.

Banco de Oro, East-West Banking Corporation, Allied Banking Corporation, Rizal Commercial Banking Corporation and the Capital Development Bank are all owned by family companies with diverse business interests.

That the Philippines has not had more bank crashes with all this potential for loans to non-bank affiliates is remarkable. Philippine banking regulator likes to think that it is due to its careful supervision of the sector. Certainly, the central bank has been far more effective and far less corrupt than, say, its Indonesian and Thai counterparts. However, perhaps the more important reason why the Philippine banking system has more integrity and better asset quality than elsewhere in the region is because Manila hasn't experienced the same degree of property speculation as the other Asian capitals such as Bangkok.

Indonesia's banking sector is the most compromised of all of Asia's banking sectors. Not surprisingly, it's also in the biggest mess. When the economic crisis set in, in 1997, there were more than 200 private banks in Indonesia, and every one of them was part of a larger conglomerate of non-banking activities such as property and manufacturing. Many — probably most — of Indonesia's banks were in various stages of collapse by 1998 because of the loans they had given to affiliated companies. The economic crisis exacerbated the problem, but many banks were on the verge of collapse even before the crisis.

Indonesia's biggest private-sector bank is Bank Central Asia (BCA). It was controlled by Liem Sioe Liong's Salim Group, Indonesia's largest and most diversified conglomerate before it was seized by the government after it had to be bailed out in 1998. The second-biggest private bank was Bank Danamon. It was placed under government management in early 1998 after its near collapse from excessive loans to property development companies owned by the bank's founders. Another big private bank is Bank Lippo, controlled by the Indonesian-Chinese Riady family. It too has enormous real estate holding and retailing and manufacturing interests across Indonesia.

Even oil-rich **Brunei** hasn't managed to avoid the private bank/ conflict of interest trap. Its first private bank was closed down in 1986, after loans to the bank's owners drove it to insolvency. Today, Brunei has just one private bank, the Baiduri Bank. It is owned by Prince Mohamed, a brother of the Sultan of Brunei. But it too is part of a wider group of interests. The Baiduri Group has links to at least 24 other companies, mostly outside the financial services sector, including a food distributor, local newspapers, an Internet service provider, supermarkets, luxury car importers, and other import-related companies. These interests are covered in more detail in Chapter 11.

Malaysia's banks are relatively independent of non-financial interests — thanks largely to tight central bank rules on who can buy into a bank. Applicants must be practically free of debt, for instance. Consequently, the country's banks are generally owned by principal shareholders whose core and practically only interests are in banking. Hence, Malaysia stands out as something of an oddity in Asia. However, there are several major exceptions. Quek Leng Chan's Hong Leong Group, a massive and diversified conglomerate, includes Hong Leong Bank (formerly owned by Khoo Kay Peng when it was known as MUI Bank). It shares its owner's attention with some of Malaysia's bigger companies, such as Hume Industries, Nanyang Press, Hong Leong Properties, and Hong Leong Industries. The other exception is the smaller Multi-Purpose Bank, which is part of the Multi-Purpose Group. The group also has enormous and diversified interests that stretch across gaming, property development, shipping, and hotels.

So, many of Asia's banks are potentially compromised by their owners' other business interests. But what, in practice, does this really mean? Rather a lot, as we are about to see.

IN-HOUSE LENDING

Any conglomerate that features a degree of vertical integration where the output of one subsidiary is the input of another has, by definition, related-party transactions. If they are all on a fully commercial basis, all is well and good. If they are not, then they amount to profit and revenue shifting around the group. Perhaps the most potentially pernicious related-party transaction is in-house lending. This practice is rife among Asia's conglomerates, with the group's bank becoming an important and sometimes the prime source of funds for the group's activities. 'We own a bank because what is the point of giving others the spread?...Our chairman thinks there is no sense in one division borrowing while the other has deposits,' Jimmy Hidayat, a director of Indonesia's Dharmala Group, was reported as saying.[2] Why indeed? Except that borrowing from the one source — a source that is an affiliate — can make a conglomerate wholly unstable. Banking works by having the assets of the bank — its loans — subject to as many independent fates as possible. When a multitude of loans are made to a range of companies that are not independent but affiliated, the fate of the loans are no longer independent and the risk attached to the loan portfolio escalates dramatically. Adverse conditions that affect one affiliate are likely to affect others, thereby increasing the risk of a series of defaults rather than just one or two. When loans to affiliates reach more than half of a bank's net assets, as was the case with the Philippines' Orient Commercial Bank Corporation, then the risks are very high indeed.

Indonesia provides an example of how fraught excessive in-house lending can be in South-East Asia. Many Indonesian conglomerates established their own bank for no other reason than to act as the banker to the group. As an earlier chapter noted, Asia's business families often don't trust one another. Besides, as Jimmy Hidayat pointed out, borrowing from someone else's bank means giving them the interest margin. The result is that Indonesia is over-banked. Supervisory resources are stretched and virtually no bank is independent — all are linked to other companies through their common shareholders. Thus, there isn't a local bank in Indonesia that doesn't sit amid a web of vested interests.

The Indonesian government has rules against banks lending more than 20% of their capital to any single borrower or a group of related borrowers; in the case of a borrower that is affiliated with the bank, no more than 10% can be lent. The rules look good on paper but they have been enforced only half-heartedly. In October 1995, no less than 77 banks were found to be in breach of these rules — up from 33 the year before.[3] The small Bank Anrico was the worst offender. It had lent a whopping 1,925% of its net capital to its sister companies. Those who make the rules didn't necessarily keep to them either. Bank Jakarta, owned by Probosutedjo, a half-brother of Soeharto, was found to have extended to its affiliates credit of more than two-and-a-half times its capital base. Clearly, the two banks were asking for it. And they got it. They were among the 15 Indonesian banks that were closed down in late 1997 at the behest of the IMF. At the time, Probosutedjo didn't seem to understand what he had done wrong. Why should his bank have been closed down when it had only 'a harmless cold,' he protested.[4] At the same time, a bank partly owned by Soeharto's son, Bambang Trihatmodjo, was also closed down. He too thought the closure was wholly unreasonable. His defense: most other banks had violated capital and lending rules and he was simply doing what everyone else did.[5]

Perhaps an even more startling example of in-house lending came to light after the collapse and subsequent takeover of Indonesia's third-largest private bank, Bank Dagang Nasional Indonesia (BDNI), in mid-1998. The bank was a cornerstone of the Gadjah Tunggal group, which until that time was one of Indonesia's ten largest conglomerates. The group's founder, Sjamsul Nursalim — who, incidentally, has a controlling interest in the large, Singapore-listed property group, Tuan Sing Holdings, and, through that, controls the Australian-based Grand Hotels Group, which is listed on the Australian Stock Exchange — had ordered BDNI to lend an astonishing 76% of its total loans to other companies that he controlled, according to the Indonesian Bank Restructuring Agency (IBRA), the agency that was set up to manage problem banks. Consequently, an even more astonishing 95% of its loans were found to be non-performing.[6] That all wasn't well was suggested in September 1997 when Sjamsul was kidnapped for three days until his wife paid US$4 million for his release. The kidnappers had reportedly acted on behalf of some disgruntled BDNI customers. Ultimately, BDNI was bailed out and then liquidated by the Indonesian government. Sjamsul was given the option of either ceding control of most of his Indonesian-based companies to the Indonesian government in return, or going to jail. He opted for the former.[7]

Rules on this sort of lending to affiliates are all well and good. But even if they are complied with, they can often still be rendered useless. Frequently, banks in Asia circumvent such rules by swapping matching obligations to their affiliates with other banks. So, one bank might lend US$100 million to the property affiliate of another bank and, in return, that bank lends US$100 million to the property affiliate of the first bank. These transactions have the appearance of being at arm's length, but in reality, they are not. Transactions like these have done a great deal in undermining Asia's banking systems.

INFORMATION LEAKAGE

Excessive loans to affiliates make many Asian banks dangerous to deal with, but such loans aren't the only threat to banks' customers. Information sharing among affiliates is a common practice with Asian conglomerates. Ordinarily, this doesn't matter, but when it is a bank that is passing on information about its customers, then there is a lot to worry about, especially if that information is commercially sensitive. By comparison, banks in the West tend to concentrate on banking and have few or no non-financial sector affiliates. Thus, in the West, client information is usually safe with the bank, if for no other reason than there are few or no non-bank sister companies to which to pass the information on.

Many companies, from both within Asia and from the West, have come unstuck after having dealt with some of Asia's banks. Typically, what may happen is that a potential borrower may approach a bank or some other finance arm that belongs to a conglomerate for a loan for a new venture. A copy of the business plan will generally be required with the loan application. If the plan looks promising, the bank might well refuse a loan but pass the plan to an affiliate so that it can start up a business along the same lines. Of course, such behavior is highly unethical and even illegal — but what does this really mean in some parts of Asia? If the plan relates to a sector in which an affiliate of the bank already operates, then the bank might well choose to pass it along anyway — just to give the affiliate a close preview of the potential competition.

EARLY FORECLOSURE

The non-bank interests of banks' major shareholders pose even more threats to their customers. The conflict of interest that envelop many banks may drive them to foreclose early on the loans of their customers. This is particularly the case when a bank is affiliated with a property company — and, as we have seen, there is no shortage of this in Asia.

Many fledgling business people have had their wings clipped after having offered up real estate as collateral for loans from Asian banks. The banks' property-based affiliates eye the collateral and urge that the loans be called in. The borrower may not have sufficient cash to meet the unexpected cash call and the real estate is subsequently seized by the bank to be sold to its affiliates.

A story often told in Singapore, to the point where it has near legendary status, concerns a banker who also owned a real estate company. A local businessman had just completed building one of Singapore's first big shopping complexes in what is now its premier shopping district. The banker was desperate for a slice of the complex for his real estate company. It was the envy of many of Singapore's business families and he wanted to have a share in it. The owner of the complex, however, made the mistake of going to the banker for a loan to set up a new factory. The banker agreed, but insisted that the shopping complex be offered as collateral for the loan. The shopping complex owner took the money and duly set about building his factory. It wasn't an immediate success, and although loan repayments continued to be made, occasionally they were a little late. The banker saw his opportunity and had his bank immediately foreclose on the loan so that he could seize the shopping complex. He had only hoped for a share in it but managed to acquire all of it. The parable of the banker with many hats is one with a wide application around Asia.

KEEPING IT IN THE FAMILY

By now, it should be clear that banks controlled by a single shareholder are potentially risky propositions, particularly if the majority owner has other business interests as well. Such banks are potential threats to themselves and their owners. Furthermore, any banking system that comprises such banks — as Asia's mostly are — is at risk, particularly in the absence of adequate banking regulation and supervision. But Asia's family-controlled banks face another risk. When the crunch comes and a bank needs cash infusions to grow stronger or even simply to survive, the controlling shareholder — usually a family — is often unwilling to take the step if it means its ownership will be diluted. This was particularly important during the height of Asia's economic crisis. Many banks in Thailand, the Philippines, and Indonesia teetered on the edge of collapse and were in desperate need of more capital to cover their escalating bad loans. Despite this, many of the controlling families refused to accept a new strategic investor or to hold a new share issue to raise the required funds, as doing so meant losing control of the bank. Rather than see a dilution of their equity, many preferred to rough it out even if this meant risking their depositors' savings.

OFF BALANCE SHEET AND OUT OF SIGHT

The growth of off-balance-sheet transactions has begun to bedevil Asia's banks. In recent years, the nature of banking has changed such that there has been a significant rise in off-balance-sheet activity. An important off-balance-sheet activity is the provision of loan guarantees. These can expose banks to enormous risks but they only turn up on the balance sheet in the event of a default. Regulatory authorities that are stretched simply by supervising banks' balance sheets, don't stand a chance when it comes to effectively monitoring off-balance-sheet activity. This is a growing problem in more developed economies, too — but there, regulators are generally diligent and have enough resources to monitor the risks.

Increasingly, banks that have sought fee income have given guarantees on corporate bonds. Also, many that are attached to larger conglomerates — as are most banks in Asia — have attempted to circumvent rules on lending to affiliated companies by simply arranging for their affiliates to raise capital by issuing bonds and then guaranteeing these bonds. What happened to Indonesia's Bank Pacific (chronicled later in this chapter) demonstrates the dangers of doing this.

BUYING OFF THE REGULATORS: BANKING IN INDONESIA AND THAILAND

The structure of Asia's banks is such that a lot can go wrong. But one final aspect of many of Asia's banking systems which ensures that all that can go wrong often does, is its regulatory systems. It is no coincidence that countries with the worst banking systems also happen to have the worst central bankers.

When the Thai government closed down 58 troubled finance companies in 1997 at the behest of the IMF, rumors provided warning of impending doom — and gave ample opportunity to local politicians with stakes in finance companies to ensure that their company wasn't targeted. The Thai media also speculated openly about which Bank of Thailand (central bank) officials took bribes to remove certain finance companies from the hit list before the list was released.[8]

Indonesia's central bank, Bank Indonesia, has been riddled with fraud and corruption. Asia's economic crisis and Indonesia's particular malaise served to highlight just how bad things have been. Corruption in Bank Indonesia has been systematic. Officials responsible for ensuring private banks' compliance with prudential rules routinely accepted bribes to overlook transgressions, some of which in some instances were nothing less than extraordinary.

In late 1997, when the Indonesian government was looking for scapegoats for the country's problems, one of its first stops was Bank Indonesia. In August, four members of Bank Indonesia's audit team that had been responsible for inspecting the books of Bank Perniagaan (BP), were arrested for conspiring with BP's owners to conceal its fraud and mismanagement. The four allegedly had taken bribes to ignore fictitious loans and fake commercial paper and certificates of deposit.[9] Later that year, the seriousness of the corruption at Bank Indonesia was made clear when three of its directors were questioned and two were arrested for taking bribes. The owners of not just Bank Perniagaan but also Bank Artha Prima, Bank Dwipa, and Bank Asta — all of which were on the verge of collapse or at least should have been had proper banking and bankruptcy laws been in force — had paid off Bank Indonesia officials to overlook their fraud and mismanagement. One of the Bank Indonesia officials arrested was the central bank's director of banking supervision.[10]

With so many senior officials implicated, serial corruption at the central bank was clearly rife. Worse, the arrests seemed more a function of the Indonesian government wanting to impress the IMF as part of its negotiations for emergency loans than an actual decision to get tough on corruption. Asia's financial collapse was a rude awakening for many in

Jakarta and for their comfortable old-boy networks in which the proceeds from corruption are routinely spread around to ensure that all are implicated and no one speaks up. The regularity of the irregular in Jakarta was underscored when Soeharto's half-brother, Probosutedjo, admitted in public that when his Bank Jakarta was closed down as part of the IMF-induced reforms, one Bank Indonesia director actually offered to help restart the closed bank under a new name. Probosutedjo also protested that his bank had been closed down because it hadn't given 'gifts' to Bank Indonesia officials 'like other private banks.'[11] Probably it didn't feel it needed to. After all, Probosutedjo was a relative of the president. Connections in Indonesia usually mean more than simply being awarded licenses and other privileges. They also mean avoiding being asked for bribes.

In early 1998, the Indonesian government established the Indonesian Bank Restructuring Agency (IBRA) to take over and restructure banks that had been pushed to the verge of collapse by mismanagement and Indonesia's plummeting rupiah; the rupiah had fallen by almost 70% in less than six months. That such an agency needed to be established clearly demonstrated that Bank Indonesia wasn't up to the task. How this new agency was to be any less prone to corruption than Bank Indonesia wasn't explained. Almost immediately, IBRA was embroiled in a scandal that became known as the 'Baligate,' in which political associates of then-president BJ Habibie collected a highly irregular US$68 million 'fee' for assisting in the recovery of loans owed to the recently nationalized Bank Bali. Several senior IBRA officials were linked to the 'fee.'

The Orient Bank of the Philippines[12]

Jose Go is a prominent member of Manila's Filipino-Chinese business community. He built his Ever-Gotesco Group into a diversified conglomerate with interests that span discount shopping malls, telecommunications, manufacturing, golf courses, and resorts. But right at the center of this web was Go's Orient Commercial Bank Corporation (Orient Bank). Go was a member of the *nouveau riche*, and he was flashy. There was the yacht, the penthouses, and the helicopter. Only in his early fifties, Go had come a long way in a relatively short period of time. But it was all expansion and never any consolidation. Many of his ventures had high up-front costs but with revenues that only trickled in over subsequent years. Consequently, he built up enormous debts. His *modus operandi* was to borrow heavily and then every so often sweep out the loans by raising funds on the Philippine Stock Exchange to pay them off. In this way, he plunged large sums into six shopping centers around Metro Manila at an average cost of US$45 million a piece; US$35 million was spent on a golf course, US$95 million went into constructing a beachside resort, and in 1996, a US$134 million commitment was made for a construction project in Xiamen, China. But there was a problem. The main source of Go's borrowings was Orient Bank — his bank.

Go and his family acquired the bank, when it was known as the Bangko Silangan Development Bank, in 1994. It was a small development bank and only in February 1997 did it receive a full commercial banking license. Go made much use of the bank in a short time. It was when Asia's economic crisis broke that Go became particularly vulnerable. The option of wiping clean his debts by simply raising more funds from the stock market disappeared when it slumped along with the rest of Asia's stock markets. At the same time, short-term interest rates on peso debt rocketed to more than 30%, crippling those like Go with high borrowings. It wasn't long before he was unable to service his borrowings even if they were from his own bank. Beset with non-performing loans, Orient Bank collapsed in February 1998. A run by depositors who attempted to withdraw their savings *en masse* after rumors circulated that Go had either fled the country or had committed suicide proved the final deathblow.[13]

Investigations by the regulator revealed that a massive 75% of the bank's loan portfolio was bad and were in fact loans to the bank's directors — Go and his associates. The amount far exceeded the government's 15% ceiling on loans to affiliates. But that wasn't all. Sixty percent of Go's borrowings from Orient Bank were unsecured. The government suspended the bank's license pending Go's agreement to a restructuring.

The Philippine government made it clear that it wouldn't bail out the bank (in marked contrast to what had become common practice in Thailand and Indonesia) but instead would sell assets that belonged to the Go family and use the proceeds to repay the bank. Go insisted that he could resurrect the bank if he was allowed to reopen it, but he disputed the government's figures as to what proportion of the loan was his. Meanwhile, his financial position looked increasingly tenuous. Other creditors were waiting in the wings. One, an insurance company, seized Go's private helicopter in lieu of unpaid premiums. It was a fitting footnote to a career and a flashy lifestyle that had been built largely on debt.

The Extraordinary Case of Bank Pacific and the Sutowo Family

T he rise of Indonesia's Sutowo family in business captures the very essence of much that is wrong with business generally in Indonesia. The story is one of long-term misappropriation of funds and business mismanagement over a 30-year period. Yet, the family survives, with its wealth intact, as one of the country's most prominent business families. The key to its success hasn't been incredible business acumen, but its proximity to then-president Soeharto and senior members of the military. The saga involves much more than the mere mismanagement of a bank — although it is an important element in the family's more recent business activities. The story is so extraordinary that it is worth telling in its entirety.

Indonesia is a significant exporter of oil and a member of the Organization of Petroleum Exporting Countries (OPEC). Oil money has provided an enormous windfall for the country and abundant opportunities for corruption. This was nowhere more evident than at Pertamina, the state-owned oil company. Pertamina was the epicenter for the accumulation of new-found oil cash after the first oil shock in 1973. Lieutenant General Ibnu Sutowo served as its head then.[14] Sutowo wanted to be something more than a retired soldier shunted off to head a state-owned enterprise; he wanted to head a major conglomerate, and the swelling coffers of oil money gave him his chance. He set out on an extraordinary acquisition binge. New refineries were built, oil tankers were purchased, and diversifications were made into shipping, airlines, telecommunications, office developments, hotels, and synthetic fiber, steel, and fertilizer plants. Even a restaurant that specialized in Indonesian food was opened in New York.[15] Money gushed everywhere. Oil revenue was augmented by massive loans that washed in to finance new project after new project. Management control was at best chaotic and at worst non-existent. By early 1975, Pertamina had defaulted on a US$40 million loan from a group of US banks headed by the Republic National Bank of Dallas. Several weeks later, it again defaulted, this time on a loan of US$65 million to more US banks. Indonesia's state-owned oil company was on the verge of collapse in the middle of an oil boom. It was an extraordinary achievement, even by Third World standards. Pertamina was in a mess. The Indonesian government desperately needed to find out the precise extent of Pertamina's borrowings — but even Pertamina didn't know. The government reportedly had to go through the humiliating process of sending cable to some 200 banks around the world to ask if they had lent to Pertamina, and if so, how much.

Pertamina had many problems, one of which was massive, systematic corruption. It was common knowledge in Jakarta that a large part of Pertamina's oil revenue hadn't been paid to the Indonesian government, but had been retained by Sutowo for either 'unconventional finance' for the armed forces and other parts of the government, Pertamina's diversification, or his personal use.[16] But that wasn't all. Between 1970 and 1974, Sutowo exceeded his authority by secretly leasing large ocean-going oil tankers on behalf of Pertamina. As Pertamina had a large fleet of its own, it wasn't exactly clear for what the tankers were used. The contracts appeared to involve the payment of kickbacks, and Sutowo conceded in a later affidavit that on one occasion, a representative of the tanker leasing company, with which he had been dealing, gave him a check for US$2.5 million. He claimed the amount was a personal loan, but a year-and-a-half after having received it, it still hadn't been repaid.[17] It also emerged that Pertamina had done hundreds of millions of dollars of business with 35 companies, owned in part or in whole by Sutowo and his associates.[18] In 1971, for example, Sutowo and his family privately established PT Adiguna Shipyard, and its first order was from Pertamina for a cargo ship.[19] After that, it took orders from Pertamina for coasters, tugboats, and barge ships on a regular basis.[20] It wasn't until 1976 that Soeharto finally moved to have Sutowo replaced as the head of Pertamina. Sutowo spent a brief period under house arrest, but that was as far as it went. Sutowo was too well connected. He had always been careful to remain close to Soeharto, and it has even been suggested that he handled the Sumatra end of the smuggling network that Soeharto had run as a colonel in the 1950s.[21]

The full enormity of corruption at Pertamina was yet to be revealed. The following year, a court case in Singapore led to revelations that a Sutowo associate and senior Pertamina executive, Achmad Thahir — whose annual salary had never exceeded US$9,000 — had left behind US$80 million in Singapore bank accounts upon his death, the proceeds it seemed of kickbacks received on procurement contracts with German firms. Thahir's widow later claimed that Sutowo and others had received similar commissions.[22] (It isn't clear how much things have since changed at Pertamina. Sutowo's replacement, long-term civil servant Faisal Abdaoe, was ranked as Indonesia's 147th-highest taxpayer in 1994. At least he pays his taxes.[23])

Sutowo did what many senior officials in Indonesia do on leaving their public positions: he started a conglomerate. Although the antecedents of Sutowo's business interests today originated in the early 1970s, their serious expansion got under way only upon his departure from Pertamina. Today, he and his family are among Indonesia's wealthiest. He and another Pertamina executive, Sjarnoebi Said, had co-founded the Krama Yudha Group on the side in the early 1970s. The group is the Indonesian partner of Japan's Mitsubishi in assembling and distributing Mitsubishi cars and has stakes in many other businesses. But Sutowo's main interest is the giant Nugra Santana Group. This group comprises at least 50 companies and includes Jakarta's Hilton

International Hotel (which is reportedly one of the biggest hotels in the Hilton group), the Bali Hilton, a Hilton in Texas, a shipbuilding company, an air charter firm, and numerous ranches, trading companies, liquor distribution and duty-free stores, and tourism-related interests.[24] In 1996, the group established a mobile telephone operator as well. Its total assets amounted to at least US$800 million prior to Asia's economic crisis.

Day-to-day management is in the hands of Sutowo's son, Pontjo Sutowo, who incidentally is a co-founder of another prominent group of Indonesian companies, the Kodel Group. Another son, Adiguna Sutowo, had separately developed his own group of 31 companies, which include the Hard Rock Café franchise for Indonesia. But perhaps the most notorious Sutowo offspring is daughter, Endang Utari Mokodompit. Endang was a mainstay of the Jakarta social set. She became a member of the board of advisors of Jakarta's pseudo-luxurious Mercantile Athletic Club, where businessmen and carpetbaggers congregate and intermingle, and where Americans and others who are new in town meet those who have been there for 20 years or more (those who now may have trouble distinguishing right from wrong).

Endang's group is the ten-member Aditarina Group, which focuses on banking and property investments in both Indonesia and Singapore. Her foray into business hasn't exactly been a success.[25] Her career began with her appointment as finance and administration director of Nugra Santana's holding company in 1978. In 1985, Ibnu Sutowo gave her the family's small bank, Bank Pacific, to manage. Its assets swelled under her supervision, and in 1988, she set up her own holding company under which an array of enterprises mushroomed, many assisted by loans granted by Bank Pacific. For a time, the bank looked successful. It managed to open as many as 18 branches, making it quite large by Indonesian standards, and by 1995, its gross assets made it Indonesia's 12th-largest private bank.[26]

In 1989, Endang established Montien International, a British Virgin Islands-registered company, that became the vehicle for some of her major acquisitions in Singapore. Over a little more than an 18-month period, she acquired a controlling stake in a large Singapore shopping center development called Bugis Junction, control of the listed Singapore operations of Australian food conglomerate Goodman Fielder (which she renamed Auric Pacific), significant stakes in Singapore-listed construction company L&M Holdings and Singapore-listed Guthrie GTS, and a massive hotel and resort complex named the Lido Lake Hotel in Sukabumi, south of Jakarta. The question on everyone's mind then was: Where was all the money coming from?

The key was Endang's Jakarta-based finance company, Pacific International Finance. Between 1992 and 1995, it issued millions of dollars in commercial paper, typically with six-month maturity and all guaranteed by Bank Pacific. The fact that Endang was the owner of the issuer and head of the guarantor bank didn't deter tens of other banks and financial institutions, including some foreign investors, from buying up the paper. Each time the paper matured, new ones were issued to pay off the old, and on it went. By 1995, Endang's outstanding commercial paper debt totalled more than US$430 million. Millions more were borrowed directly from Bank Pacific. The efficacy of borrowing from her own bank didn't seem to faze Endang. Her spending spree in Singapore and back home in Jakarta had cost a great deal, but not nearly as much as her borrowings, raising the question: where did all the money go. This remains a mystery.

By mid-1995, Pacific International Finance was unable to honor its maturing commercial paper, which meant that the responsibility was passed to the guarantor, Bank Pacific. Unfortunately, by that time, Bank Pacific was also in a great deal of strife, with more than US$400 million in non-performing loans — mostly to companies related to Endang.[27] Indeed, by mid-1995, Bank Pacific could claim assets of approximately US$950 million, but bad debts totalled around US$400 million and the bank had assumed responsibility for about US$430 million in honoring Pacific International Finance's commercial paper. The bank's net capital amounted to around US$50 million, out of which depositors had to be repaid. Clearly, Bank Pacific was insolvent.

Despite the Sutowo family's enormous wealth, they weren't required nor did they feel inclined to dispose of assets to repay their borrowings from Bank Pacific. Once again, Ibnu Sutowo's connections had paid dividends. Instead, the central bank bought into Bank Pacific, which was then placed under the supervision of a state-owned trading bank. Endang was required to step down as the head of the bank. She did begin to sell some of her assets, such as her share in Auric Pacific, which she sold to Indonesia's Lippo Group. But funds raised from these asset sales didn't contribute to paying off debts owed to Bank Pacific, but to debts with other private banks. After ten years and US$800 million, Endang's ride as president director of Bank Pacific came to an end — she was removed.

It took a long time for the real story of Bank Pacific's troubles to emerge. And even when it finally did, Indonesians were deprived of reading about it. In May 1997, the Indonesian fortnightly magazine, *Swasembada*, published a series of six articles as part of a cover story on the Endang Utari Mokodompit-Bank Pacific saga. A single purchaser snapped up almost the entire print run of the edition — more than 30,000 copies. Indonesia's printing laws prevented the publisher from printing additional copies because it had exhausted its licensed print run.[28]

Bank Pacific was finally liquidated, together with 15 other banks, in late 1997 as part of the IMF conditions to the rescue package to which the Indonesian government had agreed. The liquidation took place some two years after the bank's problems first became apparent. For two years, Bank Pacific had been allowed to operate despite being obviously insolvent. No one dared to touch it given Sutowo's powerful connections. During a chance conversation with Endang on a flight between Singapore and Jakarta in early 1997, I asked her exactly what her role was in the family business. 'I just try to help out,' came the somewhat philosophical reply.

Families, Debt, and Big Business in South Korea

South Korea very nearly collapsed toward the end of 1997. Several decades of rapid industrialization had stretched the economy to breaking point. The IMF came to the rescue by putting together emergency loans worth almost US$60 billion. It was the biggest rescue package the IMF had ever assembled. The once mighty *chaebol* were humbled. The largest, Hyundai, was so desperate for cash that in early 1998, it put its US computer component-maker, Symbios, on the market and found a buyer within two weeks — Symbios went for almost US$800 million. It was interested only in cash offers.[29] What went wrong? Essentially, little different from what had gone wrong in Indonesia and Thailand, only that the numbers were bigger. There was little variation on the common themes of imprudent lending, family-owned conglomerates that were hell-bent on expansion regardless of return, and a general corporate ethos that utterly eschewed accountability and disclosure. The one major point of departure though, was the role played by the South Korean government. Its heavy-handed intervention did for South Korea what the North Koreans had been hoping would happen for 30 years. However, the victory for North Korea was a Pyrrhic one, given that so many of its people were starving at the time.

The Chaebol *of South Korea*

The degree of concentration of commercial power that South Korea's big business groups have achieved is unrivaled in the region. The top five *chaebol* — Hyundai, Samsung, LG, Daewoo, and Sunkyong (SK) — account for around half of the country's gross national product (the top 300 companies account for almost 90%). Their growth was astonishing. Daewoo, for example, began in 1967 as a textile company with US$10,000 in capital. Just 30 years later, in 1997, it was a massive conglomerate that encompassed shipbuilding, motor vehicles, electronics, and textiles, and had sales of more than US$70 billion.

Like the conglomerates of South-East Asia, the *chaebol* are family owned and managed, are comprised of a large number of relatively small companies across a wide spectrum of activities, have a mixture of listed and privately held companies that engage in a complex web of internal transactions, are relatively indifferent to the interests of their minority shareholders and have no great fondness for disclosure, and feature centralized decision making and authoritarian management.

The *chaebol* are astonishingly diverse. Beer, cement, cars, and computer chips are all typical products produced by each of the top five or so *chaebol*. ('From chips to ships' was once the proud boast.) But the rage for synergies and core competencies has yet to make it to South Korea. In 1998, Hyundai announced a restructuring plan that would leave it with no fewer than five sectors that it labeled 'core' — and that was *after* the economic turmoil of the previous year.[30] This was not enough, and by end-2000, Hyundai was still facing the bankruptcy of one of its principal subsidiaries and further restructuring.

Like the conglomerates of South-East Asia but unlike the big business groups of Japan, the *chaebol* have yet to undergo a separation between ownership and management. Indeed, among the biggest *chaebol*, as many as a third of senior executives have family ties with the owner. Chung Ju Yung, the founder of Hyundai Group, moved all seven of his sons into management positions in the group when they were at a relatively young age. Similarly, a Lee family member heads each division of Samsung.

Sometimes, new subsidiaries are set up simply to give family members something to do. It means that even the dimmest member will be put in charge of something, and for the sake of the 'face' of the family, a range of cross-subsidies and other related transactions are used to prop up badly managed companies and to protect poor managers (especially if they are family) from the consequences of their own incompetence.

But there is one major difference between the big business groups of South-East Asia and the *chaebol*: the *chaebol* aren't clustered around a bank.[31] South Korean law greatly restricts any individual shareholder (apart from the government) from amassing more than just a modicum of any bank's total equity. On the face of it, this is a very sound policy and one that all economies should ultimately adopt. It helps make banks independent of non-bank interests and less constrained to lend prudently. Independent of the *chaebol* South Korea's banks may be, but they aren't independent of the government, the other necessary criterion for a sound and prudently run banking system. Herein lies the problem.

The Dead Hand of South Korea's Government

South Korea's *chaebol* may be big, but they aren't profitable. The combined net profit of the top 49 *chaebol* even in pre-crisis 1996 amounted to a paltry US$65 million, even though their sales accounted for 97% of the country's GDP. If the results of the now bankrupt Hanbo Group are included, then the combined income of the top 50 *chaebol* amounts to a net loss. The *chaebol* show clearly that size does matter — but not in the way that one might think.[32]

That the state has played an intrusive role in this is an understatement. It has interfered with microeconomic decisions in an extraordinarily constant and vociferous fashion. The Japanese, who colonized the Korean peninsula between 1910 and 1945, started the system, but it was then-president Park Chung Hee who greatly pushed the development of the *chaebol* in the 1960s and 1970s. There was no room for Adam Smith's subtle, market-based 'invisible hand' under South Korea's military dictators. Instead, business was directed with an iron fist. The means by which successive governments directed the private sector was through their control over the banking sector. Most of South Korea's 20 commercial banks (there were 25 until the government closed five of the weakest in June 1998) are in private hands, but they are not independent. It is the government and not shareholders that chooses most of the banks' presidents and chairmen.

Credit was cheap and free-flowing if the *chaebol* did it the government's way, and the government backed up its demands by telling the banks where to lend. The *chaebol* were told which sectors to invest in, where to locate their plants, where to invest overseas, and in what. This is not to say that the government directed the whole show. But what government effectively had was a seat on the board. If the *chaebol* consented, they were allowed to stand in the floodpath of easy credit; object and they were shunted aside. Often the credit was so cheap that it was actually provided at negative real rates of interest. The *chaebol* quickly grew into massive multi-billion-dollar concerns. But they also carried billion-dollar debts. Samsung, for example, entered 1998 carrying US$23.4 billion in debt — about the same amount as the foreign debt of the entire Venezuelan economy. And Samsung was by no means unique. The *chaebol* didn't evolve through a process of natural selection. They grew because the government had selected them and then puffed them up with debt.

The government allocation of credit on the basis of who was in favor was complemented by a comprehensive system of bribe-taking and campaign donations. The *chaebol* bribed politicians, bank officials, or both, to ensure that their access to cheap credit wasn't obstructed and that prudential safeguards (small that they were) would be ignored. This is precisely what Chung Tai Soo, the founder of Hanbo Group, did. He founded the group in 1974. How he had accumulated the capital to found the group was a matter of open speculation. He had been a government worker in the Office of Tax Administration for the previous 23 years.[33] During much of that time, the administration of tax allowed for a great deal of discretion on the part of tax officials and hence their likelihood of being offered bribes. What Chung learned at the office appeared to have put him in good stead for later life.

In 1989, Hanbo was South Korea's 44th-largest *chaebol*. Eight years later, it had shot ahead to 14th place. If only it was because Chung was a masterful entrepreneur. Debt was the elixir, and to ensure that the credit kept rolling in, Chung bribed numerous bank executives and senior politicians. Hanbo grew too quickly and ventured into unprofitable areas. Debt outstripped profit and the group eventually collapsed in early 1997 with total debt being no less than 16 times its total equity. It was quite an achievement. Chung went from being one of South Korea's most prominent 'entrepreneurs' to being disgraced and put in jail. Embezzlement convictions were added to Chung's bribery convictions and he faced a total of 16½ years in jail. The son and aides of then-president Kim Young Sam were also implicated and soon joined Chung.

The rush by the *chaebol* to outdo each other in becoming too big to be 'allowed' to fail only exacerbated the decoupling of loans from the ability to repay them. Banks too accepted the line that being big equated to creditworthiness. There was no great need for close credit analysis when it came to lending to a major *chaebol* because the accepted wisdom was that they couldn't fail. There was an implicit sovereign guarantee. This approach meant that by mid-1998, South Korea's 25 commercial banks themselves were collectively on the verge of insolvency.

The families that own the *chaebol* tend to treat their business empires as a singular entity. The boundaries between companies are porous, especially where the flow of funds is concerned. The *chaebol* tend to be built around one or just a handful of highly profitable non-bank companies. For example, each of the top three *chaebol* consists of more than 100 subsidiaries, but 80% of their revenue comes from just 20% of their subsidiaries, and almost all of their profit from just one or two subsidiaries.[34] These become the cash cow for the entire group, providing credit and subsidies and raising loans. Samsung Electronics, for example, is the world's largest manufacturer of memory chips. Its sales are enormous. The controlling Lee family has routinely used it as their prime fundraiser — to supply loans and loan guarantees to other Samsung companies — much to the irritation of Samsung Electronics' other shareholders. In 1997, it guaranteed hundreds of millions of dollars of loans of Samsung's fledgling automobile division. (Several minority shareholders believed that some US$136 million in guarantees weren't even declared.[35]) Overall, Samsung Electronics is believed to have guaranteed the debts of other Samsung companies to the tune of US$4.5 billion.

Similarly, the shipbuilding and car component Halla Group, which collapsed in 1997, had only one really profitable subsidiary, car component producer Mando Machinery. Mando sold most of its output to just one customer, Hyundai Motors, South Korea's largest car manufacturer. Mando was also the cash box for Halla, but it was a dangerous combination: just one revenue earner to subsidize 14 other affiliates and then have that one company dependent mostly on a single buyer. It was only a matter of time before the inevitable happened.

Obtaining and marshaling loans for and around the rest of their respective *chaebol* gave Samsung Electronics and Mando Machinery a unique role that went beyond simply being the star manufacturer and revenue earner for the group. Assessing creditworthiness and handing out loans is the function of the banking system in any economy. But in South Korea, it was the leading *chaebol* companies that assumed this role. So, effectively, the *chaebol* flagship companies worked *as if* they were the bankers for the group — which closes the major difference between the *chaebol* of South Korea and the conglomerates of South-East Asia.

By the end of 2000, the South Korean government could claim some success in forcing some of the *chaebol* to restructure. Samsung Group, for example, closed down or sold off loss-making divisions and is now better streamlined. Other groups, however, used South Korea's more buoyant stock market condition to issue more shares and take even tighter control of affiliates. For every two steps forward, there seemed to be at least one backward. It wasn't always clear that reform was heading in the right direction.

CHAPTER 6

Lambs to the Slaughter: Investing in Asia's Stock Markets

No stock market in the world is perfect. But Asia's stock markets, in general, are less perfect than most. In fact, the structure of most Asian companies makes Asia's stock markets potentially quite dangerous, especially for minority shareholders — people like you and me.

S hares have been traded on Wall Street for more than 200 years. In that time, trading has developed to a fine art, as have the regulations that set the parameters for trading. The same cannot be said for the stock markets of Asia. There, the laws that govern transactions are new and enforcement is patchy.[1] Very often, families who list their businesses on the stock market find it difficult to accept the obligations that listing requires. Many seem unable to comprehend that once they list their companies, the companies are no longer exclusively theirs. 'It's my company and I'll do what I like with it' is commonly the attitude. Confusion abounds as to what their obligations are — not just on the part of the families, but also on the part of regulators.

Yet a well-functioning stock market is essential to any modern economy. It must allow companies to readily raise cash to fund their expansion. But this need must be tempered with the need to protect shareholders, particularly minority shareholders, from unfair practices. Asia's stock markets, by and large, don't fit this bill. If anything, they function more like casinos and the dice all too often are loaded in favor of the rapacious and marauding majority shareholders — usually the companies' founding families. All this is very important to the West, because much of the money that is sunk into Asia's stock exchanges doesn't come from Asia but from the pension and mutual funds of the United States and Europe. Foreign investors accounted for as much as 80% of the funds that flowed into the stock markets of Indonesia and Thailand throughout the 1990s — and they almost always invested in a minority shareholding capacity.

But there is another problem, and it has to do with how minority shareholders are perceived in Asia. In Asia's business world, minority shareholders are 'outsiders.' We are told that in Asia, personal connections and relationships are everything, particularly in business, so the whole concept of a minority shareholder is an anathema to the prevailing culture. That complete strangers should entrust their money to each other and hope to make a profit is simply ridiculous to many Asian entrepreneurs — and yet, that is precisely what a stock exchange is all about. In Asia, social interaction is at its most decent among individuals who have a personal connection. It is at its most indecent when it is among strangers. And minority shareholders in listed companies are perhaps the ultimate strangers. There is no personal relationships — they may not even be recorded on the share register by name. The anonymity of the stock market is seen as a great virtue in the West; in Asia, it is nefarious to conventional business wisdom. Who, after all, would invest their money with people whom they have never met? Perhaps those with too much money or who aren't too interested in what returns they get. This may be the thinking of entrepreneurs inculcated with Asia's personalized way of doing things. Traditionally, Asian entrepreneurs, particularly the overseas Chinese, have the reputation of being frugal and having conservative habits. But that's with their own money. It can well be quite a different matter with other people's money, as we shall see.

TWISTED MOTIVES

Apart from the purpose of raising cash, listing is an excellent way to achieve a market valuation for a company. This explains why so many firms across Asia have listed just 15% or 30% of their shares. More than 90% of all the companies listed on the Jakarta Stock Exchange had less than half their equity traded publicly as at June 1997. Two-thirds had less than 31% of their stock in public hands.[2] Little had changed as at the end of 2000. Listing establishes a value for the shares and, hence, for the total company. With such a valuation, owners can go to a bank and use their equity in the listed firm as collateral for raising loans. By floating as little of the firm as possible, the owner achieves a valuation without ceding much control to outsiders.

SHAKING THE MONEY TREE: EXCESSIVE RIGHTS ISSUES AND RELATED-PARTY TRANSACTIONS

There are three bad things that companies listed on Asia's stock exchanges repeatedly do to their minority shareholders: they have far too many rights issues, they buy assets from their controlling shareholders that they shouldn't, and they trade with related companies on an unfair basis. To top it off, controlling shareholders have often been none too interested in achieving a fair rate of return on shareholders' funds. They ensure that they do quite well — usually very well — but their returns may be at the expense of their minority shareholders.

A rights issue is the issue of new shares to existing shareholders — this ensures that the founding family's control isn't diluted or lost. Minority shareholders find that unless they subscribe to each new rights issue, their equity, and hence often their returns, are diluted. Asian companies have a voracious appetite for cash so as to be able to keep on expanding and making acquisitions. Frequently, this has more to do with fulfilling the ambitions of their owners than with producing sensible returns for shareholders.

Companies controlled by Hong Kong billionaire, Li Ka-shing, are perennially accused of having too many rights issues, as well as asset shuffling, which have the effect of benefiting Li and his partners but at the expense of minority investors. A column in a January 1997 issue of the *Far Eastern Economic Review* that accused Li's Cheung Kong Group of having 'never in its history ever done anything for the express benefit of its shareholders' apart from Li himself was certainly over the top, but it evoked the indignant but rather lame reply from the group's deputy chairman that Li had never drawn a salary from the group (apart from negligible director's fees) despite his 'very considerable input' (he did not mention the millions of dollars in dividends and capital gains that Li has received), and for the good of the company, had chosen to forgo some dividend entitlements in 1976 — some 21 years ago![3]

Companies in the West tend to list on the stock market so that they can raise funds to expand. There is really nothing complicated about this. But the situation is often quite different in Asia. In Asia, listings all too frequently are little more than exit strategies, as founding families seek to off-load assets that no longer perform well and that they no longer want. 'What is profitable is mine, but what is not is yours,' is nowhere more true than in Asia. The result: many stock exchanges in Asia could well be characterized as little more than a dumping ground for companies that no one really wants.

This brings us to the second major sin committed against minority shareholders: the sale to the listed company by the controlling family of assets it no longer wants. These may be old plants and equipment or even entire companies, which end up as subsidiaries of the listed company. There is nothing wrong with this practice if the acquisition price that the listed company pays is fair. But often it isn't — and the controlling family has every incentive to ensure that it isn't. Inflated prices paid by listed companies for assets sold to them by their controlling shareholders are regularly used by Asia's founding families to strip listed companies of their profits. This practice isn't so much endemic to Asia but is an epidemic in Asia. Indonesia's Salim Group has tried to make ample use of the procedure. On just one occasion, in early 1997, it managed to sell, in one fell swoop, six companies that had been privately held by the controlling family to one of the group's listed arms, but not before minority shareholders threatened a revolt over the price the listed company was asked to pay.

Nor did the 1997–98 Asian economic crisis necessarily put an end to this practice. In November 1999, Hong Kong-listed Pioneer Industries International pulled off what appeared to be a spectacular example of making full use of minority shareholders' relative powerlessness. Its executives decided to sell a basket of Pioneer's key assets — shares in other listed companies and US real estate — to an offshore company linked to its two controlling families for US$68 million, or less than a third of the prevailing market price of US$222 million. This was after the company gave its directors a 200% raise in performance-related pay for the 12 months ended March 31, 1999 despite a six-fold increase in Pioneer's net loss for that year. Unaudited interim results for the next six months showed a positive net profit, but it transpired that this was only because the company had changed its accounting policies. The results would have shown yet another loss otherwise.

The rules governing most of Asia's stock markets require that minority shareholders must approve acquisitions such as those in the Salim case. But these rules are often circumvented by the majority shareholder covertly controlling some of the shares believed to be in the minorities' hands. These interests side with the majority shareholder if the acquisitions are put to a vote and the rules are thereby rendered useless.

Another consequence of asset injection is that shareholders find themselves holding stock in companies that are nothing like the companies they first bought into. Perhaps an investor wants to invest only in retail stocks, so it buys shares of a department store chain. However, the controlling shareholder might happen to own a coal mining company that is no longer profitable and decides to sell it to the listed department store. Minority shareholders who have invested in the retail stock suddenly find themselves exposed to the global market price of coal. Minority shareholders constantly endure this sort of maneuver in Asian stock markets.

The third major sin against minority shareholders in Asia is usually termed 'transactions with affiliates.' These are transactions between the listed company and other companies or people whom either the listed company or its major shareholder is connected with. In themselves, they need not be bad, but once again, the controlling shareholder faces all the incentive in the world to leech on profits from the company through such transactions. For example, the listed company might buy all of its input from a company that is owned solely by the founding family. Funds can be transferred from the public (the minority shareholders) to the family by having the listed company pay grossly inflated prices for the input. The listed company's profits are lowered because its costs are too high, the founding family is enriched, and the minority shareholders are left out of pocket. The web of privately held and publicly listed companies that comprise most Asian conglomerates means that such transactions face a far greater risk of being unfair to minority shareholders in Asia than practically anywhere else.

Unfair transactions with affiliated companies and unfair purchases of assets from controlling shareholders mean that Asia's controlling families have been able to achieve very high rates of return on their invested equity even though their listed companies may not be all that profitable. Asia's rapid economic growth, at least prior to the region's 1997–98 economic crisis, was very much a function of this region-wide sleight of hand. Capital was attracted to Asia on account of very high economic growth rates, but a great deal of it was invested in projects that simply weren't ever going to generate market rates of return. But that didn't stop Asia's business families from pushing ahead with them, because they counted on getting their returns through the means just described.

South Korea's *chaebol* have been beset by related-party transactions. Many of these have been particularly insidious and have taken the form of off-balance-sheet guarantees of the debts taken on by affiliates. Not only are these transactions difficult to detect, but they also expose companies to a great deal of risk. When the company that acts as the guarantor is listed, the practice exposes minority shareholders' funds to risks to which they are often oblivious. This risk can even spread across *chaebol* — some are dependent on each other as their controlling families are related. The founder of the Halla Group happens to be the younger brother of the head of the Hyundai Group, and after Halla collapsed in 1997, Hyundai's minority shareholders were aghast to discover that their company had provided Halla with at least US$1 billion in loans and debt guarantees.[4] Another risk comes from secret cross-shareholdings; rules designed to stop cross-shareholdings are easily circumvented. It is common for one *chaebol* member that wants to buy a stake in another to lend the money to an outside company, which buys the stock in the affiliate in a nominee capacity. The purchase looks like an external transaction, but it isn't.

Needless to say, very few listed South Korean companies have independent directors on their boards to safeguard the interests of minority shareholders. To cap it off, some South Korean companies have even been known to mobilize their workers to intimidate and stand over difficult shareholders at annual general meetings. The IMF sought to require South Korea to change some of these practices as part of its demands for the rescue loan package that it assembled for the country in 1997. Unless there are genuine reforms in this area, investments in the South Korean stock market by foreign investors will continue to be more like donations.

ONE ASSET, SEVERAL COMPANIES, AND LOTS OF RELATED TRANSACTIONS

Asia's entrepreneurs are as adept at utilising the stock market as entrepreneurs anywhere. The perception once was that they were loath to list their companies because it meant having to accept a measure of disclosure and the loss of some management control, but not any more. Robert Kuok, the Hong Kong-based Malaysian-Chinese entrepreneur, is one of Asia's most successful businessmen. There are at least 12 Kuok companies listed on stock exchanges across Asia. Among the ones with the most high profile are those that hold his Shangri-La Asia and Traders hotels.

When one walks into any Kuok hotel, they all naturally appear as one. But the tranquility of the lobby hides the reality. It is actually a labyrinth of related-party transactions — a hive of activity with related companies all selling goods and services to one another. Each hotel is stripped apart, with the various functions that contribute to its running being divided among various Kuok companies. Many of the higher-margin operations are performed by a company called the Shangri-La International Hotel Management (SLIM) group, which is where the real expertise and money-making ability lies. Many of the lower-margin activities are left with the listed Shangri-La Asia.

By early 1998, 19 of the Shangri-La group hotels paid fees to SLIM for management services, copyright, and trademark use of the Shangri-La brand. Payments were also made for access to the management company's centralized reservation system. The amount paid for licensing fees for the use of the various hotel names and logos is as high as 5% of each new hotel's monthly gross operating revenue.[5] Even the secretarial, legal, personnel, and financial services that the hotels need in order to operate don't reside with Shangri-La Asia but are provided by another privately held Kuok company, Kerry Trading Co.[6]

The chain's popular Shang Palace Chinese restaurants that are located in each hotel pay further management fees — as much as 1.25% of monthly gross operating sales. These are made to a SLIM subsidiary company, Shang Palace Restaurant Services Ltd.[7] The less popular restaurants, such as its upmarket but low-volume French restaurants, Margeaux, on the other hand, don't pay management fees to privately held Kuok companies.

In late 1997, Kuok moved to end the carving up of the functions of his hotel empire between his listed and privately held companies by selling the SLIM group (which was bundled into a new company, Slim International Ltd) to Shangri-La Asia. While he received US$155 million in stock, minority shareholders in Shangri-La Asia could now claim ownership of whole hotels and not just those parts that Kuok didn't want for himself.[8] The Shangri-La Asia hotels provide a good example of the mix of transactions between publicly traded and privately held companies that is common around Asia.

PRICE MANIPULATION

Floating as little of a company on a stock exchange as possible makes the price of the stock much easier to manipulate. The shares can be 'ramped' — a common practice in Asia — that is companies vigorously trade their own shares to force the price up and then sell out at a profit.

Very few of Asia's stock exchanges have the depth — the trading volume and the number of shareholders — to ensure that they function well. In the absence of good rules that are actually enforced, most of the region's stock markets are prone to price manipulation and wild price swings. Rumors are often deliberately started by traders in order to manipulate prices. This is the case not just in the stock markets but in the foreign exchange markets as well. In the latter years of the Soeharto presidency, the rupiah was buffeted constantly by rumors that the president had died, was ill, had had a stroke, had fallen off his Harley Davidson, or whatever — and it rose and fell accordingly. Buyers moved in to take advantage of the new lower price and would sell out at a profit when the rumors were verified as just that and the market had picked up. Traders in Singapore were routinely blamed for this.

Rumor-induced share runs are regular features of stock markets across Asia. So is share 'pooling,' where several wealthy investors collude so that shares in a particular company are bought and then sold successively from one member of the pool to another so that the reported turnover and price are both boosted. Other investors see that trading in the shares of the company has involved in the pooling suddenly become quite active and buy into the stock as well, hoping for a capital gain. The initial pool of investors then sell out, taking profits as they do so. A similar practice is share 'churning,' where a single investor can simultaneously place large buy and sell orders for a particular stock, but at ever-escalating prices. The stock's volume and price both increase, usually attracting other investors into the market. The process then takes on a life of its own, which allows the initial investor to sell out at a higher price and take a profit. Another practice is 'cornering.' Given that many companies in Asia, particularly in South-East Asia, tend to list only a small proportion of their capital on the stock market, their shares are prone to being cornered. An investor may quietly build up a large proportion of the publicly available shares, then place a large number of orders with various brokers for the delivery of more shares at a certain price and by a specified date. With relatively few shares left in the marketplace, brokers bid each other up to acquire the shares they have contracted to sell. The price of the remaining shares skyrockets. And who should be the seller of the shares to the brokers so that they can fulfil their contracts? The investor who placed the orders in the first place, usually via nominees to make the transactions appear independent.

These practices have been promoted by the extraordinary growth in short selling and margin trading on Asian bourses. Allowing investors and speculators to trade in shares they currently don't own or in order to borrow large sums of money, often from brokers themselves, has added much-needed liquidity to Asia's stock markets but has also made them far easier to manipulate in the manner described. Another factor that has been critical to these practices is the growth in the number of Asian conglomerates that own broking houses. This means that not only can they keep their trades secret from outsiders, they can also internalize the brokerage fees and hence reduce the cost of engaging in manipulative practices. Clearly, the practice of stock churning can occur cheaply if it is all done through one's own brokerage.

The shares of Bank Pikko, a small Jakarta-based bank with just four full branches and as few as 20,000 depositors, were subject to a cornering exercise in 1997. During the afternoon trading session of April 8, its shares more than tripled in price on the Jakarta Stock Exchange. There was no legitimate justification for such an astonishing price rise. With less than

22% of its stock in public hands and being a low-price, low-capitalized stock, it was just ripe to be cornered. In the months leading up to April, local stockbroker Benny Tjokrosaputro and an associate used 13 nominees to place buy orders with eight brokerages. One of the brokerages was owned by Tjokrosaputro. The plan worked — perhaps a little too effectively. On that April day when the market was effectually cornered and Pikko's share price skyrocketed, four brokerages were unable to deliver Pikko shares to buyers. The regulators' interest was aroused (after a series of similar instances on the Jakarta Stock Exchange) and the affairs of 138 exchange officials and family members were investigated. Tjokrosaputro and his associate were fined and new trading rules were introduced.[9] New rules are fine, but they must be enforced. The Pikko case and the subsequent fines came after the stock exchange was severely criticized for not pursuing other serious breaches.

INSUFFICIENT RESEARCH

Not all listed companies in Asia are the investor death traps described here. But many are. One might wonder how international stockbroking houses pick their way through Asia's bourses to look for stocks that they can recommend to their clients. Unfortunately, here too the usual safeguards fail. The research divisions of many of Asia's stockbroking houses — many of which are the Asian arm of big Western brokers and financial services houses — produce endless company research reports that simply fail to mention that a given listed company is part of a wider conglomerate, the bulk of which may be privately held. All too often companies are researched as if they are standalone entities independent of outside interests and influences. They are written as if they are stocks listed on the New York Stock Exchange — where management revolutions that have brought us downsizing, the stripping back of corporations to their core competencies, de-conglomeration, and getting rid of family control have already swept through.

Many securities houses have a distorted view of what the 'fundamentals' really are in Asia when it comes to assessing local shares. Their preoccupation with the minutiae of financial analysis leads them to utterly miss what is staring them in the face: that many of Asia's publicly traded companies, particularly in the South-East Asian markets such as Thailand and Indonesia, engage in practices that would probably preclude them from being listed at all in the West. What could be more fundamental than that?

Thailand's Surat Canning

South-East Asia's political leaders were shocked when their countries' economies collapsed in late 1997. But they shouldn't have been. The case of Surat Canning provides an excellent example why. Surat Canning was formed in 1984 and listed on the Stock Exchange of Thailand in 1990. It is principally engaged in the production and export of canned seafood such as crab meat, shrimp, and sardines under various brand names, most prominent of which is the Samui Island brand. Surat Canning has also been in an astonishing mess with regard to corporate governance and accountability almost from the day it was listed. After going public, the company decided to try its hand at expanding overseas, first to Vietnam where it established a fishing joint venture. However, at about the same time, in 1991, it made the first of a string of losses.

In early 1992, the board approved a major purchase of land from a company called Ekpanich Farm Co. The board of Ekpanich included a Surat Canning director and the wife of another Surat director. The purchase was major. But not only did Surat Canning not alert its shareholders or the stock exchange to the fact that the purchase was from an affiliated source, as was required by the exchange's rules, it also failed to inform them that the purchase had occurred at all. The details of the transaction came to light only four years after it took place. But that wasn't all. In 1996, the stock exchange warned Surat Canning that it was in danger of being delisted on account of it not having turned in a profit since 1990. So, the company hired the first of two Thai finance companies to assist it in the management of its operations. In late 1997, both of the finance companies were closed down by the Thai government, along with a raft of other poorly managed and indebted finance companies, as part of its obligations under the IMF's 1997 emergency loan package. In September 1996, Surat Canning announced that Song Karnjanachusak, the head of a major tapioca flour producer, SP Solid Group, had bought a 20% stake in the company. Song happens to be the father-in-law of Surat Canning's then-managing director. The acquisition gave the company a much-needed capital infusion and also strengthened its political connections. Song is the father of the then-Palang Dharma Party (PDP) Member of Parliament, Orathai Karnjanachusak.[10] Minority shareholders probably didn't know whether to laugh or cry with this news. Political connections can help companies win contracts and licenses in Thailand, but they can also help majority shareholders avoid having to comply with rules designed to protect investors.

In 1997, Surat Canning began selling off its core assets — at amounts that were radically below what they had been valued by the company. In early 1998, the company came up with another surprise — its entire board resigned. After a month without a new board, seven straight years of losses, and having sold off many of its core assets, the Stock Exchange of Thailand finally decided to delist Surat Canning from the exchange. A journalist who attempted to contact the company for comment on its delisting found that the address listed as its Bangkok headquarters was actually home to a cable manufacturing company that had no connection to Surat Canning, and the listed telephone number was answered by a woman who described herself as an assistant to the senior officials of Surat Canning; she then declined to say who those officials were.[11] That a company like Surat Canning can list and then stay listed for as long as it did is an appalling indictment on Thailand's stock exchange officials. When investors buy shares on a stock exchange, they reasonably expect that the companies have been subjected to and passed a test of minimum corporate governance standards. Not so in Thailand, it seems.

CHAPTER 7

Polygamy and Family Squabbles

Not too long ago, many of Asia's most prominent entrepreneurs had multiple wives. Even today, some of Asia's richest businessmen have as many as eight or more wives. This makes for large and complex families — and large and complex businesses. Family infighting has brought down more than one Asian business house. Polygamy leads to further complications in an already complicated Asian corporate landscape.

Families own most of Asia's private sector firms outside Japan and mainland China, be they large or small. The firm and the family are synonymous. Outsiders who deal with such firms face the added complication of dealing with not just the firm but also the family that comes with it, and that means taking on board what can sometimes be a hefty load of additional baggage.

Family-owned businesses in Asia routinely feature family members in management — and not just members of the immediate family unit, but often cousins, uncles, second cousins, and so on. Frequently, businesses grow to match the structure of the family. New divisions are added to give family members something to do when they come of age, and restructuring of even quite large conglomerates can be brought about as much by a need to reallocate responsibilities among family members as for prudential management and financial reasons. This point was made in respect of South Korea's *chaebol*, but it holds for corporate South-East Asia as well. Further complications arise from the fact that many of the older generation of entrepreneurs in Asia indulged in the practice of polygamy, where the family patriarch had more than one wife concurrently. This is particularly the case with Asia's overseas Chinese entrepreneurs.

Polygamy has a long history in Asia. Sultans, kings, and other nobles of South-East Asia routinely had concurrent multiple wives. This practice produced large, complex families, to the point where in many countries in the region, a significant proportion of the population is able to claim some link to one royal house or another. In China too polygamy was widely practiced. Second and subsequent wives were labeled concubines, and the Chinese who emigrated to South-East Asia in the 19th and early 20th centuries took this practice with them. Even in British-ruled Hong Kong, the practice of polygamy wasn't outlawed by the colony's Legislative Council until 1971, when concubinage became bigamy and thus illegal.[1]

Polygamy has some very practical aspects, especially as far as the running of a business is concerned. A common problem for Asian family-controlled businesses has always been the growth of the family's business interests being constrained by the availability of family members to manage them. Many a business opportunity has been lost simply because all the available family members had their hands full managing their existing interests. One way around this manpower constraint was for the patriarch to take several wives to ensure bountiful progeny. However, polygamy as a business management strategy has its drawbacks, and the cost of the practice by many of Asia's first-generation entrepreneurs is reverberating around Asia today. One significant problem is that complicated families make for complicated corporate structures. If the rationale for a conglomerate's structure is not the business itself but the family behind it, then appeals to restructure on the basis of prudential corporate practice tend to fall on deaf ears. Reports commissioned from management consultants like McKinsey & Co and Booze Allen and Hamilton tend to miss this point. Another is that families that are structured around a single patriarch but several mothers can be a recipe for rival factions to develop around each mother. This is perhaps the greatest danger that polygamy now poses for corporate Asia.

The potent mix of siblings, half-siblings, endless cousins, and so on, coupled with sometimes enormous corporate assets that are often not owned by individuals but by the more vaguely defined 'family,' is beginning to lead to many family bust-ups in Asia. Rival factions within a family usually do great damage to the family's business interests, not least because individual family members take their eye off management while they fight each other.

The ownership of many family-controlled companies is structured to make it difficult for individual members or factions to withdraw their equity. This is to force the family to stick together. But when personal enmities grow particularly intense, it isn't uncommon that the good of the family business is subsumed by internal family rivalries. This is all right if the effects of such family indulgence are contained. But usually they aren't. Family members refusing to talk to one another even though they have management positions in the same company is obviously unhelpful to sound management and good corporate governance. Family infighting in Asia's companies often means that minority shareholders, business partners (local and foreign), and the companies' clients invariably suffer collateral damage.

BIG FAMILIES

Many of history's most prominent overseas Chinese businessmen were polygamists. The legendary 'Sugar King' of South-East Asia, Oei Tiong Ham, who made his considerable wealth by growing and refining sugar on the northern coast of Java in the early 20th century, had one wife and no less than 16 official concubines.[2] Today, as a result, it is possible to run into Oei's many descendants all over Asia. Aw Boon Haw and Aw Boon Par, the builders of the Tiger Balm empire, had four and three wives, respectively.[3] Boon Haw's daughter by his favorite wife ('second mama'), Sally Aw, now heads the Sing Tao newspaper publishing empire in Hong Kong. C.Y. Bao, the founder of Taiwan's Chung Shing Textiles who died in 1989, had three concurrent wives.[4] The Thai-Chinese businessman, Tiang Chirathivat, who founded the Central Group, a massive Bangkok conglomerate of department stores, factories, hotels, and property, had several wives who produced the extraordinary total of 14 sons and 12 daughters, and more than 40 grandchildren. Chin Sophonpanich, the founder of one of South-East Asia's biggest banks, Bangkok Bank, had two wives. His first wife, Lau Kwei Ying, gave birth to two sons. The first is Rabin Sophonpanich, who now lives in Hong Kong where he is known as Robin Chan and runs the Asia Financial Services Group, quite separate from the family's Bangkok Bank interests. The second is Chatri Sophonpanich, the current chairman of Bangkok Bank. Chin's second wife, Boonsri, had five children. Among them are Charn and Chote Sophonpanich. Relations between the two groups of half-brothers haven't always been smooth. Both Charn and Chote joined their half-brother, Chatri, in the management of Bangkok Bank, but by 1990, both had left to pursue other interests, amid rumors of family friction. Chatri and Rabin grew up when the Sophonpanich family was still struggling in business. Money was tight and they missed out on undertaking tertiary studies. Their younger half-siblings, however, came along after the family's position had improved and were mostly educated abroad — an apparent source of contention between the two sets of half-brothers.[5]

One of the more celebrated cases of polygamy today involves the Indonesian-Chinese businessman, Eka Tjipa Widjaja (also known as Oei Ek Tjong), who heads the Sinar Mas Group. Sinar Mas is Indonesia's second-largest conglomerate, with operations in the United States,

Australia, Singapore, China, and Hong Kong, as well as in Indonesia. It is very diverse and has at least 150 subsidiaries in Indonesia alone. Its principal interests, however, are in cooking oil, banking, and paper manufacturing.

Eka is said to have many wives. The usual figure mentioned is eight, but one report claimed the true number was 'easily' in double digits.[6] They are installed in various houses around Jakarta. Many wives mean many children, and Eka has fathered more than 40.[7] Indeed, he is still siring progeny. Every few months, staff at the Sinar Mas headquarters in Jakarta find themselves ordering flowers to send to their chairman for the birth of yet another child. Although age has slowed things, it has not stopped it altogether. Another son was born in 1997 when Eka was 73 years old.

Each wife and her children constitute a separate family branch. Some wives have many children; Eka's principal wife has six. Succession problems have been sorted out for now by treating the children by the first wife as the 'official' children and, hence, the official heirs of the Sinar Mas Group. Four of the five sons from the principal wife have each been given a Sinar Mas division to manage. Sukmawati, Eka's only daughter from his principal wife, has been appointed group vice chairman. The desire to keep it all in the family was underscored when Sukmawati married Eka's nephew — her cousin — Rudy Maeloa, and he was marked out as the heir apparent. But these plans fell apart with Rudy's death from cancer in 1988.[8]

Offspring by the other wives have been assisted with loans and start-up capital so that they can operate their own businesses. Mellieh Pirieh is one of Eka's other wives. She has seven children. Mellieh and her children have established at least 26 active companies in Indonesia, most of which are grouped under the Duta Dharma Bhakti Group, which operates separately from the Sinar Mas Group.

Another child by yet another wife is Oei Hong Leong. He is based in Hong Kong where he runs China Strategic Holdings, a large, listed company that concentrates on investing in mainland China. Again, this operation is run completely separately from the Sinar Mas Group. One of its subsidiaries, China Tire Holdings, is listed on the New York Stock Exchange. Another, MRI Holdings, is listed on the Australian Stock Exchange.

Whether these arrangements will ensure that family squabbles will be avoided after Eka passes on remains to be seen. In any event, it seems quite possible, and even likely, that Sinar Mas will split up after Eka's death into four separate companies, each of which will be headed by a son of Eka's principal wife. In this way, today's divisions may be tomorrow's mini-conglomerates. Recent corporate restructuring appears to allow for this. Thus, should a family squabble break out, at least the business break-up will be smooth. Complex and costly legal battles to sort out a maze of cross-shareholdings and overlapping ownerships should be unnecessary. However, those foreign companies that have memoranda of understanding with the Sinar Mas Group as opposed to its subsidiaries may find themselves in trouble should the group evaporate. But these are the risks of doing business with Asia's family-controlled conglomerates.

The Yeo family of Singapore wasn't nearly as fortunate when intra-family rivalry emerged among their ranks. The Yeos controlled Yeo Hiap Seng Ltd, a food and beverages manufacturer founded in 1935 and with a market capitalization today of around US$400 million. There are no less than six separate but related branches of the Yeo family that collectively controlled Yeo Hiap Seng through their private family holding company, Yeo Hiap Seng Holdings. In 1994, a bitter family dispute emerged, centering on some controversial and ultimately costly investments that the company had made. Several of the six Yeo family branches wanted to withdraw from the family holding company and go their separate ways. The Yeo family subsequently split into two camps, leading to complicated and lengthy court proceedings.[9] A hitherto private family suddenly found itself in the courtroom fighting itself, with the increasingly bitter exchanges appearing on the front pages of the local newspapers. Family members who contradicted their affidavits in court didn't help to sort out the confusion over who owned what. Ultimately, the squabble led to the family's loss of the business, Yeo Hiap Seng. While the Yeo family fought each other, two corporate raiders bid against each other for control of the company. Eventually, Robert Ng Chee Siong and Ng Teng Fong of the Sino Land Group won control of the company. They acquired almost 86% of its stock, leaving the Yeo family with almost no equity in the company it founded but which continues to bear its name.[10] The Widjajas and the Yeos are but two examples of complex families and their impact on corporate structures. There are many more.

Polygamy and the complexities of Asia's business families are obviously not at the top of the agenda of any typical American or European executive when he or she travels to Asia to sign a deal. But they are important. All too often, foreign firms commission due diligence assessments on their potential local partners but completely forget to commission due diligence on the family behind the local company. Given the role of families in corporate life in much of Asia, such a mistake, though common, is barely forgivable.

Below is a case study about a South-East Asian family that controls companies listed on the local stock exchanges. The family's business interests are intricately tied to its fortunes. The Singaporean-Indian Jumabhoy family's squabbling greatly exacerbated the problems their Scotts Holdings was facing. The affairs of the Jumabhoys serve as yet another warning to outsiders of the risks of investing in the stock of Asia's family firms.

 ### Singapore's Jumabhoy Family[11]

Almost 80% of Singapore's population is Chinese, but there is also a significant Indian population, comprising about 6%. Many are descendants of gem and textile merchants who, in the early part of the 20th century, set up trading houses that stretched from India to Hong Kong, the Dutch-East Indies (now Indonesia), and Singapore. One such family is the Jumabhoys.

The Jumabhoys are rich. In fact, they are probably the wealthiest Indian family in Singapore. The family's patriarch is Rajabali Jumabhoy. He arrived in Singapore from Gujarat state in India in 1918. In Singapore, he was involved in trading. He imported dates from Persia and exported timber from Java. Over time, he amassed a small fortune, which he used to branch into other businesses. In 1952, the elder Jumabhoy passed control of what was by then the family's property and development business to his son, Ameer Rajabali Jumabhoy. Ameer is still active in the family's business, but his sons, Rafiq and Iqbal, both in their forties, are also now involved in the family's activities.

The Jumabhoys' flagship company was the publicly listed Scotts Holdings. Worth around US$440 million, it has assets that include the luxury Ascott and Palm Courtt apartments in London, Jakarta, Singapore, Bangkok, Kuala Lumpur, and Saigon, as well as food court and shopping center management companies in Singapore. The Jumabhoys control the listed vehicle largely through their private holding company, Scotts Investments (Singapore) Pte Ltd (SIS). Outside Scotts, the Jumabhoys also hold the A&W Restaurants fast food franchise in Singapore, and substantial duty-free shopping concessions at Singapore's renowned Changi Airport.

Rich though they may be, the Jumabhoy family isn't a happy one. The genesis of their problems dates from 1992, when patriarch Rajabali quietly gave his grandson, Scotts Holdings' then-managing director Rafiq, a five-year stock option to buy a large tranche of Scotts Holdings' shares and, with it, the possibility of control of the company. The option, for over 100 million shares, had a par value of almost S$101 million

(US$70 million). It was an extraordinary gesture — and seemed borne out of Rajabali's belief that Rafiq was the most entrepreneurial member of the family. The option would also stop the control of Scotts falling to Ameer's brothers, Yusuf and Mustafa, in whose business abilities Rajabali didn't have a great deal of confidence. Rajabali's move was calculated to help the family and its investment. But if he had been looking for a way to intensify sibling rivalry, he had certainly found it.

In 1994, Scotts Holdings made a fateful decision to invest in a real estate project in Gurgaon, near New Delhi, in India. Rafiq's younger brother, Iqbal, shepherded the deal. This was fine except that Scotts' board of directors, including Rafiq, were not advised of irregularities that arose from the acquisition of land; that meant that several million dollars weren't properly accounted for. Subsequent developments in the Indian deal brought further disquiet to Rafiq who, again, wasn't kept abreast of what was happening. In July 1995, he formally advised the Stock Exchange of Singapore of the stock purchase option he had been given by his grandfather, after having kept quiet about it for almost three years. A month later, Iqbal attempted to claim a half share in the option. By this stage, the friction between Iqbal and Rafiq became open and more intense. Accountants Ernst & Young were appointed by the board to investigate the Indian land deal.[12] A month later, officers from Singapore's Commercial Affairs Department raided Scotts' offices and seized documents related to the deal. Apparently, the officers knew exactly what to look for, which fueled rumors that they had been tipped off by interests aligned with Rafiq.

Rafiq was deposed as Scotts Holdings' managing director soon after, his relationship with brother Iqbal and father Ameer hitting a new low. In October 1995, Ameer's brothers, sister and their children, and founder Rajabali sued Rafiq, Iqbal, and Ameer in an attempt to have Rafiq's stock option annulled. They claimed that even though Scotts Holdings had generally been profitable, the family holding company, SIS, was not because Rafiq had encouraged excessive speculative investments.[13]

Scotts Holdings' board appointed Chng Hee Kok as chief executive in late 1995 in an acknowledgment that the affairs of the family, and with it the company, were descending into chaos. Chng, a ruling People's Action Party Member of Parliament, had already established his credentials in sorting out corporate entanglements left by imploding controlling families. He had been brought in to help manage Yeo Hiap Seng Ltd in 1994 when the various Yeo family factions fought over (and ultimately lost) control of their family firm.

Rafiq's fortunes appeared to turn around in April 1996 when he had himself appointed as managing director of SIS, the family holding company, with the help of two uncles. Rafiq and Yusuf then replaced Ameer and Iqbal as the SIS representatives on the board of Scotts Holdings. Several days later, the newly rebalanced board voted to remove Ameer as executive chairman. Rafiq was back in control after having been fired as managing director several months earlier.

Iqbal and Ameer didn't accept the turn of events quietly. They responded with a series of legal actions against the family holding company and demanded that the courts appoint a manager to run the company. On top of this, Iqbal commenced proceedings against Scotts Holdings to seek a declaration that he was wrongfully dismissed as executive director and to order that he be reinstated, or alternatively, be provided with damages for wrongful dismissal. Ameer followed suit and commenced legal proceedings to seek a declaration that the termination of his contract was null and void. But the writs didn't stop there. Iqbal launched two further actions — defamation suits, this time — one against Scotts Holdings and the other against three of its officers. The sight of the Jumabhoys suing each other and their company must have had Scotts Holdings' minority shareholders aghast. (It wasn't until early 1998 that Iqbal agreed to withdraw his three suits against Scotts Holdings in return for a settlement equivalent to US$200,000 — a payment that probably paled in comparsion to the company's lost management time and legal expenses.[14])

Relations among the various Jumabhoys at the end of 1996 strained. But the situation worsened as 1997 wore on. The Stock Exchange of Singapore censured Ameer, Rafiq, and Iqbal in March for breaches of the listing requirements that relate to third-party transactions and for misstatements in the prospectus they issued for Scotts Holdings in 1991. It transpired that Scotts Holdings had entered into a series of transactions between 1993 and 1996 with the Jumabhoys' private holding company, SIS, as well as with other companies privately held by various members of the Jumabhoy family. The approval of Scotts Holdings' minority shareholders was needed under the Stock Exchange of Singapore's rules, but none was sought. Among the transactions was a series of ten interest-free cash advances for more than US$1.5 million to the family's private holding company, the leasing of two Scotts Holdings' premises to enterprises controlled by the Jumabhoys outside the Scotts Holdings structure, and renewal of leases on Scotts Holdings property to the Jumabhoys' A&W Restaurants even though the restaurants' rental payments were substantially in arrears. Also, a company controlled by Naseem Jumabhoy, a daughter of Ameer, had supplied furniture, fabric, and other materials for the refurbishment of Scotts Holdings' luxury apartment tower, the Ascott Singapore, the Palm Courtt complex, and Scotts Holdings' head office.[15] These represented yet more transactions for which approval from minority shareholders should have been sought, given the obvious conflict of interest they entailed.

In light of all these revelations, the stock exchange demanded that the family ensure there was a majority of independent directors on Scotts' board to safeguard the interests of minority shareholders. This wasn't done and the state of the Scotts Holdings board worsened when managing director Chng Hee Kok resigned at the end of June 1997, and was followed shortly after by other independent directors. The following month, the stock exchange met with Ameer, Rafiq, Iqbal, and Yusuf to discuss how the Jumabhoys intended to arrange for a majority of independent directors. In the typically understated words of the exchange, 'it was apparent ... that there were differences of opinion among the Jumabhoy directors ...'[16] In the end, it decided that it would ban Ameer, Rafiq, and Iqbal from holding any directorships in companies listed in Singapore other than Scotts Holdings on account of the serious disputes among them and their various transgressions of the listing requirements. The stock exchange added that it viewed 'with serious concern that the disputes among the Jumabhoy directors have detracted them from their primary duty to the company, which is to ensure that Scotts' board has a majority of independent directors and that the company could function effectively and in the interest of all shareholders.'[17] Effectively, the Jumabhoys had taken their company public, but acted as if it were still private.

The exchange's concerns proved to be justified when Scotts Holdings' results for 1996 were released. It showed that the company had made a loss after tax and extraordinary items of S$8.3 million (then US$5.7 million) — the first loss incurred in many years.[18] Squabbling that shouldn't have gone beyond the kitchen table had been carried into the boardroom, with all the company's shareholders having to foot the bill.

Next, Singapore's High Court ruled in June 1997 that Rafiq's stock purchase option was indeed invalid.[19] But he immediately appealed against the decision. To support his claim that his option was valid, Rafiq declared to SIS his intention to exercise the option over the next few months. Each intention was rejected, but speculation grew that should his appeal succeed he would then turn around and sue SIS for refusing him from exercising his option before its expiry date.[20] So the Jumabhoys' minority shareholders had to endure another few months of having absolutely no idea of where Scotts was going and who would control it. Scotts' share price didn't collapse, but it didn't rise either. This was at a time when other listed property companies in Singapore had risen substantially.

The uncertainty continued into 1998. It wasn't until Rafiq withdrew his appeal to the High Court in March and resigned from the Scotts Holdings board, that it seemed it would become clear as to which Jumabhoy would eventually control Scotts Holdings. Around the same time, Scotts Holdings released its interim results for the second half of 1997, which showed that its full-year profit forecast wasn't to be met; in fact, the interim results showed a loss of S$5.05 million (US$3.10 million) and a loss for the full year of S$1.22 million (US$0.75 million).[21]

The Jumabhoys were in disarray and their company suffered accordingly. By June 1998, the family had tired of Scotts and they announced that they intended to sell out of it entirely. No doubt it was a relief to Scotts' minority shareholders — and the company's share price surged on the announcement. Once again, an Asian business family had shown that buying into the family's company also meant buying into the family — warts and all.

CHAPTER 8

Asia's E-Boom and E-Bust

The Internet boom was overhyped everywhere. Nonetheless, it proved a good tool for making money — especially for Asia's conglomerate owners. They managed to hijack what had been driven in the United States by a myriad of small and independent entrepreneurs. It was the new economy versus old economy and in Asia, the old economy seemed to have won.

Jack, can you please make some money?' asked the venture capitalist of Jack Ma, founder of China-based Alibaba.com. 'But the company's still a baby,' replied Jack. Ma's company was only two years old. 'And besides, I don't believe in child labor!'

Ma recounted this conversation to the audience at an Internet conference in Hong Kong in late 1999. They went wild with applause. The idea of taking an investor's money and giving him no return was a hit. Egged on by the support, Ma proclaimed that his business plans look no further than the two days ahead. The audience erupted with more excitement. The clincher was that on the strength of no real business plan and no claim whatsoever about profit or revenue, no less than 30 venture capitalists had queued outside Ma's door. He had the luxury of being able to select the five that he most preferred. They proceeded to cough up several million dollars. Ma's approach seemed to be a good one. Two months after his appearance at the Hong Kong conference, Alibaba.com, which provides a virtual meeting place for buyers and sellers (it's a nice thing to do but I have yet to work out how the website makes money), was given another round of investments, totalling US$20 million. Getting rich quick has never been so easy.

There's no doubt that Ma is a smooth talker and is very amusing at conferences. This and the fact that he is from mainland China, where he works with the Internet, saw millions of dollars flow his way. You know that you are riding on bubble when having a good sense of humor becomes a substitute for a business plan.

The problem Ma and others like him face is the reason why the Internet is so popular — it's basically free. Just because people flock to something doesn't make it a good investment. (People, after all, have a habit of flocking to traffic accidents.) But charging them for it does. Internet firms can do a lot of things. But the one thing that they haven't mastered very well is making money. I once sat through a presentation by Nasdaq-listed China portal, Chinadotcom, and the entire expose was on how it would spend money. What it would do to make money wasn't actually spelt out. That reminded me of sitting in on a government department presentation.

But getting consumers to part with their cash online is difficult enough even in mature economies such as the United States. Getting them to do it in Asia, where legal structures are often poor, credit card penetration rates are low, and business is usually conducted through personal connections, seems an almost impossible task. Never mind. Western investors in particular have not been discouraged from tipping hundreds of millions of dollars into Asia's e-sector. They had trouble making money in Asia from investing in ventures that actually made things such as cars and chemical plants. (A 1998 AT Kearney survey found that of the 50 multinationals engaged in manufacturing in China, only 38% were turning in a profit.[1]) But now, they expect to miraculously generate big profits from a sector that was largely untried in Asia and, it is service-oriented, against which the cultural cards are stacked even higher.

Many start-ups in Silicon Valley obtain venture capital because their founders are former employees of Microsoft or Sun Microsystems. In Asia, start-ups get funding because their founders are from mainland China, are able to assert some sort of connection with a government official no matter how unproven or tenuous it is, and can exhibit infectious enthusiasm or at least be amusing. Asia is after all the 'mysterious' East and the affectation of 'mysterious' seems to obviate the need for anything so transparent as a business plan or revenue projections, especially as far as many Western venture capitalists are concerned. It's as if insisting on such formalities would be culturally insensitive.

But unlike Asia's property bubble, which took years to build and did not catch on evenly across Asia, the Internet bubble has taken off everywhere. When an Internet World exhibition and conference opened in New Delhi in September 1999, the organizers expected a good turnout. What they didn't count on was the attendance of more than 25,000 industry representatives over three days and a further 50,000 members of the public who crowded the exhibition hall. Security guards and New Delhi police had to be called in for crowd control. Many dot-com companies will never make money. But clearly, organizers of Internet conferences at least were making a killing.

WHERE IT'S AT

The speed with which the dot-com craze caught on in Asia was astounding. What is a fad in the United States can become a panic in Asia, especially in Hong Kong. When the offer for shares in Tom.com — Hong Kong billionaire Li Ka Shing's Chinese-language Internet portal — opened in February 2000, long queues formed for application forms, and within two hours, all copies of the prospectus had been snapped up. Many potential investors told the media that they had no idea what the company did but they wanted its shares anyway. Their behavior was justified, at least initially. In the first few hours of trading on March 1, 2000, the company's stock, which had an issue price of HK$1.78, hit a high of HK$9.05. Any talk of Tom.com turning in a profit from its Internet businesses was superfluous, however. At the time, it didn't even have any revenue. Within six months of listing, Tom.com had fired 80 employees, or 16% of its workforce, to cut costs and had made a second-quarter loss of US$19 million. Revenue had yet to hit US$1 million, and when asked to give a breakdown of its revenue, the company's CEO declined because he felt that public would not be interested.[2]

Asia's e-boom has been driven by both local and foreign investors, particularly those from the United States. An American CEO of a US-based Internet firm who was at the conference at which Jack Ma spoke, mentioned that he had been in China for the past few days. The news of his presence drove up his company's stock price on the Nasdaq, so that within a few days, his company's market capitalization had grown by as much as US$550 million. Obviously he was in China to sign some deals, or at least that was the rationale. Pity, if he had simply been there on vacation. The CEO quipped to his staff that he should have stayed on in China for a few more days to see if he could push the company's market capitalization up 'by a billion.'

By and large, Asian businesses still think in terms of commodities rather than services. Traditionally, Asian firms under-acquire services as inputs, be it research and development, staff training, legal advice, accounting advice, marketing, and so on. There is a cultural bias toward tangibles, and the biggest tangible of all is land. Accordingly, some of Asia's biggest attempts to get aboard the Internet revolution are thinly camouflaged as real-estate plays.

Both Hong Kong and Malaysia have decided to establish their own versions of Silicon Valley — Singapore was keen to hop aboard too —

but their emphasis seems to be on infrastructure instead of entrepreneurship and clever thinking. Hong Kong's much-publicized Cyberport, for example, allows for almost three times the amount of luxury housing as it does for industrial space. The Internet kiosks that first sprung up along Orchard Road in Singapore in 1999 seem to be more about the well-placed and very expensive poster advertising on their outsides than the computer terminals within. People seldom use them. Why would you stand in the street to order something online when you could simply walk into the shop behind you? Malaysia's Multimedia Super Corridor too has a strong property focus. It seems to be more about the corridor than about the multimedia. Splendid facilities are one thing but a culture of creativity is quite another. Asia's grappling with the Internet has a light side. But there's also a dark side.

START UP AND CASH OUT

Some companies don't make any money but their founders become fabulously wealthy anyway; some companies list on the stock markets and still don't make any money but their founders grow even richer — it's almost as if the Internet boom was tailormade for Asia's conglomerate owners. The dot-com craze would have been irresistible to those who had sat on real estate while its value skyrocketed and who were already well-acquainted with manipulating stock markets and minority shareholders to further increase their wealth. At the start of 1999, no major conglomerate owner in Asia was significantly involved with the Internet. By the year-end, it was a question of who wasn't or at least planning to be. In Hong Kong, there was Richard Li with his Pacific Century CyberWorks, Richard's father, Li Ka Shing, with Tom.com, the Kwok brothers of Sun Hung Kai Properties with their SUNeVision, and Robert Kuok's Kerry Properties and Lee Shau Kee's Henderson Land, both of which had taken stakes in Internet start-ups. None of these forays into the new economy had a singular aim — each encompassed a range of businesses, just like their parents that spawned them. In Asia, conglomerates beget conglomerates.

Indonesia's property and banking Lippo Group, which is controlled by the Riady family, has been among the most vociferous in utilizing stock markets to build up its wealth. It was only a matter of time before it too diversified into Internet-related businesses and floated the results on the stock market. As it turned out, the Riadys did it in quick time. One Lippo company had some Internet-related assets injected into it in the second half of 1999, and within a few weeks, its stock price on the Jakarta Stock Exchange had risen by 400%. Another of their lesser-performing companies, the not-so-glamorously named PT Asuransi Lippo Life, was renamed Lippo e-Net in January 2000, and within a week, its stock price had more than doubled. It soon transpired that the company's core business would still be insurance. In their public utterances, officials of the group seemed unsure about how the company would participate in the Internet. It all looked a bit too opportunistic and the company's share price plummeted as quickly as it had risen. The company was subsequently investigated by the Indonesian financial regulators for allegedly issuing misleading statements that caused the stock price to rise, and the company and the Riady family were fined a total of more than US$600,000.[3]

Unfazed, the Riadys repackaged more assets and bundled them into a new company named AcrossAsia Multimedia. It was an ambitious name, given that almost all of the assets were in strife-torn Indonesia. There was, however, the almost obligatory if vague mutterings about investing in China's Internet sector. The company was next floated on Hong Kong's then new Growth Enterprise Market (GEM). Apart from the Riadys, other significant shareholders included a company ultimately owned by the Chinese government and a close Riady friend, former Arkansas governor, Jim Guy Tucker, who was convicted of fraud in the Clinton-Whitewater scandal. (The Riady family had earlier been at the center of the improper Clinton political donations scandal that became known as 'Donorgate'). According to analyst Gene Galbraith of web-based newsletter *Asiawise*, the company's prospectus stated that the company had 'no track record of revenue, income and cash flow' on which to base a forecast and that the group had 'no prior experience in its portal and e-commerce businesses.' A majority of the directors joined the company only six weeks prior to its IPO and in the previous four months, there had been 28 individual transfers of share agreements, 24 changes to the share capital of subsidiaries, 26 contracts outside the ordinary course of business, and 8 shareholders resolutions were prepared.[4] It was easy to see what AcrossAsia Multimedia was all about. Unfortunately, it wasn't about the Internet. And how much was all this worth? Just after listing, it managed to garner a market capitalization of more than US$2.5 billion.

But were Asia's conglomerate owners really interested in the Internet and the new economy? That each was keen to list their Internet vehicles as quickly as possible suggested other motives. An IPO translates to money inflow — particularly for the founding shareholder. If Asia's conglomerate owners were genuinely interested in building new economy companies and thought that these companies would be profitable, they would have done it with their own money, as each of the conglomerate owners was sufficiently wealthy to fund at least the first phase of their companies growth and so did not need to raise funds via an IPO. Chapter 6 made the point that profitable companies are privately held and those that are less so are listed. And so it was with the tycoons' Internet companies. Indeed, their move to list their newly created Internet ventures on the stock markets occurred with unusual haste. Never listen to what an Asian conglomerate owner says. Just watch what he does.

ASIA'S E-BOOM GETS HIJACKED

If there is a U.S. model of the Internet boom, it would be something like this: Young, tech-savvy employees of high-tech companies have an idea for an Internet company that they feel might be viable. They resign from their jobs, seek seed funding, and go about establishing their firms. Second-round venture capitalists provide more funding, and so on. Eventually, the firm might list on the Nasdaq. The main thing that drives the market's assessment of the prospects of the firm is the idea behind whatever it is that the company does. The company usually remains focused and sticks to the initial business concept.

The Asian model goes something like this. Many young educated Asians set about establishing Internet firms, but most of these do not get the funding they need to advance beyond the initial stage. Instead, the money goes elsewhere. Asia's conglomerate owners see the Internet as another opportunity to wring more money from the stock market and so quickly establish companies with a grab-bag of potential Internet-related businesses that can be pushed onto the stock market as quickly as possible. Funds are raised and they are spent acquiring stakes in other Internet ventures. So Asia's conglomerates spawn mini-conglomerates centered on the Internet. But like their parents, these companies lack focus and comprise many companies that are pushed together rather than a single company that is built up over time. The main thing that drives the market's assessment of the prospects of the listed company is not its technology or the cleverness of its main business (usually neither of these is clear), but everything that the new economy is not supposed to be — the founder's big name, his other businesses — and possible political connections.

Heaving together existing companies into Internet conglomerates has become the name of the game in Asia. In the guise of venture capitalists and incubators, Asia's conglomerate owners started the process by picking their way through Asia's small start-ups. In the United States, new economy companies tend to be lithe, focused, and independent entities. What Asia's conglomerate owners managed to do with the e-boom was to snatch it from the hands of young Asian entrepreneurs, use it to wring out more cash from the stock markets and then spend the proceeds on a buying spree for other companies. In the United States, the e-boom is about entrepreneurs. In Asia, it's in danger of being 'conglomerated.' Asia will still have its technical revolution, but thanks to the opportunism of the conglomerate owners, it will take place in a corporate setting that is still very much of the old economy.

Within a matter of months of Hong Kong-based Chinadotcom's sensational debut on Nasdaq in July 1999 — its stock price soared 235% above the offer price on the first day — it set about spending the proceeds, not so much on building its business but on acquiring approximately 25 stakes in companies and partnerships. The company freely admitted that its strategy was to 'build through acquisition'.[5] Hikari Tsushin of Japan and Creative Technology of Singapore also quickly acquired stakes in Asia Internet start-ups, although Creative Technology at least tended to invest in businesses that were related to its core business of making sound cards.

In Malaysia, there was Vincent Tan of Berjaya Group with his Mol.com. (Mol actually stood for Malaysia Online; it wasn't another sex site.) In early 2000, it was a lackluster fluorescent lamp maker called Dijaya Enterprises. By mid-year, it was controlled by Tan and had spent more than US$63 million acquiring stakes in 20 Malaysian Internet companies.

Japan's Masayoshi Son and his Softbank Corp provided another example, although Son's interest, at least initially, was to take stakes in US-based Internet firms. This he did with large stakes in the likes of Yahoo!, GeoCities, Buy.com, and E-Loan. And when their market capitalization exploded, so did Softbank's. By early 2000, it had reached the equivalent of US$44 billion. The only place to go after that was down. By mid-2000, the stock price had fallen by 80% from its peak. It had been a remarkable ride, but even new economy Softbank suffered from many of the corporate governance problems associated with Japan's old economy companies. Analysts complained that there was too little disclosure with regard to the company's balance sheet, its fund raising capacity was unclear, as was its future business plan. If there was one champion of the 'conglomeration' of the e-boom in Asia, it was Richard Li.

PUTTING THE BOOM IN A BOX

The entry of Hong Kong's Richard Li Tzar Kai to the Internet world was a cathartic event for Asia. Thereafter interest in the Internet literally exploded over night. In April 1999, Li acquired a small telecommunications equipment distributor that was listed on the Hong

Kong stock exchange. He renamed it Pacific Century CyberWorks (PCCW) and declared that he would turn it into the world's largest high-speed Internet access provider. By the end of that year, its share price had soared by 1,400% and the company had risen from nowhere to be the seventh-largest company on the Hong Kong market by market capitalization. Li's founding of PCCW caused everyone in the region to sit up and take notice — both of the Internet and what he was doing. His entry triggered many 'me-too' investments in Hong Kong as the scions of other property-based dynasties decided to hop aboard and found their own Internet companies.

PCCW is a rarity among Asian Internet companies. It started with a well-defined business plan. Its initial aim was to bring the Internet into the homes of millions of subscribers across Asia via satellite link-ups, although that brief has since been expanded upon. Until its audacious but ultimately successful US$38 billion bid in early 2000 for Hong Kong's main telecoms company, Cable & Wireless HKT, the company's most tangible asset had been a stake in Hong Kong's controversial Cyberport development, as well as a myriad of stakes in start-ups around Asia. (Through subsidiary CyberWorks Ventures, PCCW had spent more than US$600 million buying stakes in more than 30 Internet companies.) By early 2000, there were 129 PCCW-related registered domain names, which suggested that PCCW was also planning to construct many websites.

Among PCCW's investments were a stake in U.S. Web incubator CMGI, which in turn established a 50:50 joint venture with PCCW in Asia called CMGI Asia; 5% of Singapore portal Horizon.com Ltd; 22% of Nasdaq-listed U.S.-based broadband Internet service provider (ISP) SoftNet Systems, Inc; 25% of Singapore Web design and incubator SilkRoute Holdings; and approximately 20% of Hong Kong entrepreneur Yat Siu's Web design company, Outblaze Ltd. And in early 2000, PCCW acquired Hong Kong Telecom (HKT), as well as announced a regional alliance with Australia's main telecom company, Telstra Corp, to offer Internet services. Li's big grab occurred with such haste that it barely seemed possible that each acquisition could have been as judicious as the last. That was soon proven correct. By mid-2000, the US$129 million spent on the SoftNet stake in October 1999 was worth around US$65 million, for example.

What PCCW had become though was another Asian conglomerate. The unit sported eight divisions: broadband business-to-consumer (B2C) Internet services, business-to-business (B2B) Internet services, data centers and web hosting, Internet protocol backbone and satellite, mobile telephone services, Internet incubation, fixed-network services, and real estate. Thus, within a year, Li had managed to create Asia's first e-conglomerate, albeit with a hefty old economy telecommunications component from the gobbling up of HKT. PCCW might have encompassed new economy businesses but arguably it had an old economy structure — it was just another Asian conglomerate that lacked in focus, and had many small companies pushed together and given definition as a group more by sharing a common shareholder than anything else.

But PCCW's most important asset remained its executive chairman, Richard Li. With its founder being the son of Li Ka Shing, the billionaire-owner of Cheung Kong Holdings, PCCW had a direct link to Hong Kong's business and political elite. Li junior though was keen to underplay the fact that he is his father's son. PCCW's media officers had been known to request journalists not to refer to Richard as the 'son of Li Ka Shing' in their stories about him. But it's hard to hide what is obvious, and besides, the Li connection gave the PCCW stock a type of Li premium. Richard was able to leverage that premium to keep the deals flowing and PCCW's stock price soaring. He then used that as a basis to grab control of HKT — a real business with several billion dollars in annual revenue. Asia's e-boom had proven a means to an end for Li. PCCW's stock price then collapsed but Li got what he wanted — control of HKT.

FROM START-UP TO FAST BUCK

There is no doubt that the Internet and e-commerce represent a sea-change in how we do business, but a bubble is a bubble. The dot-com fever has been likened to an old-fashioned land grab, and accordingly, even Hong Kong's property tycoons rushed to stake out their plots of Internet territory. The trouble is, land in Hong Kong — or anywhere else for that matter — is in fixed supply, but Internet space is completely infinite. There is some logic to skyrocketing prices for land, but for a commodity for which supply always expands to meet demand? Pegging out your claim in cyberspace is fine, but why the rush when there's space for everyone?

But that's not the only problem. Documenting the precise dimensions of it all has proven difficult. Internet usage figures in Asia are extremely rubbery. They're almost certainly exaggerated, possibly greatly. Too many people have a vested interest in that being the case. Further, meaningful figures are very hard to come by. Accounts with ISPs tend to be counted rather than the individuals who use the Internet. This means that individuals with multiple ISP accounts are counted more than once. Infrequent users are counted too. For example, users who have accessed the Internet at a friend's house six months ago could still be counted as a user in a survey. Free users are counted too. ISPs hand out countless of start-up CDs that come with perhaps a month's free access. Many people use the free access but thereafter do not sign up, but they still get counted as users.

Websites like to use the number of registered users that they have as a basis for getting venture-capital funding, so they face an incentive to fluff up their registered user base. I have been harangued in Hong Kong and Singapore by operators at Internet trade shows begging me to register online with their sites there and then. They even promised small gifts such as pens, business card holders, mouse mats, and the like if I did. The fact that the sites were only useful if you lived in Hong Kong or Singapore — and I live in neither — and that I professed absolutely no interest in visiting the sites thereafter seemed to count for nothing. Nonetheless, if I registered, for my trouble I could get a free pen. For theirs, they would get another registered user with which to impress the next venture capitalist as to the size of their online 'community.'

Accompanying rubbery usage figures are astonishing projections for e-commerce growth in Asia. Seemingly, there is competition to generate the most fabulous forecasts. Investment bankers Salomon Smith Barney estimated in 2000 that Internet revenue (from advertising, e-commerce, and network services) in the Asia-Pacific region (excluding Japan, Australia, and New Zealand) would be US$4,465 million in 2001. But by 2005, it would be US$92,072 million — a 20-fold increase in four years.[6] Maybe, but then maybe not. And who will know?

Internet stock analysts have been forced to contort themselves in extraordinary ways in attempts to give their analyses at least the illusion of scientific underpinnings. The thinking seems to be: there is a model out there to value Internet stocks; it just hasn't been found yet. Could the problem be that stock market bubbles just haven't any structure? Sometimes, Internet companies are valued based on their customer growth rates. But this makes little sense because it is so difficult to retain customers on the Internet. Customer loyalty really means being able to raise prices without having customers leave in droves; but the freedom to desert in droves is the essence of the Internet. Also, discounted cash flow models of Internet companies are relatively meaningless because many firms change and add to their businesses very quickly, causing their revenue to bounce around a lot. Amazon.com started out as an online book retailer. It is now a retailer of many other things, from plants to pet food. It has also become an auction site.

Internet stock analysts often seem to assume an advocate role for the sector rather than remain mere analysts of it. I have seen them at Internet conferences almost begging the audience to be swept up in the enthusiasm that has picked them up. I watched one Goldman Sachs analyst on a public platform in 1999 produce slides to 'demonstrate' why the stock price for Yahoo! was 'cheaper' than that for the highly profitable Hong Kong and Shanghai Banking Corporation (HSBC). Based on some extraordinary assumptions, he produced figures to show that the projected price-earnings multiple for Yahoo! was 20 while that for HSBC was 25. 'Go home now and sell HSBC and buy Yahoo!', he exhorted his audience. His projections would have made more sense if he was assuming that Yahoo!'s stock price was about to collapse, but he wasn't.

A contributing factor to the very high stock valuations of many Internet firms is that so little of their equity is actually available for trade. This is exactly the same problem with most old economy firms that are listed on stock exchanges around Asia. With just 10–20% of a company's stock available for public trading, it's much easier to ramp up the price of the stock. (Hong Kong's Tom.com offered only 15% of its total stock during its IPO, which caused much fuss in early 2000). It also means that when fund managers decide that they need to acquire, say, some PCCW or China Online stocks in their portfolio, the heavy volume for only a small number of shares tends to over-magnify the interest in these stocks.

In late 1999, the thirst in Hong Kong for Internet-related stocks was so strong that companies with the merest association with the Internet — or even no association at all — were bid up. The stock price in Hong Kong of building contractor, China Prosperity Holdings, surged by 35% within one trading day on the strength of rumors that it was planning an Internet venture. As it turned out, the rumors were untrue. The casino that is otherwise known as the Stock Exchange of Hong Kong is clearly well-suited to the 'bubble.com' craze. Hong Kong's technology stocks have become the new red chips.

The rush to claim a link to the Internet sometimes led to some very silly outcomes. In September 1998, Hong Kong-listed loss-making retailer, Iwai's International Holdings, changed its name to Fronteer International Holdings. This did little to lift its share price. So less than a year later, the company added the online sale of clothes to its other activities and used this as an excuse for yet another name change, this time to the very grand sounding eBiz.hk.com. The trouble was that the new name was an existing subdomain name held by another company. So it was forced to change its name a third time, to eBizhk.com (one dot less).

The share price of 20 Hong Kong-listed companies that changed their names to suggest a connection with the Internet (for example, by adding a '.com') in the first nine months of 1999 rose on average by 319%, compared to a 25% rise in the market index during the same period. South Seas Development's stock price rose by more than 20% on the day

(14 September) it changed its name to Sino-i.com. This when its only e-commerce-related asset was an unused option to buy a stake in a Chinese info-tech company, an option the company had had for some time prior to its name change. Another company, shoe distributor Silver Eagle Holdings began making video compact disc (VCD) players (which has nothing to do with e-commerce) and changed its name to Cybersonic Technology. Its share price rose by almost 400%.

Some companies did well simply by announcing a modest connection to an e-commerce venture. China property developer Dong-jun Holdings saw its market capitalization soar by 90%, or US$42 million, in one day in October 1999 after it announced that it had taken a 4% stake in a loss-making Chinese website for children.

Nasdaq-listed Chinadotcom's share price tripled soon after its 1999 IPO and rose ninefold six months later. None of the company's main lines of business was profitable. Its China portal ranked only 39 in the list of the most-visited Chinese websites. The company did actually show a profit in the second quarter of 1999, but that was only because it gained a US$5.1 million windfall when a brokerage accidentally sold its entire stake in another Internet company instead of part of it. Chinadotcom's executives and founders wasted no time in taking advantage of market conditions. In January 2000 — precisely upon the expiry of the six-month moratorium on directors selling their shares after an IPO — the directors partly cashed in their holdings and netted themselves US$395 million.[7]

Asia's governments regarded the e-boom as a very healthy development. Notwithstanding the economic crisis the region had just been through and the fact that lax corporate governance had been a key contributing factor to the crisis, they embarked on a round of competitive regulatory loosening to attract a greater share of the e-boom to their shores. Taiwan eased its rules in late 1999 to allow Internet companies to list on the local exchange when they otherwise wouldn't have qualified. Internet firms with as little as NT$50 million in capital and have made a 'moderate' loss in the previous year were allowed to list with Industrial Development Bureau approval. The Bombay Stock Exchange changed its rules to allow IT companies to offer as little as 10% of their stock to the public instead of the usual 25% as long as at least 2 million shares were issued to the public and they were worth more than 500 million rupees in total. This change in listing rules enabled founders of start-up companies in India to achieve more easily a market valuation for their companies — and ramp up more easily the price of their shares at the same time.

Meanwhile, Singapore changed its rules so that 'promising' Internet companies could list on the local bourse even if they had never made a profit but provided their market capitalization exceeded S$80 million. Hong Kong decided that its stock exchange, notoriously lax as it is with its regulations, was still too strict for Internet start-ups. So it set up an entirely new exchange for small stocks, the Growth Enterprise Market (GEM). Listing on the GEM was made easier than on its bigger cousin, but disclosure rules were made tougher, at least in theory. High-tech South Korean companies that wanted to list without having to comply with all the usual restrictions could do so on the Kosdaq. In May 1999, the government relaxed regulations and offered tax incentives to encourage further listings on the Kosdaq.

REVOLUTIONIZING THE ASIAN FIRM

But it's not all corporate shenanigans with Asia's Internet boom. The Internet revolution will undoubtedly bring important technological change and innovation to Asia. Geographical considerations are important to conventional shopping: consumers choose where to do their banking and buy their books and groceries because the relevant facilities are located near their homes. But the Internet is changing this. Asian retailers, like retailers everywhere, have existed with semi-captive markets. They have a margin of market power over their customers simply because they know it's too much of a bother for many of their customers to go elsewhere. This margin permits a certain degree of slack in customer service and a slightly higher price that retailers can charge. But the Internet is now opening up conventional shops to competition from retailers potentially from around the world. A bookstore in Hong Kong that faced almost no competition in its neighborhood and so could afford to offer an outdated range of books at high prices suddenly finds that thanks to the Internet it now faces competition from cheap bookshops around the world with huge backlists, as well as all the latest releases. It's a phenomenon that's hardly unique to Asia but will be important in waking up many Asian retailers from their complacency.

There is much talk about building Web-based 'communities.' But really, such talk is over-blown. Real communities, such as those comprised by a town or a village, are given definition because exit is difficult and costly. It takes time and money to move one's house and possessions, to find a new job, and make new friends. Internet 'communities' have no such exit costs. People are free to surf any website, to shop with any e-tailer, and to jump from one chatsite to another. There is little or no loyalty on the Internet;

that's the very reason for its appeal. In commerce, everything becomes commoditized on the Internet — the only relevant consideration is price. Hence, talk of building an e-community, particularly in terms of buying and selling, is nonsense.

This of course runs completely counter to the traditional functioning of Asian businesses where personal connections are very important. Think of the traditional Chinese shop with its eclectic array of goods that may include rubber gloves alongside sticks of celery and childrens' toys. Goods are sourced not with the customer in mind but based on which suppliers the proprietor has good personal relations with. But when it comes to the Web where anonymity rules, personal connections are irrelevant. Once customers are satisfied that their credit card details are safe on the Net and that their purchases will be delivered, what matters is price.

The only retailers on the Web who are likely to be able to claim a meaningful online community will be those whose wares are so obscure that their customers have to keep coming back because there's nowhere else to go.

E-commerce does, however, provide a useful tool for retailers to build databases about customer preferences. Each time a customer of Amazon.com returns to the site and places new orders, information on that customer is gathered. When the customer next visits the site, the site can better cater to the customer according to his tastes. Thus, e-commerce is less personalized but more individualized. This is the exact opposite of where many traditional Asian firms are today. They tend to be strong on personalized business, but when it comes to customer service and individualized service, they are very weak. The mismatch between what is demanded by e-commerce and what conventional firms have is greatest in Asia than in, say, the United States.

But it is Asia's corporate sector that is likely to be the most affected by the coming e-commerce wave. Many of Asia's companies are old-fashioned and poorly structured by modern standards. E-commerce will only exacerbate their backwardness, leaving them even more exposed and under threat from external competition. The Internet is also likely to change the internal operations of Asia's companies.

The offering of employee stock options has been critical to Internet start-ups in the United States. Typically, these start-ups are cash-poor in their early days and stock options are the only way to attract good staff. But traditional family-owned overseas Chinese companies generally do not readily welcome external investors, and certainly not if they threaten the control of the founding family. In addition, stock options demand accountability and transparency of a firm's books, things that were not requied of Asian businesses until now.

E-commerce will increase the numbers of businesses engaged in international trade but reduce the average transaction size. A website, unlike a retail store, is open for business 24 hours a day, 365 days a year. Accessibility in terms of time (and not just spatial convenience) will favor retailers who decide to trade online.

The Internet will ultimately threaten the structure of traditional Asian conglomerates. Corporations will become looser knit, with greater numbers of smaller units of employees. Management will become less structured and less patriarchal, thus challenging typical patterns of Asian management. Ultimately, the Internet will also break down the vertically integrated Asian conglomerate. Under competitive pressure, individual companies within a conglomerate will be run more as discrete profit centers. This will encourage them to cut their costs and, rather than buy their input from other members of the group as they might have done in the past, they will seek external suppliers if cheaper. The Internet will provide an excellent means for sourcing inputs from as wide a field as possible to allow greater price competition. Bids will be received from anywhere in the world instead of from just the immediate locality.

When the Internet becomes embedded in corporate management culture in Asia, it will weaken divisions between departments and also weaken middle management — junior staff can send e-mail messages directly to senior staff. This has been the practice in the West. If sending an e-mail to a senior manager seems too direct, the more indirect (if you like, more 'Asian') mode will be to 'c.c.' the message to senior managers. This way senior managers can be kept informed without the obligation of having to respond. This will help break down the rigid hierarchies within many Asian firms.

REVOLUTIONIZING ASIAN SOCIETY

The Internet will see the inversion of the home and office. More and more companies will be run from people's homes. This has significant cultural implications in Asia. Already, Singapore has amended its laws to allow a wider range of small businesses to be run from homes. Previously, this was not allowed at all. In South Korea, there is tremendous social pressure against men in particular, from staying at home even if it is to work. This is an important cultural constraint that will need to change if South Korea is to fully catch the e-commerce wave.

Another challenge posed to Asia by the Internet revolution relates to existing social hierarchies. The Internet threatens to upset traditional family and workplace relations. Traditionally, older people both in the home and the workplace are accorded much respect and their authority is rarely questioned. However, it is the young who are the most Internet-aware and at the forefront of the e-commerce revolution; this will realign the knowledge balance between generations.

But perhaps the most dramatic social impact the Internet will have in Asia will be in the position of traditional overseas Chinese trading networks. The informal networks that the overseas Chinese have around the world have been the key to their success. A brother here, a sister there, and maybe cousins everywhere facilitate trade across borders, and even more importantly, the flow of information across borders cheaply, so that commercial opportunities and market niches can be quickly identified and exploited. Networks of friends and relatives are leveraged upon to find the right goods at the right price.

These overseas Chinese traders are analogous to the Internet. Although they are spread out across the world, they are nonetheless connected, but without any centralized coordination. They operate like an organic World Wide Web that gathers, processes, and distributes information. Traditional overseas Chinese commerce is often portrayed as being 'borderless.' But increasingly, it is the Internet that is providing the technological means for a truly 'borderless' trade. E-commerce is also about shaving margins and treating the customer as king. It undermines long-term relationships between buyers and suppliers — the sort of *guanxi*-type relationships favored by traditional overseas Chinese business.

When it comes to business, the Internet has greatest implications for middlemen. The overseas Chinese have been one of the world's great middleman minorities. They have performed this role as shopkeepers and traders, providing the link between buyers and producers. But the whole point of e-commerce is to cut out the middleman. Independent travel agents handled 80% of travel reservations in the United States in 1996, for example. Two years later, they handled just 50%, with much of the loss being attributed to online ticket wholesalers. International commodities markets too are moving online. Producers can deal directly with customers in online markets. There's no need for middlemen. Already, almost the entire Dutch cut-flower market (Europe's major cut-flower market) is conducted online and commodities such as chemicals, metals, tea, and coffee are increasingly being traded online via Internet-based commodity exchanges. Right now, much of the world's international rice and sugar trade is in the hands of overseas Chinese traders. But for how much longer?

CarOrder.com and other similar US-based online car retailers allow Americans to buy cars on the Web. These e-tailers place orders directly with the manufacturer, thus cutting out the car dealer/franchisee and saving the consumer US$2,000–$4,000 per vehicle. These savings will drive out conventional middlemen from many markets. Possibly as many as 500,000 cars were purchased in the United States from websites in 1999. If this is where the United States is today, perhaps it is an indication of where Asia will be in 10–20 years.

As Asia's economies tend to have more of a middleman component than the more mature economies of the West, any reduction in the need for middlemen will be more socially dislocating and could also lead to greater economy-wide cost savings than in the West. There might be as many as 16 middlemen between a producer and an exporter in an economy like Indonesia. Eventually, e-commerce will provide the means for both parties to get in touch directly, cutting out the 16 steps between them and the associated cascading margins. Substantial cost savings will result. But before that happens, there will need to be a mini-revolution within companies when it comes to purchasing. Purchasing executives taking 'commissions' on their firm's purchases is standard practice in many Asian companies. They will be loath to use e-commerce, which tends to be impersonal and undercuts the personal relationships that allow a culture of commissions and kickbacks to flourish. But ultimately, managers will see that e-commerce will provide the means not only to reduce the regular costs of purchasing but also provide the opportunities for their own staff to accept kickbacks from suppliers.

The trend towards disintermediation will have significant implications for many overseas Chinese businesses, and thus for Asian commerce in general. Not only will the middleman role be severely diminished for individual companies, but the role of trading entrepôts — middleman economies — such as Singapore and Hong Kong — will also diminish, with significant restructuring implications. As companies in Guangdong and Fujian in China, Indonesia and Malaysia find that they can deal directly with their customers instead of going through middlemen in Hong Kong and Singapore, the traditional entrepôt role of these economies will diminish. Fortunately, the services-orientation of these two economies will mean that in place of their entrepôt role will be businesses centered on the provision of other types of services.

The Internet will thus provide a fundamental challenge to traditional overseas Chinese businesses and Asia's entrepôt economies. But what about the 'non-resident' or overseas Indians who number almost 20 million? As a group, they show a greater appreciation for business services and intellectual property than do traditional overseas Chinese business people — many overseas Indians work as consultants, accountants, and researchers. They are also more prepared to work as employees — they are not as strongly inclined to work for the family firm or for themselves. These aspects, and their greater proficiency in

English, help make overseas Indians (and indeed skilled Indians in India) well placed in the emerging world of e-commerce. (It has been estimated that 80% of the world's information stored on the world's computers is in English and 70–80% of all the information on the Internet is in English.)

Already, Indians are over-represented in Silicon Valley. Further, they tend to be concentrated in the software industry. Professor AnnaLee Saxenian of the University of California, Berkeley, has found that 69% of the high-tech start-ups established by Indians in Silicon Valley between 1980 and 1998 are in software and business services, compared to only 36% of the start-ups founded by Chinese. The Chinese tend to make and distribute hardware, again reflecting an age-old bias towards tangibles. And in India itself, two of the three biggest listed companies by market capitalization are software companies.

So, the e-commerce revolution will see a shake-up of the relative commercial positions of Asia's overseas Chinese and overseas Indians. This will shift the power balance within and between Asia's economies. The Indians who have hitherto not realized their commercial potential as a group are likely to at last see that potential realized.

B2B IN ASIA

It is in B2B e-commerce that the Internet has really come into its own. Retail e-commerce constitutes only about 10% of all e-commerce worldwide; B2B accounts for the rest. Retail sales has received much attention — but that's partly a function of the problems of e-tailing. Consumer e-commerce requires huge promotional costs. We know a lot about Amazon.com and eBay because for them to survive, they have to ensure that we do indeed know a lot about them. That costs money. This is one of the unavoidable realities of retail e-commerce. Meanwhile companies are quietly getting on with trading with each other via the Internet and slashing their transaction costs as a consequence. Sometimes they do it among themselves and at other times, with the aid of an online B2B retailer. And so it will be in Asia. B2B e-commerce will be the real e-commerce opportunity in Asia. While it has more promising prospects in Asia than does consumer e-tailing, it does not mean that Asian B2B e-commerce will not be without problems.

B2B e-commerce is not being driven in Asia by Asian firms but by multinationals who source input from Asia. To cut their costs, they are demanding that they be able to deal with their Asian suppliers (and their suppliers everywhere) via the Internet. Doing business in, say, China can be a real chore for outsiders. Their very physical presence in China on a buying mission confers on their hosts the obligation to take them on banquets followed by the almost mandatory heavy drinking sessions. It would be far better if such buying can be done over the Internet. B2B e-commerce with China can cut out much of the business costs — and hangovers. By 1998, GE had more electronic trade with its suppliers than all the retail e-commerce on the Internet combined; 100% of Intel's business with its suppliers in Taiwan was conducted electronically. So it's more push than pull in Asia, even with B2B e-commerce.

Another reason why it is U.S. firms rather than local ones that are driving B2B e-commerce in Asia is that many local firms often don't trust each other sufficiently when it comes to conducting business over the Web, particularly in those economies where legal structures are weak. Selling to a GE or an Intel doesn't require the same leap of faith as does dealing with a local firm without any global reputation to protect.

Another problem with B2B e-commerce between Asian firms is that many of them, especially smaller ones, are not good payers. They also tend to pay in cash instead of credit cards when they do eventually pay. Many companies in Asia carry enormous accounts receivables — goods sold but not yet paid for — in their annual accounts. China companies, Sichuan Changhong Electric and TCL, a television set maker, posted extraordinarily high receivables of 44% and 59%, respectively, of sales in 1999, for example.[8] And this is when suppliers and customers deal with each other in a more personalized fashion than via Net-based B2B trades with their accompanying potential for anonymity. There is a tendency for many Asian firms to want plenty of free samples first. Again, this is not a practice that lends itself well to B2B e-commerce.

THE INTERNET IN ASIA — WHAT'S TO COME?

Will East Asia with its particular culture and mindset prosper or fail in the new economy 'where advances in information technology, communications, and science are transforming the way the world lives and does business?' This was the question posed by Singapore's ambassador-at-large, Tommy Koh, in an essay published in the *International Herald Tribune* in July 2000. 'The honest answer is that we do not know,' was Koh's less than optimistic response. 'The political culture of East Asia tends to suppress rather than foster creativity' as does the over-emphasis on 'hierarchy and conformity.' Koh felt that the respect for learning, which has deep roots in Asia, was a promising sign but that the region's educational institutions 'are not world class.'[9]

However, there can be no doubt of the deep interest in the Internet as it swept through Asia from 1999. But to what degree was this a top-down phenomenon created by Asia's tycoons for whom the Internet was just another way to screw more cash from Asia's stock markets? What had been started in the US by young, small entrepreneurs seemed to have been hijacked in Asia by the region's tycoons.

Still, an array of small Internet-based companies has emerged across Asia. Most will go nowhere. There are some interesting and more serious concerns. One is EggSystems.com, a Singapore start-up that has developed technology to manage buildings remotely using the Internet. The company can manage an office tower's air conditioning, security, fire alarm, and closed-circuit TV systems and asset tracking from afar — even from another country. With wide area network (WAN) capability, the firm manages numerous buildings over the Internet in real time. It has used its technology to control from Singapore buildings in Pittsburgh, Washington DC, Minneapolis, and Dallas.

Another interesting venture is the Ayala eCenter. Hundreds of thousands of Filipinos live outside the Philippines, working as expatriates and guest workers. They represent a potentially huge overseas market for consumer products that are unique to the Philippines. To tap this market, the Philippines' Ayala Group established the Ayala eCenter. Through its website, expatriate Filipinos can order a large range of Philippine goods. The idea looks like a good one given the huge numbers of expatriate Filipinos but whether it will work remains to be seen.

Asian versions of what had been done well elsewhere might have less of a bright future. The best-known search engines such as Yahoo! and Excite! covered perhaps 20% of all the content on the Net in 2000, and they were fighting a losing battle. With the number of websites growing exponentially, there were projections that within a year or two, these search engines would cover perhaps only 5% of the Net. Of what value is a company that claims to search the Net but in reality can only search a small and declining corner of it? And if this is the case for the more established and cashed up US-based search engines, what hope is there for the small Asia-based search engines such as Singapore-based Catcha.com? By mid-2000, Catcha.com had postponed its plans for listing and cut staff and salaries. Asianizing parts of the Net when its very attraction is the fact that it is a global phenomenon, may not be the way to go.

Staff management is always a problem in Asia, more so with fast growing start-ups. Traditionally in Asia, management is patriarchal and staff are expected to follow orders rather than show initiative. The pattern has been to hire staff on the basis of personal connections rather than on merit. But Internet companies have specific technical and human resource management needs. Asian start-ups must realize that they need to hire on the basis of expertise. Internet firms are also intellectual-capital intensive. The main assets of these firms are not actually owned but rented by them. The main asset walks out the door each evening, and the trick is to make sure that it comes back the next morning. So staff management is extremely important.

China, that fabled gold mine that has so often produced disappointment rather than the hoped-for ore, undoubtedly will be an enormous Internet market one day. The billion-dollar question is: when? Right now, the Internet in China is not as big as it could be because it is not easy to use in many locations. Telephone connections drop, it can be difficult to log on and connections can be extremely slow. Dramatic projections in China that forecast 30 million or 100 million Internet users by a certain date are all very well, but the main obstacle to such projections being met is not the disposable incomes of potential users but simply, that the Internet is not enjoyable to use in many parts of China. Emerging competition between domestic telephone companies will be essential to improving the quality of telephone services. The price of a personal computer has fallen dramatically in China, due in particular to local production and more intense competition. Telephone lines and calls too are now cheaper, as are Internet service provider (ISP) charges. Developments are heading in the right direction. Only with time will such lofty forecasts have any real meaning.

To some extent Asia's e-bubble has been imported from the United States, but the U.S. bubble has some reasonable foundation. People in the U.S. tend to be connected to the Internet. In Asia, people tend not to be. In fact, they tend not to be even connected to a telephone. Broadband is a big issue in the United States, Western Europe, Australia, and Singapore. But for much of the rest of Asia, the big issue is getting a good quality telephone connection. What was hype in the U.S. had become mega-hype in Asia. But that didn't worry Asia's conglomerate owners. They had made the e-bubble their own.

SECTION 3

ASIA'S TWO GIANTS

CHAPTER 9

What's Wrong with Japan?

Japan likes to think of itself as a step up from the rest of Asia. But when it comes to poor corporate governance, insufficient accountability, and corruption, Japan might as well be a part of South-East Asia. Only when Japan decides to upgrade its corporate structure and governance to the same standards as the rest of the developed world will its economy revive.

The 1990s have been referred to as Japan's 'lost decade.' At best, its economy was sluggish, at worst, it was in recession. The venerable department store chain, Sogo, collapsed in mid-2000 with almost US$10 billion in debts. More broadly, many of the *keiretsu* (large, highly diversified groups of companies that usually center on a trading house and a bank, and which dominate Japan's economy) were stumbling and most of the major banks either had just been or still were on the verge of technical insolvency. Executives at the Yasuda Group, one of the top six *keiretsu*, learned to worry less about which foreign market they should jump into and more about how to cut costs and restructure at home to ensure the group's survival. In 1987, Yasuda Marine and Fire Insurance made world headlines by paying almost US$40 million for Van Gogh's *Sunflowers*. The price was absurd. But it was symbolic of the madness that was Japan in the 1980s. By mid-1998, the group's Fuji Bank was practically insolvent under the weight of bad loans, its trading house, Marubeni, had posted its first loss in 46 years, its Yamaichi Securities had collapsed amid scandal, and the debt of its Yasuda Trust and Banking had just been awarded junk bond status by major rating agencies. What's more, the group's situation was little different from that of most other *keiretsu*. It barely seemed possible that the Yasuda Group and its fellow *keiretsu* were the large Japanese business houses that threatened America in the 1980s. What went wrong? Blame is heaped mostly on the so-called bubble economy. Banks lent for property investment, property values skyrocketed, and the banks kept on lending because the ever more valuable property meant greater collateral for loans. This incestuous cycle of lending, rising property values, and hence more lending, came to an abrupt end in late 1989. There was nothing special or unique about all of this. The Dutch, after all, did it with tulips some 350 years earlier.

But another factor — and perhaps one that is the root cause of the bubble economy — is Japan's abysmal systems of corporate governance and corporate accountability. Japan simply doesn't have a regime of corporate ethics and governance that is commensurate with the size and maturity of its economy. Japan's institutions (in both the public and private sectors) have conspired to defeat, neuter, or nullify the internal checks and balances that an economy requires to reduce the incidences of waste and misappropriation. Japan has sought to deliberately institutionalize the organic disdain for accountability and transparency that has arisen naturally in many of the economies of South-East Asia. In effect, what the Japanese have done is to build a large, modern industrial economy on a Third World frame of corporate governance and accountability. The consensual, cooperative ways of a traditional rice-cultivating society aren't appropriate for the competitive ways of a modern and diverse trading economy. In a modern economy, what was once cooperative becomes collusive. Something had to give — and it did.

CORRUPT INSTITUTIONS

The task of reviving Japan's economy is a difficult one. At the heart of the problem are demographics. Government statistics released in mid-2000 show that Japan has 21.19 million people aged 65 or more — that's 16.7% of the total population. There are also more people in this age group than those under 15 — the only mature economy in the world where this is so. Not only that, about a third of all households have one or more members older than 65. Japan simply doesn't have enough young people forming families and new households, and all the spending that goes with it to keep the economy humming along. Instead, it has a lot of older people who are retired or are facing retirement and have spent their lives acquiring all the goods they need and are now more concerned with looking after their savings. And those savings amount to a very large pool — the average savings balance of elderly households is a whopping ¥25.27 million (US$240,000), which is more than 50% higher than that of all households. Loosening these purse strings would go a long way in reviving economic growth. The trouble is that the most conservative section of society that has little reason to spend holds these purses.

It is the elderly who are among the stalwart supporters of the Liberal Democratic Party (LDP). Even if dissent was widespread among Japan's young (and it isn't), they are too few of them to effect significant change.

This is important because among the three monoliths that share institutionalized power in Japan — the government, the bureaucracy, and big businesses — it is only the government that can be changed through direct external pressure.

The nexus between big business, the bureaucracy, and the LDP is one that is complex and mutually reinforcing, so much so that it is scarcely possible to treat each of the three as distinct entities. Moreover, the mutually reinforcing nature of the relationship means that attempts to reform any one pillar of the structure represents a direct attack on all the sections. It simply isn't possible to rope off one part of Japan Inc., remodel it, and then move on to the next part. The interconnectedness of the system of client-patron relationships means that it is all or nothing. The buck doesn't stop there, it just keeps circulating, and any attempt at reform, even if relatively minor, is met with resistance from the entire establishment as each part moves to safeguard its self interest.

Japan is changing though. But the change is taking place at the speed of a glacier. Talk of policy big bangs is an overblown hyperbole. The system simply won't allow anything dramatic to occur and if by chance it does, then the conspiracy of interests that is Japan moderates it to ensure that any revolution is quickly softened to an evolution.

The Law

One fundamental problem is the Japanese approach to law. Corruption, particularly at senior levels of society, is endemic and seems closer to the chronic corruption among Indonesia's elite than most Japanese would probably care to admit. More broadly, laws are seen in more of a relative than an absolute light — this has parallels with much of the rest of Asia. In Japan, the law serves more as a guide than a straitjacket. It is also designed more to protect the established social hierarchy of Japanese society than the rights of individuals. Also, the adversarial nature of Western legal practice is somewhat at odds with the more consensual nature of Japanese society.

Accordingly, contracts in Japan tend not to spell out every contingency, which in the view of many Japanese business people, would serve only to reduce flexibility. Why agree to a contract that is very precise in its terms when conditions might change so as to render the contract no longer optimal? To many in Asia, including Japan, such an approach simply makes no sense. Verbal agreements and trust are the preferred frameworks for commercial exchange and, failing that, contracts are specified only in general terms. Should a dispute arise, mediation behind closed doors is the choice mode of resolution. To the

Japanese, this allows all concerned to avoid public embarrassment, but to those in the West, it might well seem like another excuse to avoid transparency and disclosure.

Corporate Japan's somewhat dismissive regard for the rule of law helps render many of the country's regulatory agencies impotent. The Fair Trade Commission (FTC) is Japan's sole fair competition body. It was created by the Allied Occupation authorities in 1947, modeled on the United States' Federal Trade Commission. Only very rarely has the FTC pushed for criminal charges against companies. (It doesn't have the power to prosecute criminal charges itself.) In fact, between 1974 and the end of 1990, it pushed for criminal action against just one company.[1] Things improved after 1990, when the FTC decided it was time to get tougher. It has since brought several criminal charges against pricing cartels, and mediated successfully for the end of some other restrictive trade practices. But these achievements are still minor given the enormity of the problem of anti-competitive behavior.

It has long been the contention of the United States that the FTC is under-resourced, under-staffed, and under-empowered to pursue anti-competitive behavior. From about 1993, the FTC received greater funding, but its problems are structural, as well as financial. The FTC's funding isn't guaranteed or determined independently, which means it is susceptible to political pressure. It is no exaggeration to say that it is one of the weakest agencies in the Japanese government. The chairman of its five-member board usually comes from the Ministry of Finance, and of late, the Ministry of International Trade and Industry (MITI) and the Ministry of Justice have been represented as well. None of these ministries has been a strong advocate for the reform of Japan's collusive structure. Occasionally, the ministries even tip off companies that are under FTC investigation and organize for political pressure to be exerted so that investigations are dropped.

Japan's main share-trading watchdog, the Securities and Exchange Surveillance Commission, was created in 1992, but like the FTC it too is under-resourced. With just 200 employees, it has just one-fifteenth of the staff of its US equivalent, the Securities and Exchange Commission. Listed companies are quite happy with existing arrangements and, with most shareholders being other companies, there simply is no major coalition of interests in Japan to argue for a stronger body.

One important area where business codes are relatively effective in Japan is bankruptcy. Companies do go bankrupt in Japan — relatively often, in fact. Almost 2,000 new bankruptcies a month were recorded in Japan in the first half of 1998. This, of course, is an important difference from some South-East Asian countries where petty corruption renders the bankruptcy laws useless.

Nonetheless, bankruptcy laws in Japan aren't utilized nearly as often as it could or should be. But the problem isn't with the bankruptcy codes or their enforcement but with Japan's banks, which are loath to commence proceedings against poor debtors. A company may be hopelessly in debt but be allowed to limp along because of its bank's willingness to keep rolling over the company's loans and reduce its interest obligations rather than have the loans declared 'bad.' By refinancing such debtors, Japan's banks end up keeping alive poorly managed companies at the expense of those that are relatively healthy but are denied credit. So, the effect is *as if* the bankruptcy laws are ineffective because of the banks' unwillingness to fully utilize them. Consequently, Japan's banks have one of the lowest returns on equity in the developed world. In 1997, for example, Japan's banks averaged a return of just 3.1%, compared to 17.6% in Britain, 16.9% in the United States, and 15.9% in Australia.[2]

Bankruptcy Japanese Style

The problems that corporate Japan faces are encapsulated nicely in the collapse of the department store chain, Sogo, in mid-2000. Anywhere else, the Sogo saga would look like high farce, but in Japan, the factors that led to its demise are almost par for the course.

Sogo's problems really only became apparent in early 2000, largely because its structure was so complex that it afforded little transparency. The previous year, the government had even rated Sogo, which has outlets in Japan and elsewhere in Asia including Taipei, Kuala Lumpur, and Singapore, as a healthy borrower. Listed on the Tokyo Stock Exchange, Sogo directly controlled just three stores; but via unlisted affiliates linked to it through complex cross-shareholdings, there were another 24 Sogo stores. The parent company often lent to these affiliates but did not disclose such loans to shareholders.

By April 2000, Sogo finally came clean and declared the size of its liabilities, asking its creditors to forgive almost half of what they were owed. Sogo executives went into an overdrive, visiting banks to ask for more time for repayment (Sogo owed money to some 73 banks). The typical compromise and consensus-building process was made that bit more complete with the almost mandatory suicide — one of Sogo's most senior executives hung himself in his living room by the end of that month.

By the end of June, it was confirmed that the government-affiliated Deposit Insurance Corporation planned to forgive an astonishing ¥97 billion (US$923 million) in loans to Sogo as part of a ¥600 trillion (US$5.7 billion) bailout from creditors. The company was technically insolvent and even under its own restructuring scheme was not likely to achieve positive net value for another 12 years. Was it worth saving? The government seemed to think so. With 10,000 employees and 10,000 suppliers, Sogo was deemed to be too big to be allowed to go under. It also had close links with the LDP, the dominant party in Japan's ruling coalition.

But the plan soon became unstuck. The bailout for Sogo, which essentially meant sinking a billion dollars of taxpayers' funds into a poorly managed company was met with such public outcry that within a fortnight, the government announced that it had reversed its decision. Popular feeling against the bailout was such that an informal consumer boycott of Sogo's stores in the middle of Japan's summer gift-giving season meant that Sogo's position went from bad to worse. With the two things coming at once, Sogo had little choice but to file for bankruptcy, leaving Sogo's creditors having to write-off more than ¥1 trillion (US$9.5 billion) of debt.

But was Sogo's bankruptcy a cathartic experience for Japan? Not really. First, the government reversed its decision on the bailout not because it suddenly believed that such bailouts were wrong, but because of public objection to it. The decision was born out of pragmatism rather than policy prudence. Second, other major corporate debtors — one notable example being construction giant Hazama Corp with ¥422 billion (US$4.0 billion) in group debts — quickly entered into emergency discussions with its banks on how to stave off its own bankruptcy with yet more loan rollovers and more easy credit. Ultimately, the decision to let go of Sogo was more about the greater good of the existing power structure than it was a fundamental challenge to it.

Corruption

Corruption is widespread in Japan. It isn't the petty corruption that is rife in, say, Indonesia, Thailand, and perhaps the Philippines, where almost any law is rendered ineffective by low-grade bribery. Japan's bureaucrats are paid too much for that. Instead, it is high-level corruption, involving payments of thousands and sometimes millions of dollars. In fact, one great paradox of modern Japan is that the public seems to have a healthy disgust of the corruption by their politicians, but that corruption carries on regardless. The incidence (and, of course, the scale) of high-level corruption in Japan is almost certainly far greater than in Malaysia, for example. Japan's major companies are allowed to claim a tax deduction for *shito fumeikin*, literally 'unaccounted-for-expenditure,' that is, expenditure without receipt. Payment for bribery is one obvious type of expenditure without receipt and the deduction claimed by some Japanese companies in this category run into millions of dollars each year.[3]

High-level corruption has become endemic, so much so, that the government in post-war Japan can be characterized more as a series of stumbles from one corruption scandal to another. Indeed, on average there seems to have been at least one major corruption scandal a year in Japan since the end of World War II. One of the more celebrated cases was the Lockheed bribery scandal, which was centered on 0then-prime minister Kakuei Tanaka. Lockheed Aircraft of the United States paid as much as US$13 million in bribes to more than half-a-dozen Japanese politicians during 1972 and 1973 in return for All Nippon Airways (ANA) purchasing 21 L-1011 Lockheed Tristar airbus jets. This included US$50,000 paid on each aircraft to the head of ANA, bribes to the prime minister, the secretary-general of the LDP, the trade minister, the chief cabinet secretary, the Minister for Transportation, the chairman of the LDP's Special Committee on Aviation, and both the former and then vice-ministers of transportation.[4] No one could have accused Lockheed of not being thorough. Tanaka was arrested in 1976 and later convicted, along with other senior government officials, for taking bribes from Lockheed. But the delivery of justice wasn't exactly swift. When he died in 1993, Tanaka still hadn't exhausted the appeal process through Japan's glacial court system — a full 18 years after he was first arrested. Corruption, it seems, is no great crime in Japan. The real crime is getting caught and then living long enough to serve a custodial sentence.

Another prominent corruption scandal was the 'Recruit scandal,' which emerged in 1988. It was notable for its contagion-like spread throughout Japan's upper echelons, with dozens of casualties across Japan. Recruit, an information services company, offered shares in an unlisted real estate affiliate, Recruit Cosmos, to politicians and bureaucrats at heavy discounts in return for favorable treatment. Once Recruit was listed, the recipients of the discounted stock were to be able to sell out and realize large profits. Many were implicated in this scandal, and allegations poured out over many months. By then, three cabinet ministers had resigned, 13 top businessmen and bureaucrats had been charged with bribery, and then-prime minister, Noboru Takeshita, had resigned after it was revealed that he too had accepted the discounted shares (in fact, he had been one of the biggest recipients), but not before he had lied to Parliament in an attempted cover-up.[5] The Lockheed and Recruit scandals certainly received much prominence, but they are by no means the most spectacular examples of corruption in Japan. The construction industry is the place to look for those.

Japan has been referred to not as a welfare state or a military-industrial state but as a construction state.[6] Japan's national and local governments spend extraordinary sums on public works — in fact, almost 10% of the annual GDP is spent on such projects.[7] The Tanaka faction within the LDP, forged by Tanaka after his arrest in connection with the Lockheed scandal, funded itself largely from taking a mandatory 3% cut on all major infrastructure projects. In this way, hundreds of millions — and probably billions — of dollars in bribes flowed its way. To this end, the Tanaka faction always made sure that one of its members was appointed construction minister. It claimed the justice ministry as well, just in case Tanaka's conviction should be upheld and he could be pardoned. The faction also reserved a veto-right over the prime ministership. All of this was quite extraordinary considering that Tanaka had resigned from the LDP in the wake of the Lockheed scandal. Indeed, although he was nominally in disgrace, he was actually at the height of his powers and able to control the ruling party even if he didn't technically belong to it. The key to it all was being able to spread around the largesse garnered from the construction industry. The more corrupt Tanaka was, the bigger his faction grew; and the bigger the faction, the more corrupt he and his faction had to become to support it.

Japan's construction industry was a fat honey pot and there were plenty of bees — but they weren't all politicians at the national level. In 1993, Toru Ishii, the mayor of the northern Japanese city of Sendai, was arrested along with six construction executives in connection with US$94 million in alleged bribes. Ishii had accepted large campaign donations in return for helping some of Japan's largest construction companies win local infrastructure contracts.[8] A string of similar allegations followed, and it became clear that Japan's entire construction industry was utterly riddled with corruption. Barely a single government-funded construction contract had been given in years that didn't involve bid-rigging and bribery. Even foreign governments weren't immune. In 1994, the U.S. government filed a law suit in a Tokyo court against 53 Japanese firms, which it alleged had rigged bids for contracts at an American naval base in Ayase, west of Tokyo.[9]

Sporting events weren't spared either. Amounting to almost US$14 billion in infrastructure and other spending, the 1998 Winter Olympics held at Nagano in the Japanese Alps was billed as the most expensive ever — but really it wasn't a feat to be too proud of. Like most other major construction projects in Japan, massive sums were apparently dissipated in corruption and bid-rigging. The site for the games happened to be in the constituency of Tsutomu Hata, who served briefly as prime minister in 1994. Hata's close friend and biggest financial backer was Yoshiaki

Tsutsumi, one of the world's wealthiest men and the head of the railway and real estate, Seibu Group. He also happens to be the single biggest landowner in Nagano. The billions of dollars in public funds spent on infrastructure in the area for the Winter Olympics made Tsutsumi's landholding much more valuable.[10] The profits from this were then used to further bankroll Hata. To complete the conflict-of-interest circle, Tsutsumi is a past president of the Japan Olympic Committee.

In late 1996, a former vice-minister for health, Nobuharu Okamitsu, was arrested for allegedly accepting US$600,000 in cash and two cars from a developer who won government-funded contracts to build nursing homes.[11] In February 1998, Shokei Arai, a Member of Parliament, committed suicide just prior to a parliamentary vote to lift his immunity from prosecution for accepting illegal payments from brokerage houses. Arai, who incidentally was an ethnic Korean, had been heavily involved in drafting banking legislation. Nikko Securities later admitted to paying the legislator more than US$200,000.[12]

In late 1997 and early 1998, yet another major scandal erupted, though this time it struck at the very heart of the Japanese government. It began with six of MITI's top officials being disciplined for allowing as many as 52 other MITI staff to be entertained in restaurants and on golf courses by an Osaka businessman who was notorious for his underworld connections, bribery, and tax evasion.[13] But that wasn't the end of it.

It soon emerged that the nation's most prominent banks and insurance companies had systematically spent enormous amounts on entertaining government bureaucrats in exchange for confidential information, tip-offs when bank inspections were about to be made, advance notice of changes to banking laws, and helping to conceal damaging records.

Ninety-eight senior staff at the central bank, the Bank of Japan, were disciplined for accepting lavish entertainment from private banks and other financial institutions. One official was arrested and both the bank's governor and his deputy resigned to 'take' responsibility. Around the same time, an internal probe at the Ministry of Finance found that 112 of its officials had similarly accepted 'excessive' entertainment from private financial institutions — but not before several ministry officials had committed suicide during the investigations. Several had even accepted cash bribes. Among the 112 was the vice-finance minister for international affairs. Two officials were arrested and another resigned. The finance minister also resigned. One of the finance officials had been entertained 'excessively' on almost 170 separate occasions over a five-year period by insurance companies and the like — the very firms he was supposed to be regulating.[14] The punishment meted out to those who remained was hardly devastating. Some took a voluntary 20% pay-cut for all of one month; the rest received a 'warning.' Whoever said that crime doesn't pay obviously hasn't been to Japan.

It isn't just the big businesses that fete officials from the Ministry of Finance. Smaller companies do too. The chief of the finance ministry's Banking Bureau admitted that in 1994, Takefuji Corporation, a consumer finance company, allowed him to buy thousands of its shares at an enormous discount. To compound the apparent felony, he did so in his daughter's name.[15] And it's not always the businessmen who do the favor-buying either. Local governments are responsible for providing most government services, but it is the central government that raises most of the taxes. This fiscal-expenditure imbalance means that at Budget time each year, hundreds of local government officials flood into Tokyo to embark on a round of begging, disguised as lavish entertainment for finance ministry officials. Ben Hills, a foreign correspondent in Tokyo, tells of one party that officials of the Hiroshima prefecture government held for a select group of finance ministry bureaucrats where the drinks bill alone was US$10,000. The need to lobby and entertain in Tokyo is so great that 39 of Japan's 47 prefectures maintain 'representative offices' in the capital for this purpose.[16]

But in Japan, it isn't just hospitality and gift-giving that ensures a convergence of interests between big businesses and bureaucrats. The other major contributor is the practice of hiring ex-bureaucrats by big businesses. This is known as *amakudari,* or 'descent from heaven,' which is interesting in itself. Given the low regard — even suspicion — in which public officials are held in much of the West (the United States and Australia, particularly), the practice in those countries would be regarded more as an 'ascent' than a 'descent.' It underscores the power of the senior levels of bureaucracy in Japan.

In the mid-1990s, former finance ministry employees headed almost a quarter of Japan's top 150 private banks.[17] In early 1998, the Japanese Parliament was told that local banks, brokerages, and insurers had hired 164 former finance ministry staff as executives in just the brief period beginning from the previous July.[18] In 1995, no fewer than seven ex-officials of the construction ministry had found their way into the board of directors of Sumitomo Group's Kajima Corporation, Japan's second-largest construction company.[19] *Amakudari* arises partly because government officials in Japan, virtually without exception, retire in their early to mid-fifties. One of the reasons for this is due to the extreme age grading and sensitivity to seniority in Japan's bureaucracy, when one man from a recruitment year becomes vice-minister (the head of the ministry), the rest of the intake from that batch face heavy pressure to retire so that he will have complete seniority within the ministry. The new vice-minister is then obliged to find suitable positions in the corporate sector for those who bow out.[20]

In a way, this practice promotes a type of reverse corruption. If the bureaucrat isn't antagonistic to and does the right thing by a company that he is charged with regulating, then when he retires, he can expect the company to employ him with an enormous salary simply out of gratitude. This expectation has meant that many regulatory agencies in Japan lose their teeth because their officials don't want to be over-zealous in carrying out their responsibilities lest they offend anyone and thereby close off a future private-sector job opportunity.

There is another danger as well. Existing bureaucrats are less inclined to closely monitor the activities of their former colleagues. To do so would be a considerable 'loss of face' for all concerned. Dairy product company, Yakult Honsha, revealed in early 1998 that it had suffered a loss of US$1.23 billion from stock index futures and currency swap trading. The head of the company's financial operations at the time was Naoki Kumagai — an ex-finance ministry official. Kumagai's activities went largely unsupervised and unchecked. After all, someone with good finance ministry connections should be able to get problems sorted out should they arise. The trouble on this occasion, though, was that the problems went way beyond what ordinarily a wink and a nod could fix. Kumagai's losses wiped out Yakult Honsha's profits for the previous ten years.

There are rules against *amakudari*, but they are barely enforced. The public and the media are also critical of the practice — some companies are teeming with ex-bureaucrats that they are referred to by the media as *amakudari* companies — but still it continues.

BREAKFAST-FOOD AISLE ECONOMICS

A walk down the breakfast-food aisle of any American, Australian, or British supermarket will take you past a bewildering array of products and brands, all geared to do just one thing — filling the cereal bowl at breakfast time. The dozens of names such as Cornflakes, Coco Pop, and Special K suggest that the breakfast-food market must be one of the most competitive segments on earth. But it isn't. How can it be when what is for the most part, a mixture of simple carbohydrates and air combined in garish packaging, costs so much? The reason, of course, is that while there might be many brands, there are relatively few producers. The segment looks competitive, but in reality it is dominated by only a handful of large companies, each with many brands that compete on the basis of the brightest packaging, the most extravagant claims of nutritional value, the most sugar — anything, in fact, but price.

Japan's economy too is like that — a handful of large *keiretsu* that produce a spectacular range of brands and products. What do the names Mazda Motors, Asahi Beer, Nippon Electric Company (NEC), and Kajima Corporation have in common? They are all part of the Sumitomo Group. Likewise, Marubeni, Hitachi, Fuji Bank, Canon, Taisei Construction, Nissan Motors, and Sapporo Beer are all part of the Yasuda Group. Isuzu Motors, Kawasaki, and Fujitsu are part of the DKB-Itochu Group; and Kirin Brewing, Isetan, Asahi Glass, and Nikon are part of the giant Mitsubishi Group, along with the more obvious Mitsubishi Motors Corporation, Mitsubishi Paper Mills, Mitsubishi Plastics, and Mitsubishi Petroleum Development.[21] Like the breakfast-food oligopolists, Japan's *keiretsu* traditionally have been loath to enter price wars (especially within the domestic market), but instead compete over product quality, customer service, and product innovation. Price became more important, though, throughout the 1990s, but the domestic market for consumer and other goods is still a long way from being cut-throat. And it's the domestic market that is central to Japan's economy. The rest of the world hears a great deal about Japan as an exporter, but its current account surplus (the surplus of payments for goods and services and unrequited transfers) usually makes only a small contribution to the overall economy — it was just 4% of GDP during the first half of 1998, for example. The real engine of Japan's economy is domestic and not foreign demand.

THE *KEIRETSU* — A FANCY NAME FOR A STALE CONCEPT

The collusive nature of Japan's economy is carried through to the structure of its big business groups. The *keiretsu* were instrumental in building Japan's economy after the war. The big government–big business formula worked very well — for some time. The anti-competitive practices embedded in the Japanese economy saw many of its companies grow into some of the biggest and most impressive corporations in the world. But through their system of mutual support and cross-subsidies, weak companies and poor management have survived and accumulated, clogging the arteries of corporate Japan and draining the reserves of stronger companies. What was once dynamic and instrumental to prosperity is now sluggish and a threat to it. More than two million non-financial corporations exist in Japan today, and the *keiretsu* (including affiliates and subsidiaries) account for only a small proportion of the total. But in terms of capital and output, they account for much more. In fact, the six biggest *keiretsu* account for more than a fifth of Japan's total economy.[22]

It's not always easy to tell where a *keiretsu* starts or ends. Their member companies do not tend to be independent of each other nor fully integrated. They tend to exist like the wagons in the days of the American Wild West — they all broadly travel in the same direction, but their real relationship only becomes apparent in the face of some threat, when they form themselves into a circle.

Usually, they comprise a series of core or inner companies — usually the largest — and a raft of smaller companies that are less intrinsic to the group. Mitsubishi, one of Japan's largest and most cohesive *keiretsu*, has 28 core companies, but possibly more than 1,000 group members overall — it all depends on how membership is defined.

Those *keiretsu* that are highly integrated so that their members sell much of their output to other members are sometimes called the 'vertical *keiretsu*'; those that are less integrated, at least in terms of the integration of their production processes, are the 'horizontal *keiretsu*.' (In practice, there is a continuum between the two, and attempts to draw a sharp distinction between them are bound to be arbitrary.)

Before World War II, Japan's economy wasn't dominated by the *keiretsu* but by the *zaibatsu* — large industrial conglomerates that were structured more like today's Western conglomerate, with each of the companies grouped under a series of holding companies. Three versions of such *zaibatsu* — Mitsubishi, Mitsui, and Sumitomo — survive, as three of today's big six *keiretsu*. The other three are Yasuda (sometimes called Fuyo), DKB-Itochu, and Sanwa, each being centered around a bank — Fuji Bank, Dai-ichi Kangyo Bank, and Sanwa Bank, respectively. The *zaibatsu* of old were generally owned by families, although by 1930, these families had largely turned the management over to professionals. Family ownership ended with the Allied victory over Japan in 1945, when the occupying Allied administration ordered the large family trusts to deposit their holdings with the Commission for the Dissolution of the *Zaibatsu*.[23] These were then sold to the public. In practice, this meant that they were sold to other companies, as most Japanese families at the time were more concerned with getting enough to eat than with building a handsome share portfolio.[24]

Holding Companies

The distinguishing feature between the *zaibatsu* of old and the *keiretsu* of today is that the *keiretsu* are not grouped under holding companies. Holding companies were held responsible for the rise of the pre-war *zaibatsu* — the collaborators of the militarists — and were outlawed by the occupying Allied forces in 1945 to prevent the *zaibatsu* from reforming. Not until late 1997 were holding companies legalized again, and even then with some limitations.

Nevertheless, the post-war ban on holding companies wasn't effective. Big business groups were formed anyway. They just used ways other than sharing a common parent company to define themselves. What the ban did mean though, was that those groups that emerged didn't have the openness, transparency, and corporate governance they otherwise might have had.

In forming, the *keiretsu* contravened the spirit but not the letter of the law. But why bother? Clearly, there is some rationale for disparate businesses to form themselves into a group, even though in some instances it might not be all that cohesive. The rationale is trust. As is the case elsewhere in Asia, relationships and connections very much facilitate business. Trade that occurs between two parties that already know and trust each other is trade that can occur quickly, efficiently, and without the need for detailed contracts and costly legal advice. The *keiretsu* were formed to cut the costs of doing business ('transactions costs'). One *keiretsu* member might pay more for an input from another member than can be had by going to outsiders, but that difference might well reflect a premium paid for trust and reliability. 'Better the devil you know,' as the saying goes.

With holding companies banned, the individual members of a group had no legal ties with each other, so they sought to find definition as a group using other methods. They did so in at least nine different ways:

- through cross-shareholdings
- by making use of presidential councils
- by establishing a group office
- by buying each other's output
- by clustering around a common bank
- by exchanging staff
- by clustering around a common trading company
- by setting up joint ventures and undertaking joint research
- by using the same real estate company

Cross-shareholdings

Japan's large business groups have managed to pull themselves together by having their companies take shareholding in one another (*mochiai*). In 1988, for example, almost 60% of the shares of Nippon Trust and Banking was held by other Mitsubishi Group companies; around half of the shares in Mitsubishi Motors were similarly owned, as was a third of

Mitsubishi Corporation and a quarter of Mitsubishi Chemical Corporation.[25] Mitsubishi Group itself endorses the estimate that today around a quarter of the shares in each of its 26 biggest companies are owned by other group members.[26] Cross-shareholdings like this mean that the main stockholders in Japan are not individual investors or even mutual funds; they are companies. In fact, around 60% of Japan's outstanding company shares are held by other companies.[27]

Cross-shareholdings stem from several factors.[28] The ban on holding companies is one. As mentioned, another is the historical factor of only companies having the necessary funds at the end of World War II to buy shares when Japan's *zaibatsu*-owning families were forced to give up their shares. Yet another factor is Japan's Commerce Law which allows the board of a company to increase its capital simply by assigning new shares to other firms without seeking formal approval from the existing shareholders. This has greatly facilitated the ease with which companies have been able to exchange their shares to promote cross-shareholdings. Finally, when Japan began to liberalize its capital markets in the 1960s, clusters of major Japanese companies took passive shareholdings in each other to protect themselves from hostile takeovers from abroad.

There is, however, one constraint on the ability of the *keiretsu* to structure themselves via cross-shareholdings. Japanese law prohibits banks from holding more than 5% of a non-financial company's stock. The limit is 10% for insurance companies. As if to emphasize the importance of cross-shareholdings, banks often hold stock right up to the permissible maximum (4.99%) of many of their *keiretsu* associates. But this constraint isn't as tight as it might be, and in late 1997 the ceiling was actually raised to 15%. The United States, for example, prohibits banks and their holding companies from owning any stakes in non-financial companies altogether.

The sometimes large, defensive stockholdings that *keiretsu* companies have in each other and the subsequent reduction in the threat of a hostile takeover attempt means that managers aren't under the same pressure to perform as they are in, say, the United States. The managers of companies that have exchanged stock are also able to effectively agree to turn a blind eye to each other's transgressions. This has been an important contributor to Japan not having a regime of corporate ethics and governance of a standard appropriate for an economy of its size and advancement. The lack of a threat of hostile takeover also takes the pressure off the need to have high short-term profits. In one sense, this can be useful as it allows companies to have longer time horizons and to embark on loss-lead investments. But at the same time, short-term profits also serve as a barometer of management's performance. It is one less constraint on Japanese management compared with Western management.

Presidential Councils

Presidential councils, another link in the *keiretsu* chain, comprise the presidents of the main companies in a *keiretsu* who come together perhaps once a month to discuss topics of mutual interest. The presidents of the 24 core Mitsui companies meet on the second Thursday of every month, for example. There is a second meeting, too, held on Mondays, which is attended by the presidents of 62 non-core Mitsui companies.[29]

Decisions at such meetings might be made on establishing joint ventures, undertaking group research or marketing, overseas expansion, the reform of troubled member companies, important personnel appointments, and political donations. The councils are perhaps less important than they once were, but are still influential. They act as de facto board for the *keiretsu* — much like the informal management board of some South-East Asian conglomerates. They have no legal status but constitute the real power. However, these councils are supposed to, and they usually do, pay due regard to collusive behavior and insider trading restrictions, so items that might be prejudicial to these considerations tend to be at least omitted from the formal agenda list.

Not all the get-togethers of the senior figures of a *keiretsu* are formal. The chairmen of the 28 core Mitsubishi companies meet once a month on a Friday at the group's very own Mitsubishi Club. The main function of such lunches — the so-called Friday Club — is to maintain the personal connection among the executives, as much as anything else. They might be informal, but they are very important. Personal connection is the cement of business tie-ups in Asia.

Establishing a Group Office

Although holding companies were banned in Japan between 1945 and 1997, it didn't stop some *keiretsu* from setting up an office to represent them as a group. Toshiba, for example, comprises approximately 53 core companies but has ties with more than 600 affiliates. The group finds some definition through its core members' sponsorship of the Affiliated Companies Office of Toshiba.[30] The office has only a small staff size, yet plays a role in positioning the Toshiba brand name.

Mitsubishi has its Mitsubishi Public Affairs Committee. Founded in 1964, today, it is sponsored by all of the group's 28 core companies, plus some non-core ones. Its main role is to promote the group's image. It publishes a monthly group magazine, the *Mitsubishi Monitor*, and plays a role in directing enquiries to the relevant group member.

Some *keiretsu* find further definition by having their member companies located close to each other. Typically, the core companies of a *keiretsu* don't have their head offices in one building. They tend to be distinct and separate. They might even be in different cities. However, some do co-locate their offices. Mitsubishi is the most obvious example. The corporate headquarters of the group's shipping company, NYK Line, today is in a 15-story building that overlooks Tokyo's Imperial Palace. Not far away is the historic Tokyo Station and in between the two points is Marunouchi, Tokyo's central business district. Within a block of the NYK Building are the head offices of Mitsubishi Electric, Mitsubishi Heavy Industries, Tokio Marine and Fire Insurance, Mitsubishi Estate, and Mitsubishi Chemical Corporation. Within another block or two are Nikon, Mitsubishi Corporation, Meiji Life Insurance, the Bank of Tokyo-Mitsubishi, the Mitsubishi Trust and Banking, and several more. Altogether, the head offices of 25 of Mitsubishi's core companies are within a ten-minute radius of Tokyo Station. That includes 18 companies headquartered in Marunouchi, four in nearby Otemachi, and three on the other side of Tokyo Station, such as Mitsubishi Rayon, in Kyobashi. There are so many Mitsubishi companies in Marunouchi that it has earned the nickname 'Mitsubishi Village.' And yet Mitsubishi goes to some lengths to emphasize the independence of its companies. But Mitsubishi's institutional arrangements suggest a higher degree of coordination and cooperation.

Buying from Each Other

Large companies in Japan are typically far less diversified than their counterparts in, say, the United States. They have only a few product lines, one or two of which usually dominates in terms of earnings. Similarly, they also tend to be smaller and have fewer employees. The entities that are diversified, large, and have large numbers of employees are the *keiretsu*.

Diversified though they may be, many *keiretsu* are also highly vertically integrated. The most important customer of one group member will often be another group member. For example, Toyota (which is described variously as part of the Mitsui Group or a smaller *keiretsu* in its own right) relies on more than 20 major affiliated companies for much of its supplies, including Toyota Auto Body, Koito Manufacturing, and Aichi Steel Works.[31] In turn, these rely on literally thousands of smaller suppliers and component manufacturers. Toyota also owns dealerships and a finance arm. Sellers like Toyota's many component suppliers don't present buyers with a completed product as *fait accompli* — on a like-it-or-leave-it basis. They cooperate closely with the buyer so that the buyer participates in the design of the products and will even examine the supplier's books to suggest where savings might be made. The relationship is anything but arm's length. This aspect of the buyer–supplier relationship within the *keiretsu* makes the relationships stable and difficult for outsiders to break into. An external component supplier might want to sell into a *keiretsu*, but how many are prepared to offer their books for examination?

The cross-shareholdings that companies have in one another also encourage them to do business with each other. After all, if a company buys from another company in which it is also a shareholder, then some of its payments for goods and services will flow back to it in the form of dividends. Doing business 'in-house' keeps the margins in-house as well. Rarely can outside firms — be they foreign or Japanese — break into these relationships by simply undercutting on price.

Close links between buyers and sellers within the *keiretsu* obviate the need for Western-style contracts that spell out every possible contingency. They have agreements more than contracts, and much of the relationship is based on trust built over time. This aspect, of course, is quite similar to how business is largely conducted in the rest of Asia. Trust underpins commercial relationships rather than expensive and time-consuming legal processes that reduce flexibility and betray subconscious undertones of distrust, confrontation, and suspicion. The trouble is, arrangements that hold companies to one another also mean that genuine competition is stifled, and so too are the normal checks and balances that go with it.

A Common Bank

Just like their South-East Asian counterparts, few of Japan's banks are independent of non-financial interests. Many Japanese corporations have traditionally had 'main bank' relationships, where one bank is their long-term provider of much of their financial services needs. The ties are cemented by the bank taking a stake in its client. Over time, some banks have established many relationships — a process that gave rise to the bank-based *keiretsu*. Other *keiretsu*, although not built around a bank, nonetheless feature a bank as one of their core companies.

Some, like the Mitsubishi Group, have more than one finance arm. Its Tokyo-Mitsubishi Bank (the result of a 1995 merger between the Bank of Tokyo and Mitsubishi Bank) is the centerpiece, but there is also the separate Mitsubishi Trust and Banking Corporation and the Tokio Marine and Fire Insurance.

Banks are an important provider of credit and other financial services for their associated companies, as well as hold shares in their associates. In turn, the associates often place significant funds (though for the sake of prudential management, rarely all their surplus funds) on deposit with the bank. But an important role the *keiretsu* banks play is as a central clearing house for information for the group.

Typically, the *keiretsu* banks don't provide favorable interest rates on loans to their affiliates; rather, they might offer favorable terms of repayment and loan extensions and might step in and provide management assistance when an affiliate is at risk of bankruptcy. In this situation, it might also act as the lender of last resort. When Mazda Motors faced bankruptcy in 1974, the Sumitomo Group's main bank, Sumitomo Trust, intervened by keeping the credit lines open, and reorganizing Mazda's management and production techniques. Other members of the group also lent a hand by reducing the prices of the input they sold to the company and by switching their automobile purchases to Mazda.[32]

Exchanging Staff

One important and yet informal way in which the *keiretsu* tie themselves together is by exchanging personnel. The boards of affiliated companies tend to share directors, for example. More than half of the 80 or so major companies in the DKB-Itochu Group have at least one director from the group's Dai-ichi Kangyo Bank.[33]

But perhaps more importantly, managers tend to rotate from one affiliate to another. This is very important for promoting intra-group business and trade. It means that a manager in one company might choose to buy input from an affiliate simply because he previously worked there, and knows the product and the staff. Such personal connections and bonds do much to facilitate cross-purchasing.

A COMMON TRADING COMPANY

General trading companies in Japan are known as the *sogo shosha*. The biggest *sogo shosha* are enormous. In the past, Japan's nine leading trading companies accounted for more than half of Japan's international trade, although today, their importance in marshaling goods and services to and from Japan isn't as important. But this doesn't mean that their survival is threatened. They remain very important to their respective *keiretsu*. They provide many of the physical input and services required by other group members, procure raw materials (mostly from overseas), distribute a large proportion of their output, and play a general coordinating role. Since the late 1980s, they have cut costs, restructured their activities, and poured billions of dollars into direct investment in the United States, Europe, Australia, and the rest of Asia.[34] These investments are now providing Japan's major trading houses with enormous earnings and have made them significant multinationals in their own right.

The *keiretsu* still rely greatly on the overseas arms of their trading house affiliates for the procurement and supply of foreign goods and services. Japan's trading houses have thousands of offices abroad. DKB-Itochu Group's Itochu Co has no less than 122 joint ventures in China alone. Yasuda's Marubeni has 57.[35] Offices like these remain very important for feeding the *keiretsu* back home with the raw material that they need. One study found that the main *keiretsu* purchase just 5% of their imports from unrelated foreign companies and just 6% from other *keiretsu*.[36] So, contrary to U.S. perceptions, Japan's big companies don't especially discriminate against U.S. or other foreign companies. It's simply that they avoid doing business with all outsiders, be they Japanese or foreign.

Some trading companies handle as many as 20,000 product lines, which allows them to offer multi-product deals. A construction company might source all the building and other material it needs from just one trading company, for example. The *sogo shosha* (see Table 9.1) wield significant market power, not simply because of their buying power. They control shipping facilities and the ports as well, which helps to extend their influence over what is imported to Japan and by whom.

Joint Research and Joint Ventures

Keiretsu often form committees with representatives from various member companies to study new markets, to develop market entry strategies, and to establish joint ventures. The committees identify emerging opportunities and then match the various synergies of group members to establish new companies. Some, like the Mitsubishi Group, have even formed permanent research institutes. The Mitsubishi Research Institute was established in 1970 by various core members of the Mitsubishi Group to undertake research at group level.

Group-level research and market-entry coordination is an important benefit for member companies and acts to keep them in the *keiretsu*. Once a new joint venture is established and production is under way, the other *keiretsu* members form an immediate and sometimes large market for its products. This gives the joint venture the time to establish economies of scale and to generate cash flow while it searches for external markets.

Table 9.1   The *Sogo Shosha* of Japan's Leading *Keiretsu*[37]

Group	Trading Company
Mitsubishi	Mitsubishi Corporation
Mitsui	Mitsui and Co
Sumitomo	Sumitomo Corporation
Sanwa	Nissho Iwai Corporation Nichimen Corporation
Yasuda	Marubeni Corporation
Tokai	Toyo Menka Kaisha
DKB-Itochu	Itochu Co Kanematsu Corporation

A Common Real Estate Manager

The member companies of some *keiretsu* occupy land and office towers owned by a common group real estate company. Mitsui has its Mitsui Real Estate, Mitsubishi its Mitsubishi Estate, and Sumitomo its Sumitomo Realty and Development. Some of the big *keiretsu* have enormous holdings of central business district and industrial land. Like Bangkok's Crown Property Bureau, they can diversify into almost any land-intensive industry because they can usually supply the land. So the relative scarcity of land in Japan hasn't been a problem for the major *keiretsu*. In fact, their access to land partly explains their diversity. Opportunities to enter new industries or to set up new car plants or chemicals factories don't have to be forgone because land can't be accessed.

Of late, some real estate affiliates of the *keiretsu* have been able to stave off bad annual results by selling some of the properties occupied by their affiliates to them. In 1998, for example, Mitsubishi Estate announced it would sell a downtown Tokyo property to the group's trading company, Mitsubishi Corporation, which occupies the building and rents it from Mitsubishi Estate. Future rental earnings are lost, but at least the sale meant that Mitsubishi Estate's current-year losses would be made up.[38]

THE *KEIRETSU* UNDER PRESSURE

The 1990s has seen the biggest economic downturn in Japan since the end of World War II. Declining profits, rising debts, and massive asset depreciation, most notably in real estate prices, put the *keiretsu* under a lot of pressure. Many of their practices and structure that were formerly appropriate, or at least had been masked by the extended post-war boom, were no longer optimal. The practices that saw the arteries of the Japanese economy grow also carried with them the plaque that would eventually clog them. The changed economic circumstances forced Japan's big business groups to reassess their strategies.

Many attempted to unravel, at least in part, some of their cross-shareholdings, though the move wasn't so much out of a newfound desire to improve transparency as to access the funds the shares represent. By selling them, they could at least stave off having to declare a loss for another 12 months. But even with this trend, cross-shareholdings remain important, if marginally less so. Similarly, the more difficult economic times put the intra-group transactions of the *keiretsu* under pressure. Declining corporate profits made the *keiretsu* more cost-sensitive and thus more likely to buy their input from outside the group.

But corporate restructuring is best done when funds are available to undertake them. Similarly, shareholdings should be sold at the peak of the market and not when share prices are recessed. For Japan's *keiretsu*, it was all too little, too late.

JAPANESE AND SOUTH-EAST ASIAN BIG BUSINESSES

Japan's big business groups were under enormous pressure by the end of the 1990s as were South-East Asia's conglomerates. But how similar are these two sets of organizations? The Japanese occupy a position on the cultural continuum that is neither fully in the Western camp nor fully in the Asian camp. In keeping with this, large Japanese business groups share some similarities with the conglomerates of South-East Asia — but there are also some important differences. Table 9.2 lists some of these.

There are plenty of significant similarities, too. Many are at the root of the problems that corporate Japan faces today. Both sets of business groups feature cross-shareholdings, often arrayed without the benefit of holding companies to provide a clear and transparent structure. Both sets usually feature a bank or some other finance arm. There is a preoccupation with real estate holdings. Both tend to be highly diversified, with large numbers of member companies that have a high volume of internal transactions. Audits and disclosure are generally not high priorities for the *keiretsu* or South-East Asia's conglomerates; nor are the interests of minority shareholders. Business tends to be done on the basis of trust and personal connections, and there is little reliance on, and even a suspicion of, formal legal procedures that facilitate trade. Also,

Table 9.2 Differences between Japanese and South-East Asian
Big Businesses

Japanese *Keiretsu*	South-East Asian Conglomerate
Professional management	Family management
Wide ownership	Family ownership
High expenditure on research	Low or no expenditure on research
Strong brand development	Poor brand development
Emphasis on formal internal rules	Rules are at the whim of management
Very well-defined career paths	Poorly defined career paths
Entry to firm based on merit	Entry to firm based on connections
Decision making by (apparent) consensus	Management is dictatorial and almost feudal

where the *keiretsu* has the presidential council, the South-East Asian conglomerate has its board 'at the group level.' There are other similarities. In fact, there are probably more similarities in relation to the structure and attitudes to corporate accountability between the big business groups of Japan and South-East Asia than most Japanese would care to acknowledge. The most important similarity is a cavalier attitude toward corporate governance.

BIZARRE CORPORATE GOVERNANCE

Japan doesn't have a strong culture of corporate governance. In fact, only recently has there been a Japanese word for it — *koporeito gabanansu* — the obvious origins of which are as foreign to Japan as the concept itself. Most listed companies don't have independent non-executive directors to safeguard the interests of minority shareholders. To exacerbate this problem, directors aren't required to fully disclose their current or former relationships with the company or its affiliates. Directors are appointed not so much because they are good managers or will be exemplary in carrying out their fiduciary duty, but more as a reward for long service and loyalty; it is a conferral of status for those at the end of their careers. Activist directors are unusual and are generally unwelcome. Also, many boards are simply too big. It's not uncommon to have between 20 and 60 members on a board — compared with the typically ten or fewer in the

United States, Western Europe, and Australia. Such boards are simply too large for effective decision making. In 1997, Sony was among the first to reduce its board to a managable size. The old board of 38 directors was replaced by a new one with just ten. To really break rank with the rest of corporate Japan, three of the ten were from outside the company.[39] In 1999, Nissan Motor, which had just accepted Renault of France as its new 37% owner, also cut its board from 37 to ten. But Sony and Nissan largely remain as exceptions. Larger Japanese companies are required to have an audit committee of three members, one of whom must be 'independent.' However, 'independence' is so widely interpreted that companies commonly appoint their retired executives to the position. The abuses and absurdities don't end there.

Minority shareholders are even denied the annual general meeting (AGM) as a forum where they can air their grievances, question management, and attempt to share some input. Instead, what they are given is a farce. Most Japanese public corporations hold their AGMs during a single two-day period each year. Out of the 1,864 listed companies that closed their books at the end of March 1996, 1,766, or 94.2%, held their AGMs on the same day — on June 27 that year.[40] Investors who own stocks in several companies find it difficult to attend the AGMs of all their companies, because of the inevitable time clashes. Investors who dare to have a diversified portfolio haven't a hope. Not surprisingly, 90% of AGMs conclude without there being a single question from shareholders. Even if they do manage to get to an AGM, investors might wonder why they bothered. The average length of an AGM in 1996 was an astonishingly brief 26 minutes. It's not only investors who are disadvantaged by these practices. Financial journalists, too, are unable to cover very many AGMs — which is just how Japanese companies want it. Openness and scrutiny are really not part of Japan's corporate culture, whereas minimizing the opportunities for possible embarrassment is. That a shareholder should feel the need to ask a question might be construed as a loss of 'face' to management.

Racketeers were able to make the most of corporate Japan's disdain for accountability during the 1980s and 1990s, particularly given the environment of falling profits in the wake of the collapse of the bubble economy. Racketeers would purchase small parcels of stock in various companies that allowed them to participate in those companies' AGMs. They then studied the companies and all their businesses so that they could draw up long lists of embarrassing questions. They would threaten to ask these questions unless they received payments from company directors not to do so. The practice of extorting such illegal payments — the perpetrators are known as the *sokaiya* — affected many major companies, which were mired in scandal when the practice became known. More than 20 companies faced criminal prosecution for secretly paying off racketeers. Mitsubishi Motors, Kirin Brewery, Takashimaya, Hitachi, Nikko Securities, Daiwa Securities, Toshiba Corporation, and Mitsubishi Estate were among the companies targeted. Eleven of Dai-ichi Kangyo Bank's executives were jailed in 1997 and the bank's former president, Kuniji Miyazaki, committed suicide. He didn't seem to be directly implicated but he hanged himself anyway.[41]

THE CONSPIRACY OF INTERESTS THAT IS JAPAN

Shareholder value is very low on the list of concerns of many of Japan's larger listed companies. Cozy cross-shareholding arrangements, where companies mutually turn a blind eye to each other's inefficiencies, have seen to this. But sticking together ultimately hasn't helped the individual members of Japan's *keiretsu*. All it's done is to reinforce each other's inefficiencies and mismanagement. In other economies, the market picks off those companies that are underperforming and have weak corporate governance, management, and internal checks and balances. They are either taken over and knocked into shape or they go bankrupt. In Japan, weak companies have tended to huddle together to seek comfort and protection from other *keiretsu* members, which ultimately leaves the whole group weakened. Inefficiencies and mismanagement aren't owned up to in a misplaced sense of corporate pride, and ultimately, instead of one or a few companies facing insolvency, the whole group does. Cross-shareholdings in the 1980s meant concentrating wealth and success. In the 1990s, they have become the means for cross-infection.

Those companies in Japan that have fared the best out of the financial crisis have tended to be those that are not directly attached to diversified *keiretsu*, namely, Sony, Toyota, and Honda. They are more agile and focused, and cannot hide behind their affiliates to make up for losses and poor management.

Many Japanese companies that belong to a *keiretsu* have been loath to write off bad debts of affiliates. This has meant that throughout the 1990s, many simply accumulated them. Had the debts been of non-affiliated companies, it is unlikely that they would have been carried for so long. Part of the problem is insufficient taxation incentives to write down bad debts. Part of it is also a problem of 'face' and honor. Acknowledging a bad debt suggests defeat; to declare a low profit or even a loss is to confirm it. Similarly, many bad initiatives or ventures take a lot longer to be killed off than they otherwise should. Again, doing so is an admission of failure and not something to be done lightly or without consensus.

Throughout the 1990s, corporate Japan slowly awoke to the need to write off bad debt. Many companies delayed doing this until there was little choice but to do so, by which time the size of the bad debts had grown enormous. In 1998, for example, Taisei Corporation, a construction giant affiliated with Yasuda Group, wrote off US$925 million in bad debt — much of it belonging to troubled affiliates.[42] The country's 19 largest banks also decided to come clean that year. Collectively, they decided to write off a whopping US$74.1 billion in non-performing loans.[43] Unfortunately, the wave of corporate *mea culpa* that washed through Japan wasn't so much because of a sudden collective desire to do the right thing, but more because things had reached such a bad state that there was little else they could do.

Many banks today face difficulties because of lending for real estate, not to outsiders but their affiliates. Some even specifically established affiliates to speculate in real estate and to which they extended loans for that purpose. Fukutoku Bank, Bank of Osaka, and Hanwa Bank, for example, each established non-bank affiliates to which they gave loans for real estate investments in the late 1980s. Property prices collapsed not long after that and the banks found it impossible to dispose of the real estate-backed loans of their affiliates.[44]

In March 1995, Japan's central bank created a new bank, Tokyo Kyodou Bank, from two failed Tokyo-based credit cooperatives, Tokyo Kyowa Credit Cooperative and Anzen Credit Cooperative.[45] The two cooperatives had gone bankrupt with almost US$1 billion in bad loans. Violations of legal lending limits to a single client were partly behind Tokyo Kyowa's collapse. And why had the cooperative chosen to exceed the lending limits? Its head, Harunori Takahashi, also happened to head the EIE International Group that received the loans. EIE poured millions into real estate in Japan and elsewhere around the world. It paid top-of-the-market prices for five-star hotels and office towers in Japan, Hong Kong, Australia, the United States, and elsewhere. Japan's Long-Term Credit Bank funded much of the expansion. In the early 1990s, EIE was technically bankrupt but senior Ministry of Finance officials insisted that the bank keep on lending. It transpired later that the officials involved had been wined and dined, provided with free weekends at EIE's golf courses, and flown to casinos in Macau and Australia where they could gamble with chips paid for by EIE.[46] When the bank eventually turned off the credit tap in mid-1993, Takahashi turned to his Tokyo Kyowa Credit Cooperative.

When Asia's property prices came crashing down, so did EIE. And with it went the Tokyo Kyowa Credit Cooperative. That was when it was merged with the Anzen Credit Cooperative to become the Tokyo Kyodou

Bank. The new entity was given enormous cash infusions by the Japanese government to keep it afloat. It was yet another example of the excesses of Japan, Inc. Many ordinary Japanese didn't believe that taxpayers' funds — the grants and low-interest loans amounted to US$1.3 billion — should be used to bail out lending institutions that had failed because they had broken the law. The government's problems were compounded when it was revealed that the two cooperatives had provided cheap credit to politicians and others with political connections to speculate in real estate during the 1980s.

Japan's culture of non-confrontation makes internal checks and balances difficult. Rogue copper trader, Yasuo Hamanaka, at Sumitomo Corporation was found to have accumulated US$2.6 billion in copper trading losses throughout the 1990s. He had managed to hide the losses by rolling over contracts. The enormous profits that he booked — fictitious though they were — allowed him to build up an enormous reputation, so much so that it seemed that no one at Sumitomo felt able to challenge or monitor Hamanaka's activities, thus allowing him to hide his deceit for so long. Hamanaka was eventually jailed for eight years.

The collapse of Yasuda Group's Yamaichi Securities in late 1997 was yet another example of the consequence of a lack of checks and balances. The company had illegally compensated favored corporate clients for share trading losses starting from as early as 1992. It did this by selling Eurobonds to the clients and then buying them back at more than the market rate. This allowed clients' accounts to be topped up for losses arising from other transactions. It then hid the losses through off-balance-sheet transactions. Initially, the losses were hidden by transferring them from client to client in such a way that no client would show a deficit during their accounting periods. But after a while, the clients refused to go along with the charade. So, where next to hide the losses? Yamaichi decided to move them right out of Japan and booked them with a subsidiary in Australia. To further conceal its actions, the company then issued false balance sheets and paid dividends to shareholders out of profits that simply didn't exist. It was always meant to be a temporary solution until the losses could be recovered when the stock market recovered. But it didn't.

The company's then-president later claimed that the suggestion to hide the losses came from none other than the director-general of the Securities Bureau of the Ministry of Finance.[47] Given the ministry's track record, many were prepared to believe him.

Typically, a company might set up internal risk management procedures and believe that the mere act of setting up procedures equate to the job having been done. The fact that these procedures may not be followed is immaterial. Once again, the problem of 'form over content' makes its appearance.

Accountability isn't simply a problem among companies. It is also a problem within them. The response of many companies in 1998 to Japan's worsening corporate environment was to cut the salaries of their staff across the board. Yasuda Trust and Banking, for example, cut the salaries of its staff irrespective of their division. The aim was to share the burden equally across divisions. But in practice, it meant that better-performing divisions were equally punished as the laggards. The more prudent measure would have been to give each division its own budget and to remunerate on the basis of performance. Many Japanese companies have still to learn that accountability isn't something that only starts beyond their front door. Actually, for many it doesn't start there either; it just doesn't start at all. But where are the auditors in all of this?

Auditing Japanese Style

Unfortunately, auditing in Japan can be almost as lame and ineffectual as many other aspects of the country's corporate governance regime. It is also as compromised as accounting elsewhere in Asia, some of the many transgressions of which were alluded to in Chapter 2. Financial accounting standards for companies in Japan are determined by the Business Accounting Deliberation Council, which is housed in the Ministry of Finance. The arrangement is a cozy one, indeed. Not only is the council not independent, but it is located in the ministry that has been a foundation stone for Japan, Inc. in its formal role, and informally has been at the center of some of Japan's most damaging corruption scandals. Auditing is about accountability and disclosure, and yet the body that oversees the profession in Japan represents the antithesis of these principles. The accounting profession itself has little say in the formulation of accounting standards, although it does make recommendations. The profession is small, and has a relatively low status compared to its position in, say, the United States. It is, after all, charged with undertaking a task that most Japanese corporations are utterly uncomfortable with (injecting scrutiny) and for which they see little value anyway. To underscore this, the auditing fees that large Japanese corporations pay, even to big-name international accounting firms, are typically little more than 10% of the fee equivalent-sized corporations in the United States pay.

The cross-shareholdings and other arrangements that are used to hold a *keiretsu* together generally aid secrecy rather than transparency and disclosure. Because of the long absence of holding companies, the identification of subsidiaries is difficult and thus so is determining the appropriate scope of companies for consolidation. For this reason, a consolidated statement is often an inaccurate portrayal of a company's actual performance. Earnings and assets tend to be grossly understated. Listed companies are required to report the assets and liabilities of only the companies in which they hold at least a 20% stake. But if, say, a company directly owns just 5% in another but holds a far greater indirect stake through other unlisted subsidiaries, it can avoid reporting its exposure. So, accounting and auditing in Japan aren't easy and they are hampered by regulatory standards that are remarkably lax anyway. An additional problem is international accounting firms don't operate in their own right in Japan but with local partners, just as they do in some other Asian countries. All partnerships involve compromise and a sharing of control, and there is no reason to suspect they are any different in Japan. The performance of corporate Japan since the end of the bubble economy has put the spotlight on the efficacy of auditing. And with good reason. It was the local offices of the Big Five (then the Big Six) accounting firms that audited the companies that were responsible for Japan's four biggest corporate scandals in recent years. Table 9.3 tells the sorry tale.[48]

Japanese companies have also been able to keep transactions that pose extraordinary large risks off their balance sheets. A company's books are supposed to indicate its financial health, but in Japan, time and time again, they bear little relevance to reality. Some companies offer verbal guarantees for the borrowing of affiliates, and these rarely show up on balance-sheets. Yamaichi Securities is perhaps the most celebrated example. It collapsed in 1997 with US$2 billion in off-balance-sheet debt, which until its collapse had largely been hidden. Listed construction company Tokai Kogyo's 1997 audited balance sheet showed assets of US$3.9 billion and liabilities of US$3.8 billion. Not a great result, but solvent nonetheless. What the company didn't do, however, was disclose loan guarantees of US$1.8 billion. Just a month later, the company went bankrupt and its revised statement told a very different story. In just four weeks, its actual assets had slid to US$1.6 billion and its liabilities had blown out to US$5.7 billion. Part of the reason for the dramatic turnaround was the fact that it had failed to disclose the guarantees in the first statement.[49] Of course, if a company deliberately hides such contingencies from its auditors, then it isn't completely fair that the auditor be blamed. But it's also the case that it's the auditor's job to expose such deceptions. Otherwise, what are they for?

Table 9.3   Scandals and Auditors Japanese-style

Company	Scandal	Local Auditor	Big-Six Affiliate
Daiwa Bank	US$1.1 billion lost by a bond trader (1985–95)	Showa Ota & Co	Ernst & Young
Sumitomo Corporation	US$2.6 billion lost by a rogue copper trader (1985–96)	Asahi & Co	Arthur Andersen
Yakult Honsha	US$1.23 billion lost in derivatives trading	Tohmatsu & Co	Deloitte Touche Tohmatsu
Yamaichi Securities	US$2 billion lost in off-balance-sheet activities (1991–97)	Chuo Audit	Coopers & Lybrand

Smoke and Mirrors

Assets are largely valued in balance sheets on a historical basis in Japan — that is based on the actual payment made for them. This is especially important given the cross-shareholdings within the major *keiretsu*. The Tokyo stock market peaked in 1989 when the Nikkei hit 38,916 points. Between then and mid-1998, the Nikkei didn't reach more than 60% of its 1989 peak and by mid-1998, it was in fact less than half of that amount. This meant that by mid-1998, many Japanese companies were sitting on shares that were grossly overvalued in their books. Banks, however, were required to value their stockholdings at the prevailing market prices for the purposes of constructing their accounts — at least, that was the case until the fiscal year that ended on March 31, 1998. Just prior to the end of that year, the Japanese government changed the rules and allowed banks to value their stocks at what they had actually paid for them — thus giving many banks' profits an artificial boost given the then-parlous state of the stock market. The change allowed the already loss-making Yasuda Trust and Banking to avoid a further US$450 million in losses, for example.[50]

Allowing banks to value their shareholdings at their historical value meant that by mid-1998 many, despite being in serious trouble, were actually in even worse situations. It was believed that Daiwa Bank, Long-Term Credit Bank of Japan, Nippon Credit Bank, Yasuda Trust and Banking, and Chuo Trust and Banking — some of the country's biggest banks — had significant losses hidden in their balance sheets given that the market value of their stockholdings was likely to be below their historical or book value.[51]

Disarming the Media

If internal accountability, external competition, regulators, the legal system, and auditors all fail to adequately constrain corporate managers in Japan from anti-competitive behavior, corruption, and taking advantage of their minority shareholders, then what role does the media play in exposing the rorts and the rip-offs? The answer: not a good one.

It's not only government officials who are the targets of largesse from big businesses. Japan's journalists too are targets for being wined and dined, paid off, and compromised. This is an insidious overlay on a media that is already relatively compliant. Some sections of the media are quite independent and investigative. The practice of *amakudari* is one aspect of corporate Japan that is routinely exposed and criticized in the media. Other aspects of corporate Japan are sacrosanct. Occasionally, a scandal becomes too big and Japan's media organizations arrange for teams of journalists to investigate and report every twist and turn; but other than that, many smaller scandals receive little attention. Media outlets readily accept gifts such as free telephone calls, temporary broadcasting facilities, and so on from the very organizations they are supposed to cover. Journalists can even join clubs to report on each company and actually sit in offices provided by the companies. It is all too reminiscent of the practice in Thailand and Indonesia, where companies pay local journalists to attend their news conferences, albeit at a more sophisticated level.

Industry associations and government agencies even informally grant exclusive rights to a chosen news organization to cover their affairs. Such cozy arrangements mean that other news organizations are denied access to interviews, information, and news conferences. They also mean that should the news organization become too investigative, its exclusive coverage rights will be dropped in favor of a competitor. Investigative reporting in Japan all too often is confined to revealing the marriage plans of local rock stars, sumo wrestlers, and Japanese baseball players who make it big in America; rarely does it involve breaking stories about the misdeeds of Japan's corporations.

Elsewhere, the media is one of the vital institutions that helps hold corporations and managers accountable and ensures that they don't ride roughshod over their minority shareholders. But like so many of the checks and balances necessary for a well-functioning economy, the media in Japan has some way to go before it can adequately fill that role.

The *Yakuza* in Business

Organized crime syndicates (*yakuza*) wield considerable influence in Japan. The official estimate of *yakuza* members and associates is almost 80,000. The three biggest *yakuza* syndicates are the Kobe-based Yamaguchi-gumi, and the Tokyo-based Inagawa-kai and Sumiyoshi-kai. (The Yamaguchi-gumi and the Inagawa-kai entered a pact in late 1996 so that they could concentrate less on their old animosities and more on their commercial interests.) Two-thirds of Japan's known *yakuza* members and associates belong to either of these two groups.[52]

Like organized criminals everywhere, the *yakuza* are heavily involved in the narcotics trade and prostitution. But they also have strong links to the construction, entertainment, trucking, and meat processing industries. Some of Japan's senior politicians are believed to have *yakuza* links and are known to have solicited campaign donations from them. Former Prime Minister Noboru Takeshita, who resigned in 1989 amid a bribery scandal, was dogged by innuendo concerning his alleged *yakuza* associations.

The police too are compromised by the *yakuza* in some parts of Japan. An associate of mine had the misfortune of stepping out of a bar in Osaka without paying for a drink that he had consumed. (He absent-mindedly thought that he had.) Unbeknown to him, many bars in Japan are obliged to have 'protection' arrangements with a *yakuza* gang — and several *yakuza* thugs pursued him down the street, where they punched and kicked him to the ground and continued to kick him as he lay there. They finished the job by picking him up and throwing him head-first through a plate-glass window. In the melee, one of the thugs had his eye-glasses broken. Eventually someone called the police. When they arrived, they refused to take the victim to a hospital until he had paid for his drink, for the damage he had caused to the window by allowing himself to be thrown through it, and for the broken eye-glasses of the *yakuza* thug.

In some parts of Japan, such cooperation between the *yakuza* and the police makes an unassailable combination. It explains how the *yakuza* have managed to survive for so long and how its influence in certain sectors has continued with little challenge. Furthermore, the effects of the *yakuza* aren't all bad. The tacit cooperation between the gangs and the police is why there is little obvious street crime in Japan — the *yakuza* keep it under control.

THE CULTURAL CONTEXT

Corporate Japan's problems with accountability and corporate governance seem as widespread as they are intractable. What clues does Japanese society offer for why this should be so? Japanese society has in many respects some fundamental similarities with society in South-East Asia and North-East Asia. It is hierarchal, the concept of 'face' (or perhaps more precisely, the strong desire to avoid embarrassment), the submission of the individual's aims to those of the group, the preference to avoid direct confrontation, and knowing one's place in society, are all important. But there are some subtle differences as well. Group identification is stronger in Japan than elsewhere in Asia. Whereas a South-East Asian worker typically owes his loyalty to his boss alone, the Japanese worker owes it to the whole of the company.

There is also a greater emphasis on consensual decision making, particularly in the workplace. Japanese workers tend to be consulted on management decisions. Generally, this isn't the practice in the workplaces of South-East Asia, Hong Kong, and Taiwan. But this isn't to say that Japanese workers play a key role in decision making in their companies. Like workers elsewhere in Asia, they are mindful of the prevailing hierarchy and their place in it, so they are likely to suggest only what the boss wants to hear. Once again, form over content is as important in Japan as elsewhere in Asia. Ideas on product innovation are more likely to percolate to the top from workers than is the case elsewhere in Asia, but it's easy to overstate this.

The greater importance of social cohesiveness in Japan than elsewhere in Asia — the desire not to stand out but to fit in with the group — no doubt has its roots in the greater homogeneity of Japanese society. Society is fractured along ethnic lines in most of the other Asian countries, particularly in South-East Asia. This isn't the case in Japan, where the few ethnic minorities that do exist are insignificant as a proportion of the whole population and are mostly pushed to the outer margins of society, where they are pressured to adopt the cultural trappings of the Japanese.

The importance placed on social cohesiveness in Japan implies a disdain for the measures that promote accountability. The unwritten inference of a desire for disclosure and transparency is mistrust and suspicion, and these run counter to the prevailing culture of cohesion and 'oneness.'

The Japanese individual finds self-esteem, meaning, and definition in his or her membership of a group. This makes the group terribly important to the typical Japanese. Very often, the most important reference group — the source of the individual's relevance and place in society, especially for Japanese men — is his place of employment. A threat to the group — the company — by implication is an attack on the individual, so Japanese employees are generally prepared to go to great lengths to protect it. This might even mean engaging in cover-ups, corruption, and fraud. It is the group that is the arbiter of what's right and wrong, not society at large (as it is in say, the West). So for the Japanese, corrupt behavior adopted for the sake of the group or firm is seen as less 'wrong' than it would be in the West. Again in Asia, there are no absolute truths; what is 'right' is relative.

In Japan, the concepts of honor, dignity, and 'face' have reached levels far higher than elsewhere in Asia. Honor is a commodity seemingly more valuable than money itself. In the past, if a company damaged the environment through its actions or perhaps even its customers through negligence, it tended to pay only a token amount of money. Such amounts were in no way financial compensation for the damage caused.[53] But that isn't to say that they weren't punitive. The real pain was in the admission of guilt — the blow to corporate dignity. From the point of view of the company and its executives, the indignity of an admission of culpability was punishment enough. Of course, the victims might have seen it differently.

Direct confrontation is generally avoided in Japan, as is elsewhere in Asia. Labor relations tend to be consensual rather than adversarial, the legal system is a last resort, and the general checks and balances on companies that tend to be present in the West either don't exist in Japan or exist in form only. Neither is there the separation between business, government, and the bureaucracy that at least is the aspiration in the West, if not always the practice. So, Japan, Inc. is every bit a component of the wider problem of Asia, Inc. And as elegant as Japan's cultural pretensions may be, its corporate structures and governance are considerably less so.

CHAPTER 10

China: Rising Star or Black Hole?

China has big plans for its corporations – but are they good ones? Its choice of role models suggests not. Unwieldy conglomerates, petty corruption, a poor legal framework, and crony capitalists all threaten China's future prosperity — and now they threaten Hong Kong's too.

C hina — Asia's other mega-economy — has immense potential. It is an export-driven giant and a low-cost producer, and it has enormous critical mass. Give or take a few sidelined ethnic minorities, it also has the homogeneity of population to ensure considerable potential single-mindedness when it comes to national pursuits and global expansion. When times are tough on world markets, its manufacturers can turn to domestic markets to tide them over. Most of Asia's other economies lack this advantage. But will China's full potential be realized? Eschew corporate accountability, checks and balances, and sound corporate governance, and China will find itself subject to erratic and deep booms and busts like much of the rest of Asia. Get it right, and China will be unstoppable.

A-WINK-AND-A-NOD BUSINESS

Connections (*guanxi*) are critical for doing business in China. Why? Not because the Chinese are inherently interested only in doing business with their friends but because the legal system in China is among the poorest in Asia. Contracts are difficult to enforce and the behavior of many government officials is so rapacious and corrupt that they really have little choice but to do business with those they know and can trust. China has made significant progress in recent years in drafting laws, particularly for business, albeit from a remarkably low base. Having said that, it remains the case that many of the laws promulgated by China's National People's Congress are contradictory, poorly drafted, vaguely worded, and might not even be known to members of the legal profession or fully understood by the officials responsible for enforcing them. The opportunities for discretion on the part of officials who are invariably poorly paid are many and the consequences obvious. Bribery renders the rule of law patchy and inconsistently applied in many parts of China. Corruption doesn't exist only at the petty level either. In 1998, China's government disclosed that an extraordinary US$25.8 billion had disappeared from the state grain purchase funds during the previous six years, due to a combination of ineptitude and corruption.[1] And in 1999, government auditors declared that some US$15.1 billion in state funds had been either misused or embezzled that year alone.

Contracts too may not be regarded as confidential or necessarily binding. There have been documented instances where an American company signs a contract in China with a local company, lodges the contract with the relevant ministry, which then allows other Chinese companies that are also negotiating with the American company to read it so that they will know ahead what terms the American company is likely to agree to.[2]

In this environment, personal connections are needed to find opportunities, obtain the necessary approvals from local authorities, protect the investment once it has been made, and resolve disputes. A lack of connections means a lack of protection, and this is a significant barrier to entry for investors who are outsiders. It is no accident that cultural insiders — ethnic Chinese from abroad — have contributed to the bulk of foreign investment in China (as high as 90% in some provinces). Foreign investment figures hide this because they record only the source country of the investment and not the investor's ethnicity. An electronics assembly plant set up by a Californian-Chinese near the village where his parents were born is recorded as investment from the United States, for example, and not as investment from the overseas Chinese diaspora. It is small-scale investments like this, poured in via family and other personal networks, that has driven much of China's recent development, rather than the mega-plants established by foreign multinationals.

The problem with investment that is driven by *guanxi* is that those who have the connections to investment, as well as the inclination and funds to do so, are eventually exhausted. Investment slows, and with it, the economy. At that point, a growth-driven economy has little choice but to start examining its legal and corporate governance infrastructures. If these can be fixed so that anyone can invest without the need for local connections, then investment by a whole new range of investors is made more feasible. Investment becomes less risky for those without local connections and over time, *guanxi* becomes less important. Look at Singapore. Its population is almost wholly ethnic Chinese, but good local connections aren't a prerequisite to investment there because Singapore's excellent legal system provides enough protection, rendering connections unnecessary.

But in China, *guanxi* isn't necessary for only those who want to invest. The prices of many input and other commodities in China are controlled. This means that instead of prices adjusting to equate demand to supply, goods simply become scarce should there be excess demand. There might be plenty who can afford to buy them but only a few who will get them. Who wins and who misses out often comes down to *guanxi*. Interest rates too are controlled by the state, and again, when credit is in short supply, it's handed out to those with the best connections. Markets that clear via *guanxi* are hardly efficient. They are critical for getting investment under way, which allows the recipient economy to experience a growth spurt, but such growth is unsustainable. *Guanxi*-driven growth spurts can only ever be temporary.

CORPORATE CHINA

There are five main types of business entities in China:

- state-owned enterprises
- town and village enterprises
- urban collectives
- private and individual enterprises
- joint ventures with foreigners and wholly foreign-owned enterprises

The 1990s saw an enormous repositioning of these five categories with respect to their share of national production. The state-owned enterprises (SOEs) — there are as many as 370,000 of them — are largely as moribund and inefficient as one would expect. Many — probably, most — survive only because of direct and hidden state subsidies. They are China's greatest threat to future prosperity. The other four categories together comprise the non-state sector, and by the mid-1990s, produced two-thirds of China's industrial output. The town and village enterprises are owned either by local government authorities or groups of businessmen, but they generally operate as private or labor-managed enterprises. Their proximity to the government hasn't deadened them because the lower levels of government are usually too poor to subsidize them if they make losses and so they are left to limp along in immortal decline. Consequently, they and the foreign-invested sector have been at the forefront of China's newfound vigour. There's a lot to be said for natural selection in business, even in China.

State-owned 'Enterprise'

More than half of China's industrial SOEs are loss making, and often chronically so.[3] If the range of direct and hidden subsidies were removed, probably three-quarters of the SOEs would slide into bankruptcy. Generally, they are poorly managed, pilferage-ridden, over-staffed, have excess capacity, are anti-competitive, and are mostly subject to 'soft-budget' constraints, which means that if they run out of money they are topped up by the state (or its banks), so there is little need to be prudent. Many still work to production quotas. Staff perfunctorily plod their way through assembling computers or whatever else it is that their factory makes, and once the day's quota has been met, they knock off — regardless of demand or even if there are still more hours left in the working day. It's hard not to feel incredulous when, on visiting a state-owned factory in the mid-afternoon, one finds that production has ceased and the staff are milling around because they have 'met their quota.' Still, such apparent indolence might be a blessing in disguise. The products produced by many plants are of such sub-standard quality that the plants might do more for their country's prosperity by not producing them at all.

That the SOEs are inefficient is beyond doubt and also something of an understatement. They produced less than a third of China's industrial output by the mid-1990s but absorbed almost 60% of its industrial investment. Just 1% of net industrial profits came from the SOEs.[4] And the inefficiency isn't getting any better. The low or no return on the hundreds of billions of dollars in capital that is tied up in the SOE sector represents an extraordinary loss to the economy and to the welfare of the Chinese people.

Collectively, SOEs have managed to soak up most of China's available bank credit. The fact that much of it is at subsidized interest rates is irrelevant because a great deal of it simply isn't serviced. Credit is often allocated based not on a demonstrated ability to repay but on a combination of connections and government direction. A typical bank manager's idea of risk assessment is to assess who will be offended if he refuses a loan and what they might do to him. Not surprisingly, in such an environment, loans are handed out often without there being any credible repayment plan. The four large commercial state banks didn't even have the right, in 1998, to refuse government directives to lend to SOEs no matter how insolvent they were, although there was a promise that, formally at least, things would change. In effect, the government simply orders the banks to knowingly take on bad loans. By 1998, they had only negligible capital, derisory reserves, and huge amounts of non-performing loans. They had almost certainly been technically insolvent, although a massive recapitalization plan launched by the government kept them afloat. With the state owning both the banks and many of the enterprises, lending to the SOEs isn't an arm's-length affair, which is a necessary condition for an efficient and well-run banking system. In essence, the situation in China is little different from that in South-East Asia, where the owners of the banks simply order the banks to lend to the owners' other businesses.

At the beginning of 1996, the SOEs are believed to have had debts that were, on average, almost six times their equity, excluding pension liabilities and receivables.[5] The head of China's central bank conceded in late 1997 that some US$120 billion was needed to bail out the entire sector.[6] The problem has since improved little. But the problems don't end there. Not only are many SOEs hopelessly indebted to the banks, they have also racked up enormous debts with each other through trade credit and inter-firm lending. These so-called triangular debts are estimated to have amounted to US$120 billion by the end of 1996.[7] The problems are compounded by the actions of many managers and workers who believe that their companies will collapse and so strip them of assets by awarding themselves unsustainable salaries and bonuses, as well as by overtly pillaging state assets. Not surprisingly, the prophecies of doom become self-fulfilling.

Some managers even corruptly deposit the funds of their SOEs into their private bank accounts, either permanently or so that they can pocket the interest. In July 1998, for example, China's official news agency reported that some US$1 billion in pension payments that SOE managers should have paid to their retrenched workers was 'missing.'[8] The extent of misappropriation of public funds had reached such proportions that the amount of money held in private bank accounts across China rocketed by almost 70% in the 30 months to mid-1998 — way in excess of what had been expected from the normal growth of workers' savings.[9] This practice is so rampant that the size of bank account deposits in China is no longer a useful measure of household savings.

Even determining the full extent of the country's problems is difficult. China has a long history of manipulating statistics, or outright fabrication of it. It was perhaps at its most extreme during Chairman Mao's Great Leap Forward when provinces all over China submitted highly inflated production statistics to Beijing to please the chairman. The practice has since reduced but not eliminated. Faking financial data is illegal, but it doesn't stop many from trying. Audits of 6,000 mills and factories in Anhui province in 1997 found that at least 16% had deliberately falsified financial reports by inflating revenues or claiming fictitious profits. A profit of US$5.92 million was claimed for one bankrupt textile mill, which seemed ambitious, but only more so when it was discovered that the mill had been closed for two years. Another plant, a paper mill, reported a gross revenue of US$3.9 million. That figure too had been somewhat embellished. The real figure was just US$146,000.[10] Bad news might travel fast, but rarely in Asia, and particularly in China, is it allowed to travel up, even if it means falsifying documents and figures in order to keep superiors happy.

Bankruptcy — the ultimate sanction over aberrant companies and management — is infrequently and unevenly applied. An enormous number of SOEs are technically bankrupt, but the government has been loath to pass and then implement effective bankruptcy legislation for fear of the social problems that would arise from the large numbers of workers who would lose their jobs if firms were rationalized. It's not just the salaries that workers lose when they are laid off from SOEs, but also housing, healthcare, education, and pension benefits. Consequently, mergers and acquisitions are the preferred route, even if it means weakening strong firms by forcing them to absorb the ones that are technically bankrupt. When SOEs are closed down it is the result of a government decision rather than through the actions of creditors petitioning a bankruptcy court. China's government won widespread praise in October 1998 for closing down the Guangdong International Trust and Investment Corporation (GITIC) when it couldn't pay its debts. But the fact that the closure was at the behest of the government served to highlight the need to streamline the process by which China's delinquent debtors can be closed down.

The need to reform the SOEs is obvious and incontrovertible. Even the most aging, backward stalwarts of the National People's Congress agree that something must be done. The big question though, is which way to jump.

To Form a Conglomerate or Not To

China unveiled its plans for corporate reform in 1996. 'Grasping the big, releasing the small' was the catch-phrase. Larger SOEs were to be merged and smaller ones would either be sold off, closed down, or rehabilitated if possible. The plans were expressed in typically vague terms — by not committing to detail, the government allowed for greater flexibility and avoided giving criteria against which it might later be judged. A secret list of 1,000 large SOEs (or 500, or 3,000 — it all depended on who was asked) that were selected for reform and to be kept under government control was drawn up. Included were existing large SOEs plus new entities formed by merging some of the smaller ones. The 'reforms' weren't exactly a wholesale leap into the free market. Some of the mergers since then have been more like shotgun marriages ordered by the authorities than natural pairings. Sometimes there was wisdom in forcing the mergers; at other times, they served simply to weaken existing strong companies.

A case in point is what happened to Hainan Development Bank, a regional bank based in Hainan province. In 1997, the government forced it to absorb 28 failed local credit unions. The credit unions had succumbed to a property bust, poor management, and fraud. The bank was already relatively weak, and the mergers weakened it further. Within a year, it too was insolvent.

The plans called for the specially selected SOEs to become the 'pillars' of the economy. They will be placed under separate holding companies, which will report directly to the relevant ministry, 'corporatized' so that they will be run by boards of directors and given distinct budgets, be given greater managerial autonomy, and have their capital bases restructured, including being allowed to sell shares in their subsidiaries. They will also be encouraged to become fully fledged conglomerates that branch into new sectors, including finance. Essentially, this meant they would become like the conglomerates of South-East Asia: diverse, sprawling, encompass a banking arm to serve as the banker to the rest of the group (irrespective of whatever rules may be drawn up), and have a mixture of listed and privately held companies complete with a myriad of related-party transactions. Add lashings of state-directed credit and some state direction and the South-East Asian model becomes the South Korean model.

An oft-stated goal of China's rulers is to have many Chinese companies among the Fortune Global 500 list of the world's largest companies. (As of 2000, it had just ten, compared to Japan's 107 and South Korea's 12.[11]) China's former measure of success was the production of huge output of steel, shovels, and the like — regardless of demand and quality. Now China intends to judge its companies by how big they are. Shanghai Automotive Industry Corporation (which has a joint venture with Germany's Volkswagen), Shanghai's Huadong Electric Power Co, and crude oil producer Daqing Petroleum Administration are the three biggest existing SOEs in terms of sales. They aren't exactly household names around the world the way Motorola and Ford are, but if China has its way, in the next few decades they will be. Big is best and might is right, or so it seems. China still appears unable to accept that the most appropriate measure of success is not size nor output, but the rate of return on invested capital. When it does, it will be the day that China truly awakens.

The Bigger the Better

The state-owned monoliths, China National Petroleum Corporation (CNPC) and China Petrochemical Corporation (Sinopec), were among the first candidates for the Fortune 500 treatment. Dozens of smaller oil-related SOEs were merged with the two larger companies, some of their regulatory functions were stripped off, and assets were traded between the two so that CNPC's holdings would be concentrated in China's north and west, and Sinopec's in the east and coastal regions. Between them, they also acquired (without compensation) around 10,000 gasoline stations that formerly had been held by local authorities and dozens of provincial oil distributors. Sinopec also absorbed China Eastern United Petrochemical, which had itself been formed only shortly before by merging five petrochemical SOEs. Yizheng Chemical Fibre, which is listed on the Stock Exchange of Hong Kong, was part of the booty that came with China Eastern. The asset swapping and mergers left China with two large state-controlled integrated oil companies. The chance for a vibrant and competitive oil and gasoline sector was forsaken for a duopoly.

China Ocean Shipping Co (Cosco), which reports to China's Ministry of Communications, is another of the country's more prominent SOEs. It is one of the world's top four shipping companies and has more than 600 vessels. But Cosco is no longer just a shipping company, nor is it exclusively based on the mainland. Port facilities, power, banking, and insurance are now a part of the Cosco empire. Its rapid diversification and expansion has been funded mostly by debt. It spent around US$1.1 billion on non-core assets such as real estate in 1997. By early 1998, its net debt was more than twice its equity — it was well on the way to assuming all the trappings of a South Korean *chaebol*.[12]

Cosco has a big presence in Hong Kong. Its interests there include a travel agency, which in turn owns at least four hotels in China, a real estate arm that owns residential and office towers in Hong Kong and China, an information technology subsidiary, and Yinfeng Fruit Juice Beverage Co in Shandong province. At least two subsidiaries are listed on the Stock Exchange of Hong Kong: Cosco Pacific and Cosco International Holdings. The latter (formerly Shun Shing Holdings) was a small engineering company owned by Hong Kong's Tse family until Cosco bought it and used it to achieve a 'backdoor' listing. After the takeover, Cosco injected some of its mainland assets into it, including a stake in a power plant in Henan province. Not long after, the company announced it was to construct in Shanghai a residential complex of ten blocks of 29-story towers.[13] Cosco, the shipping company, had decided, that it should be in residential housing as well. Cosco Pacific has also been a vehicle for the group's diversification plans. Its core operations are in container leasing, but in 1997, it bought 20% of Hong Kong's Liu Chong Hing Bank, which has branches across Hong Kong and in the mainland. This followed its parent's purchase of 20% of Hainan Development Bank (which was later closed down) and almost 15% of China Merchants Bank, both of which are in China. Banking had become another diversification and another diversion.

Cosco has sought to reach out beyond Greater China, but the expansion hasn't been without controversy. The company has a container terminal on a 40-hectare site at Long Beach in California, but by 1997, it had outgrown these facilities. Its plans for a US$200 million redevelopment of the old U.S. Navy facilities at Long Beach ran afoul of political opposition in the United States. Demonstrations were organized at the terminal, and some members of Congress argued vociferously that Cosco's state ownership meant that its staff were little more than agents of 'communist China.'

Cosco has run into controversy in Australia too. A consortium between Cosco and Orient Overseas Container Line (OOCL), a Hong Kong-based firm controlled by the family of Hong Kong's chief executive, Tung Chee-hwa, explored the possibility in late 1996 of setting up facilities in the port of Melbourne.[14] But these plans too were stymied when the consortium refused to go along with the Australian government's desire that new stevedoring facilities in Melbourne should be operated with non-unionized labor. The main sticky point for OOCL was that it operates container terminals on the West Coast of the United States and these are controlled by the International Longshoremen's Warehouse Workers Union, OOCL was concerned that it risked retaliation from this union in the United States if the Maritime Union of Australia (MUA) was squeezed out of its port operations in Australia. The consortium decided it would only set up in Australia if the MUA was involved. It was a perverse result, because it wasn't Cosco from communist China that was most concerned about utilizing unionised labor in Australia, but OOCL from 'free' market Hong Kong.

In mid-1998, China announced plans to merge Cosco with another massive state-owned enterprise, the China National Foreign Trade Transportation Corporation (also referred to as 'Sinotrans'). Sinotrans is one of China's largest road transportation companies. The merger would see the creation of a massive multinational shipping, warehousing, freight forwarding, road transportation, and logistics conglomerate, not to mention the banking, construction, power station, and fruit juice arms.

The push to form a conglomerate and diversify has caught on all over China. Xinhua, China's official state-run press agency, owns property in Hong Kong and elsewhere. In 1997, it bought into a Hong Kong telecommunications equipment supplier. A year later, it was even awarded a license by the Australian government to become Australia's 21st telecommunications carrier. It planned to offer Australians cut-price international calls and to service data markets. Xinhua, it seemed, had decided to drop propaganda for profits.

As should be evident, the sprawl of China's SOEs isn't contained within China itself. Their managers' aspirations are not simply to make them big but also global. The management of Cosco and Xinhua obviously have this in mind. Among the other worldwide assets of Chinese SOEs are oil wells in Kazakhstan and Venezuela, a copper mine in Zambia, aluminum mines and abattoirs in Australia, iron ore mines in Peru, and timber plantations in the United States and Canada.

Regulators in Business

Xinhua isn't the only quasi-regulator that has gone into business. That many of its regulators have also set up businesses is an enormous headache for China. This much was acknowledged by the Fifteenth Communist Party Conference in 1997, which repeated earlier calls for the separation of government from enterprise. Similar calls have been made in the past, but little has changed. Being both umpire and player is like holding a license to print money — something not to be given up voluntarily. Examples of the problem abound. The Civil Aviation Administration of China (CAAC) regulates the airline industry but also chances its arm at business. Chinese airlines cannot develop or buy their own computerized reservation systems, but are forced to buy them from a company owned by the CAAC, which has monopoly import rights for such systems.[15]

The People's Liberation Army (PLA) is big in business too, although in July 1998, President Jiang Zemin ordered that the PLA should begin to dispose of its commercial holdings. But the first problem was to work out exactly what they were. Estimates of the number of PLA companies range up to 50,000 in the mainland and overseas, that employ in total as many as two million workers. Many of these companies are only small or medium-sized. The PLA's portfolio includes hotels, pharmaceuticals companies, an airline, steel pipes factories, passenger car plants, nightclubs, and karaoke bars. The largest PLA holding company, the Xinxing Group, at the time had around 100 subsidiaries, but each of these had subsidiaries in turn. Another prominent PLA-backed group is the China Poly Group, which is also believed to have around 100 subsidiaries including some prominent Hong Kong companies, two of which are listed on the Stock Exchange of Hong Kong: Continental Mariner and Poly Investments.

The PLA isn't easily pushed around and attempts to rein in its business interests are always a delicate matter. The extent its holdings and its ability to ride roughshod over regulators and competitors alike because of its military backing saw it becoming a considerable nuisance to legitimate businesses. Smuggling too has been a favorite and highly lucrative earner for the PLA. But its other businesses tend to be more conventional. J&A Securities, one of China's top three stockbroking firms, was controlled by the PLA. (Its name seems to confirm this — 'Jun' means 'military' in Chinese and 'An' means 'security.') But it too proved hard to control. Several of its senior staff reportedly used the firm's heavy-duty backing to refuse it being audited, thus giving the staff the cover to amass huge private fortunes in personal bank accounts held in Hong Kong.[16] J&A Securities had also been implicated in providing kickbacks to win underwriting contracts. Ultimately, Beijing ordered J&A Securities to merge with the Shanghai-based China Guotai Securities.

The Ministry of Foreign Trade and Economic Cooperation (MOFTEC) is another example. It is responsible for approving all foreign investment plans in China and is charged with interpreting China's Foreign Economic Contracts Law — the law that governs trade and other commercial contacts between China and foreigners. But MOFTEC also happens to have a business arm of its own, China Resources. Mao's Communist Party established the company in 1948 to act as the trading interface between China and the rest of the world. For most of its existence, it monopolized China's international trade. It is now a conglomerate in its own right and is particularly active in Hong Kong, where its main partner is the local arm of Indonesia's Lippo Group, which became embroiled in the 'Donorgate' scandal that arose out of the 1996 U.S. presidential election campaign.

China Resources has as many as 150 subsidiaries and affiliates. Three are listed on Hong Kong's stock exchange. The largest is the increasingly diversified China Resources Enterprises. There is the food distributor Ng Fung Hong and the diversified China Resources Beijing Land. Most of Hong Kong's fresh vegetables, fruit, pork, and poultry are imported from China by China Resources. There are supermarkets, cold storage facilities, advertising agencies, a port facility, winery, and brewery interests as well. Group revenue is believed to be as high as US$10 billion annually. It sounds like a lot, but it's no great feat given that China Resources' parent has a hand in regulating many of its markets.

The Rush to List

It wasn't until the early 1990s that China officially allowed two stock markets to open — one in Shanghai and the other in the southern boom town of Shenzhen. The rush to list has been extraordinary. By 1998, almost 800 mainland Chinese companies had offered shares on either stock market. Two types of shares are traded — A and B shares. Foreigners are restricted to owning only B shares in an effort to protect China's closed exchange rate system. By mid-1998, just over 100 Chinese companies had permission to offer B shares. Collectively, the offerings had raised about US$4.4 billion.[17] The real action is in A shares — those bought and sold by mainland Chinese investors. Accordingly, share trading offices have sprung up in China's major cities. They have become popular forms of entertainment for housewives, retirees, and others who meet, chat, and watch the prices of the stocks flash on screens, while they enjoy a cigarette. Most other forms of gambling are banned in China.

SOEs can also list on the Hong Kong stock exchange. These offerings are known as H shares. More than 40 SOEs had issued H shares by 1998. Some have listed on the New York Stock Exchange as well. Yanzhou Coal Mining is one such example, which listed in 1998. It joined eight other mainland Chinese companies on the exchange. The chairman of the New York Stock Exchange was even able to meet with Jiang Zemin on a visit to China in early 1998. President Clinton reciprocated when he called in on the Shanghai Stock Exchange on his visit to China in mid-1998. How times have changed!

Listing as Dumping

The development of stock markets in China is one of the country's great milestones along the road from economic irrelevance to economic super-power status. But there are plenty of potholes. President Jiang Zemin claimed at the Fifteenth Communist Party Conference in 1997 that 'socialism need not mean public ownership.' It was another catchy slogan, even if it was somewhat internally inconsistent — but that's the way of socialist dictatorships: anything can be justified and sold to the masses if it can be sloganized. Jiang's new mantra sanctioned the large numbers of privatization and listing of SOEs that had already occurred and signaled that corporate China's long march onto the stock exchanges of the world was about to break into a run. Had Jiang suddenly decided that owning shares was a good thing? Not really. For China, listing is more a means to an end. It's viewed as a solution to China's hemorrhaging state sector. Funds raised from the public could be used to pay off old debts rather than to create new wealth. All too often, growth and evolution aren't the real purpose why companies list. It is to raise cash for their parents. The nation's banks have been bled dry, so now it's the turn of minority shareholders.

Not only is China's push to develop its stock markets driven by the need for a quick repair job on its SOEs, but the stock markets are embracing much of that which is wrong with the stock markets of South-East Asia. China's SOEs are becoming increasingly diversified with a growing web of internal transactions, are not exactly imbued with a culture of disclosure and transparency, and tend to list only a subsidiary rather than the parent, allowing plenty of scope for fleecing minority shareholders and passing the cash back to the unlisted parent.

Cash is raised when the subsidiary lists, when it buys assets from the parent, when its plants buy their input from the parent, and when it pays out its dividends. The dividend payouts have been a particularly preferred mode of stripping listed companies of their cash. Normally, a listed company declares a profit but retains a significant proportion of it to fund further expansion. But often this isn't the case in China.

In 1995, for example, Shanghai Diesel Engine, a company listed on the Shanghai Stock Exchange, paid out 80% of its earnings in dividends. This was abnormally high by any standards but absurdly high given that the company needed the funds for further investment and that its accounts receivable had soared over the previous year. The high dividend payout was driven by the cash needs of its parent and 61% shareholder, the state-owned Dongfeng Machinery Group. Some listed subsidiaries of SOEs have even declared dividends that are in excess of the available cash on hand.[18]

The development of the stock market is a way of reducing state ownership. But there's a risk: in Jiang's China, socialism is being redefined to mean that it is the losses of China's SOEs that are being socialized, by being passed to private shareholders. But the profits are being privatized by remaining with the SOEs and the cadre elite that run them.

CHINA'S BURGEONING PRIVATE SECTOR

China's non-state sector is both its salvation and its ruination. The dynamism of the new China is almost entirely a phenomenon based on the non-state sector. But the better the non-state sector becomes, the more the state sector bleeds, and the more its inefficiencies appear stark. The non-state sector dominates the light industries, and this caters to the massive and growing domestic consumer market, as well as the export markets. It's the non-state sector that earns China billions of dollars in foreign exchange, has absorbed millions of workers displaced from the state sector, and has driven economic growth to double digits. The paradox is that it will save China even though China has done all it can to suppress it. Even now, it's a creature of circumstance rather than design.

The village collectives and other enterprises centered on Huaxi village in Jiangsu province have become rich very quickly. They have earned Huaxi the sobriquet of 'China's most prosperous village.'[19] Huaxi itself has a population of just 1,200. It boasts a large farm revenue, factories, and other plants. The Huaxi Group, as the enterprises are known, stunned the rest of China in 1993 when it placed a single order for 250 Audi sedans. Farmers in China had not long before been able to afford only bicycles or perhaps a motorcycle. So the effect was cathartic. Senior Chinese leader Li Peng even wrote an inscription for the village: 'Where the hopes of China's rural areas lie.' Huaxi had reached the pinnacle of success for non-state enterprises. But it was to be short-lived, or so it seemed. A new tax law, introduced in 1994, required collectives to send the bulk of their earnings as tax to the central government. Many of the newly profitable Huaxi enterprises began to lose money, and other cities and towns appeared to be doing better, particularly those where the local enterprises were purely private and not collective. The prosperity of China's 'most prosperous village' seemed to have come to an end. Many of the collectives were sold off — usually to their former managers. But it was found that once the collectives were converted into joint stock companies, they suddenly prospered again. What was happening? It emerged that the local managers had used their positions to enrich themselves and to build up their private capital, and allowed their collectives to record losses so that they might be offered up for sale. Once on sale, usually at very low prices given their newly loss-making status, the managers used their newly acquired capital to buy them and return them to prosperity. It's a story that has been repeated across China.

Yet another 'model' non-state enterprise is the household appliance, Haier Group, located in Qingdao, Shandong province. It was held up at the 1997 Fifteenth Communist Party Conference as an example of how to proceed. Within 13 years it had risen from being a lackluster collective to a conglomerate of 104 subsidiaries and 18,000 workers. Along the way, it also managed to absorb — by choice — 18 troubled SOEs. In 1996, it sold 1.68 million refrigerators, 1.01 million washing machines, and 460,000 air-conditioners. It ranks among the ten biggest refrigerator manufacturers in the world. It has also established assembly lines in South Carolina in the United States, Malaysia, the Philippines, and Indonesia, and is investigating opportunities in eastern Europe. Its total sales in 1999 was US$3.2 billion, of which US$1.4 billion was to customers outside China. Haier's owners hope to make the Haier brand name as well known overseas as it is in China.[20] It's a success story that would be nigh impossible to find in the state-owned sector.

But the one major constraint on the Huaxi and Haier groups and other non-state enterprises like them is the problem of accessing credit. About 70% of the credit in China's formal banking system is lent through the four main state banks, and the SOEs receive as much as 90% of all that is lent.[21] With most of the credit being soaked up by the thousands of SOEs as they go through various stages of collapse, the town and village enterprises, in particular, must forgo much-needed capital to expand. Furthermore, even when the state banks can be accessed, the range of services they offer is very narrow. With their one major task being to shovel endless sums of cash into the furnaces that are the SOEs, the state banks have had little time and little reason to investigate innovative financial instruments to cater to the needs of other potential clients.

Consequently, an enormous black market in banking services has emerged in China to meet the capital requirements of the non-state sector. This in itself is a good thing. The danger, though, is that many of the underground banks and credit cooperatives are themselves poorly managed and attached to non-financial interests. Like elsewhere in Asia, where banks and other finance arms aren't independent of real estate and other non-finance businesses, there's the risk that they will lend excessively and imprudently to these interests. Such a black market springs up to meet a legitimate need, and for a while is enormously useful for bolstering economic activity. But among the seeds of success are sown the seeds of disaster, and a crash is almost guaranteed. Thirty-four credit unions in Hainan province were ordered to close or to merge in 1997. Although legal, they were supervised poorly by the authorities. Many had lent improperly to their managers for real estate speculation. Black market finance companies, of course, aren't supervised at all.

Another problem faced by non-state enterprises is the sometimes constant demands by officials for informal taxation. Strictly, such payments aren't bribes because they don't go into the pockets of officials, but they do go to support the officials' favored causes or projects. Some jurisdictions have telephone hotlines that allow foreign-owned businesses to report attempts to collect unauthorized taxes.[22] But usually these services aren't made available to local non-state enterprises. This leaves the enterprises even more vulnerable to such demands because local officials know that they are relatively cashed up and demands for levies will go unreported.

MORE DIVERSIFICATION

It isn't just China's SOEs that are diversifying; many non-state enterprises are as well. Why? Some of the diversification occurs for much the same reasons as the conglomerates of South-East Asia have chosen to diversify — a distrust of outsiders that comes from the legal infrastructure. If contracts are unenforceable or too expensive to enforce, then far better to supply as many needs in-house, or so seems to be the rationale of many non-state firms. Some of the diversification has no organizational logic, however. The Haier Group, which has been so highly successful in its manufacture of household appliances, recently branched out into health tonics and Chinese medicine.

Another successful non-state firm, technology group Stone Holdings, has also joined the diversification fray. It's one of China's largest non-state companies. Founded in 1984 by a group of researchers who were angered that their inventions usually ended up being filed away and never utilized, the group has retained much of its collective ownership. It started out by designing software and distributing Compaq computers, but grew quickly to become one of the largest computer companies in the country. It hasn't looked back since — although there was one hiccup in 1989, when its then-chairman, Wan Runnan, was involved in the Tiananmen Square democracy demonstrations and had to flee the country in the wake of the government's subsequent crackdown. Stone's diversification began in 1994 when it set up a joint venture to make chocolates and other confectionery in Beijing. That was followed by moves into securities, cement, real estate, pharmaceuticals, baby food, soft drinks, light fixtures, and furniture interests. In less than 15 years, a tightly focused computer company had transformed itself into an unwieldy conglomerate.[23] It might not be too long before China's corporate sector looks very much like those of the rest of Asia — and be destined to repeat the same mistakes.

Bureaucrats for Hire

Premier Zhu Rongji unveiled a plan in early 1998 to reform China's ministries and sack many senior officials. This was aimed at improving efficiencies and reducing costs. The plan wasn't met with quite the outrage that some were expecting. Many of the senior bureaucrats whose jobs were abolished, quickly found well-paid jobs in the burgeoning non-state sector. When news spread that a large numbers of officials might be available for hire, many of China's larger private enterprises descended on Beijing with one purpose in mind. The Huaxi Group signed up 87 of the 400 or so newly available top officials. Sichuan's Fangzhou Group hired at least nine, and Guangdong's Meidi Group, one of China's top three air-conditioner systems manufacturers, reportedly had places for at least 41.[24] This has close parallels with the practice in Japan known as *amakudari*, or 'descent from heaven,' where retiring bureaucrats take lucrative jobs in the private sector. It's one of the factors that has bred the cozy relationship in Japan between big businesses and its regulators — and contributed to the long-term malaise of Japan's economy.

CRONY CAPITALISM IN CHINA

China's crony capitalists are known as the 'princelings' (the *taizi*). They are the sons and daughters of senior Communist Party officials. Today, they can be found in senior positions in the most profitable commercial arms of the state or running prominent non-state firms. They have two things going for them: connections and education. Connections are useful for gaining approvals, credit, and the like, or simply because others think they are useful and on that basis are willing to invest millions of dollars in their enterprises. The other important attribute is that the *taizi* tend to be relatively well-educated. Parents of *taizi* used their positions to ensure that their offspring had access to the best schools in China and abroad. It isn't always fair to blame the success of all the *taizi* on their connections. Their education means that many would have been successful anyway. Coupled with connections, they are guaranteed of reserved seats among China's elite.

One of the more prominent *taizi* is Wang Jun, the son of China's late vice-president, Wang Zhen. Wang joined the China International Trust and Investment Corporation (CITIC) when it was founded in 1979 and rose to head it. He was also appointed president of the state-owned arms trader, Poly Technologies. He has used his connections to grow CITIC into China's largest investment company, although this involved more the accumulation of existing assets than actually founding new ones and building them up. CITIC holds hundreds of subsidiaries in China and overseas, including factories, office towers, toll-roads, and telecommunications interests in China. It also has timber plantations in Washington, Oregon, and Alaska in the United States, and these are held by its U.S. arm, CITIFOR, Inc.

Wang might be one of the best-known *taizi*, but he is also one of the less polished. He lacks the education that many of his contemporaries enjoy and was described in a 1995 magazine by those who have dealt with him as 'boorish,' something of a slob, and a 'classic caveman.'[25] At least, he's well connected.

Other so-called *taizi* include Ye Xuanlian, who was appointed as a senior manager at Poly Technologies and is a son of prominent military figure, Marshal Ye Jianying; Wang Xiaochao, who was a general manager at Poly Technologies and is a son-in-law of former president, Yang Shangkun; Ye Xuanning, who was appointed president of the PLA's Kaili Corporation and is another son of Marshal Ye Jianying; Wang Zhi, who was appointed general manager of the SOE, Great Wall Computer Co, and is Wang Jun's younger brother; and Larry Yung, who was made the head of CITIC's Hong Kong arm and is a son of vice-president Rong Yiren, who founded CITIC.

The family of China's late paramount leader, Deng Xiaoping, has engaged in its share of profligacy. The Dengs were reported to have had at one time significant interests in no less than 14 companies listed on the Stock Exchange of Hong Kong.[26] The family's emergence in business only during the twilight years of Deng's influence meant that its members had the connections to open doors but not always to keep them open. Deng's oldest son, Deng Pufang, who had the misfortune of being thrown out from a third-floor window during the Cultural Revolution and has been wheelchair-bound ever since, had his Kanghua Group closed down by the authorities in 1988 for 'financial irregularities.' Several organizations set up by Pufang ostensibly as charities for the disabled have since been the targets of tax evasion and misappropriation investigations. In early 1998, criminal charges were filed against the former senior executives of a company called Hainan Minyuan Modern Agricultural Development for fraud. A major shareholder was a trust fund managed by Pufang.[27]

Deng's niece, Ding Peng, was at the center of a disagreement with a former business partner, Australian James Peng, in the early 1990s. The dispute led to the Australian losing Shenzhen Fountain, a firm that he had founded. He was kidnapped from a Macau hotel room, spirited across the border into mainland China, put on trial for embezzlement, and jailed for 18 years. He was finally released in November 1999 after six years of imprisonment and much lobbying from the Australian government. Meanwhile, Ding Peng took control of Shenzhen Fountain, and under her stewardship it became embroiled in allegations of fraud, embezzlement, and crooked accounting.[28]

Deng's youngest son, Deng Zhifang, has had his share of controversy too. Soon after his arrival on the corporate scene in Hong Kong, he became entwined with the local arm of the large mainland state-owned steel-making Shougang Group, run by Zhou Beifang, another *taizi*. Zhou's father, Zhou Guanwu, was the head of the parent company in the mainland and served under Deng Xiaoping in the 1930s. The younger Zhou appointed the younger Deng onto the board of one of Shougang's subsidiaries. In turn, Shougang in Hong Kong linked up with local billionaire Li Ka-shing, who bought into the local arm. But in early 1996, it all unraveled. Zhou Beifang and his wife — a daughter of an influential Beijing vice-mayor — divorced and she left for Europe with their child. It might have been a serious lapse of judgment on Zhou's part. Not long after, he was called back to the mainland and charged with 'economic crimes' and rewarded with a suspended death sentence for his trouble. Zhou senior was relieved of his job as well. The precise nature of the 'economic crimes' was never specified, but there was no doubt that the money flowed thick and fast at Shougang. For example, there was the matter of the Shougang parent having paid US$312 million for a Peruvian copper mine in 1992, reportedly twice the price offered by the next highest international bidder.[29] Was it a gross miscalculation by Shougang's management, or did some part of the US$150 million-plus premium reflect kickbacks to the buyers? It was one of the many curious transactions undertaken by Shougang. Deng Zhifang resigned from his positions with the group. Meanwhile, his wife, Zhou Lin, was said to have attempted suicide.[30] Deng Zhifang distanced himself from the ensuing corruption scandal and, has since wisely kept a low profile.

Another Deng-linked company ran into trouble in 1997. Shenzhen Non-Ferrous Metals Finance Co — a subsidiary of China National Non-Ferrous Metals Corporation, which at the time was managed by Deng's eldest son-in-law, Wu Jianchang — cooperated with the Shenzhen-listed Hainan Minyuan Modern Agriculture Development Co (in which it was a significant shareholder) in improper Beijing property and banking transactions that added about US$100 million to its 1996 profits and capital reserves. Hainan Minyuan's share price surged by more than 12 times its initial value in less than a year, thanks to the fictitious profits. To compound Hainan Minyuan's links to the Deng clan, the China Disability Fund Association, chaired by Deng Pufang, was also a significant shareholder.[31] Charges — including fraud and insider trading — were laid all round, although no member of the Deng family was charged.

The Dengs aside, China has made some encouraging moves in the direction of minimizing crony capitalism. Various *taizi* have been removed and even charged, as was the case with Zhou Beifang. But it's never clear if such moves are more to do with the *taizi's* actual wrongdoing or with shifts in the power balance among the Beijing elite. In 1998, the country's corruption watchdog, the Central Discipline Committee, banned top officials at provincial and ministerial levels from naming their relatives to key corporate positions. How stringently this will be enforced remains to be seen. By 2000, questions were being asked about the fast-growing business links of Jiang Mianheng, eldest son of President Jiang Zemin. Mianheng's Shanghai Xintai New Technology Co had just announced plans for a US$75 million semiconductor joint venture. One thing remains clear, though. Crony capitalism is another aspect of business that China has in common with much of the rest of Asia.

NEW WAYS, OLD MISTAKES

China's attempt at reform isn't without some virtue. Undoubtedly, the changes now under way will leave China's corporate sector in an improved state. But there is plenty that is wrong with the new approach.

Better laws are being drawn up, but as we have seen in South-East Asia, well-drafted laws are only half the solution. The other half is their enforcement. And while petty bureaucrats are prepared to look the other way for the equivalent of $10 and a packet of cigarettes, new laws are little better than no law.

Enterprises in both the state and non-state sectors are being encouraged to turn themselves into conglomerates but without due regard for core competencies and accountability. 'Big is best' is the new mantra, but what about the rate of return?

Stock markets are being developed, but much about them and the structure of the companies that list on them almost guarantee that minority shareholders will be disadvantaged. There are moves to suggest that the reliance on state-owned banks will be reduced. But it seems that the private banks and finance companies that will emerge will be attached to conglomerates, as they are in South-East Asia. In the absence of genuinely enforced regulation (which, for China, seems some decades away), this will simply mean that the next financial collapse will originate from within the private sector rather than the state sector.

Crony capitalism is alive and well in China, but it is more secretive and thus more pernicious than it is in South-East Asia. Most people have heard of Marcos and know what he did (only its extent is open to question), but how many can name more than a handful or even one of the many *taizi* currently amassing large amounts of private wealth in China?

China's tardiness on genuine reform is only afforded by the fact that its currency, the yuan, cannot be traded freely. The messenger is in a straitjacket. Once it is free, the rest of the world will deliver its verdict on the massive conglomerates bereft of transparency, accountability, and the basic checks and balances needed to ensure some semblance of sound corporate governance. It will be as swift as the message that was delivered to South-East Asia in 1997–98 once its currencies were free to convey it. After years of putting up with a corporate framework that is the equivalent of a horse and cart, China is now aiming for a Volkswagen. It should be aiming for a Mercedes.

THE TAIWAN 'MODEL'

Taiwan ranks highly in surveys of corporate governance among emerging markets. A 1998 survey by Jardine Fleming ranked it as the third-best performer on this score among all emerging markets around the world. Taiwan looks to the United States for direction on corporate matters, as it does for many other matters. One of my most enduring impressions of Taiwan is being told by almost every cab driver I hailed that his cab had been manufactured in the U.S. and not Japan.

Taiwan, like South Korea and Japan, has petrochemical and high-tech companies, but its economy isn't dominated by large, lumbering, and overly diversified conglomerates. Instead, the economy comprises thousands of small and mid-sized companies, all of which compete with each other without the 'benefit' of government 'assistance' or direction. Many of Taiwan's large banks are still owned by the state, but the government has little role in telling them to whom to lend. Most probably this was by default rather than by design. Taiwan's government has been too busy fighting battles in the international arena to be concerned with meddling excessively in the affairs of private business.

The small size of the bulk of Taiwan's companies has kept them flexible, responsive to market needs, focused, and disciplined. The checks and balances in Taiwan's competitive market-based system forces accountability on all the players; it also weeds out those that are poorly managed. The economy is totally driven by exports, which account for between a third and a half of Taiwan's GDP. The focus on exports has served as an added competitive constraint on Taiwan's firms and government. Indulge in the poor corporate governance and regulatory practices that bedevil much of the rest of Asia and Taiwan will lose its competitive edge on world markets.

Taiwan's economy has many informal cliques of businessmen, but generally, its companies are too numerous and fractured for such informal associations to become noticably anti-competitive. The most prominent clique in Taiwan is the so-called *Tainanbang* (literally, the 'group from Tainan'). Tainan is a prominent commercial city in southern Taiwan and the *Tainanbang* can count among its ranks many of the senior members of the city's business community. But even here, the clique tends to comprise businessmen who operate in different sectors. Occasionally, such cliques form consortia. In mid-1998 for example, reports appeared in the media that a consortium of Taiwanese companies that included President Enterprises, Prince Housing Development, Tainan Spinning, Kun Ching Textiles, President Chain Store, President International Investment, and Universal Cement had paid US$350 million for a tract of land in the eastern part of Taipei.[32] There was nothing unusual about this consortium, except for the fact that an investigation into the background of the companies reveals that each is a member of the *Tainanbang*.

Much of Taiwan's industry is reliant on retained earnings for expansion. Very few companies are attached to a finance arm, so even if they wanted to take on debt, it would be done at an arm's-length basis. For those larger business groups that incorporate a bank, there are strict and enforced rules that prohibit excessive lending within the group. Most enterprises are family-owned, but rarely have they sought to diversify beyond their core focus. Profits (and thus, the rate of return) are of a greater concern to Taiwan's entrepreneurs than notions of size, corporate grandeur, or market share.

Larger companies tend to have open, modern structures. One reason for this is that Taiwan's government operates various schemes to promote research and development, and only companies with sound and transparent accounting may qualify. The larger companies also have a reputation for being cautious and prudent. But perhaps their most important aspect is that they comprise only a relatively small part of the economy.

Bankruptcy laws in Taiwan are relatively simple and are enforced. Firms that become insolvent are readily pushed into bankruptcy, their assets seized and sold. The state makes little attempt to prop up ailing companies. All this encourages managers to operate well or face the consequences, which are quick and ruthlessly efficient.

There is corruption in Taiwan, but it's nowhere near as rampant as in some other Asian countries and considerable state resources are now being directed into rooting it out. Petty corruption isn't a major issue, as

Taiwan's government workers tend to be relatively well paid. It's the more spectacular cases of corruption that are more problematic. The trial of Hong Kong tycoon, Lim Por-yen, the patriarch of the property and textiles Lai Sun Group, for allegedly paying US$7 million to an official so that a Lai Sun subsidiary could secure a plot of land, received widespread coverage during 1998.[33] Taiwan is now a democracy, the vibrancy of which was demonstrated in March 2000 when the opposition Democratic Progressive Party's Chen Shui-bian was elected President. The political process helps to act as a constraint on corruption at senior government levels and does so in conjunction with a relatively unfettered media. All this is a far cry from the earlier Kuomintang (KMT) rule, which was famous for its corruption when it ruled the Chinese mainland prior to its fall to communism.

Taiwan is largely free from the ravages of crony capitalism too. The KMT does, however, have substantial business interests in Taiwan, but these serve as investments to generate earnings to run the party rather than for the benefit of any one individual or family. There are more than 100 KMT companies that operate in textiles, finance, real estate, petrochemicals, construction, and news media, to name a few. They are grouped under about seven holding companies.[34] Total assets may be as high as US$20 billion. The KMT's corporate holdings themselves suffered from many of the ills that plague companies around Asia — poor management, poor accountability, low transparency, a web of cross-shareholdings, and related-party transactions. They were also riddled with personality cliques, were overly bureaucratic, and were managed by party appointees, rather than by professionals. Past KMT governments rewarded the inefficiency and sloth of the party's companies by giving them supply and infrastructure contracts, cheap loans, and other privileges. In turn, whenever the KMT needed additional cash, it simply listed one of its many companies on the local stock exchange and raked in the proceeds of selling shares to independent shareholders.

But a concerted effort has been made since 1993 by the KMT's Business Management Committee to modernize and restructure. Together, the companies generate at least US$200 million annually to fund the political activities of the KMT. The KMT companies also have considerable investments overseas. Some are in Hong Kong, where the KMT's flagship company is the Hong Kong-Taiwan Trading Co. The United States, Singapore, Japan, Vietnam, and Indonesia are also home to the KMT's investments.

Apart from questions about whether the KMT should be involved in business at all, it is the Taiwan 'model' that mainland China should follow and certainly not the South-East Asian, Japanese, or South Korean models. These models have demonstrated ways to grow rich, but only Taiwan has shown how to do it without sowing the seeds of a collapse. Simply, there is no substitute for accountability, checks and balances, and competition to ensure high standards of corporate governance, not just in respect to the firms at the top, but across the entire economy. If China produced as much as Taiwan on a per capita basis, its economy would be more than twice the size of the United States. China should think about that.

THE SPOILING OF HONG KONG

So much for mainland China, but what about its glittering new prize, Hong Kong? Hong Kong was returned to China at midnight on June 30, 1997 after 150 years of British rule. Particularly during the latter years of their stewardship, the British were content largely to establish the legal and institutional framework within which commerce in Hong Kong could take place and then stood back. It's not the free market that made Hong Kong what it is today, but commerce that is unfettered *within* the confines of its legal parameters, yet constrained without exception beyond them. Make the exceptions and the framework loses its integrity altogether.

The results, as everyone knows, were astounding. The fabled barren rock of Hong Kong Island was turned into one of the most dynamic centers of world commerce with one of the world's highest per-capita incomes. The major concern with the handing back of Hong Kong to China was whether the Special Administrative Region (SAR) would be allowed to thrive, or whether it would be plundered. Nightmarish predictions of convoys of PLA tanks thundering their way into Central (Hong Kong's business heart) proved false. It's now clear that heavy-handed intervention from China isn't the real threat to Hong Kong, but rather a slow, unrelenting chipping away at its regulatory and corporate governance framework.

In China, people think that a market economy amounts to the buying and selling of goods and services for profit. They couldn't be more mistaken. After 50 years of the culture of socialism, they have yet to fully appreciate that trading for profit is only half the story — sound rules of the game and a sound framework that governs the buying and the selling are also preconditions for a successful market economy. Buying and selling without a strong framework that is impervious to favoritism degenerates quickly into corruption — this is what China has today. The rules must rule everyone, including the rulers.

The chipping away at Hong Kong's framework currently exists in several guises. There is the obvious danger of corruption. During the first six months of 1998, the number of incidences of corruption filed with Hong Kong's Independent Commission Against Corruption leapt by almost a quarter over the previous year — the largest increase in five years.[35] It's important not to read too much into one figure, but the result was hardly encouraging. Business people who haven't cut their teeth in a commercial environment that is bound by a strict, inflexible framework are moving into Hong Kong. This in itself will see a cultural shift in the regard for rules. Hong Kong's China-backed administration too has commenced the softening of the SAR's institutions. Exemptions to local laws have already been permitted. Hong Kong's media too is under threat.

Hong Kong's position is not unlike that of the proverbial boiling frog — drop it into hot water and it will jump out. Drop it into cold water, slowly heating it, and it will stay there. The PLA-tank scenario would have been hot water. Instead, the slow but sure erosion of Hong Kong's structure of rules means that it is being heated slowly.

The Mainland Buys up Hong Kong

Acquisition of assets in Hong Kong by mainland companies accelerated as the island's handover in 1997 neared. Many of the investors were state-owned companies — so their purchases amounted to the quasi-nationalization of assets in Hong Kong that previously had been in private hands.

Thousands of mainland companies now own assets in Hong Kong. During a six-month period in 1997, mainland-controlled China Everbright bought almost 8% of Hong Kong Telecom; 20% of fashion retailer, Theme International; 11% of engineering company, Chevalier International; and 10% of office equipment company Chevalier (OA) Group. It was around this time that Cosco bought 20% of Liu Ching Hing Bank. By the following year, China Resources had acquired a stake in the Hongkong Chinese Bank. CITIC owned Hong Kong's Ka Wah Bank. Its Hong Kong arm, CITIC Pacific, had a significant stake in the Hong Kong-based airlines, Cathay Pacific and Dragonair, as well as a 20% stake in China Light and Power, Hong Kong's main supplier of power. The PLA alone now controls a total of four companies listed on the Hong Kong stock exchange and, overall, operates more than 200 companies registered in the SAR. As has been mentioned, China's state-run press agency seems intent on turning itself into a diversified media conglomerate. In July 1997, it bought a 20% stake in the Hong Kong firm,

CCT Telecom. This acquisition was notable for the fact that CCT Telecom's share price shot up by 69% in the ten days *prior* to the deal being announced. There could barely be a stronger hint of insider trading than that. The steady commercial takeover of Hong Kong by China promises to change Hong Kong's corporate environment forever, but not necessarily for the better.

Red Chips

Hong Kong was built by the market, by the pursuit of profits from production. It wasn't built by the pursuit of profits from asset shuffling and rent-seeking. But that is precisely what has been a big preoccupation in the SAR since mainland companies first began to set up there and then list on the local stock exchange in significant numbers in the 1990s. The culprits are the so-called red-chip companies.

Typically, mainland SOEs establish a company in Hong Kong, then list it, or better still, simply buy a small (and therefore cheap) local company that's already listed, and then inject it with mainland assets. They are Hong Kong companies, but they have mainland parents.[36] Many red-chip companies are managed by mainland Chinese businessmen who claim strong connections back home. The hope that these businessmen would leverage on their connections to buy state-owned assets in China at favorable prices and then inject them into their Hong Kong companies saw a red-chip bubble build up throughout the 1990s. The prospects that the red chips might have an inside running on lucrative infrastructure and supply contracts also helped fuel the boom. The public's eagerness to hand over cash to buy shares in such companies saw a rush by various SOEs to set up red-chip arms in Hong Kong. By mid-1998, some 40 red chips were listed on the Hong Kong stock exchange.

Beijing Enterprises Holdings is a typical example. It was listed in Hong Kong in 1997 and is ultimately controlled by the Beijing municipal government. An eclectic range of assets has been poured into the company. There is a brewery, several food companies, a hotel, a travel company, two wineries, a toll-road, a water treatment plant, a department store group, and a half-share in the Beijing outlets of hamburger chain, McDonald's. It's difficult to see the synergies between toll-roads and beer, for example, but that didn't perturb investors. It was, after all, a red chip and they rushed to invest in the company. So many small investors withdrew their savings to send off with their applications for stock in the company's initial public offering, that inter-bank interest rates in Hong Kong were pushed higher as banks chased funds to cover the shortfall.

The fervor for red chips reached absurd heights just before Hong Kong's handover to China in mid-1997. Share prices soared way above all rational price–earnings multiples; perhaps the premium over each stock's underlying value could be best described as its *guanxi* premium. The high price–earnings ratios were way out of kilter with the more traditional stocks listed in Hong Kong — those that happened to be less risky and with far greater history and commitment to transparency and disclosure. The share price of the red-chip CITIC Pacific soared by 25% during the three months before the handover, for example, based on nothing more than the hope that its presumed good connections in China would lead to more sweetheart deals.

The red-chip bubble went the way of all bubbles — it burst within 12 months of the handover. By the end of 1997, the rapid acceleration of asset injections from the mainland had failed to materialize and the region-wide crash in stock markets saw a flight to quality stocks, which left the red chips among the hardest-hit stocks on the market. Beijing's announcement in early 1998 that it intended to abolish or merge 15 ministries delivered another shock. The reforms meant a substantial reordering of the relationships between the red chips and their supervising ministries. Some saw their ministries merged with others that formerly had been hostile. Others saw their ministries disappear altogether. Such is the fickle nature of *guanxi*.

China Telecom holds a lucrative monopoly over China's national fixed-line telephone network. Its owner, China's Ministry of Post and Telecommunications, went to great length to protect the monopoly. China Telecom also established a Hong Kong red chip, China Telecom (Hong Kong), which was awarded several mobile telephone licenses by the ministry. In 1994, the Ministry of Electronics Industry set up China Unicom in an attempt to break China Telecom's monopoly. Rather than act as an impartial referee and regulator, the Ministry of Post and Telecommunications did all it could to shackle China Unicom. The fledgling company was prevented from connecting to the national network, for example, so as to protect China Telecom's monopoly. The good connections that China Telecom's Hong Kong red-chip arm had with Beijing helped to make it a star red-chip stock. At least, that was the case until the March 1998 reforms saw the Ministry of Post and Telecommunications abolished and its functions folded into a new super-ministry, the Ministry of Information Industry. The problem for China Telecom was that the Ministry of Electronics Industry — China Unicom's patron — was also folded into the new ministry. So, the new ministry now encompasses several rather than one telecommunications companies. Within the space of a few months, China Telecom's monopoly began to crumble when China Unicom was allowed to link up with a fixed-line network based around the city of Tianjin. The red chip had lost its shine.

The reforms threw the price of the other stocks into confusion as well. CITIC and its Hong Kong red-chip arm, CITIC Pacific, found that they were no longer under the direct authority of China's State Council (effectively, the cabinet), but were placed under the control of China's central bank. Investors suspected that this meant both companies would lose their influence and ability to secure good deals in China. CITIC Pacific's share price plummeted accordingly by a third in the two months after the change was announced.

The flood of mainland Chinese companies into Hong Kong has become like a battering ram at the castle gates — and the gates are showing some damage. Corporate transparency and disclosure are being eroded. With state backing, corporate secrets take on an air of being state secrets, which raises the stakes for those interested in subjecting such companies to scrutiny. What is the precise position of Larry Yung, the head of CITIC Pacific, for example? In late 1996, he bought 291 million CITIC Pacific shares from its parent, CITIC, at a 24% discount to the market price. This yielded an immediate paper profit of around US$400 million. What portion of his shareholdings in CITIC Pacific are truly his and which portion belongs to the state of China? In 1993, Yung purchased a 335-hectare country estate and a 14-bedroom mansion in England that were once owned by Britain's former prime minister, Harold Macmillan. On what basis can an executive of an arm of the Chinese state make such private purchases? None of these things is clear, and yet CITIC Pacific is one of the most prominent companies listed on the Hong Kong stock exchange. The inner workings of many mainland-backed companies in Hong Kong — even those that are listed — are a mystery.

The resources devoted to Hong Kong's red chips has meant a diversion of venture capital from companies with a strong fundamental to those that are more speculative and priced on the basis of who knows who, rather than on their estimated earnings. The red-chip phenomenon has significantly damaged the allocative efficiency of the market for capital in Hong Kong, as investors sought easy earnings from asset shuffling in China rather than from the creation of new businesses and productive capacity. The red chips have succeeded in accentuating the Stock Exchange of Hong Kong's casino qualities. This much was acknowledged by the chairman of Hong Kong's Securities and Futures Commission in July 1997 when he said that the red chips were in danger of earning Hong Kong the reputation as the 'Wild West of the East.'[37] Hong Kong wasn't always like this. Of course, every stock exchange has its frontier stocks, but they don't normally succeed in becoming the market's glamour stocks. The red chips did just that.

Eroding the Framework

There have been several well-publicized erosions of the supremacy of law in Hong Kong since its return to China. Just a few days before the handcover, the local administration exempted a company called SAFE Investments, which had been set up in the territory by China's State Administration for Foreign Exchange, from the oversight of the local Securities and Futures Commission.[38] This exemption was granted even though the company was authorized to engage in foreign exchange transactions and to underwrite bond and share issues. Hong Kong's previously impervious legal framework had suddenly sprung a leak. This was a forerunner of things to come.

In early 1998, the Hong Kong administration decided not to prosecute the local branch of China's government-run Xinhua News Agency, when it had clearly broken the law. A local politician, Democrat Emily Lau, applied to the agency for information on any dossier it might hold on her as was her legal right. The agency was obliged to respond within 40 days. It only did so after a great deal of prompting and after ten months had elapsed. The lack of prosecution seemed to imply that Xinhua was above the law. It wasn't long before that supposition became reality. Hong Kong's Beijing-appointed legislature rushed through new laws that exempted Chinese-backed institutions such as Xinhua and the PLA from local laws. The leak in Hong Kong's legal framework threatened to turn into a flood. Many wondered if the local arm of SOEs might one day also be exempted from local laws. The thin edge of the wedge, after all, had just made its appearance.

The sanctity of the law looked as if it was dealt another blow when the local administration decided that newspaper proprietor, Sally Aw, wouldn't be prosecuted even she had been named by prosecutors as a co-conspirator in an attempt to artificially inflate the circulation figures of one of her newspapers. Aw's employees, on the other hand, were charged. The affair led to accusations that the law had been applied selectively. Many didn't miss the fact that Aw's newspapers had always taken a sympathetic approach toward China, that she had good connections with the Communist Party leadership in Beijing, and was a close friend of Hong Kong's chief executive, Tung Chee-hwa, who had actually served as a non-executive director of Aw's Sing Tao Holdings between 1989 and 1996.[39] In another instance in late 1998, Tung revealed that he had taken the unusual step of appealing to the authorities in

Beijing and Taiwan over the treatment of Hong Kong businessman and close personal friend, Lim Por-yen, during his corruption trial in Taiwan. Tung's move angered some Hong Kong legislators and evoked accusations of favoritism.[40] Had crony capitalism finally made its way to Hong Kong's local business community? There were those who were willing to argue that in a low-key way, perhaps it had — another thin edge of the wedge.

A friend of mine relayed another worrying sign to me. He had attended a meeting with one of the SAR's most senior government officials in mid-1998. During the meeting, the official let slip that Hong Kong's quarterly GDP figure had shown an unexpectedly sharp decline in output. There were two problems with this. The figure hadn't been released publicly and wasn't due to be for several days. Furthermore, and perhaps of most concern, the official belonged to an agency that had no reason to be privy to such information ahead of its release. It would be unthinkable for such commercially sensitive information to be parlayed around the bureaucracy of the United States, Britain, Australia, or even Hong Kong when it was under British administration. Perhaps it was a one-off occurrence. The fact that it occurred at all suggested otherwise.

But perhaps the move that shook confidence in Hong Kong's institutions more than anything was the Hong Kong administration's decision in August 1998 to step in and support the local stock market. Over a matter of days, the government spent almost US$16 billion buying up local blue-chip shares. Its splurge on the stock market was absolutely unprecedented. The strategy, which ultimately worked very well, was part of a bid to defend the Hong Kong dollar's peg to the U.S. dollar against hedge funds, but it left the government holding large stakes in big companies. It was a form of nationalization. At the time, a Hong Kong-based fund manager remarked to me that the SAR had in just two weeks succeeded in Hong Kong what the communist forces in China took more than two years to achieve after their takeover in 1949. The SAR's purchases made it the largest single shareholder in HSBC Holdings, the owner of HongkongBank, with almost 9% of its stock. More than 12% of Swire Pacific and around 10% of Li Ka-shing's Cheung Kong Holdings were also purchased.[41] While the intervention might have stopped speculative attacks by hedge funds, it heavily distorted the market. The SAR's decision to buy the various stocks had nothing to do with their underlying values. The administration simply went for the big ones. Allegations were also made of widespread insider trading just prior to the intervention.[42] The three days leading to the initial intervention saw the heaviest stock buybacks in 1998. Genuine buyers were also frustrated. Those who had been waiting for key stocks to become cheaply priced before buying them, found that the Hong Kong administration was to get in before them. The regulator had become a player. Hong Kong's free market system was now anything but free.

The Media

Hong Kong's other great institution — its unfettered and highly competitive media — is also under threat. Media outlets that criticize senior mainland officials run the risk that their proprietors' other interests (particularly if they are on the mainland) might be damaged in retribution. This is a subtle attack that is difficult to prove, so it's an ideal form of control. Chapter Three, Article 27 of the Basic Law for Hong Kong, of which was agreed upon by Britain and China in 1984, provides for 'freedom of speech, of the press and of publication.' This was no great concession on the part of China, when media proprietors can so easily be subtly pressured via their non-media assets.

Chapter Three, Article 23 of the Basic Law permits the China-backed Hong Kong administration to pass laws that prohibit 'treason, secession, sedition, subversion against the Central People's Government, or theft of state secrets.' All of this seems quite reasonable, until it comes to defining what each of these transgressions might actually be. What are 'state secrets,' for example, when increasingly much of what had been owned by the private sector in Hong Kong is now owned by arms of the Chinese state? The creeping quasi-nationalization of assets in Hong Kong means that, increasingly, many privately owned assets are seeping into the realm of the state. To what extent might media exposés of rorts and other misdemeanors within them constitute threats to 'national security' in future?[43] China sentenced to jail a Hong Kong newspaper's Beijing correspondent in 1993 for 12 years (he was released after three years) for reporting that China planned to sell a significant part of its gold holdings on the world market. The news scuttled the plans and the journalist was charged with reporting on 'state secrets.' Might revealing a plan by a red-chip company to spirit profits out of Hong Kong to its mainland parent, which would seriously disadvantage minority shareholders one day, be considered reporting on 'state secrets'? Now that Cosco owns 20% of Liu Ching Hing Bank, will it mean that one day its internal machinations will constitute 'state secrets'? Hopefully not, but then who would have thought that the Hong Kong administration would have become one of the largest single players in the local stock market?

Publishing the results of opinion polls is something that no longer appears to go down well in Hong Kong too. Local pollster Robert Chung claimed in July 2000 that the vice-chancellor of the widely respected Hong Kong University had warned him not to publish polls that were critical of SAR Chief Executive Tung Chee-Hwa and his administration and that if he continued to do so, university funds for his work would 'dry up.' Chung also claimed that the pressure originated from Tung's office although Tung's staff denied this. The episode not only raised questions about the freedom of speech in Hong Kong but also academic freedom.

One final indication of the fate that awaits Hong Kong's media was provided by the SAR's most senior civil servant, Anson Chan, during a late-1999 visit to the Australian city of Melbourne. I was in Malaysia at the time, but had written my regular column for the local *Age* newspaper on the erosion of Hong Kong's institutions. Anson Chan responded by making an unscheduled visit to the newspaper's offices on the day that the column appeared and vociferously complained about what I'd written. Most disturbingly, one of her main complaints was not so much what I'd said but the fact that I had said it while she was visiting Australia. As it happened, neither I nor the newspaper's editors was aware that she was in Melbourne. It seemed extraordinary that any civil servant feels that the media should take into account his or her travel plans when deciding what and when to publish. Slowly, Hong Kong's rulers are converting respect for office into respect for those in office. It will be the media that will be among the first institutions that must show appropriate obeisance.

SECTION 4

THE MINORITY THAT COUNTS

CHAPTER 11
Asia's Overseas Chinese

Asia's overseas Chinese are the most commercially successful minority group the world has ever seen. Much of what happens in Asia occurs because this group makes it happen. The group's rise, fall, and rise again is in its hands.

A former king of Thailand once famously referred to the overseas Chinese as the 'Jews of Asia.' But the overseas Chinese have been far more successful in their domination of many of Asia's economies than the Jews ever were in Europe. So, perhaps the Thai king had it wrong. Perhaps what he should have said was that the Jews are the overseas Chinese of Europe.

Apart from Japan and South Korea, business in Asia largely consists of ethnic Chinese businesses. In South-East Asia, they absolutely dominate business and yet, form only a small minority of the population. Approximately 6% of the combined population of the five main South-East Asian economies (Indonesia, Malaysia, the Philippines, Singapore, and Thailand) is ethnically Chinese, but this 6% controls perhaps as much as 70% of the region's private corporate wealth (see Table 11.1). This tiny minority also accounts for all but one of the 18 South-East Asia billionaires identified by Forbes magazine in 2000.

Table 11.1 Indicative Overseas Chinese Economic Power[1]
(Prior to the 1997–98 Asian economic crisis)

Country	Total Population (millions)	Ethnic Chinese as % of population	% Control of Ethnic Chinese over Private, Corporate, Domestic Capital
Indonesia	201	3.5	70
Malaysia	20	29	60
Philippines	73	2	55
Singapore	3.5	77	80
Thailand	60	10	75

The dominance of the Chinese is perhaps at its greatest in Indonesia. In fact, of Indonesia's top 300 conglomerates just prior to the 1997–98 economic crisis, 217 (72%) were either wholly or mostly owned by Indonesian-Chinese — not a bad result for an ethnic group that comprises just 3.5% of the country's population. The concentration of ownership was even greater if the assets of the top 300 conglomerates are considered — almost 83% were in the hands of Indonesian-Chinese. This disparity has grown, not reduced, in recent years (see Table 11.2). This is despite the Indonesian government's exhortation (and little else) for a better distribution of wealth between Indonesian-Chinese and indigenous Indonesians. The statistics say a lot about the business talents of the overseas Chinese — and also a lot about the Indonesian government. They also show a recipe for calamitous social unrest, which, as we shall see later, is precisely what Indonesia experiences on a regular basis.

Hong Kong and Taiwan, both of which are ethnically Chinese, are powerful business forces in the world in relation to their size. Their population aren't normally referred to as overseas Chinese, but like the Chinese of South-East Asia, the bulk of Hong Kong's Chinese and a significant minority of Taiwan's population aren't indigenous to their areas of residence. Around 1.5 million mainland Chinese poured into Taiwan when the communist forces took over the mainland in 1949. Similarly, in 1945, Hong Kong's population was just around 600,000, but ten years later, it swelled to 2.6 million, with the refugees from the mainland. In fact, one of the most influential groups in business in both islands isn't native to either place but to Shanghai. Technically, many of the Chinese in Hong Kong and Taiwan aren't overseas Chinese on account of their geographic location, but on account of their migrant status: in spirit, they are.[3]

Table 11.2   Indonesian-Chinese Control of Indonesia's Top 300 Conglomerates[2]

	1989	1993	1997
Number of conglomerates	197	212	217
% of the top 300	66	70.6	72.3
% of total assets	75.6	81.9	82.6

A BRIEF HISTORY

Approximately 29 million ethnic Chinese live in South-East Asia as of end-2000. They are most assimilated in Thailand, where because of a high degree of intermarriage, the precise number of Chinese is impossible to estimate; elsewhere, intermarriage has really only occurred at the edges. The forebears of the majority of Asia's overseas Chinese emigrated from China comparatively recently — mostly in the 19th and early 20th centuries. They were economic migrants, and often their departure from China coincided with famines or other upheavals. Today, China has 29 provinces, but the vast majority of Asia's overseas Chinese ancestrally come from just three of them: Guangdong (Kwangtung) and Fujian (Fukien) provinces on the South China Sea in the south-east corner of China, and Hainan province, an island off the southern tip of Guangdong. China may have over a billion people, but the overseas Chinese have cultural, family, and language ties with relatively few of them.

The early Chinese were usually dirt-poor when they first emigrated. Many died, and over time, the cumulative effects of high rates of mortality and the self-selection that migration entails, where those most able to succeed are usually the ones who leave, meant that South-East Asia soon played host to a hardened ethnic minority well equipped for survival and succeeding in business — because the best way to survive was to make money.

One of the key factors of their success was how they migrated. They didn't so much as pour into any one location, but fanned out across Asia. One clansman from a particular village in China would migrate to, say, Bangkok, and another would settle in Singapore. The way the Chinese settled across Asia ensured that they had a ready-made international network of connections within which they could trade and raise capital. The legacy today is a web of personal connections that allows commerce to proceed on the basis of trust — and if one betrays the trust, one is soon frozen out of trade and other business opportunities. It's a powerful enforcer. This type of commerce doesn't need sound laws to function. This is why the Chinese have been so astoundingly successful in South-East Asia. For much of the 20th century, practically all of South-East Asia has been relatively lawless, making the networks invaluable. The Singaporean who trades with a Bangkok relative or another contact knows that he will be paid. Pre-existing networks of trust mean that opportunities can be exploited quickly. While the trade of the overseas Chinese gets under way, their Western competitors must arrange buyers, letters of credit, and the like, which means losing time and opportunities.

The ability to do business in business environments that are so rough that they are no-go areas for anyone else, means that the Chinese get in on the ground floor when an economy is about to take off. It's the early bird that catches the highest margin. The overseas Chinese are currently instrumental in the build-up of the economies of Cambodia, Burma, Vietnam, and even Laos. U.S. companies rushed into Vietnam as soon as the U.S. embargo on trade with the country was lifted. Their collective enthusiasm resulted in little more than an investment bubble that has now burst. Overseas Chinese investors, on the other hand, have the local connections to protect their investments, and thus have a better chance of making them a success. As a Chinese businessman in Rangoon once said to me, the reason he had been successful in business was wherever he goes in Asia, even if he has never been there before, he is always able to find a fellow Chinese there with whom he can identify some connection. Sometimes the link could be their parents were born in the same village in China, they speak the same dialect, or even they are distant relatives. Once a link is established, it's a basis for trust and then trade. I once asked a senior manager in one of Robert Kuok's companies if his company intended to invest soon in Vietnam. 'No!' came the emphatic reply. 'Let the Americans go in there first and spend all their money. We will come in after and buy up their assets cheaply after they withdraw.'

Cambodia's commercial resurgence is almost an exclusively ethnic Chinese one. Around half of the country's ethnic Chinese population died or was murdered when the Khmer Rouge was in power. Such harsh punishment simply meant that their resurgence was even stronger. Cambodia's private sector now lies almost entirely in the hands of the overseas Chinese, and at least 90% of the foreign investment into the country has come from overseas Chinese sources.

The often conscious effort to fan out across borders has other advantages. If, say, one branch of a family or clan has all its wealth wiped out by a local natural disaster, riot, or some other calamity, the wealth of the entire family or clan isn't wiped out. This contrasts sharply to the indigenous people of South-East Asia. Entire families tend to be concentrated in the same village or locality. If they suffer the same calamity, all the family's capital is destroyed, leaving them with almost no chance to start again.

> *'The reason why I stress on spreading out in the region is the inherent danger of operating only in one country, particularly for a Chinese. Spread out the way we are, we can survive. A loss in one place would not wipe me out.'*

So said Y.H. Kwong, as quoted in an article in *Fortune* magazine in 1971 — one of the very first articles on the overseas Chinese.[4] Kwong was a Burmese-Chinese entrepreneur who had learned at first hand the virtues of fanning out. He was driven out of Burma in 1959 after the dictator, General Ne Win, came to power. This all but wiped out his holdings in the country. Kwong sought refuge in Hong Kong, where he was based until his death.

DIALECTS

The native tongue of almost three-quarters of all the Chinese who live in China is Mandarin (or some version of it), but it is the ancestral tongue of only a tiny proportion of the Chinese who live in South-East Asia — perhaps less than 5%. Mandarin is the language of northern China, but because most overseas Chinese have their ancestral origins in China's south-east, their languages are the languages of that part of China. In fact, the ancestral languages of most overseas Chinese are nothing like Mandarin; they are as foreign as French is to English. The one thing, though, that is the same is its written form. In the absence of some common third language or an interpreter, someone who speaks Cantonese and no Mandarin has the possibility of conversing with a Mandarin speaker by exchanging written notes.

The main dialects of the overseas Chinese in South-East Asia are linked closely to the province from which their ancestors originated.

- Hokkien is the dialect of those with origins in southern Fujian province
- Fuzhou is the dialect of those from around Fuzhou city in the northern tip of Fujian, Hokchia is the closely related dialect of those from the area around nearby Fuqing, and Henghua is the dialect of those from the Putian area, also in northern Fujian
- Hainanese (or Kheng Chew) is the dialect of those from Hainan province
- Cantonese is the dialect of those with origins in much of Guangdong province and Hong Kong
- Teochiu (or Chiu Chow, as it is spelt in Hong Kong) is the dialect of those from the Shantou area of northern Guangdong
- Hakka (or Keh) is the dialect of a group of Chinese who in recent centuries have been sprinkled throughout northern Guangdong, southern Fujian, and further inland.[5]

The Chinese who originated from Fujian province and who speak the Hokkien dialect form the largest single group among the overseas

Chinese. However, it's the Cantonese who are perhaps best known in the West because of their association with California's goldfields in the 1850s and their ubiquitous Chinese restaurants in most Western cities in more recent times. In 1996, the Second World Fujian Convention was held in Malaysia and more than 2,500 Fujian descendants from around the world attended it. Delegates came from San Francisco, Sydney, London, and Vancouver, as well as from around Asia, for three days of networking, conferencing, and dining. Increasing wealth, and fast and cheap international air travel have encouraged a resurgence in such overseas Chinese self-awareness.

When the Chinese groups arrived in South-East Asia, they tended to join their fellow clansmen in their trade or occupation. Specific occupations became synonymous not so much with the Chinese but with certain dialect groups. The link between occupation and dialect group has now largely been broken down — but it remains useful to explain much of what can still be seen today. The Hakkas usually owned the optical shops, Chinese pharmacies, and pawnbroking shops. It's no accident, for example, that it was the Aw family that created the world-famous Tiger Balm medicinal ointment. They were Hakkas, and Chinese medicine was their preserve. In 1996, Singapore's National Museum played host to an exhibition on Hakka culture. Among the sponsors were the Singapore Optical Trade Association, the Singapore Pawnbrokers Association, and the Singapore Chinese Druggists Association. The link between the Hakkas and these associations is obvious only to those aware of the historical links between dialect and occupation.

The association of dialect grouping with occupation might be dying out, but pockets of it still exist within Asia's Chinese communities. The Hock Hua Bank in Malaysia is still seen as very much a 'Fuzhou' bank. Many of its customers and most of its senior staff speak the Fuzhou dialect. Hong Kong's mid-sized Liu Chong Hing Bank is still regarded as a 'Teochiu' bank, with its majority shareholders, traditional clientele, and senior management having Teochiu origins. And in Penang, in Malaysia, most of the antique and curio stores are run by Teochius, which explains the preponderance of Thai artefact among their stock — most of Thailand's Chinese are Teochiu and Penang's antique-shop owners rely on their Teochiu networks to stock their shops.

INTERNATIONAL LINKAGES

There are dozens of international overseas Chinese associations around the world. Many have as their focus an international gathering usually once every two years, similar to the Fujian Convention already described. The one get-together that cuts across all Chinese dialects is the World Chinese Entrepreneurs' Convention. Its inaugural convention was held in Singapore in 1991. Since then, others have been held in Hong Kong, Bangkok, Vancouver, and Melbourne. They tend to be lavish three-day affairs that allow overseas Chinese business people from around the world to meet and form or renew acquaintances. The Singapore government helped the first convention get under way. It has also supported the establishment of the Chinese Heritage Centre in Singapore — a small body that commissions academic work on the overseas Chinese. What is particularly interesting about the center is its 16-member board of governors. It comprises a mix of academics and business people. With seven of its members being billionaire businessmen drawn from across Singapore, Thailand, Taiwan, and Hong Kong, the board is like a who's who of the overseas Chinese business world. There is Jeffrey Koo of Taiwan's massive Koos Group, Li Ka-shing of Hong Kong's Cheung Kong Group, and Chatri Sophonpanich of Bangkok Bank. Board meetings take on the appearance of a de facto world Chinese chamber of commerce more than anything else.

A number of international consortia of some of the most prominent overseas Chinese in Asia have been established in recent years so that they can jointly exploit opportunities. One of the first was the Malaysian-based Camerlin consortium. It brought together a group of ethnic Chinese investors that included the Quek family of Malaysia; the related Kwek family of Singapore; Haw Par Brothers, which is controlled by Singaporean billionaire banker, Wee Cho Yaw; Indonesian billionaire Liem Sioe Liong, and several Singapore government-linked companies. The grouping came together largely at the instigation of the Singapore government, although it is dominated and driven by Quek Leng Chan. One of its first acts was to launch a hostile takeover bid in 1995 for the Singapore-based beverage and condiments manufacturer, Yeo Hiap Seng Ltd. The bid wasn't successful, but when the consortium sold the stake in the company that it had amassed, it realized a profit of US$30 million. It made another US$10 million by buying and then selling shares in Australia's National Foods, in 1997. Another investment was a 20% stake in a New Zealand-registered company, Brierley Investments Ltd (BIL). The stake made Camerlin by far the largest shareholder in BIL and gave it effective control of the company. In turn, BIL's assets included the largest single shareholding in Australia's Fairfax Holdings, which publishes the *Australian Financial Review*, the *Sydney Morning Herald*, and Melbourne's *Age*, and almost half the equity in the London-based Thistle Hotels Group.

The day that BIL became the single largest shareholder in Fairfax, journalists at the Sydney headquarters of the *Australian Financial Review* jokingly claimed they would have to learn to speak with a New Zealand accent. They didn't understand what one of their South-East Asian correspondents meant when he said that actually, a Malaysian or an Indonesian accent might be more appropriate. The journalists at Australia's premier business daily hadn't realize that their newspaper had come into the orbit of a group of South-East Asian conglomerates.

Another predominantly ethnic Chinese international consortium to have been set up is KG Investments, a Hong Kong-based investment bank that was put together in 1997 by the Koo family of Taiwan. Their Koos Group holds half of the shares in the consortium. Bangkok Bank, Liem Sioe Liong, Wee Cho Yaw, Filipino-Chinese Alfonso Yuchengco, and CITIC (an investment arm of the Chinese government) hold most of the rest. The consortium was formed to look for investment opportunities around Asia.

But it's not all work and no play. There are plenty of more informal get-togethers as well. One of the more memorable was Liem Sioe Liong's 60th wedding anniversary, which was held in Singapore in April 1994. It was quite an event. Many of the invitees lived in Jakarta, so a schedule of charter flights from Jakarta to Singapore and back, paid for by Liem, accompanied the invitation, and invitees had to state their preferred flight time with their acceptance slip. The celebration was held at Singapore's Shangri-La Hotel, which is owned by Malaysian Robert Kuok, a business partner and fellow Fuzhou. The 2,000 guests were seated in the hotel's two ballrooms and ten other function rooms, all of which were connected by closed-circuit television. Two thousand servings of lobster and abalone and US$1 million later, Liem could certainly say that his wedding anniversary had been well and truly marked. The event brought together some of Asia's most influential business and political leaders — it was certainly an invitation that one would have been unwise to refuse.

Similarly, the Chinese in Indonesia, Thailand, and elsewhere are noted for their massive wedding receptions that are sometimes attended by thousands of people. Of course, not everyone enjoys these events, but that isn't the point. The real reason for attending them is to be seen to have attended, more than anything else — more form over content. The more people who do that, then the more 'face' given to the parents of the bridal couple. These weddings also provide an opportunity to catch up with others and renew old acquaintances — the lifeblood of overseas Chinese commerce. Wedding invitations aren't so much selectively and discreetly sent out, as broadcast to all and sundry.

Receiving one can occasionally be a source of annoyance more than anything else. The obligation to attend has been conferred, in duty-bound Asian society. The weddings are usually very formal and staid affairs. But the troubles begin before one is even inside. One of the biggest problems in attending a wedding reception with 3,000 others is working out where to park the car.

DIASPORA WITHIN THE DIASPORA

The overseas Chinese represent one of the world's great diaspora, but within it are a number of important sub-diaspora. Political upheavals in South-East Asia have at various times forced large sections of overseas Chinese communities to flee en masse. Although conditions might improve in their home country, often they continue to stay abroad and from their relatively safer vantage point, use their connections back home to trade and invest there. In this way, they become instrumental to the country's economic recovery and future development, and an important part of its external economy.

The Burmese-Chinese are a case in point. After General Ne Win (himself a half-Hakka) seized power in Burma in 1958, he cracked down on the businesses of the country's Chinese population. (Running the economy was never really Ne Win's strong point. One of his other acts was to replace some of the currency notes then in circulation with new ones in denominations of 15, 45, and 90 — numbers that his astrologer had told him were 'lucky.' Rocketing inflation and rapid exchange rate depreciation made transactions difficult enough, but having to conclude them in a currency whose denominations didn't add up to 100 made life just that little bit harder.) Many Burmese-Chinese had their businesses either closed down or nationalized, and they saw little point in staying on. Burma's Chinese, particularly in and around the capital, Rangoon (now Yangon), were largely either Cantonese, who tended to migrate to the predominantly Cantonese Hong Kong, or Hokkien, who tended to flee to Singapore where the Hokkien are in the majority. Today, Singapore and Hong Kong are major investors in Burma — but it's the Burmese-Chinese who live in Hong Kong and Singapore who have facilitated much of the investment.

Today, the military junta that governs Burma is one of the most oppressive in the world. In April 1997, the U.S. government decided to ban new U.S. investments to Burma in an attempt to force the junta from power. Eastman Kodak, Levi Strauss, Walt Disney, Hewlett-Packard, Foster's Brewing, Motorola, Heineken, Apple Computer, and Pepsi Co. are among the Western multinationals to have withdrawn their investments from

Burma. But while admirable in intent, the United States' prohibitions and other Western sanctions are ineffective. The large numbers of small investments — and sometimes not so small — that find their way to Burma via families and other connections simply won't be halted by calls for sanctions delivered from Western governments.

Examples of this type of foreign investment abound in Burma. The US$16.5 million refurbishment of Yangon's colonial-era Strand Hotel was undertaken by a consortium put together by Hong Kong-based Dutch-Indonesian businessman, Adrian Zecha, but the investment was facilitated by Bernard Pe-Win, an overseas Burmese appointed by Zecha to head the company in charge of the refurbishment. Further assistance was provided by Anthony Gaw, head of Hong Kong's Pioneer International, and another foreign-based Burmese-Chinese.[6] Another foreign company with local connections to have invested is Singapore's PL International. It invested in a US$6.4 million joint venture, Myanmar Seafoods Ltd, in Yangon. The principal of the company, Peter Lee, was born in Burma but now lives in Singapore. Lee's brother, who still resides in Burma, was to handle the Burmese end of the operations.[7] Another is Robert Kuok's Shangri-La Group, which constructed a hotel in Yangon.[8] Kuok himself doesn't have Burmese origins, but Halpin Ho, a Burmese-Chinese now resident in Bangkok, helped to facilitate his initial investments. These are the types of investments made possible by overseas Chinese networks and which Western sanctions cannot stop.

The Indonesian-Chinese who live outside Indonesia are another large overseas Chinese sub-diaspora. One of the first major outflow of Chinese from Indonesia occurred in the late 1950s, after the government introduced laws prohibiting ethnic Chinese from operating shops and other businesses in rural areas. The country's economy then was absolutely dominated by rural production, so the legislation was repressive indeed. Coupled with serious rioting (an Indonesian-Chinese friend of mine lost his grandmother during these riots — she was beaten to death in a town in central Java), Indonesia's Chinese soon got the message. They fled the country by the hundreds of thousands. Beijing even dispatched several 'rescue' ships, which sailed to Indonesia to pick up the Indonesian-Chinese so they could resettle in China. For many, the move to communist China meant a leap from the frying pan and into the fire, so they quickly made their way to Hong Kong. Today, there are at least 250,000 Indonesian-Chinese who live in Hong Kong. They keep a low profile except at sporting events where, say, Hong Kong might be playing Indonesia in the world badminton championships. Most of Indonesia's top badminton players are ethnic Chinese, and such matches in Hong Kong play host to the curious spectacle of a huge number of

Chinese faces in the audience raucously supporting the Indonesian side against Hong Kong. They are Hong Kong's Indonesian-Chinese.

There is also a big Indonesian-Chinese community that lives permanently in Singapore. It has used its connections with Indonesia to invest there. One of the more prominent examples is Ong Tjoe Kim, who left Indonesia for Singapore in 1957 and set up the Metro Department Store chain, the flagship of which has a key location in Singapore's main shopping district of Orchard Road. Ong has expanded Metro to Indonesia, where there are now several large Metro stores.

CHRISTIAN NETWORKING

Although dialect and family links are still important among the older generation of overseas Chinese businessmen in Asia, they are less so among the younger generation. This isn't to say that networking and relationships are no longer important. They are, but it is the mode that has changed. Many Asian families now select the business school in the United States to which to send their children on the basis of the connections they might make there with the sons and daughters of other Asian business families. Friendships made at university tend to endure, and often not by accident. A conscious effort is made to maintain them. After all, you never know where someone might end up and how they might be of use.

Classmate connections are important, but one of the most important venues for fervent networking among overseas Chinese in Asia has become the church. A growing number of overseas Chinese business people are Christian — and often they are fundamentalist. In Indonesia, the vast majority of ethnic Chinese are Christian. (This tends to compound their problems because, after all, they are living in the world's largest Moslem nation.) A growing number of Chinese in Malaysia and Singapore are also Christian, as is just over 7% of Taiwan's population.[9] Inreasingly, overseas Chinese conglomerates start the business day with morning prayer meetings. Indonesian-Chinese businessman, Ferry Teguh Santosa, conducts regular prayer meetings at the Jakarta headquarters of his Ometraco Group, as do Mochtar and James Riady at the offices of their Indonesian Lippo Group. Indonesians Wilson Pribadi of Napan Group and Peter Gontha, a part-owner of the Soeharto-controlled Bimantara Group, are also strong Christians — they attend the same non-denominational church in Jakarta as the Riady family and have joined their respective companies together in several business groups, particularly the massive petrochemicals companies, Tri Polyta Indonesia and Chandra Asri. Hong Kong's Thomas Kwok and his family, who control Sun Hung Kai Properties, one of Hong Kong's four major property developers, are also staunch Christians. They participate in Christian outreach programs around Hong Kong. They are just a few of Asia's senior business figures to have fervently embraced Christianity.

Christian networking can pay dividends, and not just in the ecclesiastical arena. Some of the senior executives of the Bank Danamon Group in Jakarta, which is owned by the Indonesian-Chinese Atmadjaja family, are strong Christians. They are said to have had a direct line to the country's indigenous but Christian finance minister, Johannes Sumarlin, who was dropped from the Cabinet in 1993. Family patriarch, Usman Atmadjaja, and Sumarlin apparently attended the same church. This link proved helpful when Bank Danamon needed quick access to government credit to keep it solvent. (By 1998, when the bank again needed to be bailed out, there was a Moslem finance minister in place. The bank was seized by the government.) But one of the more prominent overseas Chinese Christian networks in Asia is that which centers on the Indonesian-Chinese Riady family, who own the Lippo Group.

With Chinese chambers of commerce and other Chinese associations banned in Indonesia, the country's ethnic Chinese have few opportunities open to them to legally meet in groups. Christianity is one of the several state religions permitted under Indonesia's constitution, so Christian get-togethers provide one way in which Indonesia's Chinese can legally assemble. The Riadys' Lippo Group and the Maspion Group, which is owned by Indonesian-Chinese Alim Husin and his family and based in the Indonesian commercial city of Surabaya, heavily support Christian networking events in Indonesia. One such event took place in a five-star resort on the island of Bali in late November 1997. The three-day Christian fellowship meeting was organized by a group of Surabaya-based Christian Chinese. Attendees included Mochtar Riady, and the Maspion Group family members. Ostensibly, the meeting was for Christian fellowship, but with a heavy overlay on dining and sporting activities. In reality, it was a big networking exercise, with shared religious beliefs being the common factor. More than 100 Chinese Christian from around Indonesia attended the event.

Chinese chambers of commerce were never solely devoted to business, either. Their most important function was to help the members of the Chinese business community keep in touch with one another. In this regard, Christian churches across Indonesia have replaced the traditional role of the now banned Chinese chambers of commerce.

PERSECUTION AND SUCCESS

The Malaysian government introduced its New Economic Policy (NEP) in 1971 after communal rioting in 1969 led to the deaths of 196 Malaysian-Chinese. The NEP was designed to expand the economy and then give indigenous Malaysians (the *bumiputras*) a bigger share of the larger pie. The program met with moderate success in terms of evening out the share of national income and wealth among the various ethnic groups. But in terms of buying peace among them, it has been a great success — and this is the real measure by which it should be judged. At first, Malaysia's Chinese hated the NEP. While it didn't act to directly distribute their existing wealth away from them, it put in place social measures such as restricting the number of places in Malaysia's universities for the Chinese and forcing all firms (which were mostly Chinese-owned) to hire quotas of indigenous employees. Many Malaysian-Chinese are now very supportive of the NEP and its successor. The employment quotas are no longer the burden they once were because the NEP's education policies have meant that there is now a class of well-trained indigenous Malaysians who are useful and productive employees. So, what started out as a shotgun wedding between indigenous Malaysians and Malaysian-Chinese, is now more of a wedding of mutual consent. And besides, many Malaysian-Chinese concede that sharing business opportunities is a better alternative to having their businesses burned down. There can be profit in pragmatism. This isn't to say that Malaysia's race-based redistributive policies are perfect. It has, for example, bred a class of *bumiputra* entrepreneurs who are coddled by the state and who have come to expect that the government will find ways to bail them out when they get into trouble — but perhaps this is an acceptable price for racial harmony.

Shortly after the street riots that swept through parts of Jakarta in April 1996, I attended a dinner party at a house in the up-market Jakarta suburb of Menteng. Most of the guests, like the host, were ethnic Chinese. The food was fully catered from the local Grand Hyatt and was served amid the splendor of gilt French rococo furniture and Han dynasty pottery figures. I asked the middle-aged Chinese woman on my left where she was during the riots and if they had affected her. She replied that they had not and, further still, she and her husband had no idea the riots were taking place because at the time they were on 'the island.' 'Which island?' I asked. 'Our island,' she replied. Money can buy a certain amount of protection, even in Indonesia.

There is no NEP-equivalent in Indonesia. Indonesia's Chinese have been deliberately encouraged to dominate the private sector. Throughout his 32-year reign, President Soeharto sought to actively encourage a Chinese entrepreneurial class in the manner that Jews were permitted to the Spanish Court of the 15th century. No matter how successful in business they became, their ethnicity precluded them from ever becoming a political threat. The most prominent Jew-equivalents at the court of Soeharto were Liem Sioe Liong and Bob Hasan. Both are ethnic Chinese and became billionaires from the privileges, monopolies, and other concessions that Soeharto granted them. Both also acted as the president's most senior advisors on matters ranging from the economy to his personal finances. No matter how big in business they became, they would always be dependent on and never threaten Soeharto.

Almost any instance of violence in Indonesia quickly develops into an ethnic pogrom, with Chinese shophouses being burned down and looted. A spectacular example was the riots of May 1998, when IMF-induced price rises and dissatisfaction with Soeharto saw riots break out across Indonesia. Thousands of Chinese temporarily fled to Singapore, Hong Kong, and Australia, while their houses and shops back home were ransacked and destroyed by angry mobs. Many of the Chinese women who remained were subject to organized mass rape, particularly in Jakarta's Chinatown district, a fact the Indonesian government at first denied but later confirmed. And symbolically, the original two-story Jakarta home of Liem Sioe Liong was looted and burned.

The reluctance of the Indonesian government to introduce measures to curtail Chinese commercial power has bred enormous discontent among indigenous Indonesians. The Chinese are accused of having divided loyalties — but then it's probably difficult to feel too nationalistic when your house and your neighbors' have just been burned down. But perversely, the cycle of hatred and violence against the Chinese simply ensures their success.[10] The usual explanation for their success — that the Chinese 'like hard work,' value education, and are 'good' at business — have a ring of truth, but then these social characteristics tend to be present in overseas Chinese communities everywhere. It's the constant persecution and threat of violence that have made Indonesia's Chinese go that little bit further.

The vast majority of the Indonesia Chinese were born in Indonesia. Many have little direct knowledge of China and most have never been there. Even so, they face one of the most culturally oppressive regimes anywhere. All the symbols and celebrations normally associated with Chinese culture are banned or frowned upon in Indonesia. Lion dancing in the streets is largely banned. Chinese chambers of commerce are also banned. The open display of Chinese characters is frowned upon. Chinese-language schools are banned. Entry to the civil service and the military is prohibited. And at least up until 1998, the identity cards that all Indonesians must carry had a code that identified the holder as being either Chinese or not. This overt discrimination against Indonesia's Chinese is apparent even before one's arrival in the country. The customs forms handed out to passengers on flights bound for Indonesia seek declarations on all the usual nasties such as firearms, narcotics, and pornography, but Chinese medicines or anything marked with Chinese characters must also be declared — surely, the ultimate ignominy.

Indonesia's Chinese are never allowed to forget their migrant heritage, and yet are never allowed to celebrate it. The pressure is unrelenting. Consequently, they react like most other pressured minorities — they seek to protect themselves by making money. Money buys a house with high walls, security guards, the silencing of harassing government officials and, ultimately, a hasty departure from Indonesia should the need arise. For Indonesia's Chinese, wealth buys the security their government denies them.

Many forecast the end for Indonesia's Chinese population during the May 1998 riots, but actually the opposite would prove true. Persecution encourages minorities to adopt defensive strategies — and for the Chinese, one such strategy is wealth creation. What's more, overseas Chinese capitalism works best in business environments that are chaotic and where the rule of law is absent. The ability of the overseas Chinese to do business within their networks and to pull in capital as required from family members and other associates from overseas, allows them to triumph where others fail. It's only when markets mature and a sound rule of law is established that others can effectively compete with the overseas Chinese. Under these circumstances, the comparative advantage of the overseas Chinese is eroded and they must compete alongside everyone else on the same basis. It's for this reason that the chaos that is the Indonesian economy allowed its 3% Chinese population to control as much as 70% of the private local capital. But in a highly structured and mature economy such as Australia, where the Chinese also comprise about 3% of the total population, they are not spectacularly successful, and their wealth is proportionate to their numbers. The paradox of persecution is that it simply hardens the resolve of the persecuted and thereby helps their future success. For the overseas Chinese, their networks guarantee it.

What the 1998 upheavals will do for Indonesia's Chinese is to simply ensure that their absolute domination of the Indonesian economy will be more prolonged than it otherwise would have been. Not only that, but many Indonesian-Chinese left Indonesia — probably permanently — because of the riots and killings, but many remained behind. The effect of this is to rejuvenate the Indonesian-Chinese diaspora that exists outside Indonesia. And these will be an important source of capital and trading networks for those Indonesian-Chinese that remain in Indonesia, which will add further to their commercial ability and power.

SECTION 5

KINGS, CRONIES, AND PRESIDENTS

CHAPTER 12

Royal Business

The Sultan of Brunei, the family of the King of Malaysia and the King of Thailand are all big in business. The wealth of the first is probably overexaggerated, the wealth of the second is greatly underexaggerated, and as for the third — they're just getting started.

Asia was once just like Europe — dotted with royal families and their palaces. Principalities and sultanates existed all over the region. Usually, they were very small in size. The Indonesian island of Bali, which is much smaller than the southern half of England, at one stage was home to no less than nine separate kingdoms whose kings were all completely convinced of their self-importance. Today, very few kings and queens of Asia survive in any meaningful way. Those who do, usually must make do by going into business — and some have been very spectacular indeed. This chapter looks at three of them. The first, the Sultan of Brunei, is famous around the world for his extravagance, although as will be explained, the true extent of his wealth is open to question. The second, the current King of Malaysia, has gone into business in the most conventional of ways and today, his family's corporate interests form one of the country's more important business groups. Finally, the King of Thailand isn't known for his business acumen or his corporate holdings, but in fact is one of the richest men in the world today.

THE SULTAN OF BRUNEI, INCORPORATED

It was 1 a.m., Sunday morning. Everything was a blaze of colored lights. The moist, tropical air pumped with heavy metal music, and I was strapped into a seat that was slowly ascending the 30-meter-high steel tower of a device named the 'Freefall.' Once at the top, there were several seconds' view of the surrounding sea of flashing lights — until the controller flicked a switch, and I and several others went plunging to the ground in a terrifying but brief ride. Had I really found a Moslem paradise? For those few seconds, it seemed more like a Christian hell. I certainly wasn't anywhere regular. I was in Brunei.

Jerudong Park, on the outskirts of Bandar Seri Begawan, the capital of the tiny, oil-rich state of Brunei Darussalam, features an enormous amusement park. It's filled with dozens of rides set among tropical gardens, waterfalls, and fountains. The park is perhaps the most extraordinary feature of an extraordinary country. But then, in Brunei, there are many things that are out of the ordinary. Entry to the park is free to all, as are all the rides. The park, which opened in 1994, was a gift to the people of Brunei from their sultan. Music blasts from loudspeakers throughout the grounds and it stays open until 2 a.m. daily. Next door is a massive sound stage and auditorium that has a seating capacity of 4,000 people, plus private, royal boxes for the sultan and his family. Michael Jackson, Stevie Wonder, and Whitney Houston have all performed here. Again, the concerts were free to Bruneians — all paid for by the sultan. All this sits rather oddly with Brunei's state religion of Islam and with the fact that not only is alcohol banned throughout the country, but root beer is perhaps the nearest thing to alcohol you can drink during any flight on the country's international carrier, Royal Brunei Airlines. Jerudong Park wasn't my idea of an Islamic paradise, but judging by the several thousand Bruneians who had flocked to it on the evening I was there, I was in a minority.

Everyone knows that Brunei is rich, but little is known of the business structure of its ruling family. Its members go to enormous lengths to hide their assets, and the secrecy raises a lot of questions. Exactly what are those assets? The sultan is usually billed as being fabulously wealthy, but does this stand up to scrutiny? He certainly has the trappings of wealth, but has he the wealth itself? But first, some background on the country and its ruler.

Brunei, which sits on the coast of the island of Borneo next to the Malaysian state of Sarawak, has a population of just 300,000. Bruneians are said to have the highest per-capita income in the world, thanks largely to the country's oil and gas earnings. The current head of state and prime minister, since his father abdicated in 1967, is Sultan Hassanal Bolkiah. The sultan was generally regarded as the richest man in the world until recently, when he was overtaken by Microsoft founder, Bill Gates; his wealth is routinely estimated at close to US$30 billion. Stories of his personal profligacy are legendary, if not a little clichéd. His oft-cited vital statistics are: he owns 165 Rolls-Royces, Bentleys, and other cars; has a fleet of private jets and helicopters; has a palace with 1,788 rooms and domes gilded in 24-carat gold; and once famously left a US$170,000 tip for the staff at a hotel in Cyprus. Such snippets tend to be regaled uncritically and *ad nauseam* in newspaper articles, that almost without exception they are in the 'gee-whiz' genre. Certainly, the order of magnitude of the extravagance is undeniable. It is also of very recent origin. Prior to the oil price hikes of the early 1970s, Brunei was an unremarkable, sleepy backwater. In the early days, when the current sultan was growing up, the royal family lived in a wooden house built on stilts over the Brunei River. The family is royal — but it's also *nouveau riche*.

Today, the sultan's palace is off-limits to outsiders, but they are free to visit his polo club. The club really must be seen to be believed. It's so absurdly lavish that words really do fail to describe the enormity of it all. Suffice to say, when a polo match is interrupted by rain, the sultan is said to have two helicopters from the Royal Brunei Airforce fly in and hover over the polo ground until it has dried out sufficiently so that play can resume. Nearby, is the Jerudong Park Medical Centre, a hospital that was purpose-built for the royal family. (It must be one of the few hospitals in the world that has a polo club as its postal address.) It looks more like a Grand Hyatt than a hospital and has rooms that more than match its lavish exterior. Originally, it was used only by members of the royal family, but with such a restricted clientele, its medical staff weren't getting enough practice to maintain their skills. Its very exclusivity led to a deterioration in the quality of the service offered, so in the interest of the health and safety of the royal family, the hospital was opened to commoners as well. Then there are the mosques. They too are astonishingly grand. The dome and minarets of Brunei's relatively new Jame 'Asr Hassanil Bolkiah Mosque is coated in the 24-carat gold sheathing that has become standard in the country, and the interior is set with Italian marble and onyx. Somewhat unusual for a mosque, it's fully air-conditioned, and infrared beams activate the water taps in the bathing areas where worshippers undergo their ablutions before prayers.

The sultan has two wives. The first is his cousin Saleha whom he married in 1965 and the second is Mariam whom he married in 1981. He and Saleha live in the main palace, the Istana Nurul Iman, while Mariam lives in a second palace, the Istana Nurul Izzah, on the outskirts of the capital. Together, the two queens have borne the sultan ten children. The eldest, a son, Al-Muhtadee Billah, is the sultan's heir apparent and was designated the crown prince in a lavish ceremony in 1998. An official photograph of the sultan with photographs of his two queens on either side are displayed in most shops and houses in Brunei. The sultan's unusual family arrangements must cause endless protocol headaches for visiting heads of state and other notables. A photograph in a book published in 1996 by the Brunei government to commemorate the sultan's 50th birthday shows the wife of Japan's then-prime minister, Toshiki Kaifu, sitting on a couch between the queens at the Istana Nurul

Iman in 1991, seemingly unsure of which wife to address, and so looking ahead instead.

The Bruneian royal family is large, and the Bruneian capital is dotted with palaces and homes for the assortment of minor royals. When driving around Bandar Seri Begawan, one can see palaces in various states of construction. Locals show little interest in who is to occupy each new palace — one inconsequential royal is little different from any other, and open speculation about the family isn't encouraged. The sultan himself, is one of ten children. He has six sisters and three brothers. The brothers — Prince Jefri, who until 1997 served as the finance minister; Prince Mohamed, who is foreign minister; and Prince Sufri — have all enjoyed higher profiles than the sisters, who are more or less invisible. Like the sultan, two of the brothers have taken multiple wives. Prince Jefri has four and Prince Sufri, three. Perhaps, when money gushes effortlessly from oil wells, what else is there to do?

Prince Jefri is the family's most controversial member. In 1997, a former Miss USA attempted to sue both the sultan and Prince Jefri because Prince Jefri had allegedly been responsible for luring her to Brunei ostensibly to undertake modeling work but actually to work 'as a sex toy.' The former beauty pageant winner claimed she was kidnapped and held in a royal compound for 32 days and that her passport was taken from her. She claimed she was one of several young American women who have been brought to Brunei for the purpose. Her deposition to the Central District Court of California raised the specter of teams of young women being shuttled by jet to and from Brunei to entertain various members of the Brunei elite on an ongoing basis.[1] Elsewhere, it was alleged that the sourcing of women from the United States first began in 1993.[2] The US$90 million lawsuit was eventually dropped when the judge ruled that the sultan and Prince Jefri were covered by the US Foreign Sovereign Immunities Act.[3]

The following year, Prince Jefri was again the subject of a court case filled with suggestions of sexual intrigue, this time in London. Two of his former business colleagues claimed in a suit that he had paid £21 million for a house in London's Park Lane where he could 'keep his prostitutes away from the public eye.'[4] They also claimed to have sold the prince millions of pounds worth of luxury goods over many years, including ten custom-made watches with figures of copulating couples on the faces.[5] The court case produced other information on the prince's London activities, and particularly his real estate investments there. Another mansion had been created by merging two separate mansions in London's upmarket Hampstead, and half of the merged building comprised a three-story gymnasium. The prince had acquired yet another London home at 45 Park Lane, for £90 million, which had formerly been the Playboy Club. But fine homes are not Prince Jefri's only indulgence. He bought a 55-meter yacht, which is imaginatively named 'Tits.' Its two lifeboats are apparently dubbed 'Nipple 1' and 'Nipple 2.'[6]

Prince Jefri's penchant for ostentation and largesse caught up with him, however. In February 1997, he resigned as Brunei's finance minister. He and the sultan had a falling out and there were rumors of large sums of money that had gone missing. The details were sketchy and the Brunei government provided no information other than to note that the sultan had replaced Jefri as finance minister. The prince did take some remedial action — he appointed the United Kingdom's second-largest public relations agency, Lowe Bell Communications, to represent him. But it was too little, too late. The following year his private business empire collapsed and investigations began into billions of dollars that were missing from the Brunei Investment Agency (BIA), which Prince Jefri headed. But more on this later.

The Sultan in Business

Details of the sultan's personal business arrangements and those of the rest of his family are notoriously difficult to obtain. The family's financial advisors have secrecy provisions included in their contracts, as are the contracts of anyone else who is contracted to do work for the sultan and the rest of the Bolkiah family. The secrecy clause is stringently enforced. For example, almost all of the work done in Brunei on the family's many palaces and the guest-houses that are built for visiting dignitaries is sub-contracted to foreign consultants. But before they commence work, the consultants must sign strict secrecy agreements about the work they do in Brunei. These agreements go as far as preventing architects and interior designers from retaining photographs of their completed work for inclusion in their work portfolios. Those who have retained such images to show prospective clients have been threatened with legal action by lawyers acting on behalf of the Bolkiah family. Many members of the royal family also prefer to hire personal staff who are Burmese rather than locals as locals are more likely to gossip about the nature of their work.

The sultan and each of his three brothers have their separate holding companies. The sultan has the Brunei Investment Agency. Prince Jefri's private assets, until 1998, were grouped under the Brunei-based Amedeo Holdings. Prince Mohamed has his Baiduri Holdings, and Prince Sufri, the Primal Group.

The sultan's business interests within Brunei are structured relatively simply. The Brunei government has a 50% interest in Brunei Shell, the other 50% being owned by the Dutch petroleum Shell Group. Brunei Shell has two main subsidiaries: Brunei Shell Petroleum (the main oil and gas explorer, producer, and refiner), and Brunei LPG (which also includes Japan's Mitsubishi Corporation). In turn, Brunei LPG owns Brunei Coldgas, which is responsible for transportation and sale of LPG to Japan. The Brunei government (and hence the sultan) has another oil exploration company, Jasra International Petroleum. It has formed joint ventures to exploit new offshore oil discoveries with New Zealand's Fletcher Challenge Energy and Elf Aquitaine of France.

The sultan's overseas investments are principally managed by the BIA, which doubles as the Brunei government's investment arm. But since there is no separation between the government and the state in Brunei, and the head of state is the sultan (the government and his ministers all operate out of his principal residence, which tends to underscore this), then effectively what belongs to Brunei belongs to the sultan. The BIA is believed to be assisted in its task by a coterie of financial advisors that include Morgan Grenfell and Citibank of the United States, the Union Bank of Switzerland, Nomura and Daiwa of Japan, Macquarie Bank of Australia, and Singapore's Government Investment Corporation.[7] Records filed with the US Department of Justice show that the BIA uses Kaye, Scholer, Fierman, Hays and Handler, one of New York's 20 largest law firms, to handle its US legal matters. In 1995, it paid the firm just over US$2 million to provide legal advice and assistance in connection with Internal Revenue Service matters and its US real estate holdings.[8]

It is usually assumed that the principal holdings of the agency comprise a portfolio of blue-chip stocks and bonds, but that's pure speculation — the agency has never opened its books for inspection. There are some direct investments, however. A series of holding companies are used to manage the agency's direct investments. They include Sejahtera, Inc. in the United States; the Brunei Investment and Commercial Bank, which has holdings in Australia; and Audley Hotels and Resorts, which is registered in Singapore but based in London.

Also, there is a direct stake in the US$700 million Asian Infrastructure Fund. Among the other investors in this fund are U.S. billionaire George Soros and Hong Kong billionaire Li Ka-shing. The BIA also owns 9% of Malaysia's national airline, Malaysian Airlines. There are three cattle stations or ranches in northern Australia, which collectively cover 6,000 square kilometers — more than the total size of Brunei. The three stations, Scott Creek, Willeroo, and Opium Creek, supply Brunei with almost all of its fresh beef. The agency's Australia-based Glencoe Group of Companies owns the properties. Another Glencoe Group member is the Brunei Property Development Co, which undertakes residential real estate development around Australia's small northern city of Darwin.

In 1996, the BIA paid just over US$130 million to become the biggest single investor in Australia's Sydney-based Macquarie Bank (it sold out in late 1998). A year later, the agency was reported to have bought a big chunk of the French smart card manufacturer, Gemplus.[9] The agency has also been rumored to have made many other substantial purchases in recent years, including one of the twin Petronas Towers in Malaysia — billed as the world's tallest — but almost invariably, the rumors are proven false.

Among the hotels owned by the agency are the luxury Hotel Meurice in Paris, which was bought for around US$100 million from the Aga Khan, the spiritual head of the Moslem Ismaili sect, and was expensively refurbished in 2000; the Beverly Hills Hotel on Los Angeles' Sunset Boulevard, purchased for US$185 million and then later refurbished for an additional US$100 million; London's famous Dorchester Hotel; Singapore's Holiday Inn Crowne Plaza and the Hyatt Regency Hotel; and 95% of the Nusa Dua Beach Hotel in Bali (the other 5% is owned by Siti Hardiyanti Rukmana (Tutut), the eldest daughter of Indonesia's former president, Soeharto). In 1996, the BIA attempted to buy the famous Hotel George V in Paris, but was outbid by Saudi Arabia's Prince Alwaleed. The sultan is known to have bought several homes around the world, including an estate in Las Vegas, a mansion in Vancouver, and another in Auckland, New Zealand, for which he paid almost US$4 million.

The domestic investment arm of the Brunei government — and hence the sultan — is Semaun Holdings, which was established in 1994. However, its function is not so much to make profits but to stimulate private business activity in Brunei itself. It is chaired by Brunei's minister of industry and primary resources and is specifically charged with investing in all the sectors that the sultan believes will be the growth areas of the future: biotechnology, computer technology, halal food processing, industrial estate management, downstream oil and gas industries, pharmaceutical research, silica-based industries, and tourism. It is the government's main vehicle to try to reduce the Bruneian economy's almost total dependence on oil and gas.

How Rich is the Sultan, Really?

Determining the sultan's precise wealth is difficult for several reasons. The family's strong preference for secrecy is one. But the most important difficulty is definitional. Little differentiation is made between the wealth of the state of Brunei and the sultan's personal wealth. For all intents and purposes, he *is* the state. But how far does that go? Does it mean that all the assets managed overseas by the state-owned BIA should be taken as the personal property of the sultan? Most analysts do. But then, does this mean that all public works undertaken by the government in Brunei also belong to the sultan, which implies that highways and sports stadiums are his too? Then what about the unexploited oil and gas reserves onshore and just off Brunei's coast? The convention seems to be to treat those assets that are tradable and of a personal nature (palaces, cars, and Lear jets) as part of the sultan's wealth along with Brunei's portfolio of investments overseas. Thus, that part of Brunei's natural wealth that hasn't been exploited isn't included. The sultan cannot, presumably, put a 'for sale' sign up on his country and sell it to the highest bidder.

The sultan and Bill Gates tussle it out each year in the world's lists to be the richest person in the world. In 1998, Gates shot ahead. Soaring Microsoft stock saw his estimated wealth reach US$51 billion, according to *Forbes* business magazine. The sultan came in second with an estimated US$36 billion. By 1999, the sultan's wealth was down to US$30 billion. However, Bill Gates' wealth is readily quantifiable — one need only multiply his shareholding in Microsoft by its current share price to assess the bulk of his wealth. With the sultan, it is a different matter. There is no public record, and the sultan goes to great lengths to ensure that there aren't any. It is even actually illegal under Bruneian law to attempt to estimate Brunei's foreign reserves, for example. *Forbes* put the sultan's wealth at US$30 billion–36 billion, but how accurate a figure is this really? Clearly, the sultan is rich. But is he *that* rich? Possibly not.

The bulk of the sultan's earnings has come from oil and gas exports. In recent years, Brunei has exported no more than US$2.5 billion worth of oil and gas annually. But about half of this flows to Shell and Mitsubishi through production sharing agreements. Daily production of crude oil has been capped at around 150,000 barrels since 1988 to prolong the country's reserves.[10] So this puts an upper limit on oil earnings at least. Brunei did receive a surge of income in 1979 during the oil crisis when production peaked at 250,000 barrels a day. This would have generated around US$3.2 billion in 1979 — but again, approximately half of this would have flowed to Shell.

There is no income tax in Brunei, so the sultan earns little from taxation. Overall, Brunei's government earns almost nothing domestically but generates plenty of outgoings. Most Bruneians gave up productive employment long ago. Only about 60,000 Bruneians are wage earners, and the government employs at least two-thirds of them in administration. On top of that, the government provides free education and healthcare. All of this is a massive drain on the country's revenues and almost certainly soaks up most of its share of what Brunei earns from its oil and gas exports — about US$1.3 billion in 1999. So, it seems that in average years, there might be very little left over from Brunei's hydrocarbon exports that can be added to national — the sultan's — wealth. He has to make do with earnings from good years like 1979.

But there has been much unproductive expenditure on countless palaces for the many members of the royal family, three-lane highways around the capital (which at peak hour remain almost empty), helicopters and private jets, aircraft for the Royal Brunei Airforce, and enormous subsidies for the perennially loss-making Royal Brunei Airlines. There has been a lot of overt waste, too. The royal family provides rich pickings for consultants and others who pad their expenses, knowing that Brunei doesn't have an opposition to raise awkward questions about government waste or an investigative media to expose the rorts.

More waste comes in the form of hiring hotel rooms that were used. On one occasion, the sultan reserved for a week three floors in each of five five-star hotels in Kuala Lumpur but ultimately stayed only at the Palace of the Golden Horses Hotel. Rather than cancel the reservations at the other four hotels, he chose to pay for all the rooms reserved for the entire week in all the hotels. The hotels were delighted but all the more so after they were able to sell many of the unoccupied rooms to other guests and thereby be paid twice over for each room.

On another occasion, when the heir to the throne, Prince Hakim, stayed at the luxury Regent Hotel in Kuala Lumpur, he took two entire floors. He stayed in a suite with his Chinese girlfriend on one floor, with several of his staff occupying some of the rooms on the same floor. His mother stayed on the other floor with several of her staff. All in, Hakim and his party paid for 80 rooms including two suites, but only about 12 rooms were actually used. Hakim's girlfriend insisted on taking her daily baths filled only with Evian mineral water from France rather than with local tap water, claiming a variety of allergies to what came out of the tap. Wasteful spending on hotel rooms is compounded by hotel staff who might take items from the minibar and other things from the unused rooms, which are then charged to the royal family and its party.

After factoring in Shell's and Mitsubishi's cuts and the daily expenses of running Brunei, it's difficult to see how there is anything much left over for the sultan. What little there is, appears to be spent on expensive baubles and the odd 'trophy' acquisition overseas, like a hotel. The total purchase price of the sultan's *known* direct investments abroad amounts to little more than US$2 billion. Obviously, a lot has been spent on palaces, mosques, public buildings, and roads in Brunei. But these should be valued at the price they would bring in the market today and not what was spent on them. So, perhaps this palace or that road might have cost US$250 million, but who would want to pay a huge sum of money for second-hand palaces in the jungles of Borneo and highways that go nowhere? A lot of money has been made in Brunei, but an awful lot has been spent too.

Forbes magazine estimates the wealth of another oil entrepreneur, Prince Alwaleed bin Talal bin Abdulaziz Alsaaud, the high-flying nephew of the Saudi king, to be US$20 billion. He has built up large stakes in Citicorp, the Four Seasons Hotel chain, Apple Computer, TWA, Saatchi and Saatchi, Daewoo Corporation, Hyundai Motor, Planet Hollywood in the United States, and is the outright owner of the Hotel George V in Paris. It simply isn't possible to generate a list like this for the BIA or the Bolkiah family. The prince's Citicorp investment paid off handsomely. The day after the company announced in April 1998 that it would merge with Travelers Group, the market value of Prince Alwaleed's 41 million shares (about 3.5% of Citicorp's total stock) sky rocketed by US$1.54 billion, and this was after already enormous capital gains since he first bought the shares in 1990.[11] Prince Alwaleed's holdings are so big that they are difficult to hide. And yet, the Sultan of Brunei's wealth is supposed to be four times as great but is practically invisible. Is it really possible to invest as much as US$36 billion around the world and leave almost no trail? It stretches credulity. One possibility is that the figure of US$36 billion (and later US$16 billion) is overstated — perhaps grossly overstated. Between squandering money on palaces and other luxuries, and subsidizing the livelihood of 300,000 Bruneians, it's difficult to see how the sultan could have anything like this figure. Perhaps a case of the emperor's new clothes?

Bumpy Beginnings

One of the family's earliest financial advisors was the Malaysian Khoo Teck Puat. He was particularly close to the current sultan's father, Sultan Omar Ali Saifuddien III, who abdicated in 1967. Khoo started out by working as a junior clerk in a Singapore bank and rose to become deputy general manager. (His father was a banker and had helped found several Singapore banks.) In 1959, he established the Malayan Banking Corporation in Malaysia. The bank grew rapidly, but in 1966, rumors that he had channeled funds from the bank to his own interests caused a run on the bank. In the wash-up, he was ousted. But in 1965, Sultan Omar gave Khoo permission to establish the National Bank of Brunei and it became the focus of his attention after his departure from Malayan Banking. Throughout the period that Khoo ran the National Bank, he made a significant effort to draw members of the Brunei royal family into its ownership, thus hoping to leverage its operations on their name. Ultimately, the royal family's stake reportedly grew as high as 30%, leaving Khoo to hold the remainder.[12] He was able to capitalize on his links with Sultan Omar and play a prominent role in the sultanate's private sector in the 1970s and 1980s. However, being the only bank domiciled in Brunei, Khoo's bank wasn't subject to the scrutiny and prudential supervision that it might have been elsewhere. Although he owned most of the bank, its actual status was never quite clear, and many outside Brunei believed (incorrectly) that it had some kind of sovereign or government backing. Khoo borrowed heavily from the bank to expand his portfolio of other businesses outside Brunei. In 1986, Khoo's friend and protector, the former Sultan Omar, died, and his son Sultan Hassanal hired a team of investigators from the United States to examine the bank's financial standing. The investigations revealed its chronic exposure to Khoo's other companies, and the Brunei government closed it down.[13] The advisors even went as far as inviting an *Asian Wall Street Journal* reporter to the country to be briefed on Khoo's business activities as part of a strategy to have him exiled from the country. Almost certainly, this was the first and last time that a foreign journalist was *invited* to Brunei to cover business affairs that are even remotely connected to the Bolkiah family.

In November 1986, the Brunei authorities issued a warrant for Khoo's arrest on charges of defrauding the bank. Khoo's debts, however, were ultimately repaid. He raised US$340 million by selling a string of hotels that he owned in Australia, and other assets around Asia that belonged to him were seized by Brunei's Ministry of Finance with the help of the U.S. financial advisors flown in to Brunei for the purpose. Khoo's eldest son, Khoo Ban Hock, didn't escape so lightly. He was jailed for two years in Brunei for his role in illegally channeling almost US$600 million in loans from the bank to his father's other companies.[14] Khoo's family suddenly faced battles on several fronts. Around the same time, his daughter, Mavis Oei, who holds Singaporean citizenship, was fined in Singapore for acting as a nominee for her father's companies when she bought two valuable pieces of land. Foreigners are generally not permitted to own land in Singapore. The fine of S$1,000 (about US$600) was relatively light, but the real sting was that she chose to forgo the US$15 million in profit from the sale of the land as part of her mitigation.[15]

Khoo escaped from the Brunei controversy with his wealth intact and has since managed to build on it. Today, he owns almost 15% of the UK's Standard Chartered Bank, a stake he acquired in 1986 at around the time that the Brunei government accused him of removing funds from the National Bank of Brunei. He also owns most of the shares in Central Properties, Goodwood Park Hotels, and Hotel Malaysia — three companies that are listed on the Stock Exchange of Singapore. His Standard Chartered stake alone is worth around US$1.6 billion and in 2000, *Forbes* magazine estimated his total wealth to be US$2.7 billion. This makes Khoo one of the richest men in the world today. Partly, he has the Sultan of Brunei to thank.

Prince Jefri

Prince Jefri was, until early 1997, Brunei's finance minister and head of the BIA. Privately, he owned and ran Amedeo Holdings with his son, Prince Hakim, until its collapse in 1998. Among the company's 27 subsidiaries was Amedeo Developments Corporation, the prime building contractor in Brunei, which constructed most of the palaces around Bandar Seri Begawan for the many members of Brunei's royal family — in all about 40 buildings — including the sultan's main palace.[16] Its most recent major project was the sprawling 'six-star' 530-room Jerudong Park Hotel, which has full sea frontage and is wrapped around a golf course that is fully lit with sports stadium-grade lighting to allow golf to be played 24 hours a day. A power generation project was also undertaken with Siemens of Germany. With so much building activity, Amedeo was an important employer in Brunei of foreign consultants and contractors, as well as many Thai, Filipino, Indonesian, and Pakistani guest workers.

Amedeo Holdings had active offshoots overseas. Amedeo UK, for example, paid an astonishing £243.5 million for the London jeweler Asprey in 1995. Asprey also has showrooms in Paris, New York, and Singapore. In 1998, Prince Jefri merged Asprey with its subsidiary, the Crown Jewellers, Garrard, to form Asprey & Garrard. In 1997, Amedeo paid £45 million for the Hotel Plaza Athenee, considered one of the best hotels in Paris. In 1996, a Hong Kong subsidiary, Amedeo Holdings Co Ltd, signed a memorandum of understanding (MOU) to purchase half of the Meridien Hotel on the Thai island of Phuket, although the deal later fell through. A US subsidiary, Amedeo Hotels, bought the 1,000-room Palace Hotel in New York (formerly, the Helmsley Palace) in 1993 for US$202 million. Like the sultan, Prince Jefri employed Western financial advisors such as SBC Warburg, which advised him on the Asprey deal.[17]

The collapse of Amedeo brewed for over a year. By mid-1997, the sultanate was awash with rumors that some US$10 billion had 'disappeared' from the BIA. Prince Jefri, who had already been relieved of his position as finance minister, was fired as head of the BIA in mid-1998. By this time some reports suggested the missing amount was as high as US$16 billion.

The sultan appointed a task force to investigate the affairs of the BIA. The Bank of England was asked to join in the hunt for the missing billions, which appeared to have been misappropriated on non-government projects and property acquisitions.[18] The London branch of accounting firm KPMG was appointed by the Brunei government to audit BIA's accounts for the time that Prince Jefri served as its chairman. Its initial survey of the BIA's finances yielded little more than US$10 billion. There should have been several times that figure. The rest — if there was a rest — was still to be located. Two London-based partners at Arthur Andersen were also appointed to oversee Amedeo Corporation and some of its subsidiaries, including Amedeo Development Corporation, Amedeo Fishing, Amedeo Insurance, Jerudong Park Inc, and AMS Technology.[19]

Many contractors — some from the United Kingdom and Australia — were left unpaid, one to the tune of £30 million.[20] Brunei's High Court was later told that Amedeo's total debts were US$6 billion. Amedeo's collapse was accompanied by, what was by Brunei standards, a massive government shake-up. The attorney-general resigned and was fired from his position as chairman of Royal Brunei Airlines and from positions with the boards of other state-run companies. His departmental head also resigned. The deputy minister of finance was also removed from the airline's board.[21]

Prince Jefri disappeared overseas, first to Europe and then to the United States, where he was holed up at his Palace Hotel in New York. An Airbus 300 that he was using was kept on standby at New York State's Stewart International Airport until the Brunei government requested that permission for the plane to take off not be granted because its ownership was in dispute.[22] Prince Jefri returned to Brunei shortly after aboard a Gulf Stream VIP Executive Jet that had been chartered for the purpose.[23]

He claimed that the investigations into his affairs were at the instigation of 'religious conservatives' and warned that Brunei was increasingly coming under their influence. The minister of education and Jefri's replacement at the BIA denied the claim, although he did add that the investigations were being 'done solely for the sake of Allah the Almighty' and that the citizens and people of Brunei who seek the truth and obey the decree of Allah the Almighty shouldn't be easily influenced by such claims.[24] The whole affair was given widespread coverage in Brunei's *Borneo Bulletin*, and it was almost in danger of becoming exciting. Prince Jefri accused the newspaper — which is owned by brother Prince Mohamed — of 'speculation' and 'innuendo' shortly before he returned to Brunei.[25] The royal family was clearly at war.

A More Serious Attempt at Business

Prince Jefri is the most high-profile of the sultan's brothers, but it is Prince Mohamed whose business interests most resemble a conventional Asian business group. He has significant stakes in at least 25 companies, and they operate mostly in Brunei and Singapore. His principal holding company is Baiduri Holdings, which owns the Baiduri Bank, the only private commercial bank that is currently incorporated in Brunei, and the bank's subsidiaries, Baiduri Finance (also partly owned by local businessman Goh King Chin) and Baiduri Securities (partly owned by Malaysia's PhilleoAllied Group). There is also a stake in Brunei's National Insurance Co; a 12.5% stake in Boustead Co Ltd,[26] an engineering company listed on the Singapore Stock Exchange; a 20% stake in Highsonic Enterprise, which operated Myanmar Airways International, the international airline of Burma until October 1998; and 100% of QAF Brunei, another holding company. QAF Brunei, in turn, has 18 subsidiaries, all of which operate in Brunei. Generally, they are small companies aimed at providing services to Brunei's small population. Among them are grocery distributor Ben Foods, air-conditioner servicer Q-Carrier, and BMW importer QAF Auto. Another is Brunei Press, which monopolizes commercial print media in Brunei. In addition to the local *Borneo Bulletin* newspaper and its weekend counterparts, it owns the weekly Malay-language *Media Permata*, and Brunei's only Internet service provider, the amusingly named 'Brunet.' For a while, the QAF companies were listed on the Stock Exchange of Singapore. In 1985, Prince Mohamed acquired Ben and Co, a Singapore-listed food trader. He then injected the QAF companies into it, and renamed the whole entity QAF Ltd. But in 1990, he sold his controlling interest and bought back its Brunei-based subsidiaries.

The third brother is Prince Sufri. He set up his Primal Corporation in 1991. In 1993, Primal won approval from the Vietnamese government to invest up to US$9 billion in 19 projects in Vietnam, mostly in oil and gas exploration over a 20-year period. It then set about establishing a Singapore-based consortium of companies to undertake the investments. The first company to join Primal's consortium was Singapore's Asia Pacific Resources. However, since this initial burst of enthusiasm, little has been heard of either Prince Sufri or Primal, most likely on account of Sufri's reported ill-health. It is unclear what, if anything, was ultimately invested in Vietnam.

All the Trappings — But Where's the Wealth?

The world's media has played a big role in promoting the story of the fabulous wealth of the Sultan of Brunei. But much of the reporting has proceeded in a vacuum of real information and instead focused on the sultan's trappings of wealth rather than the wealth itself. More academic studies too have fallen into this trap. Routinely, the BIA is said to earn between US$2 billion and US$4 billion annually from its investments around the world. But since the agency has never published its accounts, such figures are pure conjecture more than anything else. It seems that the ultimate basis for the figure was an article on the sultan by Mary Anne Weaver in *The New Yorker* magazine in 1991.[27] The figure hasn't been corroborated or confirmed since then, but has been repeated so often that it has become conventional wisdom. Likewise, QAF Holdings is sometimes written of as if it is an enormous conglomerate ('the second-largest business operation in the country after Brunei Shell'[28]). It isn't. It comprises little more than import agents, some retail outlets, the *Brunei Bulletin*, and some other service sector firms, none of which represent interests of any size given that they feed off a population base of just 300,000.

By 1998, world oil prices were at their lowest in almost 20 years. The country's earnings from oil and gas almost certainly were doing little more than funding the day-to-day running of the government. The BIA had been gradually withdrawing its holdings in mutual funds from around the world for at least two years prior to the investigations of Prince Jefri's activities, most probably to make up for budget shortfalls. Brunei and its royal family were living beyond its means even before Amedeo's collapse and the BIA's billions were known to have gone missing. Oil prices had more than doubled by 2000, but this did little to plug the hole left by Prince Jefri.

Pressure on Prince Jefri to come up with the missing billions came to naught. So in 1999, Amedeo was wound up and the sultan launched legal proceedings against him in Brunei's High Court. The suit alleged that Jefri had misappropriated BIA assets worth US$14.7 billion. And this was in addition to the sums lost by Amedeo. When asked by the High Court to estimate his monthly living expenses, Jefri came up with the somewhat startling figure of US$500,000. The legal move was unusual. Disagreements within the royal family had always been settled in-house. And so ultimately was the Prince Jefri fiasco. In May 2000, it was announced that an out-of-court settlement had been reached and that Jefri would be returning the money he had taken. The precise terms were to be kept secret but the little that was known didn't really ring true. It had more the hallmark of a face-saving exercise than anything else. It was not disclosed exactly how much Jefri proposed to return to the BIA - in all probability it was to be nothing like what was missing. Much of it appeared to have been frittered away carelessly or lost through mismanagement, so there would be little chance that the BIA would get back what it had lost. Jefri might have been in disgrace, but he appeared to be still living a charmed lifestyle. I saw him one evening in August 2000 at an amusement park that had been temporarily set up in the Tuilleries Gardens in Paris, just opposite the BIA's Hotel Meurice. He was accompanied by several well-dressed women, some children and servants.

Sinking oil prices and the debacle at the BIA served to heighten a cash crisis that was already apparent. Long-term investments that had only been held for a short period, like the stake in Australia's Macquarie Bank, were sold off. Penny pinching became the order of the day. The sultan's contract with Singapore's prestigious Mount Elizabeth Hospital for a suite to be kept on permanent standby in case he needed it was ended.[29] Several of the sultan's prize racehorses were sold off.[30] And one report even claimed that 40 polo ponies were slaughtered simply to save on hay.[31] Brunei has never opened up its books for outside scrutiny. Estimates of the sultan's wealth have been based on guesswork at best, and at worst, all that analysts have done is to quote each other. All that has been visible to the outside world has been the trappings of wealth, but never the wealth itself. It now seems that the Sultan of Brunei's legendary wealth is precisely that.

MALAYSIA'S ROYAL HOUSE OF NEGRI SEMBILAN

Malaysia is a federation of 13 states, nine of which still have a sultan. Every five years, one of the sultans takes his turn to be the Yang di Pertuan Agung (King) of Malaysia. The Yang di Pertuan Agung for the latter part of the 1990s was the sultan of Negri Sembilan state, Tuanku Ja'afar Tuanku Abdul Rahman. It also just happens that of all the royal houses of

Malaysia, the royal house of Negri Sembilan has had the most success in business. This is quite important. The transition from being genuinely royal and living from tax revenues and other unearned income, to actively engaging in commerce isn't always an easy one. Some royal families have managed to toss off the shackles of the past and have emerged as successful business people. The royal family of Negri Sembilan is one of them. The children, brother, nephew, and nieces of the former King of Malaysia have all gone into business, mostly through the family's two business groups: the Antah and Melewar groups.

Like most other families in business, the Negri Sembilan family has had to take some risks and be prepared to occasionally fail. The family's royal status has been of no direct help in its business activities, though family members readily concede that their special status certainly opens doors and avails them of opportunities that they otherwise might not have had.

The former king's second son, Tunku Imran Ja'afar, who is in his early fifties, is the CEO of Antah Holdings, which is listed on the Kuala Lumpur Stock Exchange. (Tunku is a rough approximation for prince or princess.) Antah is a conglomerate of 71 subsidiaries and another 21 associated companies. Operations are concentrated in Malaysia, but spread around the world with subsidiary interests in the United Kingdom, Australia, Africa, Hong Kong, and even Sri Lanka. Its core operations are in food and beverages (it sold its 7-Eleven franchise for US$21 million in July 2000 but retains the Pepsi franchise for Malaysia), oil and gas interests, highway construction, financial services, and property. Overseas interests include a half-share in JW Carpenter, which has 37 hardware stores across the United Kingdom.[32] The group intended to list its Oiltools International — which it claims operates in more than 30 countries — on the London Stock Exchange in 1998.

Tunku Abdullah, a brother of the former king, and who is now in his seventies, co-founded a joint venture construction company in 1963 that has grown into the Melewar Group. Each of Tunku Abdullah's seven children or their spouses assists in the group's management — many have been provided with their own subsidiaries to run. One subsidiary, Masterconsult, is involved in arms trading and has occasionally brokered deals for Malaysia's airforce.[33] There are other subsidiaries that are involved in advertising, manufacturing, property development, electronics trading, travel, healthcare, and printing. But the most important asset of the group is the 70-branch Malaysian Assurance Alliance, which is listed on the Kuala Lumpur Stock Exchange and had a market capitalization approaching US$500 million before Asia's economic crisis set in. It is one of Malaysia's largest life insurers and is managed by Tunku Abdullah's son, Tunku Ya'acob.

Other scions of the extended Negri Sembilan royal household are in business too. The former king's brother-in-law, Tunku Shahabuddin, is the major shareholder in the profitable Malaysian computer distributor SCS Computer Systems. A niece, Tunku Zahiah Sulong, has been appointed as the Malaysian representative of art auctioneer Christie.

All in, the Negri Sembilan royals provide an example to other *bumiputra* business people. They embody Prime Minister Mahathir's dream of a commercially viable class of indigenous business people who work with, rather than are dependent on, the country's ethnic Chinese population.

BHUMIPOL ADULYADEJ, THE KING OF THAILAND

Bhumipol Adulyadej, the current King of Thailand, isn't known for his wealth. But his wealth is quite separate from that of the Thai state, and there is plenty of it. *Forbes* magazine estimated King Bhumipol's private wealth to be at US$1.8 billion in 1997. But by 1998, he had been bumped off the list, presumably due to the effects of Asia's economic crisis.[34] Crisis or no crisis, the king's private wealth seems to have been wildly underestimated. Real estate investments and massive holdings of Thai blue-chip stocks have underwritten much of the Thai royal family's private riches. The true figure of the family's personal wealth is likely to be closer to US$8 billion (split roughly between Thai blue chips and Bangkok real estate, as explained below). The king and the immediate members of his family directly hold shares in several Thai listed companies. Dhana Siam Finance and Securities PCL boasts the king and his daughters, Princess Maha Chakri Sirindhorn and Princess Chulabhorn, on its share registry, and Thai Insurance PCL can claim the king as a significant direct shareholder. But the great bulk of the family's private wealth is managed by the Crown Property Bureau.

The bureau was established in 1937 to ensure that the Thai royal family could be financially independent of the state. It also helped to keep the family's assets out of reach of Thai politicians and the military. Part of the bureau's strategy is to keep a low profile. A consequence of this is the difficulty in obtaining information on its holdings, and there is almost no reliable published account of what it owns and why.

The bureau is the country's largest landowner, and vast tracts of valuable commercial property in Bangkok are under its control. Rental income generates huge revenue for the bureau each year. But real estate isn't its only investment. There are direct stakes in at least 100 Thai companies, many of which are listed on the Stock Exchange of Thailand, and indirect stakes in hundreds of others. Indeed, at the beginning of

1997, the equity held in blue-chip Thai stocks had a then-market value of at least US$4.002 billion. With the US$77.6 million in Thai stocks held directly by the king and his immediate family, the immediate royal family's total investments in the Thai stock market stood at a minimum of US$4.079 billion, possibly much more. Asia's economic crisis saw the Stock Exchange of Thailand's market index decline by around 60% in the 12 months to March 1998, which would have seen the family's holding of Thai blue chips decline in value to about US$1.6 billion, but it has since bounced back.

The king and his immediate family stay out of the day-to-day management of the Crown Property Bureau. In effect, it functions like a personal mutual fund for the family. But members of the extended royal family do permeate its management and many sit on the boards of dozens of listed Thai companies. The head, or director general, of the bureau is Dr Chirayu Isarangkun na Ayudhya, a distant royal himself. He is the chairman of four listed Thai companies in which the bureau has significant stakes and a director of at least eight others. Altogether, at least 39 public Thai companies have one or more obvious members of the extended Thai royal family on their boards. Among them are princes, princesses, and many who, like Dr Chirayu, attach the 'na Ayudhya' suffix to their names, to denote a distant royal linkage.

In Thailand, where the king is accorded enormous respect and even seen as semi-divine by many of his subjects, Thai companies welcome him and the bureau as investors. Being able to cite the Crown Property Bureau as a shareholder confers on Thai companies considerable prestige. The bureau usually doesn't take an active role in the management of any of the companies in which it invests. But this is not to say that it's a quaint backwater for the employment of distant cousins of the king. On the contrary, the bureau is a vast, complex enterprise that manages its investments with as much acumen and intensity as any fund manager charged with managing a large portfolio. Investments are categorized into four groups: finance, which is led by the Siam Commercial Bank; basic industry, led by Siam Cement; real estate, led by Siam Sindhorn Co Ltd; and communications, led by Siam TV and Communication Co Ltd. Management is undertaken by professionals, and the bureau has a rational, modern structure. Holding companies are made use of, allowing for the group's accounts to be consolidated. The bureau isn't afraid to approach formal capital markets when it needs funds. In 1996 alone, its property arm issued US$60 million in bonds and its bank made similar issues in subsequent years.[35] All in all, the bureau is probably administered more professionally than some of the companies in which it invests.

The bureau has a controlling stake in Siam Cement, which is Thailand's largest industrial conglomerate. It's also beginning to emerge as something of a multinational. There are 69 subsidiaries, including three in the United States and two in China. Also, there are some 37 associated companies.[36] There are four joint ventures in Indonesia. Two are with the ethnic Chinese Wings Group, another with the ethnic Chinese Maspion Group, and one with Hashim Djojohadikusumo, the brother of a brother-in-law of former president Soeharto. The latter is one of Siam Cement's biggest commitments to date outside Thailand. Its Singapore-registered Tuban Petrochemicals had a 20% share in the US$2.5 billion petrochemicals complex that Hashim was to build in Indonesia, although the venture was put on hold due to the Asian economic crisis.[37] Siam Cement's holdings are extensive but are transparently structured. Subsidiaries beget subsidiaries. One of its associated companies is Siam Pulp and Paper PCL, Thailand's largest manufacturer and distributor of pulp and paper. It alone has 22 subsidiaries.

The bureau, and hence the king, is Thailand's biggest single landlord. There are enormous holdings of agricultural land in most of the country's provinces. But the most valuable holdings are in Bangkok. At the time the bureau was set up, just prior to World War II, it is believed to have owned almost one-third of the land in Bangkok. Much of this land is almost certainly still held by the bureau.[38] Assuming that as much as a quarter of Bangkok's central business area is in the hands of the bureau (Bangkok-based real estate consultants assure me this is probable), and if the business and surrounding built-up areas have a net area of, say, ten square kilometers of commercial land, then the bureau is sitting on a land bank in the middle of Bangkok of some 2.5 million square meters. Of course, Bangkok's property market was particularly hard hit in the lead-up to Asia's economic crisis. The market for prime city real estate grew increasingly illiquid as the 1990s wore on, making a true market price of such land difficult to assess. A reasonable estimate based on the transactions that occured from about 1994 is about US$2,000 per square meter. If this is the long-term value, then King Bhumipol most probably holds prime Bangkok land that has a long-term market value of approximately US$5 billion.

The bureau's enormous holdings of land in Bangkok means that it can expect to be offered a shareholding in almost any venture in the city that involves significant land usage. This means stakes in hotels, transitways, pipelines, convention centers, and so on. The bureau often contributes land, or at least its use, to a venture in return for a share in the equity. And, of course, many bureau-related companies operate from offices that are leased from the bureau's property arm. Hotels (including shares in Bangkok's famous Regent and Dusit Thani hotels), residential developments, and commercial properties are all part of the bureau's real estate portfolio. In late 1994, the bureau even had plans drawn up to develop a new, self-contained township outside of Bangkok that was to accommodate 300,000 to 500,000 people, but these are yet to come to fruition.

Diversification into communications has yet to meet with much success. The bureau's Siam TV and Communication Co has lost money every year since it was set up in 1982.[39] Today, it is a media holding company with three divisions that contain a total of 16 subsidiaries. There is also a combined 20% stake in Thailand's ITV television station and an 11% stake in *Business Day*, an English-language daily business newspaper published in Bangkok. The bureau's media interests depend a great deal on the other businesses controlled by the bureau for advertising revenue. Some of the problems that the bureau has had in this sector have stemmed from its need to stay above politics, but this is difficult when the Thai public has come to expect a daily diet of feisty political coverage. The bureau has found that there are some benefits of owning media outlets, however. When, in 1997, former Thai prime minister, Chavalit Yongchaiyudh, offered the position of finance minister to Olarn Chaipravat, the president of the bureau's Siam Commercial Bank, the bureau's ITV was the first to report that Olarn had turned down the offer.

The king and his family are, through the bureau, one of the leading commercial powers in Thailand. But in recent years, the royal family has begun to diversify its wealth beyond Thailand. Siam Cement has established operations and subsidiaries in the United States, Italy, China, Vietnam, Burma, the Philippines, Malaysia, Cambodia, and, Indonesia. And in 1995, Dusit Sindhorn, a joint venture between the bureau's property arm, several other Thai companies, and Thai hotel operator, Dusit Thani (of which the bureau also owns 14%), bought the German hotel chain, Kempinski.[40] This effectively gave the King of Thailand an interest in hotels around the world, including in San Francisco, London, Frankfurt, Munich, Buenos Aires, Montreal, Istanbul, and Mumbai (formerly Bombay).

The Crown Property Bureau has a reputation for conservatism and prudence. Nonetheless, like any other typical Asian conglomerate, it is riddled with related-party transactions. Listed companies that are controlled by the bureau routinely trade with companies that are privately held by the bureau. Listed bureau companies often announce that they have 'won' a tender or supply contract with this or that company, and it transpires that those companies are also in the Crown Property Bureau stable. Thai Industrial Gases PCL is the main supplier of industrial gas to Siam Cement, for example, and both companies are in the bureau's portfolio. The Deves Insurance was set up in 1972 by the bureau to provide fire insurance to the bureau's extensive real estate holdings. It has since branched out into other forms of insurance and is listed on the Stock Exchange of Thailand, but the bureau remains one of its most important customers and one of its largest shareholders.[41] The Siam Commercial Bank and Dhana Siam Finance and Securities handle many of the bureau's banking transactions, particularly those that are fee-based. Both are publicly listed but controlled by the bureau. Whether or not such transactions are on fully commercial terms (as, indeed, they should be when listed companies are involved) is impossible to say. Even tracking down such transactions is difficult on account of Thailand's lax rules on public companies' disclosure of transactions with affiliates.

The bureau is the reluctant star at the top of Bangkok's corporate tree. And as such, it bore its fair share of pain in Asia's economic crisis. Siam Cement particularly suffered. It had enormous US dollar debts, all unhedged, belying the usual presumption that the company was prudently managed. So, when the baht collapsed in 1997, the company's US dollar debts exploded in baht terms. In early 1998, it reported a stunning US$1.19 billion loss for the previous year — its first loss in almost a century of operating and the largest loss ever made by a listed Thai firm. Despite the apparent disaster, the company said it had no need to issue new shares to raise capital, that it fully expected to service from export earnings all its debt, and would pay off total debt within five years.[42] Other companies in the Crown Property Bureau were also badly affected by the Asian crisis. Dhana Siam Finance and Securities, in which the bureau and members of the royal family directly hold equity, was forced to issue new shares in order to double its capital base to cover dramatic increases in bad debts.[43] The bureau also announced it would cancel or drop investment projects worth a total of US$3.2 billion in response to the crisis.[44] But the resilience of Siam Cement, the jewel in the crown as far as the bureau is concerned, showed that while the King of Thailand's wealth took a battering, he was still some way from being down to his last billion.

The private wealth of King Bhumipol Adulyadej and his family has some similarities with the wealth amassed by the family of Indonesia's Soeharto when he was in power. Both are fabulously wealthy and, indeed, became the richest families in their respective lands. Both own large tracts of property. Both specialize in heavy industry — the sort of activity that requires government licensing and approvals that others find difficult to obtain; and both have media holdings, including television stations. But there is one very important difference. The Thai royal family has achieved much of its wealth from inheritance and prudent investment. Also, if they want an asset, they pay for it. The Soeharto clan, on the other hand, did not. Whereas Thai companies see it as an honor to have the Crown Property Bureau take a stake in them, Indonesian companies saw a Soeharto stake as a necessary evil. The Soeharto billions are the subject of the next chapter.

CHAPTER 13

President of the Country; Chairman of the Board

During his 32-year rule as president of Indonesia, Soeharto allowed his family to develop a business empire of unprecedented proportions. It is for this that he will be remembered. But he was not the only one.

There is little separation between politics and business in much of Asia, although, as usual, it is the degree that varies. The habits of some Asian leaders even belie a basic confusion between themselves and their families, and the state. Philippine dictator Ferdinand Marcos is a case in point. Vast sums of hard currency and gold were plundered from the country and stashed in foreign banks. Marcos and his family even helped themselves to foreign aid. And his wife, Imelda, habitually signed checks drawn directly on the Philippine central bank to pay for her purchases in the boutiques of New York's Fifth Avenue. For the Marcoses, the central bank had become their private piggy bank. *'L'état c'est moi,'* 'The state is me,' Louis XIV famously declared to the French parliament in 1651. *'Ako ang bayan'* is the Tagalog (the Philippine language) version. No doubt it was a thought that crossed the minds of the Marcos family on many an occasion. The lack of separation of political families from the state, though, is more apparent than in Indonesia, where for many politicians, elevation to high office is tantamount to an invitation to a free-for-all.

WINNER TAKES ALL?

Around April 2000, the personal masseur of Indonesia's President Abdurrahman Wahid went missing. So did US$4 million from the National Logistics Agency. The money had been paid to the masseur by an agency official in the hope that the masseur would be able to

234

influence the president into appointing him as head of the agency. As far as scandals go, this one was a ripper. But it is hardly the first.

A month or so earlier, it emerged that Wahid had appointed his brother, Hasyim Wahid, as a 'special assistant' to the Indonesian Bank Restructuring Agency (IBRA) — the agency established in part to control assets seized from the owners of defunct or illiquid banks and which by then controlled almost US$100 billion in such assets. The position came with a house, a car, and a lot of discretion to play favourites and to settle old scores. After significant adverse media comment, Hasyim announced that he'd step down from the position, but not because of the efficacy of the appointment but rather to quell the uproar that greeted it.

At the same time, the government announced that it had dropped an investigation, citing 'a lack of evidence,' into how local textiles conglomerate, Texmaco Group, had managed to acquire so much money from state banks during the Soeharto era. The group had amassed more than US$2 billion in debts that it could not repay. Wahid's critics were quick to highlight the close connection between Wahid's nephew, Syaifullah Yusuf, and Texmaco Group, and drew their own conclusions. Business, it seems, was as usual in Indonesia.

Meanwhile Wahid's vice-president, Megawati Sukarnoputri, the Jakarta housewife who against all expectations, especially her own, was appointed to that position in October 1999, remained as mute on policy as she had been prior to her elevation. She heads the Indonesian Democratic Party of Struggle (PDI-P) Party but her main political attribute is that she is a daughter of Indonesia's first president, Sukarno, who was shunted aside by Soeharto in his bid for the presidency. Her rise in Indonesian politics was no more than a calculated affront to Soeharto. She was unwittingly propelled by anti-Soeharto forces — and by her second husband, Taufik Kiemas.

Taufik stood in Indonesia's 1999 national elections as a PDI-P candidate for a South Sumatra constituency, but then so did several of his relatives, including Saridayanah Kiemas, who stood in Jakarta, and Nasrudin Kiemas, who also stood in South Sumatra. Critics were quick to cry nepotism. Indonesia had some new players but they came with old habits. Coupled with descriptions of Taufik as a 'businessman' — the family runs a chain of six gasoline stations — one might be forgiven for wondering if history was about to be repeated.

Wahid's predecessor, Bachruddin Jusuf Habibie, who served as Indonesia's president between May 1998 and October 1999, was no stranger to controversy. Indeed, his nepotism would have been considered worthy of great note had his predecessor not been the greatest nepotist of them all — Soeharto. In contrast to the wealth achieved by the Soeharto family, the commercial prominence gained by the Habibie clan was somewhat modest. The two main commercial vehicles of the Habibie family were the Timsco Group and Repindo Panca Group, which together had significant direct interests in at least 87 Indonesian companies. Many of these companies had interests that mirrored the responsibilities Habibie had as a minister in Soeharto's various cabinets. The more prominent of them owed their existence only to privileges and concessions granted to them by Habibie or his agents.

The two most notable events of Habibie's brief term as president was his decision to allow voters of East Timor a referendum to see if they wanted to secede from Indonesia (they did), and the Bank Bali scandal. This scandal ended any chance Habibie had of being re-elected president. It involved Habibie's aides being closely linked to the misappropriation of US$70 million from Bank Bali. The bank had been nationalized in 1998 after it had all but collapsed, a victim of mismanagement and the economic crisis of 1997–98. The scandal came to light when Britain's Standard Chartered Bank, which was to buy into Bank Bali and thus save it, discovered that US$70 million was missing. The imbroglio that followed led to Standard Chartered losing interest in the acquisition.

But it is the Soeharto empire that took nepotism and corruption to new heights, even by world standards. And it is still the Soeharto family that remains an important business player in Indonesia since the resignation of President Soeharto.

PRESIDENT SOEHARTO INCORPORATED

Most visitors to Jakarta throughout much of the 1990s didn't know it, but from the minute they flew into the Soekarno-Hatta International Airport, they embarked on a process of feeding the Soeharto family's coffers that ended only after they left. The management of the airport was undertaken by the Humpuss Group — owned by Soeharto's son, Hutomo Mandala Putra (Tommy). The airport ground handling services were undertaken by the Bimantara Group — owned by another Soeharto son, Bambang. Outside the airport, the visitors might have hired a Citra Taxi — owned by daughter Siti Hardiyanti Rukmana (Tutut). As they took the 30-kilometer drive to the center of Jakarta, they drove along a toll-road owned by Tutut. Along the way, they would pass billboards owned by Tommy, managed by another of his companies, and which usually displayed advertising for other Soeharto-owned companies. On the way to their hotel, the visitors would drive past Plaza Senayan, a massive shopping center in which another Soekarno daughter had a share. And eventually they would pull up at their hotel, often the Grand Hyatt, which is partly owned by another Soeharto son. All this in their first hour of having arrived in Jakarta, assuming there were no traffic problems.

In the 32 years that he was in power, Soeharto and his family enriched themselves on a scale never seen before. There have been the Marcoses of the Philippines, the Bhuttos of Pakistan, and Haile Selassie of Ethiopia, but the scale of the wealth they achieved while in power absolutely pales in comparison to what the Soehartos of Indonesia amassed. The Soeharto business empire is held by the inner core of the Soeharto family, as well as a large number of the extended family. There were also various charitable foundations (*yayasan*) that the Soehartos established. These were enormously secretive and were variously rumored to have massive corporate holdings themselves. It seems, though, that reports of their assets were greatly exaggerated. The real heart of the Soeharto business empire was the companies owned directly by individual Soeharto family members.

Some estimates put the family's wealth at its peak at as high as US$25 billion. These estimates are hard to verify, but what is verifiable is the number of companies that the family owns. At the time of Soeharto's resignation, there were at least 1,251 separate, active companies in Indonesia alone in which members of the Soeharto family had significant shares. The full list of company names — too long to replicate here — runs to dozens of pages.[1] Nothing was too big for the Soehartos to be involved in. There were satellites, toll-roads, airlines, and television stations. But then nothing was too small, either. Interests in condoms, wooden chopsticks, and mineral water bottling were acquired as well. All this was possible only because of the political power that the Soeharto family wielded. Simply, the Soeharto empire was the biggest 'kleptocracy' the world has ever seen. Its tentacles worked their way into almost every crevice in Indonesia's economy. It is for this reason that the Soeharto business empire will survive in some form or other for years to come.

THE CAST OF CHARACTERS

The Soeharto family is from central Java. Java is the most culturally, commercially, and politically dominant island among Indonesia's 17,508 islands. Soeharto's late wife, Tien, was a minor royal from one of the many royal houses that dot Java — a connection she made the most of, having the family appear dressed for official portraits in *batik* material emblazoned with the *barong* design of the royal house with which she professed a connection. The family is also ostensibly Moslem, although it is well known that Soeharto subscribes to the mystical beliefs of central Java as well. Still, in a country that claims to be almost 90% Moslem, it is politically wise to be seen as an active participant in the faith. Members of the family made several well-publicized pilgrimages to Mecca and, in 1997, Soeharto's cousin, half-brother, and four of his children announced that they had each donated between US$100,000 and US$500,000 toward the construction of a US$3 million mosque in Soeharto's honor in the Bosnian capital of Sarajevo.[2]

But business is the family's main preoccupation. The key players while Soeharto was president were each of his six children, their spouses, two of his grandchildren, a brother of one of his sons-in-law, a cousin, and a half-brother (see Figure 13.1). All were actively involved in business in their own right and all prospered during Soeharto's tenure as president. A half-brother of Soeharto's late wife and the parents-in-law of one of his daughters might also be added to the list, but their interests are peripheral to the Soeharto family's core business activities.

Eldest child, daughter Siti Hardiyanti Rukmana (born, 1949), or 'Tutut,' was the head of the Citra Agratama Persada Group of companies at the time of Soeharto's resignation. Her principal investments were in toll-roads, mostly in and around Jakarta, but there were also mining companies, a flour mill, hotels, a television station, banks, and a 14% share in Indonesia's largest private bank, Bank Central Asia. She had significant interests in at least 111 companies in Indonesia.

Indra Rukmana (born, 1948) is Tutut's husband. He had business interests with his wife and others. But unlike the Soehartos, his family has its origins in business. His father, Eddy Kowara, was the founder of Indonesia's Teknik Umum Group, in which Indra is a shareholder. The group's main interests are in construction and, until recently, it held the Coca-Cola bottling franchise for much of the country. Indra also had a share in brother-in-law Bambang Trihatmodjo's Bimantara Group. Apart from these interests, there are approximately 15 companies that Indra owns and manages in his personal capacity.

Siti Hediati Prabowo (born, 1959), or Titiek, is Soeharto's middle daughter. She headed up the Maharani Group of companies and had direct interests in 70 Indonesian companies. Her husband, General Prabowo Subianto, had a record promotion through the Indonesian military and attained the position of commander of Indonesia's important Army Strategic Reserve (Kostrad) until his removal after Soeharto's resignation. Titiek cooperated in many of her business activities with her brother-in-law, Hashim Djojohadikusumo. Many of Titiek's interests were in the financial services sector. She had interests in several banks and owned a stockbroking firm, for example. There were investments also in a major shopping center and a cement producer. One company, a finance firm, was listed on the Jakarta Stock Exchange.

Siti Hutami Endang Adyningsih (born, 1965), or Mamiek, is Soeharto's youngest daughter. At the time of his resignation from the presidency, she had been in business for only a comparatively short time, but had managed to accumulate significant interests in six Indonesian companies. Her main business activities were in mobile telecommunications, land reclamation near Jakarta, and aircraft leasing.

Pratikto Singgih is Mamiek's husband. He had business interests separate from those of his wife. He headed several chemicals companies owned by ethnic Chinese-controlled Gadjah Tunggul Group, one of Indonesia's largest conglomerates, and he was the major shareholder in at least one of those companies. Pratikto and Mamiek were believed to be estranged; he maintained a low profile in Jakarta and, unlike the other Soeharto spouses, almost never accompanied the family on overseas visits.

Sigit Harjojudanto (born, 1951) is Soeharto's eldest son. He was not actively involved in business on a day-to-day basis, but tended to take large but passive stakes in big infrastructure and heavy industry projects. He had significant interests in at least 115 Indonesian companies. He is the main shareholder in the Arseto and Panutan groups, had a significant minority interest in the Nusamba Group, and held 16% of the Bank Central Asia Group. He was a business partner of Soeharto-confidante, businessman Bob Hasan.

Elsje Anneke Ratnawati Djoefrie is Sigit's wife. She had several business interests in her own right grouped under her Wahana Group. For a while, she and a friend, Suzanna Tanojo, controlled Asia Matrix, a Singapore-based maker of injection-molded plastic components, and which is listed on the Singapore stock exchange, but they sold out in 1997. Elsje also had a small share in Tommy's hotel and tourism Pecatu Indah Group.

Bambang Trihatmodjo (born, 1953) is Soeharto's middle son. He controlled the Bimantara Group, the biggest of the Soeharto family conglomerates. It was the most professionally managed of the Soeharto business groups and made ample use of holding companies to give it a clear and transparent structure. Its holding company was listed on the Jakarta Stock Exchange and included interests in infrastructure, chemicals, telecommunications, multimedia, hotels, a television station, mining, property, and consumer goods. The single biggest contributor to the group's results was the national television broadcaster, RCTI. Bambang also had significant interests that are held separately through PT Asriland, the private holding company that he owned with his wife, Halimah. She in turn owned almost a quarter of national television station, SCTV. Altogether, he had significant interests in at least 327 companies in Indonesia via the Bimantara Group, APAC-Bhakti Karya Group (which he owned with the Indonesian-Chinese businessman Johannes Kotjo), and PT Asriland. He also has substantial interests outside Indonesia in Singapore, Canada, Australia, and elsewhere.

Hutomo Mandala Putra (born, 1962), or Tommy, is Soeharto's youngest son. He rose to prominence outside Indonesia for being the Soeharto family member behind the ill-fated national car, — the president allowed him to import, free of duty, fully assembled Kia cars from South Korea that were rebadged with the 'Timor' label and sold free of sales tax as Indonesia's national car. His Humpuss Group spans an unwieldy range of interests including petrochemicals, an interest in an airline, and even mineral water bottling. Tommy had established another, much smaller group called the Pecatu Indah Group, which was intent on turning a huge swath of the southern part of the island of Bali into a massive tourist complex, as well as building a resort on another Indonesian island, Beliting. Tommy had significant interests in at least 127 companies in Indonesia. A story that did the rounds in Jakarta is that the Soeharto family was told by a *dukun*, a traditional Javanese soothsayer, that president Soeharto would lose all his power if Tommy married. For years, Tommy remained Indonesia's most eligible bachelor. But in 1997, he married Ardhia Pramesti Rigita Cahyani (Tata), who is a distant relative of his late mother, Tien. In a little more than a year, Soeharto was forced to resign.

Probosutedjo (born, 1930) is a half-brother of Soeharto — they shared the same mother. He, his wife Ratmani, and their five children ran their Mercu Buana Group. They had significant interests in at least 119 active Indonesian companies, including one of the country's largest glassware manufacturers and the Hotel Le Meriden in Jakarta.

Sudwikatmono (born, 1934) is a cousin of Soeharto. He amassed significant interests in no less than 288 Indonesian companies, often by offering to help foreign investors and others with government approvals and then taking a share of the equity of the new venture for his trouble. He had interests in the Subentra, Astenia, Pondok Indah, Jababeka, Dwi Golden Graha, and Wijaya Kusuma Jaya groups. Sudwikatmono shares a close relationship with Soeharto. Soeharto's parents divorced when he was a child and for a time he went to live with an aunt, the younger sister of his father — Sudwikatmono's mother. Their relationship from that time has endured for 70 years.

Ari Haryo Wibowo Sigit Harjojudanto, or Ari Sigit, is the son of Sigit Harjojudanto and is Soeharto's oldest grandson. By the time of Soeharto's resignation, he had managed to acquire interests in 28 Indonesian companies under his Arha Group even if he hadn't yet reached the age of 30. His activities are particularly interesting and will be examined closely later.

Eno Harjojudanto is Ari Sigit's younger sister and thus a granddaughter of Soeharto. She had been in business for only two or three years at the time of Soeharto's resignation but had established the Mahardika Group, which has companies that operate in telecommunications, property, and transportation.

Hashim Djojohadikusumo (born, 1954) is the brother of ex-General Prabowo, Titiek's husband. Hashim controlled the Tirtamas Majutama, Swabara, and Era Persada groups. Hashim's interests stretched across banking, mining, cement, power plants, and international commodities trade. He had significant direct interests in at least 109 active Indonesian companies and had companies overseas, particularly in the mining and trading sectors.

Another Soeharto relative, Soehardjo, a brother of Soeharto's late wife, Tien, was appointed to the position of director general of customs and excise. It was a useful contact in the bureaucracy for the family to have, given the proclivity of its members to set up import-export companies that required licensing. Soehardjo resigned from the position within a month of Soeharto's resignation. Of course, his departure had nothing to do with Soeharto's. He simply wished to make way for 'the next generation,' or so he claimed.[3] So that is the clan. Now for their deeds.

GETTING STARTED — PILLAGING THE STATE-OWNED OIL COMPANY

Almost all of the Soeharto family's business groups began with lucrative government supply contracts. Often, the contracts were with the state-owned Pertamina oil company, which ever since the oil shocks of the 1970s has been used like a giant honey pot by any Indonesian with the necessary connections to be able to stick his or her paws into it. The fact that Pertamina's internal accounting has been utterly opaque and its accounts aren't made public has been an enormous help to many Indonesians who decided that they would try their hand at business and were in need of some seed capital. Contracts that the Soehartos had with Pertamina included the distribution rights for the company's products both in and outside Indonesia. Titiek's Datam Group, for example, started out as a distributor for Pertamina, but later branched out into banking and financial services. Tommy was never able to wean himself off the sustenance that Pertamina provided and, if anything, seemed to have developed something of an addiction to it. In late 1997, he signed a US$180 million contract with Pertamina to transport gas from one of its

Figure 13.1 The Soeharto Clan

Late Wife
Tien

Sons
Sigit Harjojudanto — Main business group: Arseto Group
Bambang Trihatmodjo — Bimantara Group
Hutomo Mandala Putra (Tommy) — Humpuss Group

Daughters
Siti Hardiyanti Rukmana (Tutut) — Citra Agratama Persada Group
Siti Hediati Prabowo (Titiek) — Maharani Group
Siti Hutami Endang Adyningsih (Mamiek) — Various

Daughters- and Sons-in-Law
Indra Rukmana, married to Tutut — Teknik Umum Group, Various
Pratikto Singgih, married to Mamiek — Various
Elsje Anneke Ratnawati Djoefrie, married to Sigit — Wahana Group
Halimah Trihatmodjo, married to Bambang — Various
Prabowo Subianto, married to Titiek
Ardhia Pramesti Rigita Cahyani (Tata), married to Tommy

Grandchildren
Ari Haryo Wibowo Sigit Harjojudanto (Ari Sigit) — Arha Group
Eno Harjojudanto — Marhadika Group

Others
Probosutedjo, half-brother — Mercu Buana Group
Sudwikatmono, cousin — Subentra Group, Various
Hashim Djojohadikusumo, brother-in-law of Titiek —
Tirtamas Majutama Group

---

fields to markets in Japan for 15 years.[4] It was alleged that at the time of Soeharto's resignation, Pertamina had corrupt deals with no less than 159 separate companies, mostly linked to members and friends of the Soeharto family.[5]

Other monies for the family's start-up capital came from having themselves granted import monopolies. One of the earliest such monopolies was an exclusive license for the import of raw materials for plastic, granted in 1984. Originally, three state-owned companies were given the exclusive right to import the raw materials. Less than six months later, the three appointed as their sole importing agent Panca Holding Ltd, a Hong Kong-registered company that was owned by two Vanuatu-registered companies, which in turn were owned by Sudwikatmono, Bambang and Sigit. Naturally, Panca Holding took a big cut for itself and the whole exercise added between 10% and 15% to the import price of the materials and as much as 40% to the price of the finished articles in Indonesia. The monopoly was dismantled in 1988, but not before Panca had reaped millions of dollars for the Soeharto family. In 1986 alone, Panca Holding was thought to have earned US$30 million from its import monopoly.[6]

Other early monopolies that the Soeharto family secured were Tommy's soybean crushing monopoly run by PT Sarpindo, exclusive licenses for the domestic distribution of Pertamina petrochemicals products, a clove import monopoly that Probosutedjo shared with Soeharto crony, Liem Sioe Liong, that began in the 1960s, and Sudwikatmono's monopoly on the import and distribution of motion pictures. But perhaps the most famous monopoly of all was the clove buying monopoly that Tommy established toward the end of 1990.

CLOVES — TOMMY'S LICENSE TO PRINT MONEY

Crushed cloves are the vital ingredient in Indonesia's ubiquitous *kretek* cigarettes, which are a mixture of cloves and tobacco that gives off a sweet smell as they are smoked. So much *kretek* is consumed that public places in Indonesia seem to be enveloped by a permanent haze of clove smoke. By the mid-1980s, an astonishing 80,000 tonnes of cloves were consumed in Indonesia each year, making cloves a major cash crop in the country. In 1987, a group of Indonesian-Chinese businessmen formed a clove buying consortium that initially operated in eastern Indonesia. They bought cloves but had trouble selling them. There was no need for the big cigarette manufacturers to buy cloves from the consortium when they could buy them straight from the growers. What the consortium needed was government backing for their clove buying business. That was where Tommy came in. He was invited to join the consortium, and at the age of 26, he became consortium head through his company, Bina Reksa Perdana. Tommy lobbied the government, and despite enormous pressure from the cigarette manufacturers, Tommy and the consortium won. Indonesia's clove trading monopoly, known by its Indonesian acronym, BPPC, was inaugurated in late 1990. Ostensibly, the monopoly was set up to benefit clove farmers by establishing a minimum price at which they could sell their cloves. But it wasn't the farmers who were to benefit. The BPPC bought cloves from farmers at around US$3.50–4 a kilogram and resold them to cigarette manufacturers at around US$6–7 a kilogram, the difference netting the BPPC around US$100 million a year.[7]

Like such floor price schemes everywhere, production — and hence supply — was stimulated and demand was stifled, so not surprisingly, the BPPC soon built up enormous stocks of cloves. Soon, Tommy was in need of credit to finance the activities of the BPPC. He turned to the central bank for a US$600 million line of credit but was refused. He then wrote to the Sultan of Brunei to request a US$650 million loan, which Tommy suggested could be funneled through Indonesia's central bank so that the loan would attract a sovereign guarantee; the sultan declined. Finally, Tommy asked his father, the president, to intervene, and the central bank was pressured into lending Tommy the money. The bank initially lent only US$350 million.[8] It isn't known if the loan was repaid. The BPPC didn't publish its accounts, and the central bank has never announced if it was repaid.

By 1992, the BPPC's clove stockpile had grown so huge that Tommy publicly advocated that clove farmers burn half of their stocks, which led to rarely expressed outrage by some legislators in Indonesia's Parliament. Eventually, the buying price was reduced to US$2 a kilogram, but the BPPC maintained its selling price for cloves at around US$6–7. On top of that, various farmer cooperatives were suddenly permitted to buy cloves, but they weren't allowed to sell them to the cigarette manufacturers until the BPPC had disposed of its massive stockpile.[9] But that still wasn't enough for the BPPC to get rid of its stockpile, so in late 1994, the government announced a new decree that specified how many cloves (right down to the last gram) each cigarette manufacturer should have in stock per cigarette produced.[10] This didn't work either — the stockpile remained. In 1996, the BPPC suggested and the government agreed to an initiative to replace around half of Indonesia's clove trees with other cash crops such as coffee, vanilla, and cocoa. To fund the conversion, cigarette producers were forced to pay a levy of Rp 1,000 (then US$0.38) for each kilogram of cloves they bought from the BPPC.[11] It must have been especially galling to the cigarette producers to have to actually pay a levy designed to contribute to increasing the scarcity, thus raising the price, of one of their input, and then to have payment of that levy linked to their purchase of that input in the first place. But, when it came to protecting the business interests of the Soeharto family, nothing was too ridiculous. The measure worked, however, and by late 1997, it was clear that clove demand was again about to exceed supply, so the government stopped forcing clove

244

farmers to cut down their clove trees. Indeed, one minister actually said that unless farmers went back to producing more cloves, Indonesia might have to begin importing cloves.[12] Relief appeared to be in sight for the long-suffering farmers. But it was a mirage. Lest any village cooperatives that had been authorized to buy cloves actually take advantage of the new, favorable clove demand situation by selling them directly to cigarette manufacturers rather than to Tommy's clove monopoly, the government introduced a new decree in late 1997 so that any cooperatives found engaging in such unauthorized trading would lose their right to act as clove buyers.[13] The decree ensured that any benefit from the new market conditions would flow only to the BPPC. A private Jakarta think-tank, the Institute for Development of Economics and Finance, estimated in 1997 that the BPPC's activities had cost Indonesian clove farmers the equivalent of US$761 million in lost revenue over the preceding five years and that rather than become better off as a result of the BPPC, farmers had actually grown poorer.[14] Tommy and his BPPC had succeeded in bringing Indonesia's clove industry to its knees, impoverishing already poor farmers, and bringing considerable disrepute to Indonesia by his actions — but he had made a lot of money.

TOMMY STRIKES AGAIN — THE TIMOR CAR FIASCO

Tommy likes cars. Especially fast ones. Like most young car enthusiasts, he dreamt of owning a Lamborghini. But like the Soeharto that he is, he couldn't stop at just one — so he went to Italy and bought the company. He and occasional business partner, fellow Indonesian, Setiawan Djody, together with the Malaysian company, Mycom, paid anywhere between US$50 million and US$125 million for the Italian sports car manufacturer in November 1993, buying it from the U.S. car company, Chrysler.[15]

But the Lamborghini purchase didn't satiate Tommy's interest. After mulling over the possibility for a number of years, he started Indonesia's infamous national car project in 1995. Cars were already being produced in Indonesia by joint ventures with Japanese, South Korean, and European car manufacturers. Mostly, they assembled vehicles from imported components. Tommy's plan was to use technology from South Korea's Kia Group to produce a car in Indonesia — the Timor — the bulk of which was to be made from local parts. But having absolutely no car manufacturing facility in Indonesia, it was to be many years before Tommy's dream was to be realized. What to do? Tommy hit on the idea of importing fully assembled Kia cars to Indonesia and selling them as

Timor cars. Ludicrous though this plan to fully import a car from one country to serve as another's national car was, the Indonesian government obliged and Tommy was granted a license to import 45,000 Kia cars. He then secured an exemption from import duties and sales and luxury taxes from his father, and was able to put the cars on the market in Indonesia at a price 30–50% below the competitors and still make a tidy sum on a substantial mark-up. Indonesia now had a national car that was 100% imported. Most of the cars then on sale in Indonesia had at least been assembled in the country, but Indonesia's national car wasn't even that. The absurdity of it all was plain to everyone except, it seemed, President Soeharto.

The Timor wasn't terribly popular with Indonesian car buyers. The controversy surrounding the decision to import the cars, and the fact that it was linked to Tommy, who is universally regarded in Indonesia as the most 'brat-like' of Soeharto's children, didn't help sales. Another reason was that it was simply dangerous to be seen in one. An expatriate I know had his Timor set upon four days after he bought it, by as many as 30 youths who beat in every panel with sticks while he was caught in a Jakarta traffic jam. He felt lucky to escape with his life. Not surprisingly, Jakarta motorists didn't feel like being turned into political targets simply by the choice of their car. Sales suffered accordingly.

So, Tommy was left with a large number of Timor cars on his hands. What happened next was probably predictable. It's only fitting that government departments and state-owned companies should support a national car. Indeed, it might be considered unpatriotic even to buy anything other than the national car. So the government issued a directive that all government institutions must buy the Timor. Even Tommy's brother, Bambang, complained about this latest move, especially since he had just signed an agreement with another South Korean car company, Hyundai, to produce cars in Indonesia — but without the special tax and import duty exemptions that had been granted to Tommy's Timor.[16] Other government-related entities soon fell into line, particularly those headed by officials keen to be seen doing the right thing by the Soeharto family. The governor of central Java announced a plan to buy 105 Timor cars for senior officials and regents in his province.[17] This was followed by an announcement that all 100 members of central Java's Local House of Assembly had 'agreed' to buy a Timor for themselves and to pay for them from their own pockets.[18] Jamsostek, the state-managed pension fund for workers in Indonesia, which is regularly pillaged in 'national interest,' also bought 20 Timors cars.[19] Indonesia's wealthy Chinese business community, which is regularly press-ganged into 'national interest' projects as part of the informal tax it must pay for having been allowed its success, also bought Timor cars. The Indonesian-Chinese property and industrial Mulia Group bought 144 Timors cars.[20] One was even given to Nobel Peace Prize winner, East Timor's Bishop Carlos Belo.[21] Perhaps it was thought that this might legitimize them. It didn't. After Soeharto was ousted from office, the Indonesian province of East Kalimantan held a fire-sale for the Timor cars it had bought for its Members of Parliament. It intended to use the proceeds from the sale to buy essentials for the poor, such as rice, sugar, cooking oil, and kerosene. It was all rather symbolic.

The award of the national car status to the Timor came with the proviso that Tommy's PT Timor Putra Nasional (TPN) actually had to commence assembling and then manufacture Timor cars in Indonesia. Car plants require enormous capital investments to establish. Tommy initially approached foreign banks, but after initial interest, they shied away when Japan, supported by the European Union and the United States, filed a complaint to the World Trade Organization (WTO) against Indonesia over the Timor car. Tommy then approached Indonesia's larger banks. Understandably, they too weren't enthusiastic. Part of the problem was that various companies connected to the Soeharto family didn't have a good record for actually paying back the loans from Indonesian banks, and Tommy was asking for loans that totaled US$1.3 billion. Tommy approached Indonesia's central bank to request that the private loans granted for the Timor project be guaranteed by the bank — after all, the Timor was a national car. This request too was refused, but what the central bank did, in conjunction with the government, was to order 16 Indonesian banks — four state-owned banks and 12 private banks — to provide the project financing that Tommy needed. The consortium of banks eventually came up with an offer of US$690 million, leaving the rest to be raised from a proposed share issue of TPN, the company charged with making the car. Several of the private banks were reportedly prepared to immediately write off whatever loans they had to give to TPN.[22] The central bank governor, Soedradjad Djiwandono, was known to have opposed to the plan but had to profess support for it in public, as he had done with so many other schemes in Indonesia that have involved politically powerful figures. 'I'm the strongest supporter of the national car plan,' Soedradjad was quoted as saying.[23] Such effusive support from such an unlikely source equated to a public rebuke in Indonesia's political 'doublespeak.'

Several months after the banks had been 'invited' to lend to TPN, the company still hadn't received much or any of the money, prompting it to complain publicly.[24] As the economic crisis engulfed Asia in the latter part of 1997, the banks found it increasingly difficult to find the money.

Non-performing loans had already risen dramatically, and banks simply didn't need any more such loans. When the IMF was going through the Indonesian government's finances, it found what it described as a 'well-endowed' fund. The fund was for reforestation and improving anti-fire defenses after Indonesia's disastrous forest fires in the latter half of 1997. The fires had left much of South-East Asia covered in thick smoke for months, led to the smoke-related deaths of hundreds of people, and for a time ruined the tourist trade for Singapore, Malaysia, and parts of Indonesia. 'Why hasn't the money been spent?' asked the IMF. 'The money has been set aside to help build the Timor national car,' was the reply.[25] The national car plan was abandoned as part of the conditions the IMF attached to its emergency loans to Indonesia in 1998.

THE BUSANG GOLD FIASCO

Yet another telling episode of how business is done in Indonesia was the scrum over the Busang gold deposits. In late 1995, a small Canadian mining company called Bre-X Minerals announced that it had found a significant gold deposit at Busang in East Kalimantan. The announcement set off an extraordinary chain of events that fluctuated between farce and fraud. Over the next few months, the claims as to how much gold Busang contained steadily escalated. A significant find grew into the biggest find ever. Calculations were made that the deposit contained the equivalent of US$21 billion in gold, and the rush was on. Mining companies scrambled over each other for a piece of the action, as did members of the Soeharto family. Bre-X needed a partner to help develop the mine, and Canada's Placer Dome and Barrick Gold Corporation offered themselves as suitors. The Indonesian government told Bre-X that it had to accept Barrick as its partner and, on top of that, Barrick would be taking a 75% stake in the mine. Bre-X understandably objected. Meanwhile, a local businessman, Jusuf Merukh, claimed that he held proper title to much of the land that covered the Busang site. Clearly, Bre-X needed a protector.

Bre-X announced that it had awarded a company owned by Soeharto's eldest son, Sigit, 10% of two properties at the Busang concession and also placed the firm (or more precisely, Sigit) on a US$1 million-a-month retainer for 40 months to assist in 'administrative' matters. Barrick, meanwhile, needed more fire power to back its claims, so it teamed up with Sigit's sister, Tutut. This set the scene for a public Soeharto family feud, so President Soeharto's closest friend, businessman Bob Hasan, was called in to broker a compromise among all the parties involved. He arranged for Bre-X to have a 45% share, two Indonesian companies to take a 30% share, 10% for the

Indonesian government, and 15% for the U.S. mining company, Freeport McMoRan Copper and Gold, Inc. The U.S. company had just provided Hasan with financing so that a company associated with him could buy a 9.4% stake in Freeport's Irian Jaya mine. Everything now seemed bedded down, but there was one problem. Soon after, the Bre-X geologist credited with finding the Busang deposit, Filipino Michael de Guzman, died when he fell or jumped from a helicopter that was carrying him to the Busang site. There, he was to meet several of Freeport's geologists who were at Busang to conduct due diligence on the site before their company bought into it. It's not widely known, but the helicopter from which de Guzman fell belonged to a company owned by Bambang, but that was a coincidence. Once cores from the site were taken and independently tested, it was announced that everyone had been subjected to a giant fraud. There was no gold at Busang. Perhaps the biggest casualty was Indonesia's reputation. However, for the first time, the world had a clear view of the role that the Soeharto family played in business in Indonesia. Two offspring of the president fought hard to be the first to feed at a trough before they had even checked to see what was in it — and they did it before the world's media.

MORE DEALS

Many of the Soeharto family's business ventures involved infrastructure development, but many didn't. Many ventures involved securing licenses and distribution rights that simply pushed up prices and penalized ordinary Indonesians. As has been noted, contracts with state-owned agencies were among the Soehartos' favorite sources of revenue. Bureaucrats were routinely pressured into signing contracts, even when the deal wasn't in their agency's best interest. The rub for them was that when their agencies were pushed to the brink of insolvency by these practices, they couldn't publicly turn around and blame the Soehartos, but instead had to endure castigation in public for being such poor managers. The frustration for some of them, particularly those who were competent, must have been soul-destroying. Djiteng Marsudi, the head of state-owned electricity supplier PLN, is a case in point. After Soeharto's resignation, he told of a typical incident on one of Soeharto's official trips to Germany in 1995. 'I was invited to go along, unaware that I was going to sign a power purchase agreement,' Djiteng said. 'I was taken aback and couldn't do anything but sign the contract on behalf of PLN.'[26] The agreement Djiteng signed was with a consortium that included Soeharto's children.

Loans from state banks were another favorite way of raising cash. The banks' directors were pressured into granting loans to the Soeharto companies knowing that they almost certainly wouldn't be paid back. In 1992, the World Bank offered Indonesia US$307 million in fresh bank capital in return for better banking standards. The Indonesian government readily accepted the offer and injected the funds into the state-owned bank system, where they were quickly dissipated in another round of 'loans' to companies linked to the Soeharto family and its various cronies.[27] Thanks to the World Bank, the Soehartos had found a way to pillage the funds of the international community and not just those of their countrymen.

Pillaging Telecommunications

PLN wasn't the only state-owned enterprise to have been pillaged for cash by the Soehartos. In telecommunications, they found a whole sector that was ripe for looting. In 1991, Tutut secured a license to operate a private television station across Indonesia, TPI. It was never a success. Initially, it simply borrowed equipment from the state-owned television station, TVRI, to operate. It also borrowed heavily from Tutut's Bank Yama, which contributed to the bank breaching regulations on loans to affiliates and ultimately to its near collapse. Toward the end of 1997, TPI itself was near collapse. So, Tutut had Indonesia's state-owned long-distance telephone company, Indosat, 'agree' to buy what was then US$45.4 million worth of convertible bonds.[28] The value of the bonds happened to almost match TPI's total debts, rendering it debt-free just as the country was about to slide into its biggest economic crisis for 30 years. TVRI was able to repay Bank Yama so that the bank too was saved from ruin. As awful as this deal seemed to be, at least it had a degree of transparency.

When in 1993, Indonesia's highly profitable state-owned Palapa communications satellites were transferred to a private company, PT Satelindo, which was 60% owned by Bambang, not only was there no tender, but it wasn't even clear that the government had actually received any payment for them.[29] Bambang's companies later acquired two additional satellites from Hughes Space and Communications, Inc. of the United States, made possible in part by a US$136 million loan guarantee provided by the US government's Export-Import Bank.[30]

In December 1996, strange things were again happening to Indonesia's public telecoms sector. The Indonesian government decided to sell an additional 4.15% of its domestic telephone service provider, PT Telkom — it had already floated part of the company on the local stock exchange the previous year. Investment bankers were keen to handle the sale, as the stake, though small, was to be sold for US$600 million.

Numerous bids to handle the sale were submitted to the government, but when government officials met to decide how the placement should be undertaken, just one bid was considered — that which had been submitted by a major U.S. investment bank together with well-connected local stock-broker, PT Makindo. What had reduced the field to just one bid? As the decision day drew close, potential bidders were told that they would have to meet certain unwritten conditions, one of which was that they must be prepared to place as much as half of the shares with an offshore company owned by 'a well-connected local businessman' and to provide attractive financing for that purchase to boot. Several competing investment houses withdrew for fear that the new conditions would have led to a clear violation of the United States' Foreign Corrupt Practices Act. Just who that businessman was hasn't been made public, but on the basis of previous practice in Indonesia, few people had any doubts as to which family he belonged.[31]

Pillaging Aviation Fuel

In 1989, Tommy and businessman Bob Hasan bought control of an airline — Sempati Air. Connections count for a lot in Indonesia, and soon after the purchase, Sempati was able to break the monopoly that state-run Garuda Airlines had on domestic jet services and on international routes. This was certainly one example of where the power of the Soeharto family actually benefited the public. Garuda had grown astonishingly slothful as a monopoly, and competition from the new entrant did much to improve services all round. Unfortunately, Sempati's use of its new connections didn't end there. To cut costs and bolster profits, Sempati stopped paying the state-owned oil company, Pertamina, for its aviation fuel. (It had long since stopped paying for its airport landing fees and catering bills.) No one at Pertamina dared to raise the issue with Sempati on account of its new and powerful backers. It wasn't long before Garuda found that the only way it could compete was to stop paying for its fuel too. The situation persisted for months as the two airlines worked up millions of dollars in unpaid fuel bills.[32] Eventually, Sempati ran into financial trouble and couldn't pay back its debts anyway. After president Soeharto resigned, it collapsed.

Pillaging Sport

The South-East Asian Games XIX were held in Jakarta in October 1997. Funds, ostensibly to support the games, were collected from compulsory surcharges on households' payments for utilities, such as electricity and the like. The surcharge was levied by requiring payees to also buy a sticker emblazoned with the games logo. Despite the fact that the surcharge was collected by the utilities companies and their agents, a private company associated with Bambang was appointed as the handler of the funds. At the time of its appointment, the company admitted that it intended to charge an administration fee of around US$2 million from the estimated US$16 million in funds that might be collected. But by the end of the year, the levy scheme had been extended, and suggestions appeared in the press that as much as US$40 million had disappeared.[33] Perhaps there was a logical answer to the question of the missing funds, But, as is usual in Indonesia, poor transparency hides a multitude of sins. Or it might not. You never know. The games sticker fiasco came on top of allegations that Bambang's Bimantara Group had been awarded the right by the government to print tax stamps, which was to earn the group as much as US$180 million annually.

Pillaging Farmers and their Fertilizer

Yet another example of the imposition of costs on others to reap profits was eldest son Sigit, urea fertilizer tablet monopoly. Millions of Indonesians survive by growing rice. To this end, fertilizer is an extremely important input for raising crop yields and making otherwise unproductive soil productive. Ariyo Set Wijoyo, a company owned by Sigit, suggested to the government that urea fertilizer applied in tablet rather than granular form was more effective in raising crop yields. So from 1992, the use of tablets over grains was officially encouraged. At the same time, it granted Sigit's company a monopoly to manufacture and distribute the tablets. To encourage farmers to use the tablets, the government ensured that granular urea was difficult to obtain. Many farmers didn't want to use the tablets, especially since they were more labor-intensive to apply than the grains and the necessary applicators that should have been made available with the tablets were in short supply. With rice being one of Indonesia's main crops, Sigit's company earned enormous revenue. This was enhanced by state subsidies, but even these weren't enough. In mid-1997, it was revealed by the state auditor that the government had lost US$6.2 million through a combination of overstocking of urea tablets, 'excess payments' to Ariyo Set Wijoyo, and excess payments of subsidies. And all this was for the brief period of April to September 1996.[34] Ultimately, political sensitivities aroused in the most sensitive of Indonesian sectors — rice-growing — by the urea tablet debacle proved even too much for the president's eldest son to withstand. By the end of 1996, the urea tablet monopoly was taken away from him.[35] Perhaps Sigit was a little embarrassed by the episode, but the millions of dollars he made from the monopoly undoubtedly helped to make him feel better.

Sigit's wife, Elsje, also managed to hook up to the government contract gravy train. In 1995, Solusindo Mitra Sejati, a company she set up, was appointed by the home affairs ministry as a 'consultant' to implement the mass registration of Indonesians and for the production and distribution of identity cards that all residents of Indonesia are required to carry. The appointment was greeted with understandable outrage, particularly as the government already had sufficient capability to produce the cards. But more so because the price ordinary Indonesians were initially asked to pay for the cards was almost five times the price of the old cards.[36] Big Brother comes at a price, particularly if contracted out to Big Brother's wife.

Monuments — But to What?

Toward the end of 1997, a wave of 'bigness' seemed to sweep over everybody in Indonesia's First Family. Everyone wanted to do something big.

Tutut's flagship company, Citra Lamtoro Gung Persada, announced that it would lead a consortium to build a three-tiered above-ground transitway through central Jakarta at an estimated cost of US$2.58 billion.[37] She wasn't daunted by the fact that her brother, Bambang, announced at the same time that he was heading a consortium to build an underground transport system that was to follow almost the same path. Some Jakartans wondered if the three-tier transitway might not collapse onto the underground system, leaving the city where it had started.

Tutut's sister, Titiek, wanted a big project as well. She went for something *really* big and astounded observers by announcing plans to build a bridge from the Indonesian island of Sumatra all the way to Peninsular Malaysia.[38] Her partner in the 95-kilometer bridge was to be the well-connected Malaysian company, Renong. At the time of the announcement, Indonesia's media was filled with pictures of Titiek showing her father, President Soeharto, models of the proposed bridge. Meanwhile, Soeharto's cousin, Sudwikatmono, announced that he had formed a partnership to build the world's tallest tower in Jakarta, the Menara Jakarta.[39] At an estimated total cost of US$560 million, the tower was to cost around US$1 million for each of its proposed 558 meters.

As ordinary Indonesians wondered who was to pay for all the new infrastructure projects the Soeharto family was intent on building (usually *they* did), reality struck. Asia's economic crisis hit and all the projects were either delayed or canceled.

THE THIRD GENERATION: THE RISE OF GRANDSON ARI SIGIT

At the time of Soeharto's resignation, his grandson, Ari Sigit, had managed to amass 28 holding companies and subsidiaries in his Arha Group. Not all were active, however. Some had been set up to lie in wait for the right opportunity, which could then be pushed into a pre-existing company selected from the Arha shelf.

Ari Sigit first appeared on the Jakarta business scene around 1994. He and the son of a prominent figure in Indonesia's then-ruling Golkar Party joined forces to search for business opportunities that their pooled connections could elicit. After a series of early setbacks, Ari Sigit went on to develop ever more audacious plans to generate cash. His efforts did a great deal of harm to the Soeharto family's image within Indonesia, which was quite a feat given the innuendo and scandal that had already enveloped the family.

The Bali Beer Fiasco

But what propelled Ari Sigit to national and even international prominence was the Bali beer scandal, which brewed in 1995. Bali is an island between the main Indonesian island of Java and another known as Lombok. It has its own distinct culture — most of the island's inhabitants subscribe to a Balinese version of Hinduism (most Indonesians are Moslem) — as well as stunning scenery and excellent beaches. It is a tourist mecca, earning billions of dollars in foreign exchange every year. It is also a very big market for beer, not just because of the large numbers of Australian, German, and other tourists who frequent the island, but also because local religious beliefs don't prohibit the locals from consuming alcohol. Ari, a Moslem, together with some partners, came up with the idea of forcing distributors of alcoholic beverages on the island to buy stickers to be attached to the label of each bottle of alcoholic drink sold on Bali. Their company, Arbamass Multi Invesco, collected a Rp 200 levy imposed by the local provincial government, but then added on another Rp 400 as Arbamass's handling charge.[40] The charges were imposed with the full cooperation of Bali's provincial governor, who by all accounts was in on the scheme. The Rp 600 charge added the then-equivalent of US$0.25 to each bottle and can of beer and other alcoholic drinks sold in Bali. Sales of bottles and cans that didn't bear the stickers were illegal. Given the enormous quantity of beer and other such beverages involved, the scheme was set to net Ari millions of dollars in income each year. Indonesia's major beer companies were understandably outraged by such an audacious attack on their livelihood and responded by boycotting beer supplies to the island in early 1996 until the charges were removed. Once news of the boycott surfaced in the international media, President Soeharto's attention was drawn to the activities of his grandson and he called an end to the sticker exercise, not least of all because other Soeharto family members have hotel and other tourism-related interests on the island, and the beer boycott was beginning to harm those interests. President Soeharto's move was a setback to Ari Sigit, but it didn't stop him from approaching the head of one of Indonesia's two major breweries and quietly offering to include him in the revenue generated by the beer levy if he agreed to publicly support the sticker scheme. For the executive, the offer was certainly tempting — it would have involved millions of dollars flowing his way — but he declined.

Having come so close to capturing millions of dollars in revenue from Bali, Ari Sigit searched for another source of revenue. Upsetting beer companies and foreign tourists proved problematic, as they made their grievances public. What Ari needed was a high stream of revenue from a politically weak source. Indonesia's small but wealthy Chinese minority was an obvious target.

A Taste for Birds' Nest

Many Chinese, particularly those who adhere to more traditional tastes, regard birds' nest as a delicacy. Not any birds' nests, but those produced by small birds called swiftlets in many parts of South-East Asia. The actual nest doesn't comprise the sticks and other usual building materials seen in common birds' nests, but only the gelatinous saliva produced by the swiftlets. The nests tend to be translucent, have a plastic-like consistency, and fit easily into the palm of the hand. Rich in protein, the nest is usually boiled into a soup and believed to be beneficial in aiding a multitude of ailments. A typical Cantonese recipe for birds' nest soup will include the nests, vegetable oil, fresh ginger, chicken, mushrooms, and perhaps quail eggs.[41] The demand for the nests is enormous and their production is now a multi-million-dollar business in many parts of South-East Asia. In Indonesia, the best-quality nests come from houses rather than caves, when literally hundreds of swiftlets will take over the ceiling and eaves of a house to make their nests. The only sensible thing the human occupants can do is to move out and find accommodation elsewhere, for the appearance of the birds turns the house into a gold mine. A house that has been taken over by the swiftlets can generate around US$40,000 a year in revenue, depending on birds' nest market conditions. The value of the house, as ramshackle as it might be, is transformed overnight, with hitherto almost worthless housing suddenly changing hands for as much as US$500,000. Local governments in Indonesia have been known to grant licenses for the right to harvest birds' nests from the underside of this bridge or that overpass, as well as from caves and other places inhabited by swiftlets. The birds' nest market is a buoyant one. In the lead-up to the return of Hong Kong to China in 1997, the price of birds' nests in South-East Asia soared as demand rose in Hong Kong on account of the celebratory Chinese banquets that were being held. The market is lucrative. It was also dominated by the Chinese in Indonesia, which made it fertile ground for Ari Sigit's activities.

Ari Sigit approached Indonesia's Birds' Nest Association, which was a grouping of ethnic Chinese birds' nest producers and traders. He soon organized it into a cartel and placed himself and his partners at its top. He then sought government backing to give the association monopoly rights on the export of the nests. Next, he had the association charge a fee of around US$70 for each kilogram of nests exported. The association actually didn't do anything for the money; it said it didn't have to — the money was really an export tax it was collecting on behalf of the government, minus, of course, a handling fee.

Customs officials at Indonesia's airports prohibited the export of nests unless they were accompanied by receipts from the association. But for many birds' nest producers, the fee was exorbitant. So, many exporters sought to avoid Ari Sigit's fees by bribing the customs officials to get their nests aboard planes bound for Hong Kong. One birds' nest producer told me how he managed to take out two suitcases stuffed with birds' nests — a consignment worth in excess of US$50,000 — by first calling the customs department the night before he was due to fly to Hong Kong, negotiating the 'fee' that they would require to allow the consignment through, and then, once at Jakarta's Soekarno-Hatta International Airport, handing over to customs officials his passport stuffed with US dollars. Eventually, customs officials realized just how valuable the nests were and took to confiscating them for themselves. My birds' nest informant indignantly told me how this practice had made the whole matter of exporting the nests an impossibility, because no insurance company in Jakarta was now willing to fully insure his luggage against such loss. Ultimately, what had been a thriving industry was in tatters after Ari Sigit's intervention. In 1997, Indonesia's trade ministry announced that Ari Sigit's association had no legal basis to collect the fees after all, and thus the money collected wasn't a government tax.[42] But the money collected wasn't refunded and remained with Ari and his association. Every cloud has its silver lining, particularly if your grandfather is president.

Monopolizing Chinese Medicines

Another Chinese-dominated industry that Ari Sigit moved into was the import and distribution in Indonesia of traditional Chinese medicines. In 1990, China and Indonesia normalized their relations, which led to a dramatic growth in traditional medicine imports to Indonesia from China. As the trade grew, so did its attractiveness to outsiders wanting a piece of the action. In 1996, Ari Sigit had one of his companies, PT Arvesco Husada, granted the sole right to import Chinese medicines and operate a state-sponsored compulsory labeling system. Naturally, quality issues were at stake and Arvesco's public rationalization as to why it should have a labeling monopoly was to protect consumers from improperly labeled medicines. Chinese herbalists in Jakarta claimed that the introduction of Arvesco as a middleman led to the prices of some imported traditional medicines more than doubling overnight.[43] Arvesco's annual profit from the traditional Chinese medicine trade grew to around US$7 million each year, with the company controlling more than 50% of the Chinese medicines trade in Indonesia.

Taxing Schoolchildren

In August 1997, reports began to appear in the Indonesian media that parents across the archipelago were being forced by their children's schools to buy specially branded black shoes marked with an 'OSIS' logo. The schools had said that the shoes were to be part of the national school uniform, that it would be compulsory for all school children to wear them, and that the scheme was endorsed by Indonesia's Ministry of Education and Culture. Much of the outcry from parents was on account of the high price attached to the shoes — Rp 21,000 (then, US$7.50) — which was far above the price of equivalent shoes that could be bought in market across Indonesia and was a significant amount of money in a country where the annual per-capita income then was barely above US$1,000.[44] The company that had apparently reached an agreement with the education ministry to supply the shoes was the hitherto unheard of PT Aryo Nusa Pakarti. The initial media reports didn't say so at the time, but the scheme had the hallmark of a venture designed by Ari Sigit, particularly as the company didn't actually intend to make shoes but merely act as a middleman. With 26.5 million elementary schoolchildren in Indonesia and assuming that each child would need at least one pair of shoes per year and a mark-up of 40% by the company, Ari Sigit was looking at a potential annual profit of almost US$80 million. However, that a grandson of the president was seeking to make so much money from poor families across the country was political dynamite, even for a regime that was essentially totalitarian. After the controversy raged across the nation for several weeks, the president expressed his surprise at and disapproval of the shoe plan, forcing the education department and Ari Sigit to abandon the scheme.[45]

Cash Call: Ari Gets into Telephone Boxes

In 1997, many of Jakarta's streets suddenly sprouted public telephone boxes. Often not just one or two, but sometimes as many as a dozen, and often only meters apart. A contract awarded to Ari Sigit's PT Arhista by Indonesia's state-owned domestic telecommunications company, PT Telkom, suggested an explanation. It allowed Ari Sigit to act as the middleman in procuring coin-operated public telephones, and for his trouble, he was allowed to keep an astonishing 30% of the revenue collected from each telephone.[46] The government contracts didn't end there. Another Ari Sigit company, Arvesco Ganeca, was given a contract to supply books to government schools.

And Now for Some Infrastructure

During the last years of the Soeharto regime, Ari Sigit built other interests around government contracts and licensing. His companies frequently bid for government contracts, which he then sold to others, usually companies controlled by Indonesian-Chinese businessmen, to undertake the actual work. In 1996, one of his companies was awarded the right to build a toll-road in East Java.[47] Another, a joint venture with South Korea's Kuk Dong Construction Industrial Co, was awarded a contract to build another toll-road in 1997. Yet another, Bontang Tirta Sejahtera, was awarded a US$140 million contact to build a water pipeline in Indonesia's East Kalimantan province. His Arvesco Ikabina Esindo was awarded a US$300 million contract to build a power station in the north of Indonesia's Sumatra island. And yet another company, Arvesco Internusa Engineering, was awarded a contract for land reclamation near Jakarta.[48] If rent seeking was Ari Sigit's job, then he was good at it.

Some Dabbling with the Private Sector

But not all of Ari Sigit's ventures were with the public sector. One subsidiary, PT Arha Green Invesco, assisted in land preparation for real estate developers. This largely meant clearing the land of slum dwellers and illegally constructed shanties so that the developers can move in. There were also fiberglass manufacturing interests, an interest in a palm oil plantation, and ownership of Arha Bali Semaranta Rafting, a company that takes tourists white-water rafting on Bali. Ari Sigit's rafting interests came to grief in early 1996 when several foreign tourists drowned when taking part in an expedition organized by his company. The incident led to claims soon after that the company had cut corners to reduce costs.[49]

Ari Sigit Gets Sexy

The Bali rafting mishap didn't diminish Ari Sigit's enthusiasm for business; nor did the Asia financial crisis. In early 1998, the *Asian Wall Street Journal* reported in a world exclusive that Ari Sigit was busy planning the launch of Sexy — his consumer label. The first Sexy boutique was to be opened in Jakarta by the end of the year. Its shelves were to be stocked with Sexy clothes designed by none other than Ari Sigit himself. A chain of Sexy cafés, Sexy soft drinks, and Sexy beer were also on the drawing board. Ari Sigit even mentioned plans for franchising Sexy abroad and hoped to launch the label in London in 1999.[50] Ari Sigit seemed intent on becoming Indonesia's answer to Richard Branson. Perhaps he was considering a joint venture with the UK entrepreneur. But what would it be called — Sexy Virgin?

All Good Things...

Times were tough for Ari Sigit in the immediate post-Soeharto era. No longer could he demand contracts from government departments simply because of who he was. Several of his trading concessions were also taken away. He had to repeatedly deny persistent and very strong rumors that he was behind the import of the drug, Ecstasy, that flooded Jakarta's nightclubs in the latter years of the Soeharto regime.[51] And to add insult to injury, a television soap star also took advantage of Indonesia's post-Soeharto *glasnost* and declared that she had given birth to Ari Sigit's illegitimate child when she was 16. She was paid for her silence, and the baby was taken from her and given to Ari Sigit's aunt Tutut.[52] And in August 2000, Ari Sigit's wife was arrested in Jakarta for drug possession. With Soeharto's departure went Ari Sigit's career. He was just 29 and he had already peaked.

LISTING FOR PROTECTION

An important survival strategy used by the members of the Soeharto family to prepare their business empire for the post-Soeharto days was to list as much of it as possible on stock exchanges in Indonesia and overseas. The wider ownership that comes with going public means more people and institutions have a vested interest in the maintenance of the privileges that have been granted to the Soeharto companies. And if the Soehartos were to successfully list their companies, their shares had to be seen by institutions and the public as attractive stocks to hold. There were at least 19 Soeharto family-linked companies on the Jakarta Stock Exchange at the time of Soeharto's departure from the presidency. One, petrochemicals company Tri Polyta Indonesia, is even listed on the New York Stock Exchange. But the most overt example of the rush to list was provided by Tommy's Humpuss Intermoda Transportasi (HIT), which concluded its IPO in December 1997 despite the fact the Jakarta share market had just crashed. The company's main assets are contracts with Pertamina, the state-owned oil company, to transport liquefied natural gas (LNG) from Indonesia to Japan. HIT was Tommy's only consistently profitable company, and having no other company listed, he was desperate for it to be listed prior to the March 1998 presidential elections, just in case his father didn't run.

ONE LAST FEED AT THE TROUGH

Business people across Asia had to face new realities and austerity with the onset of the region-wide economic crisis in 1997–98. This was particularly so in Indonesia, the hardest hit among Asia's economies. But there was one family that was having none of it — the Soehartos. As ordinary Indonesians faced massive unemployment, enormous price rises for basic commodities, and an erosion of their living standards not seen before, the various relatives of the president behaved as if it was business as usual. President Soeharto himself seemed to be unable to appreciate either the changed circumstances or its causes. Currency speculators and bad weather were behind the region's economic crisis, he told participants of an OPEC conference held in Jakarta in December 1997.[53] Naturally, he took no blame for the crisis. But the actions of his own family even as it was under way exacerbated it.

One of Soeharto's first moves in response to the crisis was to withhold or cancel his approval for more than 150 infrastructure projects around Indonesia. Among them were several projects linked to members of his family. It seemed like a promising start. But then six weeks later, he quietly signed a new decree that allowed 15 of the 150 projects to proceed, or to proceed pending further 'review.' Many of the 15 — power stations, airport upgrades, toll-roads, and the like — happened to be projects controlled by his children. It was a sign of things to come.

Toward the end of 1997, the government closed down 16 private banks at the behest of the IMF as one of the preconditions for providing the country with a 'bail-out' loan package. The 16 were among the worst of Indonesia's banks in terms of poor assets, loan rule violations, and capital adequacy. All the bank owners accepted their fates quietly, except two: the two members of the Soeharto family whose banks were among the 16. Both Bambang (Bank Andromeda) and Probosutedjo (Bank Jakarta) immediately launched lawsuits against the government for closing their banks. For several weeks, Probosutedjo even refused point blank to close his bank and allowed it to operate while the others were padlocked shut by security guards. Eventually, both suits were withdrawn, but only after Soeharto-confidante, Liem Sioe Liong, allowed Bambang to acquire the license and name of Bank Alfa, a small, defunct bank for which he no longer had any use. Bambang repainted the hoardings outside his bank branches to read 'Bank Alfa' instead of 'Bank Andromeda,' changed the letterhead, kept the old staff, and within three weeks of the old bank having closed, Bambang was back in the banking business. It wasn't really what the IMF had in mind.

Another IMF target was Tommy's clove monopoly. The IMF demanded that it be abolished altogether. It was indefensible even in good times; maintaining it in the middle of the worst economic crisis to have hit the country in decades was unconscionable. So, Soeharto closed down the BPPC, but in its place sprang up another of Tommy's companies, Kembang Cengkeh Nasional, from which cigarette manufacturers were required to purchase their cloves. All that had really changed was the clove monopoly's name. Growing outrage at yet another flouting of the IMF's guidelines for assistance finally led Soeharto to publicly announce that the clove monopoly really was to end and that no similar organization would replace it.

Tommy's next move was to arrange to sell stakes in two of his companies that operated large hypermarket-type wholesale stores under the Goro name in Jakarta to a company owned by the Ministry of Cooperatives. No Goro store had ever been profitable, but Tommy demanded US$13 million for them. Shortly after, the stores were looted and partially burned in the riots that precipitated in Soeharto's resignation. When the new cooperatives minister was appointed after Soeharto's departure, one of his first deeds was to launch an inquiry into the terms of the proposed deal.

Bambang too saw opportunity in Indonesia's misery. When the rupiah collapsed, President Soeharto announced that the government would consider subsidizing the import of necessities at about half of the prevailing rupiah rate. This was widely interpreted to mean that the scheme would allow for imports of food and medicine at the cheap exchange rate. Bambang had other ideas. He applied for and was given permission to import foreign-made vehicle parts at the special exchange rate. Not only that, but import taxes were waived as well. The imports were to be handled by Bimantara's motor vehicle division and were aimed at supplying minibus operators in Jakarta.

But one of the most damaging assaults on the Indonesian people was much more surreptitious. It got under way in late 1997 and continued into the early months of 1998.

Raiding the Retirement Savings of Indonesian Workers

In November 1997, President Soeharto called on Indonesia's state-owned enterprises to support the stock market by using some of their 'excess' capital to buy up shares. Jamsostek, the state-managed pension fund that looks after the compulsorily acquired retirement savings of Indonesian workers, was one of the most vociferous in heeding Soeharto's call. But its buying spree was selective. The stocks of the state-controlled telecoms were targeted, but so were the stocks of Soeharto companies such as Tutut's toll-road operator Citra Marga Nusaphala Persada and Bambang's Bimantara Citra. Jamsostek bought heavily into another Bambang company, property developer Bhuwanatala Indah Permai. It was an interesting investment given that the company was utterly insolvent. Jamsostek's buying didn't include the shares of a single company controlled by Indonesian-Chinese. All the trades were undertaken through two government-owned securities companies. Their support for the Soeharto companies kept them so busy that they even hired new staff when most private securities firms in Jakarta had all but collapsed. Jamsostek's massive buying kept the prices of Soeharto-linked shares artificially high, but it also allowed the various members of the Soeharto family to cash in their shareholdings by selling millions of dollars worth of their shares to the state-run pension fund. It was a raid on the savings of ordinary Indonesians of enormous proportions and it allowed the Soehartos to push their increasingly worthless and debt-ridden companies onto the state sector, as the nation's economy collapsed around them.

A Day of Reckoning?

Soeharto resigned from the presidency in March 1998. He had little choice. There was rioting in the streets and senior members of the government were deserting him one by one. His successor, Habibie, owed his political position, his family's business success and everything else to Soeharto. No one expected that Habibie would hold a serious investigation into the Soeharto family's wealth and they weren't disappointed. The first investigation held by the Habibie administration folded due to 'lack of evidence.' The outcry that this was met with and the fact that Habibie decided that he quite liked being president and hoped to stand for re-election induced him to announce another investigation. Habibie's Attorney-General, Muhammad Ghalib, and Coordinating Minister for Development Supervision, Hartarto Sastrosoenarto, were sent to Soeharto's house to tell him of the new investigation. The fact that two ministers went to see Soeharto rather than Soeharto being called in for questioning suggested what sort of inquiry it would be. So did the fact that the family of Hartarto had wealth that was itself worthy of investigation. Their Garama Group comprised at least 30 separate companies, which operated in sectors that closely mirrored those that Hartarto had been responsible for either as a minister or a senior civil servant. The inquiry was of course political window-dressing and was still stumbling along by the time Habibie was pushed out of office.

Soeharto and his family feigned incredulity at the need for such investigations. They couldn't see what all the fuss was about. Soeharto appeared on his daughter Tutut's TPI television station in September 1998 to say that 'I don't have one cent of savings abroad. I don't have accounts at foreign banks. I don't have deposits abroad and don't have any shares in foreign firms, much less billions of dollars.' He was probably correct. Much of the posturing over Soeharto's wealth focused on him rather than on his family. It also focused excessively on whether the family has assets abroad even though it happily admits to controlling billions of dollars of assets in Indonesia. Furthermore, Indonesia's legal system is so weak and its laws so ill-defined that when Soeharto and his family claimed they broke no law, they were probably correct. It would after all be particularly clumsy to break the laws when you in fact make them.

In May 1999, *Time* magazine published a cover story in which it was alleged that the Soeharto family had amassed a fortune of US$15 billion.

The centerpiece of *Time's* many allegations was that the Soehartos had transferred US$9 billion from Switzerland to a bank in Austria. *Time* offered no solid evidence for the allegation. Soeharto sued *Time* in a Jakarta court for defamation in relation to the entire article including the cover and sought US$27 billion in damages. I was among those who provided a sworn affidavit on behalf of *Time*. I focused on details of Soehartos' assets and modus operandi within Indonesia (I had nothing to offer on the US$9 billion allegation.) The court eventually rejected the suit in June 2000. It declared that Soeharto had not been defamed.

It has always been widely assumed that the Soeharto family has vast sums of cash stashed overseas. One or two academics have built careers on such claims. But it has never been clear to me that this is the case. There is no doubt that the Soehartos made themselves extraordinarily wealthy and they did so through corruption and nepotism, but the great bulk of what they have was and remains in Indonesia.

With President Wahid's coming to office, there was a new investigation into the family's wealth. The claims as to the size of the wealth grew ever more astronomical and some of the more extraordinary claims came from Wahid himself. There was more political impetus behind this investigation, but this time Soeharto, weakened by a series of strokes, was able to avoid intense scrutiny due to illness. Asked if it was true for example, that he had the then-finance minister issue rules in 1996 that required state banks to give 5% of their net profits to his charitable foundations, Soeharto replied that he could not remember. With the need to be seen to be doing something, the government arrested Soeharto confidante Bob Hasan in March 2000 and detained him at the Attorney General Marzuki Darusman's office, apparently in a cage that Marzuki would only confirm was of 'minimum conditions.' Soeharto himself was finally ordered to stand trial on corruption-related charges in August 2000 but these were later dismissed on the grounds of Soeharto's alleged ill-health. Tommy, too, was ordered to stand trial but managed to abscond. He was still at large toward the end of 2000.

CHAPTER 14

Other Politicians, Other Businesses

The lack of separation between politics and business is one of South-East Asia's great challenges for the future. It is a problem that cuts widely and deeply. The problem extends beyond the presidents of Indonesia.

Presidents Habibie and Soeharto are, of course, not the only Asian political figures to have used their positions to benefit their families. Many other Indonesian ministers and senior political figures have availed themselves or their families of the spoils of office. In Malaysia, the children of senior political figures have also gone into business — some legitimately, and some not quite so. In Thailand, the blurring of politics and business is such that on occasions, Cabinet meetings might well have doubled as meetings of the Thailand Chamber of Commerce. Senior executives of many of Bangkok's biggest businesses seem to rotate between the boardrooms of Bangkok and the Cabinet with astonishing regularity.

FOLLOW THE LEADER: THE INDONESIAN CABINET GETS DOWN TO BUSINESS

The Soeharto family did very well out of Indonesia. The Habibie family hasn't done that badly either. Individual members of both families accumulated great wealth during the Soeharto years, but they aren't the only ones to have benefited from their positions. Public officials at all levels in Indonesia use their positions to grant themselves or their families special privileges and benefits. The Soehartos probably aren't unusually nepotistic; it's simply that they had greater opportunities than most. The level below them in the power structure had more opportunities than the one below it, and so on. Corruption and nepotism pervade all levels; it's the opportunities that differ. Indonesia is full of potential Soeharto families. Using one's public position to provide private benefits to oneself and one's immediate family is a fundamental part of what Indonesia is today. This is borne partly from absurdly low salaries paid to civil servants in Indonesia, partly from Indonesia's legal system being so woefully inadequate, and partly from a culture that not only has few sanctions against such practices, but also actually seems to encourage them. The absence of a well-resourced and inquisitive opposition over the decades has also meant one less constraint on the rapaciousness of those in power.

In 1997, I attended a seminar at Jakarta's Grand Hyatt at which Indonesia's then-Minister for Communications, Joop Ave, was a speaker. Just before the minister took the podium, the seminar adjudicator asked the members of the audience to switch off their mobile telephones to ensure that the minister's presentation wouldn't be punctuated every few minutes by shrill ringing from around the room. The minister expressed his mock indignation. 'How dare he tell you to switch off your phones,' he barked. 'Every time one of those things rings, I make money!' He was only half-joking. The speed of change in telecommunications technology is such that every few years, new technology arrives and must be licensed by governments around the world. In Indonesia, each new communications system, and thus each new round of licensing, means new opportunities to bestow government largesse and privileges on those with political connections. Hence, the spread of new technologies to a country like Indonesia is more rapid than in many Western economies, simply on account of the opportunities for nepotism the mandate of each technology that sweeps through represents.

In 1997, the Indonesian government invited 'bids' for licenses to operate handphone systems based on the new PCN technology. Interested parties were able to pay Rp5 million (at the time about US$2,000) to purchase a pre-qualification document. But as is the way of these things in Indonesia, the formal selection criteria weren't the only selection criteria. The call for tenders flushed out an astonishing array of companies that not only were hitherto unknown in telecommunications, but also were hitherto unknown at all. The one common characteristic among them, however, was that almost without exception they were backed by politically well-connected figures. Ari Sigit put in two bids via two companies that he had created especially for the opportunity. A company partly owned by Titiek put in another bid. So did a company owned by the son of the former head of the state-owned oil company Pertamina; as did a company headed by the son of Ginandjar Kartasasmita, the then-Minister for National Development Planning; another headed by a retired general and partly owned by Ginandjar's brother; and another partly owned by a son of former vice president, Try Sutrisno; and yet another owned by president Soeharto's half-brother,

Probosutedjo; and another controlled by a son of Habibie, who was then just a minister. Only companies plugged into the political elite put in expressions of interest; others, even those with vast telecoms experience, simply didn't bother. But like Busang, telecommunications is a gold mine and the rush was on. Merit is the fundamental criterion for such tenders in most countries. In Indonesia, all too often, it's an optional extra. The nexus between politics and business is played out over and over in Indonesia. Many aspiring politicians entered Soeharto's Cabinet with almost nothing, but left with a conglomerate.

The Manggala Group of companies is owned by Tantyo Adji Pramudyo, son of Soedharmono, Indonesia's vice president between 1988 and 1993. The group is a typical Indonesian conglomerate, with a haphazard range of interests from shrimp hatching to oil drilling. As usual, many of the companies are dependent on either contracts or approvals from Pertamina or other government bodies. The group encompasses at least 39 companies.

But one doesn't need to be a president or a vice president of Indonesia for one's family to have a stratospheric rise in business. Bustanil Arifin served as Indonesia's Minister for Cooperatives and chairman of the so-called National Logistics Agency (Bulog) until March 1993. Bulog was in charge of flour milling and flour pricing in Indonesia. While Arifin was minister, his wife Christine was a shareholder in Liem Sioe Liong's flour monopoly run by Liem's Bogasari Flour Mill — the chief beneficiary of Bulog's restrictive importing and distribution policies. Arifin's daughter, Arnie, also went into business. A company controlled by her borrowed at highly reduced rates of interest from Bank Bukopin, a state-sponsored bank that was under her father's control, to buy the building that housed the bank's head office. As if that wasn't extraordinary enough, she then leased the building back to the bank.[1] After Arifin left the Cabinet, his family emerged as the controllers of the diversified Daniputra Nugra Utama business group, which encompasses at least 45 subsidiaries. These operate in property, agri-business, oil drilling, and forestry. The family also has a stake in Indonesia's paper manufacturing Pakerin Group.

Another minister who served with Bustanil Arifin was Radius Prawiro. He was the Coordinating Minister for Economy, Finance, and Industry between 1988 and 1983. In late 1997, President Soeharto again sought his help as Indonesia's economy collapsed; and in early 1998, President Soeharto appointed him to advise the government on rescheduling debt. Although a widely respected economist and seen as one of the few senior politicians in Indonesia to stand up for economic reform, Prawiro's family have not been shy about going into business.

His four children established the diversified Lumbung Sumber Rejeki Group. Altogether, the family controls at least 81 companies in Indonesia.

Hartarto Sastrosoenarto, a long-serving minister whom President Habibie appointed as his coordinating Minister for Development and National Reform in May 1998, was first appointed to the Cabinet in 1983 as the Minister for Industry. Until then, he had been a life-long bureaucrat. In the 1960s, he headed a state-owned pulp and paper mill and in the 1970s, he was the director of silicate and fertilizer industries in the Ministry of Industry. His family's business interests later matched these positions. Hartarto's three sons and two daughters founded the Garama Group in the late 1980s. The group has at least 30 separate companies, and possibly many more, which range across pulp and paper, packaging, chemical processing, manufacturing, shipping, engineering, palm oil plantations, and poultry raising. Another Hartarto company, PT Graha Curah Niaga, exports fertilizer from state-owned fertilizer factories. Some Hartarto family companies have been set up overseas. Fajar Paper Australia Pty Ltd, for example, is based in Melbourne, Australia, and was first registered in 1992. It is involved in paper export and import, and shares several directors with Fajar Surya Wisesa.

The family of Ginandjar Kartasasamita, another long-serving minister who was appointed by President Habibie as the Coordinating Minister for Economy, Finance, and Industry in May 1998, is yet another political family that is heavily involved in business. One brother, Agus Gurlaya Kartasasamita, owns a quarter of the Catur Yasa Group. It has some 18 subsidiaries, mostly involved in engineering and construction — activities that are highly dependent on government licenses, approvals, and contracts. There are also some activities in the mining and energy sector, including some that are connected to the controversial Freeport mine in Irian Jaya. (Ginandjar served as Minister for Mines and Energy between 1988 and 1993.) A Ginandjar son, Agus Gumiwang Kartasasamita, was part of a consortium to take over a failed textiles conglomerate, the Golden Key Group, and was one of the many politically well-connected scions to seek a PCN handphone license from the government.

Abdul Latief, the Minister for Manpower between 1993 and 1998, was already a successful businessman when he entered the Cabinet. But his entry to politics did his business interests no harm. His Alatief Group encompasses some 32 subsidiaries that include companies that own many non-mining assets associated with the Freeport mine. While Latief was a minister, his companies and his partners bought approximately US$370 million worth of assets from Freeport, financed by approximately US$255 million of debt guaranteed by Freeport.[2] The group also owns the

Sheraton Hotel near the mine and one of Jakarta's biggest shopping centers (Pasar Raya) and an adjacent hotel and office tower. In 1995, a consortium to which his group belonged was awarded a 15-year concession to install and operate a telephone network in Indonesia's East and West Kalimantan provinces. To complement these interests, Latief also owns several magazines and a newspaper.

Harmoko, who was appointed the Speaker of Parliament in 1997 and was the Minister for Information between 1983 and 1997, tended to own much of the ministerial portfolio he administered. While he was Minister for Information, he owned some of the country's biggest and most influential newspapers. His Pos Kota Group also has its own newsprint mill. Harmoko also has an interest in the English-language *Jakarta Post* newspaper — an interest that the owners of the *Post* gave to him when they were seeking a publishing license. When Harmoko, as information minister, closed down three newspapers and magazines in 1994, because they had allegedly strayed too far beyond what they had been licensed to report, many were especially suspicious of Harmoko's motives with the banning of *Detik* — a tabloid that was a competitor to a tabloid owned by Harmoko.

Harmoko is also close to ethnic Chinese businessman, Mohammad Lukminto, who owns the Sritex textile and clothing group of companies. Harmoko's late brother, Noor Slamet Asmoprawiro, was a partner in several of Lukminto's companies.[3] Sritex was awarded the contract to make all the yellow shirts that supporters of Soeharto's ruling Golkar Party wear while Harmoko was the chairman of Golkar. Sritex also has contracts with the Indonesian military to supply uniforms and, in 1997, was awarded a contract by NATO to make 500,000 uniforms for NATO member countries.[4] The group employs around 12,000 workers.

'Old soldiers never die, they only fade away' goes the popular saying. Perhaps the Indonesian adaptation could be: 'Old Cabinet ministers never die, they just start a conglomerate.' After Soeharto's forced resignation in May 1998, demands came from around the country for an inquiry into the wealth of the Soeharto family. But such an inquiry seemed unnecessarily narrow. The wealth of many Cabinet ministers, past and present, and of past vice presidents, is undoubtedly worthy of inquiry as well.

THE MAHATHIR FAMILY IN BUSINESS

Malaysia sits on a peninsula that juts out from southern Thailand and shares the island of Borneo with Indonesia. It is sophisticated, organized, and modern. Around 35% of its 19 million people is ethnically Chinese, another 10% is Indian, and the rest are indigenous people, mostly Malays. In many respects, it's a highly developed country. Public infrastructure is of a very high standard. The country is criss-crossed by high-quality toll-roads, and wherever you go, water can be drunk straight from the tap. The only other South-East Asian country that can claim this is the city-state of Singapore — but then, most of its water is piped in from Malaysia anyway. Much of what Malaysia is today is due to Prime Minister Dr Mahathir Mohamad.

One thing in Malaysia that is more important than first-rate highways and clean drinking water is the sense of self-confidence. This, more than anything else, is Mahathir's greatest achievement — he has taught Malaysians, especially Malaysia's ethnic Malay population (the *bumiputra*), to be confident. And if one wants to see what a nation of people with little self-confidence is like, one need only travel to nearby Indonesia where pathos is one of the few commodities not in short supply. It's for this reason that Dr Mahathir might well be regarded as one of Asia's great leaders. His relentless and self-serving attacks on the West and his ridiculous tirade against currency trader, George Soros, at whose feet Mahathir puts much of the blame for Asia's economic crisis when it first emerged, are more easily forgiven when they are seen for what they are — attempts to deflect the attention of Malaysians from their own ethnic and cultural divides so that they can stand united against a common foe. Indonesia's reaction to the crisis, on the other hand, was to look for scapegoats at home — and months of violence directed at its ethnic Chinese community was the result. To some, Mahathir's outbursts are a sign of his petulance, but they can also be seen as evidence of his nation-building. In any event, Mahathir really should be judged by what he has done instead of what he says, and his achievement is what Malaysia has become today. This is not to say that Mahathir is perfect. He is far from it — but let credit be given where it is due. Malaysia's court system works relatively well, particularly in so far as business litigation is concerned; there have been concerted efforts to stamp out official corruption, particularly at the federal level. There is great depth to the Malaysian Cabinet, as well. Throughout Mahathir's tenure as Prime Minister, there have been several ministers who could have taken over from him and the country would still have been in relatively safe hands.

Again, the contrast with Indonesia couldn't be more stark. Soeharto spent much of his 30-odd years in power eliminating rivals, leaving a power vacuum and instability as his legacy. Like the family of Soeharto, Dr Mahathir's family is prominent in business. But there are important differences here too. The Soeharto family's wealth was on a scale never before achieved by the family of any despot in history. But perhaps the main difference has to do with how the wealth was assembled in the first place. What do the relatives of Dr Mahathir really own? The main corporate players in the Mahathir family are his three sons and four of his brothers-in-law. Together, they have significant assets in Malaysia, and collectively serve on the boards of at least 17 companies listed on the Kuala Lumpur Stock Exchange. They also have interests in Hong Kong, Singapore and, in the case of one Mahathir son, a hotel in downtown Sydney, Australia.

Dr Mahathir's wife, Siti Hasmah, is one of ten children. Her father was a stern disciplinarian who rose through the ranks of the civil service. His colleagues and family alike respected him. Three of Siti Hasmah's brothers — Jaffar, Ahmad Razali, and Hashim Mohd Ali — have become prominent in Malaysian business, and one, Ahmad Razali, like the prime minister, has achieved considerable success in politics in his own right. Another brother, Ismail, who passed away in July 1998, was the highly regarded head of Malaysia's Permodalan Nasional, Malaysia's biggest *bumiputra* unit trust agency, which manages investments on behalf of the country's indigenous people. The trust controls around 22 companies listed on the Kuala Lumpur Stock Exchange and, accordingly, Ismail sat on many company boards. He also served as a governor of Malaysia's central bank and was regarded as thoroughly incorruptible.[5]

Dato' Jaffar Mohd Ali is the co-founder and chairman of Jasatera, a construction company now listed on the Kuala Lumpur Stock Exchange. He has a 30% stake in the company, which has built many of Kuala Lumpur's tallest office towers and hotels, including the city's Regent Hotel and Holiday Inn. Jaffar is a director of at least 13 other Malaysian companies, including the listed Cycle and Carriage Bintang. He also has significant interests in advertising. He and two of his brothers, Ahmad Razali and Zainal Abidin, are partners in DiBena Enterprise, a private Malaysian company. Two subsidiaries of this company have joint ventures in Malaysia with Danish firms; one is in the power generation sector, and the other distributes and markets computer software.[6]

But the brothers' business interests don't end there. They have a stake in the Goldtron Group of companies. The group's parent company, Goldtron Ltd, is listed on the Stock Exchange of Singapore. It owns around 70% of Goldtron Holdings, a separate company listed on the Hong Kong stock exchange. In turn, Goldtron Holdings shares ownership of the group's Malaysian arm, Goldtronic (M) Sdn Bhd, with DiBena Enterprise. Jaffar serves as a chairman of the Malaysian arm and is a director of the Hong Kong arm. His nephew and Mahathir son, Mokhzani Mahathir, serves as a director of the Hong Kong arm and in early 2000 was appointed chairman of the Singapore arm. Outside Asia, the Goldtron Group has operations in the United States, China, South Africa, Australia, and Russia, mostly in consumer electronics, magnetic tape, and blank video cassettes. The Singapore arm makes pagers and handphones. Many of the products are distributed under the Goldtron brand name. Jaffar's achievements in business have been considerable. Being a brother-in-law of the prime minister has helped, but it hasn't been the main factor of his success. He would have been successful anyway.

Ahmad Razali Mohd Ali's corporate involvement hasn't been as extensive as Jaffar's. He has chosen to spend more time in politics (he was Chief Minister of the Malaysian state of Selangor between 1982 and 1986), although of course in Malaysia, political and business pursuits need not be mutually exclusive. In the early 1990s, he was part of a group of *bumiputra* figures with strong links to the ruling UMNO party, which acquired stakes in a large number of publicly traded Malaysian companies. Around 1991, he acquired 7% of the listed Setron, a consumer electronics goods-related company. The stake was acquired through a Malaysian company and a Singapore company in which Ahmad Razali held 49% and 51% stakes, respectively.[7] Around the same time, he was appointed as chairman of publicly traded Golden Plus Holdings, a position he retains today. (Another brother, Zainal Abidin, is also a director.) Golden Plus is involved in quarrying, road construction, and property development, and has investments in China.

Hashim Mohd Ali doesn't appear to be greatly active in business, although he sits on the board of several important public Malaysian companies. They include Country Heights Holdings (chairman), which announced in early 1998 that it was taking a 68% stake in a £200 million international exhibition development in London's Docklands,[8] Arab-Malaysian Corporation, and Hong Leong Credit. He also serves on the board of his nephew Mirzan Mahathir's Konsortium Perkapalan.

Dr Mahathir's brothers-in-law have enjoyed success in business, and this success isn't normally linked to their relationship with the prime minister. It's a different story, though, for his sons, Mirzan, Mokhzani, and Mukhriz.[9] The three are said to hold directorships in more than 210 Malaysian companies, including around a dozen publicly listed companies. But the three have tended to stick to well-defined areas of interest in their businesses. For Mirzan, it is transport; for Mokhzani, it is healthcare; and for Mukhriz, optical fiber products and tourism.

Eldest son Mirzan's connections are impeccable. Besides being the son of the prime minister, he is married to a relative of Indonesian billionaire, Liem Sioe Liong. He also formed a joint venture with Singapore-based Kim Eng Securities, which is partly owned by Gloria Lee, a sister-in-law of Singapore's former prime minister, Lee Kuan Yew. Such connections have done him little harm — he has had a meteoric rise in business. He is a director of at least eight publicly traded Malaysian companies, and a director of a listed company in Hong Kong, S. Megga International Holdings, which is one of the world's largest manufacturers of cordless telephones.[10] S. Megga has a joint venture with a subsidiary of China's Ministry of Information Technology, as well as a cordless telephone joint venture called S. Meggatel with local businessman, Patrick Lim, in Malaysia.[11] By 1998, S. Megga faced considerable financial problems. In November 1997, it requested that trading in its shares be suspended pending a restructuring exercise but then refused to allow trade to recommence even seven months later, despite repeated requests from the Hong Kong stock exchange.[12]

Mirzan's private company, Peringkat Prestasi, holds many of his investments, including a 26% stake in Lion Corporation, a diversified Malaysian conglomerate run by Malaysian-Chinese entrepreneur, William Cheng. But Mirzan's main interest is in building a haulage and logistics empire. His flagship company is Konsortium Perkapalan (KP), which he controls through Peringkat Prestasi. KP started out as a trucking company, but Mirzan had much grander designs for it than simple road haulage. In 1994, KP bought Malaysia's second national shipping line, Perbadanan Nasional Shipping Line (which came with 14 vessels), for US$80 million. Further acquisitions consumed more cash, so in 1996, he took KP public. When it listed on the Kuala Lumpur Stock Exchange, it did so with a massive 162% premium over its offer price. Investors fought to get hold of the stock on the assumption that the company's powerful connections would generate opportunities aplenty. Soon after listing, KP was back on the acquisition trail. It paid US$240 million for control of Nasdaq-listed and Hong Kong-based Pacific Basin Bulk Shipping, which came with 25 vessels. Next, control of road haulage company, Diperdana Corporation, was acquired, giving KP control of almost half of Malaysia's road freight market. A 35% stake in air cargo company, Transmile Air Services, followed this. Mirzan was on a roll. KP branched out overseas, too. Its biggest foray abroad is its operation of India's only privatized inland container depot in New Delhi. Its partners are P&O of Australia and an Indian company.[13]

But the most ambitious and controversial part of Mirzan's empire building was his attempt to buy a controlling 30% interest in Malaysia's largest shipping company. Mirzan offered just over US$600 million for the stake in Malaysia International Shipping Corporation (MISC), which has 62 vessels and many subsidiary interests including vegetable oil refining and merchant banking. The 30% stake was held by a government pension fund and although Mirzan had offered what was then a fair price for it, it was below what the fund had originally paid for it. However, in the middle of negotiations, Malaysia's state-owned oil company, Petronas, and a business partner of KP swooped in and bought the stake. Asia's economic crisis struck shortly after and in early 1998, KP announced that it had sold all of its shipping assets to MISC. The prey had suddenly turned predator. The proposed transaction was quickly condemned as a government-sponsored 'bail-out' for a son of the prime minister. That was the charge at least until the price that MISC was to pay for Mirzan's shipping interests was revealed. At US$220 million, it was below even the bottom end of what was considered a 'fair' price by independent valuers, and meant that KP would record an extraordinary loss for the sale.[14] The deal was no bail-out. It was a fire sale.

Dr Mahathir's middle son, Mokhzani, also had a prominent rise in business, although his ambitions haven't been quite as grand as those of his older brother. Apart from his involvement with his uncles' Goldtron Group, his main interest is in Tongkah Holdings in which he is chairman. His relationship with Tongkah began in 1992 when the board approached Mokhzani to see if he was interested in joining the company to give it some greater direction. At that point, Tongkah was doing nothing great and comprised only some small tin dredging and oil and gas interests. It had also made losses for eight straight years. Mokhzani joined, taking equity as he did so, and set about turning it into one of the fastest-growing companies on the Kuala Lumpur Stock Exchange. Within two years, Mokhzani had returned Tongkah to profitability. Early moves were in all directions — seismic data processing, Internet service provision, plantations, plastic molding, granite processing, consumer goods manufacturing, and stockbroking in the form of Kestrel Securities. In 1998, it negotiated to buy another stockbroker, MGI Securities. Ultimately, Tongkah settled on three core areas of activity — stockbroking, manufacturing, and healthcare — spread across 31 subsidiaries. It has been the healthcare interests that have absorbed most of Mokhzani's time.

In 1997, Tongkah commenced a 15-year contract to provide hospital support services to 19 government-owned hospitals in Malaysia. Tongkah also acquired a majority stake in Hospital Pantai, a listed operator and supplier of services to private hospitals in Malaysia. Another Tongkah unit was established to offer telemedicine services. Hospital Pantai, in turn, became a substantial shareholder in Singapore-listed Asia Matrix, the company that had previously been controlled by Elsje Anneke Ratnawati Djoefrie, a daughter-in-law of Indonesia's then-president Soeharto. After Mokhzani bought in, it was transformed from a loss-making plastic injection mold maker into a health services company. It set up a series of healthcare ventures in Singapore and changed its name to AsiaMedic.[15] Yet another Tongkah unit signed an agreement in July 1998 with Becton Dickson & Co of the United States to exclusively manufacture syringe disposal containers for export to Australia and other markets in the Asia Pacific.[16] In all, Mokhzani has assembled a health services group that spans Malaysia, Singapore, and Australia. The expansion is part of a deliberate, careful strategy and not unexpected. Mokhzani is, after all, the son of a medical doctor.

Youngest brother Mukhriz has also made his mark in corporate Malaysia. In 1992, Mukhriz joined a company originally established by Tiong Hiew King, one of Malaysia's richest men. The company was renamed to Optical Communications Engineering (Opcom), and was to make optical fiber products. Eventually, Mukhriz emerged as its main owner with Mokhzani, and together they formed a new company, Opcom Cables, in partnership with Sweden's Ericsson Cables AB. The company's plant is capable of producing 12,000 kilometers of cable a year, and is one of South-East Asia's largest producers of high-speed fiber optic cable. Mukhriz also bought control of Reliance Pacific, a listed operator of 16 two-star hotels around Malaysia and one of Malaysia's biggest tour organizers. Reliance Pacific has also followed the well-worn route from Malaysia down to Australia to invest in property. Subsidiary Prime Heritage heads a consortium that was to build in Sydney two adjacent hotels with a total of 493 rooms. It also owns Sydney's Royal Gardens Hotel, said to be worth A$40 million (US$26 million).[17] Clearly, Mukhriz, like his brothers, has maneuvered his way to the big end of town.

But to what extent is the business success of Dr Mahathir's sons and other relatives dependent on the fact that he is prime minister? And what the inevitable comparisons with the Soeharto family? The Soeharto children's businesses are astonishingly diversified. Their strategy wasn't to develop and then build on any particular expertise over time. Rather, it was based on snatching anything and everything as quickly as possible — the plutocratic equivalent of a 'smash and grab.' Also, many of the Soeharto businesses relied on monopolies and licensing bestowed by the government. In contrast, the Mahathir sons have relatively narrow interests in which they have sought to become expert, and then to build on this expertise. Their acquisitions are based more on strategy than opportunism and generally aren't reliant on government-bestowed licensing and other privileges. It's difficult to find any national infrastructure project in Malaysia in which any member of the Mahathir family has a business involvement. Another very important difference is that debt and share issues have funded the Mahathir businesses, whereas opportunistic gifts of equity from foreign investors were important for the Soehartos' business expansion.

There's no doubt that being the sons of the prime minister has helped them — but this isn't to say that Dr Mahathir has sought to give his sons privileges. If anything, the contrary is true. Arguably, the sons — all foreign-educated and from a household where both their parents were trained as doctors — would have been successful in business anyway. None of the Soeharto children are foreign educated, on the other hand, nor were their parents. Soeharto was a soldier and a smuggler before he ascended to the presidency. To the extent that there is favoritism, at least it is openly questioned and debated in Malaysia. In Indonesia, privileges were granted to the Soeharto family regularly and without debate.

The two different styles of doing business might perhaps explain why the Mahathir family companies and the Soeharto family companies have never been easy suitors despite attempts at pairings on several occasions. In late 1995, rumors surfaced that Soeharto son, Bambang Trihatmodjo, and his business partner, fellow Indonesian Johannes Kotjo, had bought shares in Hospital Pantai just as Mokhzani was buying in. It appeared as if the trio were acting in concert.[18] Around the same time, there were rumors that Bambang was buying up shares in Goldtron in Singapore and Tongkah Holdings in Malaysia. Soon after, it transpired that Indonesia's First Family had bought a stake in Goldtron but it wasn't Bambang that did the buying, but Soeharto grandson, Ari Sigit, and a fellow Indonesian investor. Together, they captured 7.8% of the company.[19] Within a few days, Goldtron announced that it would form a joint venture in Indonesia with one of Ari Sigit's companies. The new venture, PT Arha Nusa Bhakti, was to produce pagers and cellular telephones.[20] However, by mid-1998, the venture still hadn't reached the production stage and Goldtron all but abandoned the plan.

SARAWAK INCORPORATED

The Malaysian state of Sarawak shares the island of Borneo with Indonesia. But that isn't all it shares. The families of both Sarawak's and Indonesia's senior politicians have become spectacularly wealthy in short periods of time. There is a lot of money in Sarawak. Timber has generated much of the money and underwritten a property boom and an infrastructure boom.

Sarawak's chief minister, Abdul Taib Mahmud, has been in power since 1981. He is perhaps the most powerful of all Malaysia's provincial chief ministers. This is largely due to Sarawak's unusual ethnic make-up, which means that his party, Parti Pesaka Bumiputra Bersatu, which federally is minor, is powerful at home. Many years in public life and his relatively modest income from political office haven't meant that Taib has missed out on life's pleasures. Known for his expensive tastes, he is rumored to have paid almost US$2 million for the late American showman Liberace's piano.[21] Liberace's life was filled with many strange twists, but it's unlikely that he would have ever imagined that his piano would find its way to Borneo's steamy jungles. Much of Taib's wealth comes from timber. In 1987, a political feud between Taib and his predecessor, Abdul Rahman Yaacob, saw a flurry of startling allegations made in two of Sarawak's local newspapers, one of which was owned by Abdul Rahman Yaacob and the other by interests allied with Taib. What the allegations revealed was that the current and previous chief ministers had, between them, connections with companies that had been allocated around 30% of Sarawak's forest land for logging. Companies associated with Taib and his supporters had accumulated timber concessions that covered 1.6 million hectares of Sarawak, the logged value of which was of the order of US$12 billion, according to one source.[22] Taib's attachment to forests began in 1966–67 when he served as Sarawak's forestry minister, a post which he has held again since 1985, concurrently with his role as chief minister.[23]

One of the companies that has been at the forefront of Sarawak's development is Cahya Mata Sarawak (CMS). Originally a joint venture between the government's Sarawak Economic Development Corporation and the neighboring Malaysian state's Sabah Economic Development Corporation, the company started out as the local monopoly cement producer to feed the building boom then under way in both states. In 1989, the Sabah state government sold its stake and the government of Sarawak's chief minister, Taib, decided that the company should list on the Kuala Lumpur Stock Exchange. At the same time, the chief minister's brother, Onn bin Mahmud, and his two sons, Mahmud Abu Bekir Taib and Sulaiman Abdul Rahman Taib, bought in. Originally, they held around 10%, 12%, and 12%, respectively, leaving the state through its Sarawak Economic Development Corporation (SEDC) with just 11%. However, by mid-1997, Onn had increased his share to around 33%, and Mahmud and Sulaiman had reduced their holdings to around 9% each. This meant that the family of the chief minister had acquired more than half of the equity in the formerly state-owned company by 1997. By this time, the original part-owner, the SEDC, was left with approximately 8.5%.[24] CMS hasn't looked back since the Taib family bought in.

It wasn't long before the cement company had been transformed into a diversified conglomerate that sprawled across infrastructure development, water supply, steel making, transportation, manufacturing, property development, financial services, and stockbroking. By 1998, CMS had at least 43 subsidiaries. One was CMS Transportation, which had formerly been known as Archipelago Shipping and owned by Onn until he sold it to CMS.[25]

Over the last eight years, CMS Group has moved to sew up Sarawak's construction supplies sector. The group boasts Sarawak's largest quarry operator, its largest steel-rolling mill with a local market share for steel products of more than 70%, and its biggest supplier of asphalt. There are also arms that provide shipping and trucking services, water treatment chemicals, pipes and fittings, and so on.[26] Construction supplies and political connections have proven a formula for success.

The group wins many of the Sarawak government's major infrastructure contracts. Road building, water supply, and heavy civil engineering projects are regularly awarded to CMS. Some contracts have been enormous. In mid-1997, the Sarawak government launched the first phase of what was then a US$1.5 billion low-cost housing project in Kuching. CMS was appointed as the project's joint developer.[27]

The group's Sarawak Securities dominates securities trading in Sarawak. In 1995, the company earned US$20 million in pre-tax profit, which isn't bad for a provincial brokerage in a small country.[28] In 1997, this was complemented by the acquisition of Bank Utama, a small Malaysian bank. The bank was listed separately on the Kuala Lumpur Stock Exchange and proceeded to set up Sarawak's second stockbroking firm, Utama Securities Holding. Overall, CMS withstood Asia's economic crisis relatively well, and by the end of 1997, it was still able to declare a pre-tax profit of some US$65 million.[29] CMS had engaged management consultant Boston Consulting Group, to recommend restructuring and cost-cutting, which were in the process of being implemented.[30]

But CMS isn't the only group associated with Sarawak's chief minister. Another brother, Moh'd Tufail bin Mahmud, is a partner in Sarawak's timber and real estate Sanyan Group. It has enormous timber concessions across Sarawak, as well as huge timber processing plants.

The maneuvers that saw the conversion of CMS from a state-owned enterprise to a family-owned conglomerate in the hands of the relatives of the chief minister of Sarawak raise many questions. The Sarawak experience demonstrates yet another case of an Asian conglomerate that is a creature of connections and even nepotism, rather than the much-vaunted Asian hard work and entrepreneurialism.

THAI POLITICAL PARTIES AND BIG BUSINESSES

Whether in dictatorship or in democracy, Thailand's politics have invariably been about one thing: big businesses. A great many of Thailand's senior businessmen sit in the Thai Senate — indeed, it's almost as if each major Thai business family attempts to have at least one of its members there just to look after its interests. In early 1998, after the worst of Asia's economic crisis, when the Thai government attempted to promulgate its new bankruptcy law at the behest of the IMF, the bill for the new law had to pass through the Senate, where it was met with a great deal of interest, least of all because the companies of many senators themselves were all but insolvent. Debate over the bill was actually carried on in terms of what it would mean for the family of this or that senator. Inscrutability and subtlety — traits commonly associated with those of the Far East — don't feature too prominently in Thailand's Parliament. One of the senators at the time even happened to be Charn Uswachoke of Alphatec. He had just driven his business group into the ground through mismanagement and unauthorized internal transactions.

It isn't only the Thai Senate that harbors a web of vested business interests. Some of Thailand's most prominent political parties have, in the past, appeared to be little more than a front for some of Bangkok's biggest corporations. And in Thailand, governments rise or fall on the strength of shifting alliances between Bangkok's big business families, as much as on shifts in allegiance among the Thai military.

Thailand is now a thriving democracy, but political parties engage in a level of vote-buying that is extraordinary by any measure. The Thai Farmers Bank Research Center estimated that in the July 1995 elections, Thailand's political parties spent the equivalent of US$670 million on buying votes.[31] So, obviously each election is a phenomenally expensive exercise for the parties, and appeals have to be made to big business for cash. Thai-Chinese own the majority of Thailand's big businesses, and given that big businesses in Thailand heavily underwrite the major political parties, it isn't surprising that they also choose to send their own representatives into Parliament. And, by default, they are invariably Chinese. This process has reached such a degree that many political parties now appear little more than coalitions of like-minded big businesses that line up against other political parties that represent competing business interests.

Thailand's big Chinese business families are a fractious lot and so, there are many political parties. The main parties to have contested recent elections are the Chart Thai Party, the Democrat Party, the New Aspiration Party, the Chart Pattana Party, Palang Dharma Party, the

Social Action Party, the Nam Thai Party, and the Prachakorn Thai Party. These have all drifted in and out of coalition with one another as each family has sought to better re-position itself at the public trough. In 1998, a new party, Thai Rak Thai (TRT), was formed by telecommunications billionaire, Thaksin Shinawatra.

The Democrat Party was formed in 1946 as a pro-royalist grouping. It declined in the 1950s and then re-formed in the 1970s when it retained many of its pro-royalist elements but included a much larger group of businessmen and professionals from Bangkok and the southern coastal cities and towns. It is the main party in government today in Thailand and is the party that Prime Minister Chuan Leepai belongs to.

The core of the Chart Thai Party came from the military faction that included the once powerful General Phin. Many of the members of the faction were in league with some of the budding ethnic Chinese entrepreneurs at that time. They went on to develop several of Thailand's largest business groups today. Hence, there is a historical link between Chart Thai and many of the big Thai-Chinese business families — a link that continues to this day. Bangkok Bank has had a long association with Thai politics, particularly with Chart Thai. The bank's founder, Chin Sophonpanich, greatly benefited from his association with Gen Phin during the 1940s and 1950s. Another Thai-Chinese entrepreneur close to Gen Phin was Udane Tejaphaibul whom Phin 'adopted' as a son. Udane went on to control Bangkok Metropolitan Bank and many other companies in Thailand. Consequently, both Chin and Udane became important financial backers of Gen Phin and his son, Chatichai Choonhavan, who served as prime minister between 1988 and 1991. The mixture of military and big business backing has meant that Chart Thai has played host to a variety of colorful characters. One of the most notorious in recent times is Narong Wongwan, a Chart Thai MP. He was prime minister-elect after the March 1992 elections, but the nomination was withdrawn in the face of opposition from the U.S. government, which accused him of having links with the drug trade.[32] Narong returned to prominence in 1995 under Banharn Silpa-archa's prime ministership. The narcotics claims led the United States to refuse Narong a visa, and the outcry over his alleged links prevented him from assuming a formal senior position in Banharn's administration.[33] (Incidentally, Congressional records show that Thapawong International, a company owned by Narong, paid US$25,000 that year to the Washington-based lobbyists Jefferson-Waterman International for advice and assistance to 'strengthen [Narong's] reputation in the United States.'[34] It was to no avail — he was still unable to get a visa.) In 1992, Chatichai Choonhavan left Chart Thai to form the breakaway Chart

Pattana Party. This gave big businesses two parties to back, and in effect, a bet each way. Chatichai himself went into business while managing his political career. Erawan Trust Co, Siam International Amalgamated Manufacturers, and Amherst Thailand were among his private companies.[35]

Among the main political parties, Chart Thai is the party that retains the biggest backing from big business. The Sophonpanich family (Bangkok Bank), the Tejaphaibul family (Bangkok Metropolitan Bank), and the Srifeungfung family (Thai Asahi Glass) have all bankrolled Chart Thai. The Amata, Ban Chang, and Hemaraj groups also have good links to Chart Thai. The principal corporate backers of the Chart Pattana Party are the Osathanugrah family (Osotspa Group), Adisai Bodharamik (Jasmine Inter-national), and the Tipco Group, which, along with the Phatara-prasit family (Sura Thip Group), has ties to the Democrat Party.

The New Aspiration Party, from which former Prime Minister Chavalit Yongchaiyudh came, has received backing from the Krisdathanont family (ITF Finance and Securities) and the Kanjanapas family (Bangkok Land).

Pairoj Piempongsant, who controls the Ban Chang Group, is a supporter of the Chart Pattana Party and, more recently, Chart Thai.[36] Ban Chang is no stranger to political intrigue. It employs the husband of Pauline Kanchanalak, who came to prominence in the United States in 1996 for her frequent visits to the Clinton White House and US$253,000 in donations she made to the Democratic Party that it later returned. Kanchanalak, herself a Thai-Chinese, was able to organize for President Clinton to meet with two senior executives of Thailand's giant Charoen Pokphand Group.[37]

Telecommunications billionaire, Thaksin Shinawatra, bankrolled the Palang Dharma Party and eventually became its leader and a deputy prime minister in the Banharn Silpa-archa administration. Notwithstanding his leadership of Palang Dharma, Thaksin maintained very close ties with Chart Thai's Therd Thai faction, which had links to the communications department. He exerted significant influence over government telecommunications policy while Banharn Silpa-archa was in power (1995–97).

The mutual dependence between politics and big businesses in Thailand doesn't relate to funding alone. There is something of a rotating door between the Cabinet and many of Bangkok's boardrooms. Bangkok Bank, for example, seems to have a permanent spot in the Cabinet. Over time, various former bank executives have rotated through the Cabinet. Major General Pramarn Adireksan, who was a director of Bangkok Bank between 1974 and 1975 and a business partner of the Tejaphaibul family, was a member of the Cabinet on several occasions. Arsa Sarasin, a foreign minister in the Anand Panyarachum administration, served as the bank's executive director between 1993 and 1994. He was also appointed as executive chairman of the mining group Padaeng Industries. (Anand himself was appointed chairman of Saha Union Industries.) Vichit Suraphongchai was Bangkok Bank's president but was appointed Minister for Transport and Communications by Chuan Leekpai during his first term as prime minister. Amnuay Viravan, who had also been a senior executive at Bangkok Bank, was later appointed a deputy prime minister.

Another big business executive to have rotated through various administrations is Banharn Silpa-archa. He has been both an executive and a businessman in his own right. He started out by supplying chlorine to the Public Works Department. Next, he moved into construction and, during the Vietnam War period of provincial development in Thailand, became one of the department's biggest contractors, building roads and water mains. The profits were invested in his native Suphanburi province — in a rice mill, a finance company, gasoline stations, land, and motor vehicle distributorships. He was the province's leading businessman by the early 1970s.[38] His influence broadened beyond Suphanburi and he was later appointed a director of Siam City Cement PLC.[39] He joined Chart Thai and was awarded with several Cabinet positions. Eventually, he rose to become prime minister in 1995, but his short-lived administration collapsed under accusations of corruption and nepotism.

Other prominent Thais who have shuttled between the boardroom and the Cabinet are Surat Osathanugrah, who heads the Osotspa Group and served as communications minister (1969), deputy minister of the interior (1983), minister for commerce (1985) and, between 1992 and 1994, was deputy leader of the Chart Pattana Party; Supachai Panichpakdi, who was president of the Thai Military Bank from 1990 until 1992 when he joined the Democrat Party and was made a deputy prime minister the following year;[40] Siddhi Savetsila, a former foreign minister, who serves on several of Charoen Pokphand Group's boards; Som Jatusripitak, the president of the Siam City Bank, who was appointed commerce minister in 1997;[41] and Thanong Bidaya, who was appointed in mid-1997 as finance minister and had been a president of the Thai Military Bank. Even Suchinda Kraprayoon, who led an attempted coup against Thailand's elected government in 1992, ended up as the honorary chairman of Charoen Pokphand Group's Telecom Holding two years later.

Certainly, there are aspects of the close relationships between big businesses and political parties that bear similarities to, say, the situation in the United States. But the difference is in the degree. Presidents of the

United States don't regularly appoint the head of Coca-Cola, General Electric, Chase or Manhattan to their Cabinet, and certainly not all at once. Nor is either mainstream political party in the United States the property of any particular group of big business.

Of course, there's nothing wrong with close ties between big businesses and Thailand's Cabinet if those ties don't lead to undue influence. But, of course, they do. The Thai media is filled each day with allegations of payoffs, favors, bribes, and nepotism between business and government figures. Almost every one of the governments that have fallen in recent years did so under the weight of allegations of corruption. When the baht was floated in 1997, an event that was precipitous to Asia's economic crisis more generally, Bangkok was filled with rumors of the government having tipped off its big business favorites ahead of the float to allow them to make killings on the foreign exchange market.

In 1997, a parliamentary committee dominated by government legislators recommended that the government buy a large tranche of the hopelessly indebted Muang Thong Thani Estate that had been built on the edge of Bangkok by Bangkok Land, which is owned by the Thai-Chinese Kanjanapas family. The committee argued that the estate be used as the site for a temporary Parliament building. The recommendations met with a public outcry and certainly made no sense in terms of logistics or government savings. What was clear, though, was that Bangkok Land had been an important donor to then-prime minister Chavalit Yongchaiyudh's New Aspiration Party.[42] Earlier that year, Thailand's defense ministry had also decided to buy a condominium tower from Bangkok Land, a decision approved by the Cabinet. Instances like this occur in Thailand with monotonous regularity. But Thailand has made progress. The greater feistiness of Thailand's media means that such decisions are now reported at least.

Nepotism and favoritism are one thing, but Thailand's political system also leaves its senior government officials susceptible to bribes, and allegations of bribe-taking run thick and fast. The prices of many agricultural commodities are controlled by the government in Thailand, which make various ministers susceptible to bribes from industry bodies that seek a rise in the official price of their particular commodity. In early 1998, the Social Action Party's representative in the Cabinet, industry minister Somsak Thepsuthin, was forced to defend himself against allegations that he had accepted a 200 million baht bribe (then equivalent to US$4.5 million) from domestic sugar producers for a sugar price rise of at least 2 baht per kilogram.[43]

Sometimes the largesse originates from within Parliament itself. In early 1997, Thailand's then-education minister, Sukhavich Rangsitpol, was criticized for handing out bundles of baht worth US$2,000 each to fellow members of Parliament. Ostensibly, the packets of money were Chinese New Year gifts, but at a total cost of US$244,000, the gesture seemed somewhat generous. Opposition politicians linked the gifts to the minister's desire to have a plan approved to buy computers and other equipment for which he had allegedly received commissions.[44]

Illegal donations are another problem. In 1996, it emerged that an Indian national, Rakesh Saxena, a former treasury advisor to the deeply troubled Bangkok Bank of Commerce, had given illegal donations to then-prime minister Banharn Silpa-archa's Chart Thai Party. The donations had been made in the names of three employees of a company called Zilar International Trading Co, which was owned by Suchart Tancharoen, a former Chart Thai deputy interior minister.[45] Suchart Tancharoen, it turned out, was a substantial borrower from the bank, and in the wash-up after its rescue the bank seized land and shares he had placed as collateral for the loans. The money had been borrowed via a company listed on the Thai stock exchange, Jalaprathan Cement, in which Suchart was the largest shareholder. Ostensibly, the funds were borrowed for the company, but they went straight to the company's shareholders instead. In early 1998, the company's creditors seized management control as the company slid toward bankruptcy.[46] Another borrower that the bank had to similarly negotiate with was Chucheep Harnsawat, a former agriculture minister.[47] Things went from bad to worse and were capped off when opposition MPs accused Suchart of illegally obtaining the land he had put up as collateral in the first place.[48]

Yet another frequent problem in Thailand arises when parliamentarians themselves directly hold interests in companies that benefit from government contracts. Of course, Thailand has no monopoly on this. But it is the regularity with which such allegations are made that is stunning. A classic example of these allegations are those that surfaced about Tipco Group in 1988. Tipco Group has ties to the Chart Thai Party and to some figures in the Democrat Party. Deputy agriculture minister Virat Rattanaset of the Chart Thai Party signed on contracts in early 1998 to be awarded to construction company Sisang Kanyota, which is widely believed to be owned by former prime minister and Chart Thai parliamentary leader, Banharn Silpa-archa. The bid from Banharn's company included equipment that was sourced from Tipco Group, and the tender documents were allegedly written in such a way that only Tipco's equipment matched the tender specifications.[49]

These are just a few of the more interesting examples of impropriety at senior government levels in Thailand. Thailand isn't alone in having these problems, but it's a question of degree. Thailand's political development has come a long way in recent years. The influence of the military in government is declining; by the general election of January 2001, there had been two civilian prime ministers (Banharn Silpa-archa and Chuan Leekpai), and democratic elections are now broadly accepted as the only appropriate means of removing one administration and replacing it with another. But clearly, there is still some way to go.

A MARCOS REVIVAL?

Mid-1998 saw the election of Joseph Estrada as the President of the Philippines. The former local movie star and vice president to the previous president, Fidel Ramos, saw a return to favor of a group of businessmen who hadn't been welcome to the inner circle of Manila's political elite since the dying days of the regime of the dictator, Ferdinand Marcos. Many business figures who had been close to Marcos backed Estrada's presidential campaign, which was also supported in its latter stages by Imelda Marcos.

Politics in the Philippines, like Philippine society, is a complex business. The country's population can be divided roughly into three groups: those of Spanish descent, those of Chinese descent, and those who are indigenous. The groups aren't mutually exclusive, however. Many prominent Filipinos can claim a mixed heritage from all three groups. But when it comes to business, it's the ethnic Chinese and the old Spanish families who wrestle for control of the national economy. And when it comes to politics, the game is more like musical chairs between the big business families, with each fighting for ascendancy. Election is an expensive business in the Philippines. It is more about show business than policy, and putting on a good show is an expensive business. It soaks up a lot of money, so come election time, those with cash are expected to contribute — and lately, those with the most cash have been the local Chinese business families.

There are close links between the Chinese community in the Philippines and the Chinese of Taiwan. The links are largely historical. The two groups share a common ancestry — mostly they are of Hokkien decent, meaning that they originate in the southern half of China's Fujian province. The shared ancestry has been important for the promotion of business links between the two groups of Chinese. There is a significant amount of investment in the Philippines from Taiwan (a lot of it goes unrecorded because foreign investment in land, for example, is prohibited, so it occurs using local nominees), and the Filipino-Chinese are significant investors in Taiwan. So, come election time, Taiwan is another important source of campaign funds for local politicians.

Estrada relied on a coterie of ethnic Chinese businessmen for financial support in his bid for the presidency. Among them was the head of the Fortune Tobacco Group, Lucio Tan, mining magnate Manuel Zamora, Metropolitan Bank & Trust owner George Ty, and Equitable Bank owner George Go.[50] There is nothing like backing the winner when it comes to business — especially in the Philippines — even if the candidate does run a campaign built on rhetoric that is pro-poor and vaguely anti-business. Pragmatism makes for some strange bedfellows. But Estrada's most prominent backer was none other than former Marcos crony, Eduardo Cojuangco.

Many of the businessmen that Marcos cultivated and helped to build up were local Chinese. In part, their overt 'Chineseness' made them less of a political threat. The cronyism of Marcos had important parallels to the cronyism of Indonesia's Soeharto, who also deliberately courted local Chinese rather than indigenous business people who might ultimately become an alternative source of political power. Marcos cronies operated businesses both on their own behalf and on behalf of the Marcos family in secret nominee arrangements.

Jose Yao Campos, who owns United Laboratories in the Philippines, one of Asia's largest pharmaceuticals companies, and who now lives in Vancouver, Canada, was one businessman who was especially close to Marcos. In effect, he acted as the financial advisor to the Marcos court. Another former Marcos crony, Roberto Benedicto, grew enormously wealthy under Marcos from a sugar monopoly and with his ownership of several banks. Many of his assets were sequestered by the Aquino government in the wake of the fall of Marcos, but they were returned to him after he paid a settlement to the government. Among his other assets was a bank based in California, Beverly Hills office towers, and other real estate in Los Angeles.[51]

But it was Eduardo Cojuangco who grew the wealthiest during the Marcos years. His links to the former president extended to being the godfather of his son, Bongbong. He had a near monopoly on the country's coconut industry during the Marcos years and owned more than half of San Miguel Corporation, the beer and food giant that is one of the largest companies in the Philippines. He still owns a large, multi-million dollar horse stud farm at Mudgee in Australia that he acquired during the Marcos years. The Aquino administration sequestered a large part of Cojuangco's San Miguel stake, claiming that they were ill-gotten gains from the Marcos years. This gave the government effective control of the board. (The government also sequestered his shares in the United Coconut Planters Bank.) Backing Estrada helped Cojuangco to return to the inner sanctum of Manila's elite. He bankrolled much of Estrada's campaign and served as the head of Estrada's political party. Within weeks of Estrada being sworn in as president, Cojuangco was elected chairman of San Miguel, a position that he had not held for 12 years. Cojuangco was back. The excesses of the Marcos years threatened to return with him.

By the end of 2000, Estrada was facing impeachment. He was accused of taking US$8.1 million in payoffs from illegal gambling syndicates and around US$4 million that had been meant as tobacco excise taxes. He strenuously denied the allegations and refused to resign but members of his inner circle deserted him in droves nonetheless.

Estrada had bumbled his way through his presidency. Indecision and policy infighting marked his tenure. A generous interpretation of his presidency is that he was a caretaker president at best, leaving the Philippines in little more than a holding position. This is fine in good times, but when the Philippine economy required urgent and ongoing reform, it was a disaster. Under Estrada, the country seemed governed by the so-called 'Midnight Cabinet' — Estrada's drinking buddies, who appeared to have more say than the actual cabinet. There were more overt allegations of cronyism particularly in relation to Estrada's close links to Lucio Tan who controlled Philippines Airlines and who was himself one of Marcos' best known cronies. Tan, like Cojuangco, was a big political donor to Estrada.

Marcos' inability to differentiate between himself and the state was in some respects carried on by Estrada. Marcos though did it as a calculated grab at self-enrichment. For Estrada, it was done more out of ignorance and buffoonery, as he dispensed state favors and grants to anyone whose support he needed to buy. His presidency also happened to coincide with his mistresses moving into grand mansions around Manila and his associates suddenly having the funds to acquire large, new businesses. Under Estrada, the legacy of feudalism in the Philippines was continued.

On the day in November 2000 when the Philippines' House of Representatives' Justice Committee voted to proceed with an impeachment case against Estrada, the principal index of the local stock market surged by 16% — the biggest jump in its history. This was not so much a vote of confidence in what might come next but rather the result of broad sentiment that any change would be for the better.

SECTION 6

ASIAN ECLIPSE?

CHAPTER 15

Asian Eclipse and Beyond

Given how business has been and will continue to be done in Asia, what should outsiders look for when seeking to do business there? And with regard comes to reforms, what really should be done?

King Mongkut, the King of Siam, as Thailand was then known, was a budding astronomer. In 1868, he calculated that a total eclipse of the sun would occur later that year during the morning of August 18. Not only that, but the best place to see it would be in the southern part of Siam. It was too good an opportunity to miss. The widespread belief throughout the kingdom was that solar eclipses were the result of the great dragon, Rahoo, swallowing the sun and that the only way to make him disgorge it was to frighten him with loud fireworks. Mongkut was always looking for ways to drag his country into the Modern Age, so if he couldn't slay Rahoo, he could at least show his people that science could be used to predict the exact time of the eclipse and its duration.

Invitations to Siam to witness the event were sent far and wide to foreign dignitaries and astronomy groups. For weeks, thousands of workers, under the personal direction of Mongkut's prime minister, cleared a site on a marsh alongside the beach at Sam Roi Yot — about 140 miles south of Bangkok — on which the viewing platforms and pavilions were built. A party of ten Frenchmen made their way to Bangkok as the day grew near (they had come overland from Europe — the Suez Canal was yet to be built), and the British commander of the Straits Settlements (in what is now Malaysia and Singapore) arrived aboard the steamer *Peiho* with his wife. On August 8, the king, the crown prince, an assortment of other princes and royals, and a retinue of almost a thousand left Bangkok with a procession of 50 elephants in tow and made their way to Sam Roi Yot.

The full eclipse promised to be a grand occasion — and it was. Food and wine were provided in abundance, and two brass bands regaled the revelers each night. But on the day when the eclipse was to take place, the well-laid plans were in danger of coming unstuck. A thick layer of cloud spread across the sky and threatened to entirely mask the event that everyone had assembled to see. The king no doubt felt a rising sense of despair, and the French muttered among themselves. But just prior to the time that the king had predicted the eclipse would commence, the clouds opened and the sun burst forth — allowing the party a clear view of the entire proceedings. The king and his prime minister excitedly took turns at the telescope. At the very point that the eclipse was complete and all was dark, a canon was fired, and pipes and trumpets burst forth from the royal enclosure. The king was victorious. But it was to be short-lived. The spot that had been chosen to observe the eclipse was malarious. Many, if not most, of the revelers came down with the disease, including eight of the ten Frenchmen and King Mongkut himself. He managed to return to Bangkok, but within a fortnight, he was dead.[1] Eclipses haven't been very kind to Asia.

REAPING WHAT IS SOWN

Rahoo, the dragon, was back in 1997. But this time, Asia's eclipse was economic. The speed with which economic collapse engulfed the region caught everyone by surprise. Many countries that were forecast in early 1997 to experience an economic growth of 8% found that by mid-1998, they could expect zero or even negative growth, or in Indonesia's case to contract by as much as 15% in that year. Thailand was the first to fall, and the rest of Asia followed not long after.

Investors had been forced to assess crony capitalism, poor corporate governance, and low transparency for what they were really worth without such considerations being masked by guaranteed exchange rates. They fled and Asia's exchange rates collapsed. This was no 'financial' phenomenon — it was fully grounded in the real economy. The exchange rates, initially at least, were simply catching up with reality. The trigger might have been financial, but the bullets were real.

Thailand, like Indonesia, the Philippines, and Malaysia, linked the value of its currency to the US dollar. In order to 'peg' or fix the value of their currencies, these countries' governments routinely had to enter the marketplace, alternating between buying up their currency if it threatened to fall below the peg or selling it off if it seemed like it was going to rise above the peg. The trouble with this is that when economic conditions within the country change, pressures build up which aren't reflected in the current value of the currency. An exchange rate is like a messenger. Movements in it tell how an economy is doing and where it's heading. Peg it and the messenger is gagged.

The Thai economy had been faltering, since the beginning of 1997 at least. Accordingly, currency traders saw the weakness in the economy, saw that the baht was becoming increasingly overvalued, and began to offload their baht holdings onto world markets. (The trend was magnified but not caused by some traders who deliberately 'shorted' the currency.) The more they sold down the baht, the more the Thai authorities had to buy it up to maintain its value. Eventually, with its stocks of foreign currencies almost drained, the Thai government had little choice but to step away and let the baht's value be determined by supply and demand. The implicit guarantee that Thailand's government had given to the foreign currency traders — that no matter how bad Thailand's economy became, their money would be safe — was ripped away. The day that happened — July 2, 1997 — the baht went into a free-fall.

Next, the traders turned their attention to the region's other 'managed' currencies: the Indonesian rupiah, the Philippine peso, and the Malaysian ringgit. Pressure on these currencies became enormous, forcing their governments to also fully float them. So, one by one, they too were picked off. And with each new float came a dramatic depreciation. The messengers had been ungagged and the message wasn't a good one.

Each fall meant that the US dollar loans that companies in the region had taken out grew more difficult to service. Increasingly higher amounts of local currency were required to buy the same amount of US dollars, and the more the local currencies poured into the marketplace, the more their value fell. Very few local firms had bothered to purchase options that allowed them to buy US dollars at a specified rate, which left their positions unhedged. They hadn't bothered because, after all, their governments had implicitly guaranteed the value of their currency pegs.

In just a few months, the baht fell by more than half, the peso by more than a third, and the ringgit by 40%. The rupiah's demise was the most spectacular. It fell from around 2,400 to the US dollar at the beginning of 1997 to as low as 16,000 less than a year later — an astonishing fall of 85%. The speed with which boom turned to bust was historic by world standards. And yet all of this happened when the so-called fundamentals of these economies were generally sound — low inflation, small or no government budget deficits, and strong exports. Indeed, two months before Indonesia began its rapid collapse, the World Bank had described the Indonesian economy as 'performing very well' and likely to maintain a 7% growth rate in the coming years.[2]

The Taiwan dollar had been pegged to the US dollar but it, too, came under speculative pressure during 1997. Taiwan's government allowed it to gently depreciate in the first half of the year, but in mid-October 1997 it too stepped back and allowed its currency to be determined by the market. In contrast to the other Asian currencies, Taiwan's dollar didn't collapse, although it did fall. The relative level of marketplace support that its currency received indicated the relative robustness and integrity of its economy. It was a reward for Taiwan's much stronger performance as a competitive economy with stronger governance.

The long-term fixing of the value of a currency is nearly always bad, but in South-East Asia, fixing it to the US dollar was disastrous. When US interest rates were low in the early 1990s, an enormous volume of funds rolled into the then high-growth economies of Asia. The flood of money meant that those currencies unable to vary with demand became undervalued. Each US dollar that went into Thailand, for example, bought perhaps 25 baht at the government's fixed rate. But had the baht been allowed to rise with demand, it might have bought only 15. The pegged rate being above the market rate thus meant that billions of dollars worth of extra baht were created and this washed around Thailand's economy and saw the money supply expand dramatically. The government should have borrowed back a lot of the extra baht ('sterilizing,' in economists' parlance) to take it out of the marketplace, but it didn't. Other Asian governments did make such borrowings with respect to their own currencies — but only with varying degrees of success.

So where did all the money that had been attracted to and been created in Asia go? A lot of it poured into real estate, big infrastructure projects, and heavy industry. Property prices escalated and bubbles soon emerged. Coupled with the poor governance and accountability that is endemic around Asia, the region was heading for trouble. Asia has always had problems with governance and accountability, even in the good times. But 'in a strong wind even turkeys can fly,' goes the saying. Asia was the darling of the world, and the matters of cronyism, corruption, and corporate governance were glossed over. However, while Asia boomed, its sins accumulated. Its economies weren't in fine shape — they just looked that way. And one of the facades was the regime of pegged exchange rates that were unable to reflect the real story.

A CHECKLIST FOR WESTERN INVESTORS

Crisis or no crisis, inadequate corporate governance, cronyism, and other blemishes in Asia aren't going to fade fast, so Western business must simply get better at spotting the dangers of doing business in Asia. What are some of the danger signs? Five prominent ones are examined below.

Relationships

The poor legal framework of most Asian countries means that if one must have a local partner, it needs to be one that can be fully trusted, and preferably one with whom there are long-standing personal relationships. Exchanging business cards or having met someone on several occasions doesn't constitute a personal relationship in Asia. Relationships can only be fostered over time. It makes sense to build up trust because litigation often isn't an option in Asia, if only because it's more trouble than it's worth. Moreover, the confidence-building period can also be used to gather as much information about a prospective partner as possible. Accurate information on businesses and the people who run them can be extremely difficult to obtain in Asia, so an opportunity for information should be zealously taken.

The getting-to-know-you period also inevitably will mean social functions, often at which business might not be discussed at all. Mainland Chinese businessmen have developed a great fondness for taking visiting Western business people for a gamed ten-pin bowling for example, which might be followed by a banquet, a heavy drinking session, and karaoke. Ten-pin bowling alleys might not look like substitutes for a well-functioning legal system, but when used like this, that's what they are. Probably a great many entertainment venues in China will have to shut down when it gets its legal framework right. Personal connections won't be nearly as important then for doing business; nor will be the venues in which those connections are forged.

Personal relationships as a prelude to business (rather than the other way around) are essential in Asia, but so often Western business people get it wrong — even those who should know better. I attended a dinner in 1997 at a private home in South-East Asia where the guest of honor was a visiting former prime minister of a Western country. After his exit from politics, he had set himself up in business. On entering the house he was introduced individually to all who were present. Standing next to me was a local businessman who happened to own one of the country's largest pharmaceuticals companies, and he was introduced as such. The visiting former dignitary immediately launched into his plans for setting up a pharmaceuticals factory in China and suggested that maybe he and the local businessman should get together to discuss it. The local businessman was somewhat taken aback, agreed politely that yes, they must, and then slipped away. The exchange wasn't an edifying sight.

When it comes down to business negotiations, minutes of all meetings should be kept and both sides must sign off on them. Any agreements or communications must be confirmed in writing. This is particularly the case if the language of the negotiations is in English, which will generally mean that the local side will be negotiating in a second language and so will need more time to analyze what it is they're being offered or have agreed to. Everything should be documented, and then everyone should agree as to the meaning of what has been documented.

Although legal systems in some Asian countries are remarkably poor, a recourse to the courts might ultimately be the only option. So, business arrangements should still be backed up with legal documents and contracts. What they shouldn't be, though, is overly complex. Clauses that deal with unlikely contingencies should be removed and the remainder should be expressed as simply as possible. After having devoted time and other valuable resources to forging strong personal relationships, it's unwise to then jeopardize a relationship by burdening it with a complex and excessively legalistic contract that raises the specter of distrust. The efficacy of this rule may vary from country to country, though. Business people in Singapore, Malaysia, Hong Kong, and the Philippines are more familiar with the intricacies of a modern legal system than elsewhere in Asia. Their colleagues in China, Thailand, and Indonesia, however, are a different matter.

Contracts and other legal documents should be explained clause by clause to the local party. If they aren't given the opportunity to fully understand it, they might sign it anyway, simply to save 'face.' This is no great victory on the part of the Westerner, as contracts tend not to be viewed in much of Asia as absolute and binding in the same way that they are in New York or London. If the local party doesn't understand the contract but signs it anyway, they'll be tempted to renegotiate it later.

Know Your Local Partner

Poor disclosure and lack of transparency are two of the biggest problems with corporate Asia. Very rarely will it be immediately obvious where potential local partners in Asia fit in with the local business and political scene. It always makes sense to establish — discreetly — just who it is you're dealing with. I once met two executives of a Western company in Jakarta who were terribly pleased with themselves for just having signed up for a joint venture with a local company. The executives felt that their new local partners were 'well connected,' but just *how* so they were unsure. They were horrified to learn later that the company they had been dealing with was ultimately owned partly by the Indonesian military and partly by the eldest son of then-president Soeharto. Their company had an image to maintain back home, and it wasn't one that was compatible with setting up joint ventures with the armies and cronies of developing countries.

Another aspect of business in Asia is that the vast majority of companies outside Japan and China are owned and managed by families. The fortunes of the family depend on the firm, but it can work the other way too. Asian business families tend to be more complex than their Western counterparts on account of the large numbers of children they might have, but also because of the practice of polygamy in earlier generations or even in the current generation. Complex families make for complex businesses. More than a few prominent companies in Asia have been brought asunder by family infighting. Large families with many branches are more prone to dividing into factions, which then fight over who should control the family firm. And when the family is both the owner and the manager, then family infighting can cause the firm's management to suffer as it becomes embroiled in the infighting. Western investors generally consider it essential to conduct due diligence on a company in which they are considering taking a stake. But how many consider due diligence on the family behind the company? It makes sense to establish the composition of a family and how it's structured if one is thinking about establishing a long-term business relationship with it. Western companies might need to consider, for example, what could happen if they have a business arrangement with a 'group,' but that group disintegrates into six smaller entities should the founder's six sons decide to take their inheritance and go their separate ways on his death. Business agreements and legal contracts with an entity that has simply evaporated pose complications not usually encountered in the West.

Due Diligence and Independent Audits

Due diligence is essential in Asia, but very often even due diligence by professional firms will be less than comprehensive than in the West due to the difficulty in obtaining commercial information. Due diligence is absolutely essential if a company in Asia is being bought into. When legal recourse against the vendor is unavailable, sellers of companies face a strong incentive to exaggerate or fabricate their company's positives and to hide the negatives (such as debt and taxation liabilities). Very often, a company will keep several sets of books — one for the auditors, one for the tax authorities, and one for the owners. The aim of a due diligence assessment should be to uncover the latter and then anything that the owners have missed. Forecasts of sales, revenue, and profits are another problem area. The forecasts of many Asian firms represent more of what their owners would like to see happen than what is likely to happen. At best, they will be 'targets' that the locals will hold-up as 'forecasts.' At worst, they will be overt fabrications.

Few truly profitable companies are ever sold in Asia, and even fewer to outsiders. If they were profitable, generally they wouldn't come onto the open market. The fact that companies and families tend to be synonymous in Asia means that — unlike, say, in the United States — good companies are rarely sold because the vendors have grown old and simply wish to retire. In Asia, the family firm is the main place of employment for family members and if it's any good, it almost always will be passed on to other family members when the founder wishes to take a less active role. Failing that, it will be shopped around to the founder's inner circle of friends and associates. If still no buyer is found, then and only then will it make it onto the open market. It's at this stage that investors from the West come to know that it is available for sale, and very usually companies that get this far down the chain aren't worth having.

Prospective buyers of companies in Asia must also insist on an independent audit of such companies. But the potential buyer must be assured that the accounting firm and the staff who undertake the audit don't have any commercial or personal relationships with the vendor of the company. This holds even if the accounting firm is a Big Five firm. The accounting firm might have a Western name, but that doesn't mean that the local partner in charge of the audit isn't the second cousin of the wife of the vendor of the company. A country like Thailand, for example, might have a population of 60 million, but its commercial community is relatively small and is concentrated in central Bangkok. Personal connections are the way business is done in Asia, which means everyone knows everyone. In Asia, everyone is in the loop — even the auditors. In the more 'Wild East' economies like Thailand and Indonesia, professionalism can be hoped for but is rarely guaranteed.

A problem that often won't be picked up by either due diligence or auditing is exposure to off-balance-sheet obligations, especially verbal guarantees — and again, given the personalized nature of business in Asia, these are more common there than in the West. A company owner might, for example, provide a verbal guarantee on behalf of the company for loans taken out by the company of a close business associate, but conveniently forget to mention it when it comes to selling the company.

If, after due diligence and auditing, the company doesn't look to be a good investment, then one option might be to buy not the company but its assets. This would be one way to avoid buying into existing debts, unwritten guarantees, and taxation problems. It also means not having to take all the existing local staff and thus is an opportunity to cut out the deadwood. Rules on firing staff in some Asian countries can be surprisingly restrictive, despite popular perceptions.

The Cost of Political Connections

Nothing beats the fundamentals when it comes to valuing a company and its earning prospects. A red chip in Hong Kong might take on the hue of a blue chip until its supposedly well-connected CEO is arrested for 'economic crimes' and given a suspended death sentence. Even top-level international brokerages have become ensnared in the Asian game of valuing a company because of its crony connections, rather than because it's a viable concern. Bankers Trust repeatedly recommended throughout the first part of 1997 in its *Asia Windows* publication that its clients buy the commercial paper of Bangkok Land — not because the company had a healthy balance sheet and promising prospects (it had neither), but rather because the company was believed to have good political connections and it was thought that its political benefactors would bail it out.[3] Shares in Bangkok Land nudged the equivalent of US$10 in 1996. By mid-1998, they were seven cents — and no bargain at that.

How easy it has been for all too many Western financial and other advisors in Asia to adopt local ways, rather than to import new ways and skills and generally lift standards. All too often they have contributed to the many problems of corporate Asia, rather than alleviated them. Sidling up to Asia's crony capitalists might be one way to access some short-term gains, but it's those Western companies that have remained aloof from the fickle fortunes of the region's cronies that have the longest histories in Asia.

Approaching Banks

Approaching a local bank for finance in Asia can be the nearest thing to committing corporate suicide. Most Asian banks (and in some Asian countries, *all* the local banks) are part of wider conglomerates. Hence, they sit amid a sea of vested interest and potential conflicts of interest. What guarantee is there that if you take your plans to enter a potentially profitable local niche to Bank X, which belongs to sprawling Conglomerate Y, in search of finance, the bank simply won't take your plans and pass them on to an affiliate so that it can set up a business based on your plan? Unfortunately, in some parts of Asia there is no guarantee whatsoever. That is one reason why so many business families in Asia start their own banks (remember, Indonesia, for one, has more than 200) — they simply don't trust anyone else's. The best way to minimize such a risk is to seek financing from outside the country or to seek it from the local branch of a foreign bank. Failing that, the best alternative is to approach a local bank that has as few non-banking affiliates as possible and which has a controlling shareholder that is similarly focused.

REAL REFORMS

All too often, it seems to be forgotten that economies are made up of individuals and firms. Economic reform, therefore, means reforming their behavior. It doesn't mean fiddling with exchange rates, interest rates, prices, liquidity, and the like. ('If only Japan would introduce a permanent tax cut' or 'if only Indonesia would introduce a currency board' were the catch-cries of some analysts during 1998, for example — as if that would solve all Japan's or Indonesia's problems.) If firms behaved ethically and transparently, were accountable to all their shareholders, and were allowed to fail when they become insolvent — and fail quickly, so that their capital can be seized and reallocated to those more capable — then macroeconomic variables such as inflation, employment, and the exchange rate will look after themselves. There is no such thing as 'top-down' reform when it comes to an economy. Asia's big problems are at the corporate level, so that's where the reforms must be made. And what are the reforms so badly needed in Asia? Generally, they go beyond the limited changes that were prescribed by the IMF in its various 'rescue' packages doled out to Asia in 1997 and 1998. Some of the reforms that are most needed are outlined below.

Pay Public Servants Decently

'If you pay peanuts, you get monkeys,' goes the saying. In Asia, you also get corruption. The most urgent and fundamental reform that Asia must make is to ensure that its government workers are paid sufficiently to obviate the need for them to accept petty bribes. A sound legal framework is absolutely essential for a sound business environment. But it doesn't matter how fine and brilliantly conceived that framework is on paper; if middle- and low-ranking civil servants and court officials from the judge down are easily bribed, then in reality it's utterly worthless. As mentioned in Chapter 2, you don't get a court case when the presiding judge is paid as little as US$380 per month — you get an auction. Similarly, the IMF and the World Bank can demand for all the prudential supervision of the private banking system they like from Asia's central banks, but while it remains possible for the owner of a bank to walk into the central bank with a bribe to have his balance sheet deemed to have met minimum standards, their efforts will largely go wasted. Fewer government workers that are paid more are needed across Asia.

The salaries paid to civil servants must not only be viewed as recurrent expenditure. A country's legal framework is part of its national 'soft' infrastructure, and the task of civil servants is to help build that infrastructure. Hence, their salaries have a capital component and should be viewed as such. This isn't an argument for big government, but for efficient government. 'Lean and mean' should refer to the overall operation of government and not to the physical condition of its employees on account of their pitiful salaries. What the IMF should have required of Asia in exchange for its various emergency loan packages of 1997 and 1998 were substantial reductions in the numbers of bureaucrats but the tripling of the salaries of those that remain. That would be genuine reform.

Enforce Bankruptcy Laws

Bankruptcy means accountability. Get it wrong and you're out of business. Not nearly as many Asian companies go bankrupt as should do so, and when they do, the process is usually way too slow. Often it's not for the lack of decent bankruptcy laws. We have seen how Indonesia's laws, modeled after Dutch bankruptcy codes, have failed not because of drafting inadequacies, but because it's simply too easy for companies to bribe all the officials concerned to avoid being wound up. The IMF required both Indonesia and Thailand to draw up better bankruptcy laws as part of the requirements for their emergency loan packages — but it didn't require that the officials charged with implementing and enforcing the new laws should be better paid so that they would be less receptive to bribery. Bankruptcy codes, like other laws, are meaningless if they can be avoided with a small cash payment and other gifts.

Bankruptcy laws must be enforced, and they must be enforced without fear or favor. The offending company might be owned or run by a powerful figure — a Soeharto, or a princeling in the case of China — in which case the bankruptcy court may not dare to close it down. In short, bankruptcy courts must be well resourced and transparent. Backlogs shouldn't be allowed to build up and the assets of insolvent companies should be able to be seized easily and sold off quickly. Far too much effort was expended in Asia during its 1997–98 economic crisis by companies and politicians who sought to avoid *any* bankruptcies, let alone mass bankruptcies. Asia needed large infusions of foreign capital throughout the crisis to bring it to an end. But poor bankruptcy regimes meant that assets couldn't be forced from their owners' hands and sold off to foreign investors to bring in those cash infusions. There's almost no such thing as bad assets — just over-priced assets. Most bad assets become good assets as their prices go down, and one way of ensuring this is that they come onto the market in the first place — via a bankruptcy court, if need be.

Reform Bank Ownership

The structure of the ownership of Asia's banks is a constant threat to Asia's economic well-being. Asia might overcome the crisis of 1997–98, but unless the ownership of its banks is seriously reformed, further crises are inevitable. Apart from Japanese and South Korean banks, most Asian banks have a single controlling shareholder, usually a local entrepreneur and his family. This would be alright if these families didn't have other interests, but usually they do — interests that compromise the banks' independence. Routinely, Asia's banks are pressured to extend loans to their major shareholders, say for property speculation, to build factories, and so on. Not only are loans granted on a non-commercial basis, but too much credit often ends up being given to the one client. This puts the bank and its depositors at risk and undermines the integrity of the banking system in general.

The only way to remove this risk once and for all is to ensure that banks don't have major shareholders. Generally, no single shareholder is permitted to own more than 15% of a bank's outstanding share capital in Australia, for example. Such a rule means that Australian banks cannot be beholden to a major shareholder's non-financial interests. It doesn't make them immune to mismanagement, but it does mean that they are less vulnerable. The head of an Indonesian bank once bitterly complained to me that his family would like to set up a bank in Australia but that they wouldn't bother because they couldn't have majority ownership and control. But that is exactly the point of the Australian regulations — to prevent just that, and with good reason. It's a constraint that must be replicated throughout Asia if the region's future prosperity is to be assured.

But it's not only the other interests of banks' dominant shareholders that can distort their lending policies. It's the non-financial assets that they own themselves. There are banks in Asia that also happen to own substantial stakes in cement plants, housing estates, and even pineapple canning factories. It simply is not possible for a bank to maintain its independence and credibility when it is itself involved in businesses that compete directly with those of its customers. So, another essential banking reform that must be adopted across Asia is to follow the US example and simply prohibit banks from holding stocks or managing companies outside the financial sector.

Reform Accounting and Auditing

Auditing practices in at least several Asian countries can border on the farcical. The World Bank provided funding to some Asian countries such as Thailand in 1998 to improve accounting and auditing standards. Of course, this was to be welcomed, but a big part of the problem was that accounting firms were contravening existing standards. The abuses vary in degree throughout the region with some countries showing more willingness than others in implementing international accounting standards. The head offices of some major accounting firms may also have been too prepared to sacrifice quality and integrity for growth and market share. Accounting standards need to be standardized across Asia, and the research divisions of the region's stockbroking houses should be more reluctant to accept companies' accounts at face value.

Greater Protection for Minority Shareholders

The abuse meted out to minority shareholders across much of Asia is nothing short of extraordinary. Routinely, they see the funds that they invest in a listed company siphoned off by the controlling shareholders to their privately held companies. Excessive and injurious related-party transactions, the regular sales of assets at inflated prices to the listed company by its controlling shareholders, and excessive rights issues, are among the various abuses. They occur with such monotonous regularity in most of Asia's stock markets that they are the rule rather than the exception. Genuinely independent directors are a rarity in much of Asia, which closes off another avenue of protection for outside investors. Moreover, not all Asian stock exchanges require listed companies to have internal audit committees. The United States, Canada, Australia, and the United Kingdom all have this requirement, as do Malaysia and Singapore. (It only became a requirement in Hong Kong from the beginning of 1999.) To top it off, the level of disclosure and transparency is abysmal. Capital gains on the basis of rumor have driven Asia's stock markets as much as anything else. The red-chip phenomenon of Hong Kong is an example of this wider problem. These practices aren't sustainable and ultimately are self-defeating.

The region's stock exchanges and capital markets regulators have taken steps since the 1997–98 Asian economic meltdown to tighten standards, but, as is usual in Asia, the problem often isn't the regulations but their enforcement. Infringements of the rules by listed or listing companies must not be circumvented by buying off regulators with free stock (as is done in Indonesia), by turning a blind eye because the offending company belongs to the family of an influential politician (as in Thailand), or by allowing companies to circumvent rules that require minority shareholder approval for major asset acquisitions by buying up stock in the market through nominees to shore up the minority vote (as is done across Asia). These are just a few of the problems that must be rectified if confidence is to return to Asia's stock markets. The wholesale withdrawal from Asia's stock markets by Western mutual funds, particularly, will severely limit the ability of companies in Asia to raise funds by issuing stock, notwithstanding the merits of their particular situations. Such a withdrawal is guaranteed unless Asia's stock markets can clean up their act, in practice as well as on paper.

Ban *Amakudari*

The practice in Japan known as *amakudari,* or 'descent from heaven,' where retiring bureaucrats take lucrative jobs in the private sector, has currency across Asia. The habit has caught on in China, too, where retrenched senior bureaucrats are eagerly sought for the connections they bring. There is an insufficient separation between the regulators and the regulated in Asia, and *amakudari* is one of the reasons for this. Essentially, the practice is a subtle form of corruption — be helpful when in the job and the pay-off comes when you leave. The United States is one country that has rules to prevent its senior officials from accepting jobs in sectors that are too closely tied to their former areas of responsibility. It's not a foolproof system, but it's better than nothing. It is a lead that Asia should follow.

Reform Media Ownership

In the same way that censorship of political coverage by governments is a threat to a well-functioning society, censorship of business coverage by big businesses is a threat to the efficient functioning of an economy. Information is gold in business — it is an essential input; if it's of inferior quality, then so too will be the output. Often in the West, the mere fact that the media could expose fraudulent or unethical business behavior is sufficient threat to prevent it from occurring in the first place. In many parts of Asia, this threat is blunted to the point of being non-existent. Government censorship is one thing, but censorship caused by the conflicts of interest that arise from a media outlet's non-media affiliates arguably is equally pernicious. In this way, the imperfections of Asia's local business media were a contributor to Asia's economic crisis of 1997–98. Reform of Asia's economies must include reforms to the region's business media. A good start would be for the governments of the region to require a phased sell-down of the shares in media outlets on the part of the region's diversified conglomerates.

Better salaries for journalists must complement independent ownership of Asia's local business media. Journalists, like government workers, need to be paid a decent wage. In many Asian countries, their salary is on par with officials' salary — it is abysmal; and the consequences are the same too — corruption. A significant part of Asia's local business media — especially in Thailand, Indonesia, and China — is compromised by the readiness of journalists to accept bribes from companies not to file negative stories about them. If a company can evade scrutiny from regulators, journalists, and auditors, then it's a law unto itself. And many companies, right across Asia, are precisely that.

Endnotes

Introduction

1. These examples were correct as at December 1998. Ong Beng Seng heads Singapore's Hotel Properties Ltd — one of Asia's most dynamic and better-managed companies.
2. Tomé Pires, *Suma Oriental of Tomé Pires* (1515).
3. The form of this paragraph draws partly from that used by Jonathan J. Pincus to open his book, *Pressure Groups and Politics in Antebellum Tariffs* (Columbia University Press, 1977).

Chapter 1: Bureaucrats, Bribery, and Bankruptcy

1. For more on this, see 'Indonesian judges need strong sense of integrity,' *Indonesian Observer*, April 6, 1998.
2. Cited in East Asia Analytical Unit, *The Philippines: After the Crisis* (Australian government, 1998).
3. 'China steals lead as Asia's piracy king,' *Asian Wall Street Journal*, June 18, 1998.
4. 'Jakarta tightens rules on famous brand names,' *Straits Times*, May 18, 1991.
5. 'Copyrights and wrongs,' *Business Times*, November 9, 1995.
6. T. Fang, *Chinese Business Negotiating Style: A Socio-Cultural Approach* (Linköping University, 1997), p. 104.
7. See editorial: 'Scandal, Inc.,' *Far Eastern Economic Review*, May 7, 1998.
8. 'Living dangerously,' *Far Eastern Economic Review*, February 29, 1996.
9. Christie's International auction catalog: 'South-East Asian pictures and Straits Chinese works of art,' Singapore, October 6, 1996.
10. 'Search for other seven paintings continues,' *Jakarta Post*, September 28, 1996.
11. The remarks were reported in various publications, including the *Jakarta Post* and *Inside Indonesia*.
12. E. Achmadi and J. Trommel, 'Indonesia's sound law and broken courts,' *Asian Wall Street Journal*, March 11, 1998.
13. P. Wood, *Principles of International Insolvency* (Sweet & Maxwell, 1995).
14. 'What can Indon firms do about debt?,' *Business Times*, February 20, 1998.
15. 'Legal hurdle,' *Far Eastern Economic Review*, March 5, 1998.
16. 'Bankruptcy procedures may take 7 years under new Thai law,' *The Star*, May 4, 1998.
17. 'Indon court rejects bankruptcy suit against Ometraco,' *Business Times*, September 30, 1998.
18. 'Court declares first bankruptcy', *South China Morning Post*, October 14, 1998.
19. See 'Unseen precipice,' *Far Eastern Economic Review*, April 23, 1998, for some good references to this.

Chapter 2: Auditing Asia

1. 'Wing Lee switches to Ernst & Young after turnover row,' *South China Morning Post*, January 23, 1999.
2. 'Arthur Andersen,' *South China Morning Post*, December 11, 1997.
3. 'Regulators follow money trail,' *Bangkok Post*, July 30, 1997; and 'Suthee calls VAT hike inappropriate solution,' August 15, 1997.
4. 'The flaw in the Soeryadjaja strategy,' *Business Times*, December 4, 1992.
5. 'Price Waterhouse paints bleak future for CAM Int'l,' *Business Times*, July 12, 1997.
6. 'Alphatec – an integrated vision,' *Asian Business*, June 1, 1995.

7. 'Mr Chips: Charn positions Thailand's No. 1 semiconductor maker to take on the world,' *Asiaweek*, March 1, 1996.
8. 'Alphatec woes start to hit suppliers in US, Europe,' *Asian Wall Street Journal*, June 17, 1997.
9. 'New auditor probes improper transfer,' *Bangkok Post*, August 18, 1997.
10. ibid.
11. 'Man at the top says Alphatec rescue mission doomed to fail,' *South China Morning Post*, August 2, 1997.
12. 'Charn resigns from Alphatec after audit,' *Asian Wall Street Journal*, July 29, 1997; and 'Charn quits amid money mystery,' *Bangkok Post*, July 29, 1997.
13. 'Alphatec's questionable practices foreshadowed Thai economic woes,' *Asian Wall Street Journal*, September 9, 1997.
14. 'New auditor probes 'improper' transfer,' op. cit.
15. '10 execs, shareholders of listed Thai firms blacklisted,' *Business Times*, July 7, 1998.

Chapter 3: Asia's Corrupted Business Media

1. E. Paisley, 'Buying up China with Oei Hong Leong,' *Institutional Investor*, January 1995.
2. *Thornton Guide to Companies in Thailand* (Thornton Publishing, 1996), p. 212.
3. In early 1998, the Chung family announced its intention to sever the link between Hyundai and the newspaper, presumably because the newspaper was reliant on subsidies from Hyundai, and this could no longer be afforded. The move was likely to see some job shedding had the newspaper survived. Bizarrely, Brussels-based International Federation of Journalists issued a press release calling for the link between the newspaper and Hyundai to be restored. The federation was far more interested in journalists' jobs than editorial independence, it seemed. (Media Release, 'IFJ protest as Hyundai cuts lifeline to Korea daily newspaper,' International Federation of Journalists, January 26, 1998.)
4. In 1995, Indonesian journalist, Ahmed Taufik, was jailed for three years (of which he served only two) for writing a story that revealed Harmoko's media stakes. ('Indonesia's tireless fighter for freedom of the press,' *South China Morning Post*, November 22, 1997.)
5. 'Technical problems,' *Far Eastern Economic Review*, September 4, 1997.
6. 'Businesspeople's delicate link with the media industry,' *Jakarta Post*, November 14, 1997.
7. 'Thai journalism exposed,' *Bangkok Post*, June 15, 1996.
8. '*Swasembada* swamped with complaints of lost copies,' *Jakarta Post*, May 14, 1997; and 'Free press meets the market: Buyer snaps up magazine's entire issue,' *Asian Wall Street Journal*, May 16–17, 1997.

Chapter 4: Merchants of Menace? Conglomerates Asian-style

1. Structures such as these are not exclusive to South-East Asia, but they do tend to be predominant in the region. UK entrepreneur Richard Branson's Virgin Group could be characterized by the flat, overlapping structure. However, his group is more an exception to the rule.
2. H. Sender, 'Inside the overseas Chinese network,' *Institutional Investor*, August 1991.

Chapter 5: Asia's Conglomerates and their Banks

1. 'Borrowed time,' *Far Eastern Economic Review*, May 26, 1994.
2. 'All under one roof,' *Far Eastern Economic Review*, June 17, 1993.
3. 'Banking: Time to consolidate,' *Far Eastern Economic Review*, May 16, 1996; and 'Fifty-two banks violate legal lending limit regulations,' *Economic and Business Review Indonesia*, July 17, 1996.
4. 'Bank Jakarta has "bad ties" with Bank Indonesia,' *Jakarta Post*, October 12, 1997.
5. 'Money isn't everything,' *Far Eastern Economic Review*, February 12, 1998.

6. 'Repay loans, Indonesia tells three big banks,' *Asian Wall Street Journal*, August 17, 1998.
7. 'From rags to riches,' *Far Eastern Economic Review*, October 15, 1998.
8. 'Now for the hard part,' *Far Eastern Economic Review*, September 25, 1997.
9. 'Four ex-BI staff named in $301m bank scam,' *Jakarta Post*, August 28, 1997.
10. 'Travel ban on former bank directors,' *Australian Financial Review*, December 31, 1997.
11. 'Bank Jakarta has "bad ties" with Bank Indonesia,' *Jakarta Post*, October 12, 1997.
12. This section draws on the Economist Intelligence Unit, *Philippine Alert*, February 1998; 'Go down in debt,' *Far Eastern Economic Review*, March 26, 1998; 'Manila will confiscate assets of failed bank's owner,' *Business Times*, March 16, 1998; and 'Philippine tycoon Jose Go under siege,' *Business Times*, March 30, 1998.
13. 'Rizal Commercial of Philippines withdraws offer for Orient Bank,' *Asian Wall Street Journal*, April 9, 1998.
14. Much of what appears below is sourced from many articles that appeared in the Indonesian media during 1997. One of the better articles is 'Gunung Agung to sue Jagata over bank scam,' *Jakarta Post*, May 28, 1997.
15. Interview with Masagung, *Eksekutif*, July 1980.
16. 'Artha Graha Group acquires Bank Arta Prima,' *Indonesian Observer*, May 23, 1997.
17. 'PT Gunung Agung acquires SFC stake,' *Indonesian Observer*, August 11, 1997.
18. Much of the detail that relates to Ibnu Sutowo's time at Pertamina is sourced from J. Bresnan, *Managing Indonesia: The Modern Political Economy* (Columbia University Press, 1993).
19. Pusat Data Business Indonesia, *Conglomeration Indonesia*, 3rd ed., vol. 2 (1997), p. A-631.
20. Bresnan, op. cit., p. 173.
21. ibid., p. 180.
22. ibid., p. 181.
23. '1994's top taxpayers,' *Economic and Business Review Indonesia*, February 24, 1997.
24. Alongside the Jakarta Hilton is the massive Jakarta Convention Center, which was largely funded by the Indonesian government. The family would have liked to list the Jakarta Hilton on the Jakarta Stock Exchange but one of the difficulties had been vagaries concerning which part of the hotel/convention center belongs to the family and which to the government. This sort of confusion has been something of a theme in Sutowo's rise in business.
25. S. Seagrave, *Lords of the Rim: The Invisible Empire of the Overseas Chinese* (Bantam, 1995), p. 314f.
26. A. Schwarz, *A Nation in Waiting: Indonesia in the 1990s* (Allen & Unwin, 1994), p. 138; and Bresnan, op. cit., p. 183.
27. Pacific International Finance did write to the holders of its debt to request a postponement of repayments, but they were less than comforted when it was obvious that Endang was still acquiring new stakes in companies, particularly in Singapore.
28. *Swasembada* swamped with complaints of lost copies,' *Jakarta Post*, May 14, 1997; and 'Free press meets the market: Buyer snaps up magazine's entire issue,' *Asian Wall Street Journal*, May 16–17, 1997.
29. 'U.S. firm Adaptec to buy Hyundai unit for US$775m,' *Business Times*, February 21, 1998. (Ultimately, the U.S. Federal Trade Commission intervened, and Symbios was eventually sold to LSI Logic rather than to Adaptec.)
30. The five core sectors are construction, automotive, electronics, chemicals, and finance and other services ('Chaebol in rush for restructuring,' *Korea Times*, May 8, 1998).
31. This is irrespective of finance companies and merchant banks that some *chaebol* started in an attempt to circumvent South Korea's banking law.
32. F. Hu, 'Should China grow chaebol?,' *Asian Wall Street Journal*, December 18, 1997.
33. 'House of debt,' *Far Eastern Economic Review*, March 14, 1991.
34. 'Chaebol can pin it all on Confucius,' *Australian*, December 17, 1997.
35. 'Halting pace of Korea Inc. reforms is highlighted,' *Asian Wall Street Journal*, March 30, 1998.

Chapter 6: Lambs to the Slaughter: Investing in Asia's Stock Markets

1. Singapore and Hong Kong are important exceptions. Their stock markets are governed by sound rules that are enforced.
2. Derived from the Institute for Economic and Financial Research, *Indonesian Capital Market Directory 1997* (Jakarta, 1997).
3. 'Miracle man,' *Far Eastern Economic Review*, January 16, 1997, and George Magnus's reply in the letters to the editor, *Far Eastern Economic Review*, July 24, 1997.
4. 'Web site,' *The Economist*, December 13, 1997.
5. Shangri-La Asia Limited, 'Proposed connected transactions involving the acquisition of SLIM International Limited and General Mandate,' September 3, 1997.
6. Details on payments to affiliates appear in Shangri-La Asia Limited, *Annual Report 1996*, Hong Kong.
7. Shangri-La Asia Limited, op. cit.
8. 'Shangri-La set to pay $155 million in stock for Slim,' *Asian Wall Street Journal*, August 14, 1997.
9. 'Bapepam probes 100 investors and brokers,' *Jakarta Post*, April 25, 1997; 'Families of Jakarta bourse management under probe,' *Straits Times*, May 2, 1997; and 'Tjokrosaputro denies market cornering, accepts penalty,' *Jakarta Post*, May 16, 1997.
10. 'Tapioca tycoon buys 20% Surat Canning stake,' *Bangkok Post*, October 1, 1996.
11. 'Fish packer Surat's travails are Thais' woes in a can,' *Asian Wall Street Journal*, April 2, 1998.

Chapter 7: Polygamy and Family Squabbles

1. E. Huang and L. Jeffrey, *Hong Kong: Portraits of Power* (Weidenfeld & Nicolson, 1995), p. 114.
2. E. Chin, *Gilding the Phoenix: The Straits Chinese and their Jewellery* (The National Museum, Singapore, 1991), p. 124.
3. K.B. Chan and C. Chiang, *Stepping Out: The Making of Chinese Entrepreneurs* (Prentice Hall, 1994), p. 318; and J.K. Yeap, *Far from Rangoon* (Lee Teng Lay Pte Ltd, 1994).
4. 'Relative success story,' *Washington Post*, September 11, 1994
5. 'Bangkok Bank can't rely on family ties,' *Asian Wall Street Journal*, February 12, 1998.
6. 'A maze of family connections complicates succession,' *Washington Post*, September 11, 1994.
7. The number of children was reported in 'The Cukong cover their assets,' *Asia Inc.*, July 1995.
8. 'A maze of family connections complicates succession,' op. cit.
9. 'Alan Yeo begins court bid to wind up YHS Holdings,' *Straits Times*, June 21, 1994; 'Judge takes witness to task for contradicting affidavit,' *Straits Times*, June 24, 1994; and 'Respondents "unfamiliar with assertions in joint affidavit",' June 25, 1994.
10. *thornton Guide to the Companies of Singapore & Malaysia*, Issue 1, 1996, p. 260.
11. The story of the Jumabhoys has been pieced together from various sources. They include: Scotts Holdings Ltd, *Annual Report 1996*, Singapore; Salil Tripathi's excellent 'Blood battle,' *Asia Inc.*, June 1996: and various reports in Singapore's *Business Times* newspaper.
12. At the end of 1995, Ernst & Young delivered its report, which was critical of the Indian land deal and in January 1996, Scotts sold the land for an amount generally believed to be too low, albeit at a 41% profit.
13. Part of their claim is for the transfer of 71 million SIS shares to a trust Rajabali had established for his heirs in 1957.
14. 'Iqbal Jumabhoy accepts suit settlement,' *Business Times*, January 13, 1998.
15. Media release, Stock Exchange of Singapore, 'Public reprimand statement: Scotts Holdings Limited,' March 19, 1997.
16. Media release, Stock Exchange of Singapore, 'Statement on Scotts Holdings Ltd ("SHL"),' July 3, 1997.
17. ibid.

18. Scotts Holdings Limited, *Annual Report 1996*, Singapore.
19. 'Rafiq gives notice to exercise 6m Scotts shares,' *Business Times*, September 6, 1997.
20. 'SIS rejects Rafiq's right to exercise Scotts option,' *Business Times*, September 12, 1997.
21. 'Scotts in the red with $5m interim loss,' *Business Times*, March 27, 1998; and 'Rafiq quits as director; Scotts gloomy on forecast,' *Business Times*, April 2, 1998.

Chapter 8: Asia's E-Boom and E-Bust

1. As cited in 'Accounts unreceivable,' *Far Eastern Economic Review*, July 6, 2000.
2. 'Tom.com losses reached $19 million in 2nd quarter on heavy ad spending,' *Asian Wall Street Journal*, August 2, 2000.
3. 'Lippo tests Internet waters again with this week's AcrossAsia IPO,' *Asian Wall Street Journal*, July 13, 2000; and 'Indonesian regulator cites Lippo for trade breaches,' August 4, 2000.
4. Galbraith, E., 'Happiness through another man's eyes,' *Asia Inside Newsletter*, July 28, 2000.
5. 'Shopping spree,' *Far Eastern Economic Review*, January 20, 2000.
6. As cited in 'Riding the net,' *Far Eastern Economic Review*, March 23, 2000.
7. 'China.com and founders raise US$395m from share sale,' *Business Times*, January 21, 2000.
8. 'Accounts unreceivable,' *Far Eastern Economic Review*, July 6, 2000.
9. See T. Koh, 'Knowledge workers will need a new East Asia', *International Herald Tribune*, July 19, 2000.

Chapter 9: What's Wrong with Japan?

1. D. Nanto, 'Japan's industrial groups: The *keiretsu*,' Congressional Research Service, November 5, 1990.
2. *Euromoney*, July 1998.
3. B. Hills, *Japan Behind the Lines* (Hodder & Stoughton, 1996), p. 18.
4. C. Johnson, *Japan: Who Governs?* (W.W. Norton & Company, 1995), p. 196.
5. K. Rafferty, *Inside Japan's Power Houses* (Weidenfeld & Nicolson, 1995), p. 290.
6. W. Tab, *The Postwar Japanese System* (Oxford University Press, 1995), p. 173.
7. Johnson, op. cit., p. 216.
8. 'The rot spreads,' *Far Eastern Economic Review*, July 15, 1993.
9. 'Strong foundations,' *Far Eastern Economic Review*, October 20, 1994.
10. Hills, op. cit., p. 24.
11. 'In the line of fire,' *Far Eastern Economic Review*, January 16, 1997.
12. 'Head of Nikko says that firm made illegal payments,' *Asian Wall Street Journal*, March 31, 1998.
13. 'Japan's culture of corruption,' *Age*, October 4, 1997.
14. 'Two top bureaucrats quit Japan's Finance Ministry,' *Asian Wall Street Journal*, April 28, 1998.
15. 'Scandalized,' *Far Eastern Economic Review*, July 31, 1997.
16. Hills, op. cit., p. 43.
17. 'Portrait of power,' *Far Eastern Economic Review*, April 2, 1998.
18. '"Conflict of interest" slammed,' *South China Morning Post*, February 18, 1998.
19. Hills, op. cit., p. 17.
20. Johnson, op. cit., pp. 142, 149.
21. This is not to say that all of Japan's important companies are parts of *keiretsu*. Nippon Telegraph and Telephone (NTT), Suntory, Honda, and Japan Airlines are among those that are not.
22. D. Nanto, 'Japan's *keiretsu*: Industrial groups as trade barriers,' Congressional Research Service, January 30, 1994.
23. F. Fukuyama, *Trust* (The Free Press, 1995), p. 167.
24. Japan has a significant small-business sector comprising hundreds of thousands of companies, which tend to be family owned. In this respect, this segment of Japan's

economy is similar to the rest of Asia. Many, though, are suppliers and sub-contractors to the *keiretsu*.
25. Nanto, 'Japan's industrial groups: The *keiretsu*,' op. cit.
26. Supplied by the Mitsubishi Public Affairs Committee.
27. D. Nanto, 'Japan's *keiretsu*: Industrial groups as trade barriers,' op. cit.
28. ibid.
29. W.M. Fruin, *The Japanese Enterprise System* (Clarendon Press, 1994), p. 20.
30. ibid.
31. Nanto, 'Japan's industrial groups: The *keiretsu*', op. cit.
32. Fukuyama, op. cit., p. 199.
33. Nanto, 'Japan's industrial groups: The *keiretsu*,' op. cit.
34. East Asia Analytical Unit, *A New Japan? Change in Asia's Megamarket* (Department of Foreign Affairs and Trade, Australia, 1997), p. 173.
35. East Asia Analytical Unit, *Asia's Global Powers: Japan and China* (Department of Foreign Affairs and Trade, Australia, 1996), p. 30.
36. Nanto, 'Japan's *keiretsu*: Industrial groups as trade barriers,' op. cit.
37. ibid.
38. 'Creative cooking,' *Far Eastern Economic Review*, April 9, 1998.
39. 'American accents,' *Far Eastern Economic Review*, July 31, 1997.
40. 'Scandals put corporate culture on trial,' *Nikkei Weekly*, June 23, 1997.
41. 'American accents,' op. cit.
42. 'Another Japan builder sets big write-off,' *Asian Wall Street Journal*, April 7, 1998.
43. 'Top banks set record for loan disposal,' *Nikkei Weekly*, April 6, 1998.
44. J. Choy, 'Credit union takeovers take over financial system debate,' *Japan Economic Institute Report*, April 7, 1995.
45. ibid.
46. Hills, op. cit., p. 42.
47. 'Former executives charged for hiding Yamaichi losses,' *South China Morning Post*, March 5, 1998.
48. 'Accounting faces risk of becoming exciting,' *Australian Financial Review*, March 23, 1998.
49. 'Creative cooking,' op. cit.
50. ibid.
51. 'Top banks set record for loan disposal,' op. cit.
52. United Press International (UPI) report, January 30, 1997.
53. I. Taka, 'Business Ethics in Japan,' *mimeo*, 1997, The International School of Economics and Business Administration, Reitaku University.

Chapter 10: China: Rising Star or Black Hole?

1. 'China admits to huge deficit in grain funds,' *Asian Wall Street Journal*, October 14, 1998.
2. T. Fang, *Chinese Business Negotiating Style: A Socio-Cultural Approach* (Linköping University, 1997), pp. 186–187.
3. World Bank, *China's Management of Enterprise Assets: The State as Shareholder*, June 1997.
4. East Asia Analytical Unit, *China Embraces the Market* (Australian government, 1997), p. 333.
5. 'The bigger, the better,' *Far Eastern Economic Review*, May 21, 1998.
6. 'China calls for preferred approval of listings of ailing state firms,' *Asian Wall Street Journal*, October 16, 1997.
7. 'The long march to capitalism,' *The Economist*, September 13, 1997.
8. '8.2b yuan of China's pension funds missing: report,' *Business Times*, July 27, 1998.
9. 'Corruption boosts size of savings accounts,' *South China Morning Post*, July 14, 1998.
10. 'Widespread accounting fraud tarnishes Anhui province,' *South China Morning Post*, February 27, 1998.
11. 'The Global 500,' *Fortune*, July 24, 2000.
12. 'Red-chip parents carry huge debt loads,' *Asian Wall Street Journal*, April 21, 1998.

13. 'Cosco unit moves into Shanghai housing,' *South China Morning Post*, April 24, 1998.
14. Transcript of 'Red Ships,' *Background Briefing*, Radio National, Australian Broadcasting Corporation, April 19, 1998.
15. 'Ministry shake-out,' *Far Eastern Economic Review*, March 19, 1998.
16. 'Zhu's financial clean-up takes on PLA,' *Business Times*, July 18, 1998.
17. 'Chinese firms abandon plans to offer shares,' *Asian Wall Street Journal*, February 13, 1998.
18. 'Upside down,' *Far Eastern Economic Review*, June 29, 1995.
19. 'Village boasts huge free market growth,' *South China Morning Post*, March 30, 1993; and 'Once-greedy capitalist centre outshines star of collectivism,' *South China Morning Post*, December 2, 1997.
20. 'Rising corporate star ranks first in sales,' *South China Morning Post*, July 10, 1997.
21. C. Lo, 'China can dodge a financial crisis,' *Asian Wall Street Journal*, December 29, 1997.
22. T.G. Rawski, 'Is China next?,' *Asian Wall Street Journal*, January 23, 1998.
23. 'Stone Group to continue asset injections,' *South China Morning Post*, April 17, 1997.
24. 'Ex-bureaucrats in hot demand,' *Business Times*, April 23, 1998.
25. 'Revolution's children,' *Asia, Inc.*, January 1995.
26. ibid.
27. 'Zhu pulls no punches in fight to clean up scandal-ridden economy,' *South China Morning Post*, July 24, 1998.
28. 'Accounting methods of Deng's niece's firm queried,' *South China Morning Post*, May 1, 1998.
29. 'Goodbye to all that,' *Far Eastern Economic Review*, March 23, 1995.
30. 'Pressure on the first family,' *South China Morning Post*, May 14, 1995.
31. 'Scandal touches firm linked to Deng,' *Asian Wall Street Journal*, April 24, 1998, and other reports.
32. 'Consortium bids record price for land in Taipei,' *Asian Wall Street Journal*, July 7, 1998.
33. 'Lai Sun boss targets missing aide as "real bribes suspect",' *South China Morning Post*, May 7, 1998.
34. 'The money machine,' *Far Eastern Economic Review*, August 11, 1994.
35. 'Cases of corruption filed in Hong Kong rose 24% in 1st half,' *Asian Wall Street Journal*, July 9, 1998.
36. The shares in the red chips aren't to be mistaken for H shares, which are the shares of mainland SOEs traded on the Hong Kong stock exchange.
37. 'Wild West of the East warning issued by SFC,' *South China Morning Post*, July 26, 1997.
38. 'Treasury arm wins exemption from SFC,' *South China Morning Post*, July 10, 1997.
39. 'Tycoon with close ties to Beijing,' *South China Morning Post*, March 19, 1998.
40. 'Tycoon grateful for friend Tung's help,' *South China Morning Post*, November 5, 1998.
41. 'Intervention share buys made public,' *South China Morning Post*, October 27, 1998.
42. M. Faber, 'Who profited from the intervention?,' *Asian Wall Street Journal*, September 7, 1998.
43. A.L. Neumann also makes this point in 'Will China rein in Hong Kong's press?,' *Freedom Under the Dragon: Can Hong Kong's Media Still Breathe Fire?* — a report by the Committee to Protect Journalists, September 1997.

Chapter 11: Asia's Overseas Chinese

1. The table is a combination of estimates from East Asia Analytical Unit, *Overseas Chinese Business Networks in Asia* (Australian government, 1995); M. Yamaguchi, 'The Emerging Chinese Business Sphere,' *Nomura Asian Perspectives*, 11(2), July 1993; and my own estimates. These estimates are not precise but serve to suggest the order of magnitude only.
2. Derived from data presented in: Pusat Data Business Indonesia, *Conglomeration Indonesia*, 3rd ed. (1997).
3. The debate over the use of the term 'overseas Chinese' has raged on for many years. Academics in the field have devoted considerable energy and resources to debating the nomenclature and are often critical of the term's usage. Their argument often rests

on the fact that 'overseas Chinese' is a loose adaptation of the Chinese term, *hua-qiao*, or sojourner, the term given to many mainland Chinese who left China in the 19th and early 20th centuries. They were seen as sojourners because they usually left China with the intent of returning, although of course many did not. However, I contend that the term 'overseas Chinese' has, like many other words and terms in the English language, evolved with time and thus is no longer mirrored by its original Chinese source, *hua-qiao*. I believe that when the term 'overseas Chinese' is used today, it doesn't imply that those so described have any connection with China and therefore the term doesn't have the political connotations that many purist academics contend it does. The term has broad acceptance, as does its modern meaning, which surely is the test of the appropriateness of any term. Hence, I strongly argue that the term 'overseas Chinese' is the appropriate term.

4. L. Kraar, 'The wealth and the power of the overseas Chinese,' *Fortune*, March 1971.
5. Hokchia is very close to Fuzhou and can be considered a subset of the latter. Another category, Choa Ann, could be added, although it is halfway between Teochiu and Hokkien. But, given that Hokkien and Teochiu are closely related and mutually intelligible, it really can be considered a subset of one or the other.
6. 'Heartbreak Hotel?' *Far Eastern Economic Review*, July 18, 1991.
7. East Asia Analytical Unit, op. cit., p. 185.
8. Extrapolated from Shangri-La Hotel Public Company Limited, *Annual Report 1996*, Bangkok.
9. 'In search of an Asian path,' *Asiaweek*, December 19, 1997.
10. I first developed these arguments in: M. Backman, 'Blame Indonesia's Chinese,' The 5th Column, *Far Eastern Economic Review*, March 5, 1998.

Chapter 12: Royal Business

1. Lawsuit filed on January 17, 1997, with the United States District Court, Central District of California, 'Shannon la Rhea Markatec (plaintiff) vs Kaliber Talent Consultants, et al.'
2. 'Sultan's brother took 40 prostitutes to the Dorchester at a time,' *This is London*, February 19, 1998.
3. 'Royals score immunity victory, vow to fight Miss USA sex slave case,' *South China Morning Post*, September 20, 1997.
4. 'Prince "ripped off buying love nest" in Park Lane,' *South China Morning Post*, February 14, 1998.
5. 'Prince and £21 million Park Lane sex den,' *This is London*, February 12, 1998.
6. 'Bad taste and loads of money,' *South China Morning Post*, June 20, 1997.
7. G. Hiscock, *Asia's Wealth Club* (Nicholas Brealey Publishing, 1997), p. 167.
8. Filed with the U.S. Department of Justice in accordance with the Foreign Agents Registration Act.
9. 'Brunei Sultan said to invest in smart card company,' *The Star*, February 3, 1998.
10. Other than a few million dollars worth of clothing exports and some tourism-related revenue, this comprises the sum total of Brunei's earnings from exports to the rest of the world. On top of that, very little is produced in Brunei for its own consumption. Almost all food is imported, including approximately 94% of its rice requirements. Consequently, imports chew up around two-thirds of Brunei's export income.
11. 'Buffett, Prince Alwaleed are among the big winners,' *Asian Wall Street Journal*, April 8, 1998.
12. G. Gunn, 'Rentier capitalism in Negara Brunei Darussalam,' in K. Hewison et al., *Southeast Asia in the 1990s* (Allen & Unwin, 1993), p. 130.
13. Y. Kunio, *The Rise of Ersatz Capitalism in South-East Asia* (Oxford University Press, 1988), p. 205.
14. 'Khoo Teck Puat flies off after slipping in last week,' *Straits Times*, November 1, 1989.
15. 'Hotelier's daughter fined for illegal property transactions,' *Straits Times*, April 11, 1990.
16. 'Prince "ripped off buying love nest" in Park Lane,' op. cit.
17. 'Revenue probes Asprey,' *Sunday Telegraph* (London), December 10, 1995.

18. 'Sultan seeks help on funds scandal,' *Australian Financial Review*, July 20, 1998; 'Progress in hunt for missing billions,' *Borneo Bulletin*, October 21, 1998.
19. 'Sultan of Brunei relieves Prince of Amedeo post,' *Asian Wall Street Journal*, August 3, 1998.
20. 'Brunei grapples with recession,' *Daily Telegraph*, July 16, 1998.
21. 'Major changes at RBA,' *Borneo Bulletin*, June 26, 1998.
22. 'Prince Jefri's jet attracts interest at NY airport,' *Borneo Bulletin*, September 28, 1998.
23. 'Prince stays, Gulf Stream leaves,' *Borneo Bulletin*, October 3-4, 1998.
24. 'Don't blame conservatives says Pehin Aziz,' *Borneo Bulletin*, September 23, 1998.
25. 'Prince Jefri returns,' *Borneo Bulletin*, October 2, 1998.
26. Bousteadco is majority owned and managed by Wong Fong Fui through his Janburgh Holdings. Wong is a business partner of Prince Mohamed. Wong, like Prince Mohamed, is also a shareholder in Myanmar Airways International.
27. M. Weaver, 'Our far-flung correspondents: In the Sultan's palace,' *The New Yorker*, October 7, 1991.
28. Gunn, op. cit., p. 120.
29. 'Brunei Sultan gives up Mount E suite,' *Business Times*, October 1, 1998.
30. 'Prince with penchant for pop declared heir to sultan's throne,' *South China Morning Post*, August 11, 1998.
31. 'Brothers grim in Brunei,' *Business Week*, August 10, 1998.
32. Antah Holdings Bhd, *Annual Report 1996*.
33. 'Blue blood in the boardroom,' *Asia Inc.*, May 1997.
34. 'The global power elite,' *Forbes*, July 28, 1997; July 6, 1998.
35. Dhana Siam Finance and Securities PCL, *Annual Report 1996*, p. 13.
36. The Siam Cement Group, *Annual Report 1996*. Associated companies are those in which Siam Cement has direct and indirect interests of between 21% and 50%.
37. 'Indonesia project feels Asia crisis's pinch,' *Asian Wall Street Journal*, February 13, 1998. Work on the project ceased in February 1998 due to the regional financial crisis. But US$1 billion had already been spent and construction is expected to resume when economic conditions improve.
38. K. Hewison, 'The financial bourgeoisie in Thailand,' *Journal of Contemporary Asia*, vol. 11, 1981.
39. 'Siam TV seeks clear picture,' *Bangkok Post*, April 28, 1997.
40. 'Not child's play,' *Far Eastern Economic Review*, June 29, 1995.
41. *Guide to the Companies of Thailand* (Thornton Publishing, February 1996), p. 79.
42. 'Siam Cement posts big loss on Baht's slide,' *Asian Wall Street Journal*, February 26, 1998.
43. 'Dhana Siam Finance plans to double capital to 15b baht,' *Business Times*, March 12, 1998.
44. 'Crown Property Bureau drops B143bn in projects,' *Bangkok Post*, February 14, 1998.

Chapter 13: President of the Country; Chairman of the Board

1. This estimate includes the Salim Group companies in which Soeharto's cousin, Sudwikatmono, is known to have an interest. However, it doesn't include companies controlled by more distant relatives, such as those attached to the Sahid Group nor those whose only Soeharto-link is that their partial or full ownership by a Soeharto-linked charitable foundation. Neither does it include the Astra Group and its many subsidiaries in which the Soeharto family held a small indirect stake. Also, I have used other (lower) estimates from elsewhere (such as in M. Backman, 'What now for Suharto, Inc?,' *Asian Wall Street Journal*, May 26, 1998), but these have been superseded by my subsequent research.
2. The mosque is to be called the Haji Muhammad Soeharto Mosque. 'Soeharto Mosque construction to begin,' *Indonesian Observer*, September 13, 1997.
3. 'Suharto relative quits key post,' *South China Morning Post*, June 9, 1998.
4. 'Humpuss again wins LNG contract from Pertamina,' *Jakarta Post*, December 5, 1997.

5. 'Pertamina to scrap 159 dubious deals, *Jakarta Post*, October 10, 1998; and 'Indon govt finds evidence of graft in Pertamina deals', *Business Times*, October 10, 1998.
6. J. Bresnan, *Managing Indonesia: The Modern Political Economy* (Columbia University Press, 1993), p. 249; and A. Schwarz, *A Nation in Waiting: Indonesia in the 1990s* (Allen & Unwin, 1994), p. 50.
7. Schwarz, op. cit., p. 154.
8. ibid., p. 155.
9. ibid., p. 157.
10. 'New rules are expected to benefit Indonesia's clove-trading monopoly,' *Asian Wall Street Journal*, October 28, 1994.
11. 'Govt decides to stop cutting clove trees,' *Jakarta Post*, August 13, 1997.
12. 'Clove intensification program launched in 10 provinces,' *Indonesian Observer*, August 18, 1997.
13. 'Sanctions set for violations of clove trading system,' *Indonesian Observer*, September 20, 1997
14. 'Clove farmers lose Rp2.3t in sales revenue,' *Jakarta Post*, October 1, 1997.
15. 'To market, to market,' *Far Eastern Economic Review*, August 25, 1994.
16. 'Govt directive on buying Timors unfair: Bimantara,' *Jakarta Post*, June 6, 1997.
17. 'Soewardi under fire over Timor car orders,' *Jakarta Post*, July 12, 1997.
18. 'All Central Java House members buy Timor cars,' *Indonesian Observer*, August 14, 1997.
19. 'Timor announces it sold 1,250 cars in one night,' *Jakarta Post*, July 14, 1997.
20. ibid.
21. 'Bishop Belo to receive official Timor,' *Indonesian Observer*, August 2, 1997.
22. '13 banks ordered to finance Timor car project,' *Jakarta Post*, May 7, 1997.
23. ibid.
24. 'TPN calls for quick disbursal of consortium's loans,' *Indonesian Observer*, June 3, 1997.
25. 'Indonesian fire fund steered to car project,' *Australian*, January 23, 1998.
26. 'Indon utility cancels power purchase pact,' *Business Times*, June 9, 1998.
27. 'Was the World Bank part of Indonesia's problem?,' *Asian Wall Street Journal*, July 15, 1998.
28. 'Indosat given option to buy "TPI" shares,' *Jakarta Post*, October 3, 1997.
29. Schwarz, op. cit., p. 149.
30. G. Aditjondro, 'Suharto & Sons,' *Washington Post*, January 25, 1998.
31. 'Telkom offer angers bankers in Indonesia,' *Asian Wall Street Journal*, December 20–21, 1996; 'A private affair,' *Far Eastern Economic Review*, January 30, 1997.
32. The matter was even raised by legislators in Indonesia's House of Assembly. See 'Pertamina criticized over Sempati Air's fuel debts,' *Jakarta Post*, July 22, 1997.
33. 'State firms asked to sell stickers,' *Jakarta Post*, July 7, 1997.
34. 'Sumarlin discloses huge losses,' *Jakarta Post*, June 26, 1997.
35. 'Barren business,' *Far Eastern Economic Review*, October 16, 1997.
36. 'On public service,' *Jakarta Post*, December 23, 1995.
37. 'Triple decker project goes on as scheduled,' *Indonesian Observer*, October 20, 1997.
38. 'President okays plan to establish bridge linking Indonesia, M'sia,' *Indonesian Observer*, August 21, 1997.
39. '558-meter-high tower to "lift Jakarta's image",' *Jakarta Post*, August 13, 1997.
40. Reuters report, 'Indonesia beer firms toast move to end levy row,' February 8, 1996.
41. C. Leh, *A Guide to Birds' Nest Caves and Birds' Nests of Sarawak* (Sarawak Museum, 1993).
42. 'Indonesian scion forages for revenue in bird nests,' *Asian Wall Street Journal*, February 20–21, 1998.
43. 'Monopoly of Chinese drug trade opposed,' *Jakarta Post*, May 3, 1995.
44. 'Parents object to shoe company monopoly,' *Jakarta Post*, August 23, 1997.
45. 'Soeharto disagrees with shoe plan,' *Jakarta Post*, August 29, 1997.
46. 'Ari Sigit Soeharto: Boy wonder of Indonesia's business world', *Economic and Business Review Indonesia*, July 8, 1995.

47. 'Citra Marga to build 1.1trln rupiah toll-road,' *Economic and Business Review Indonesia*, April 30, 1996.
48. 'Ari Sigit Soeharto: Boy wonder of Indonesia's business world,' op. cit.
49. 'Firm owned by Soeharto relative,' *South China Morning Post*, January 4, 1996.
50. 'Indonesian scion forages for revenue in bird nests,' op. cit.
51. The allegations were printed in 'Victoria Police investigate drug links to Soeharto family,' *Age*, October 3, 1998.
52. 'Poor little rich kids,' *Sydney Morning Herald*, October 24, 1998.
53. '"Speculators, El Nino behind economic crisis",' *Indonesian Observer*, December 2, 1997.

Chapter 14: Other Politicians, Other Businesses

1. 'A helping hand,' *Far Eastern Economic Review*, May 16, 1991.
2. 'How Suharto's circle did well together with Freeport,' *Asian Wall Street Journal*, September 30, 1998.
3. 'Sri Bintang's mortal sin,' *Inside Indonesia*, June 1995.
4. 'Sritex wins order from NATO,' *Jakarta Post*, March 4, 1997.
5. S. Cheong, *Bumiputera Entrepreneurs in the KLSE* (Corporate Research Services, 1996), pp. 165–171; and C. Cragg, *The New Taipans* (Century, 1995), p. 90.
6. Cheong, op. cit.
7. E.T. Gomez, *Political Business: Corporate Involvement of Malaysian Political Parties* (James Cook University of North Queensland, 1994), p. 151.
8. 'Country Heights takes 68% stake in London project,' *Business Times*, January 23, 1998.
9. I am indebted to Salil Tripathi for making available to me his article, 'The sons also rise' on the Mahathirs in business written for *Asia, Inc*. The article, written in 1997, wasn't published, as *Asia, Inc*. ceased publication before there was an opportunity. I have drawn on some of Salil's research and interviews in relation to the business activities of Dr Mahathir's sons for this section. Other sources include: 'Land and sea,' *Far Eastern Economic Review*, October 6, 1994; 'The M Factor,' *Far Eastern Economic Review*, July 11, 1996; 'Out of Dad's shadow,' *Asiaweek*, September 6, 1996; and 'Transmile sheds stake in unit,' *Business Times*, August 19, 1997. Additional information on Konsortium Perkapalan and Tongkah Holdings comes from corporate profiles and annual reports provided by the companies.
10. The family's Hong Kong interests haven't met with great success. Both Goldtron Holdings and S. Megga International Holdings Sectors manufacture consumer telecommunications and electronics products. These have become increasingly competitive, so that neither firm is currently profitable. In late 1997 and early 1998, S. Megga missed payment on some of the convertible bonds it has issued and was also served with a writ by one of its creditors. ('Banker serves claim on Megga,' *South China Morning Post*, December 2, 1997; and 'S Megga double blow,' *South China Morning Post*, January 7, 1998.)
11. 'Equine Park township coming up in Serdang,' *New Straits Times*, April 3, 1996.
12. 'Siu-Fung, S Megga attacked for refusing to resume trade,' *South China Morning Post*, July 14, 1998.
13. 'Bombay terminal to boost KPB business in Indonesia,' *The Star*, July 27, 1998.
14. 'The Mirzan Mahathir story,' *Business Times*, July 13, 1998.
15. 'Hospital Pantai ups Asia Matrix stake to 7.2%,' *Business Times*, November 27, 1997; 'Asia Matrix takes 60% stake in 4 ventures,' *Business Times*, November 28, 1997.
16. 'Tongkah signs up for new venture,' *The Star*, July 25, 1998.
17. 'Malaysian seeks stake in Sydney hotel,' *The Star*, November 25, 1997; 'New confidence in World Square,' *Australian Financial Review*, February 5, 1998; 'KL's Reliance in control of Sydney hotel,' *Business Times*, November 17, 1997.
18. 'Pantai shares soar as prominent trio moves in,' *Business Times*, December 19, 1995; and 'Tongkah takes stake in Hospital Pantai,' *Straits Times*, December 20, 1995.
19. 'Prominent Indon businessmen take 7.8% stake in Goldtron,' *Business Times*, October 18, 1995.
20. 'Goldtron to make pagers in Indonesia,' *Business Times*, October 13, 1995.

21. 'Stand and deliver,' *Far Eastern Economic Review*, September 12, 1996.
22. *Logging Against the Natives of Sarawak* (INSAN, Kuala Lumpur, 1994), p. v.
23. ibid., p. 5.
24. Information supplied by Investamatic Services, Kuala Lumpur, March 23, 1998.
25. *Logging Against the Natives of Sarawak*, op. cit., p. vi.
26. Information is from corporate profiles supplied by CMS Bhd.
27. 'Work on township in Kuching set to start,' *The Star*, August 27, 1997.
28. 'Stand and deliver,' op. cit.
29. 'CMSB posts RM231.3mil group profit,' *The Star*, March 25, 1998.
30. 'CMSB considering further cost-cutting measures,' *The Star*, June 29, 1998.
31. 'Promises, promises,' *Far Eastern Economic Review*, October 10, 1996.
32. 'Busted: MP's drug indictment roils parliament,' *Far Eastern Economic Review*, May 26, 1994.
33. United States Department of Justice, 'Foreign Agents Registrations Act, Annual Report for 1995' (Report by the US Attorney General to Congress).
34. 'Thailand's former PM Chatichai dies, aged 78,' *Business Times*, May 7, 1998.
35. 'Political plays,' *Far Eastern Economic Review*, July 22, 1995.
36. 'The curious cast of Asian donors,' *Washington Post*, January 27, 1997.
37. 'Probe politics,' *Far Eastern Economic Review*, September 28, 1995.
38. Pasuk Phongpaichat and Chris Baker, *Thailand's Boom!* (Silkworm Books, 1996), p. 177.
39. K. Hewison, 'The financial bourgeoisie in Thailand,' *Journal of Contemporary Asia*, vol. 11, 1981.
40. 'Compete or die,' *Far Eastern Economic Review*, August 5, 1993.
41. 'Democracy first,' *Far Eastern Economic Review*, November 6, 1997.
42. 'Surface measures,' *Far Eastern Economic Review*, April 10, 1997.
43. 'SAP ready to quit coalition,' *Bangkok Post*, February 13, 1998.
44. 'New Year gifts cause outrage,' *Jakarta Post*, February 8, 1997.
45. 'Extradition battle starts next month,' *Bangkok Post*, September 27, 1996.
46. 'Firm's liabilities total B5bn,' *Bangkok Post*, March 27, 1998.
47. 'BBC seeks to rescue B65bn in bad debt,' *Bangkok Post*, March 2, 1998.
48. 'Majority rules,' *Far Eastern Economic Review*, May 23, 1996.
49. 'Opposition bid to push Chart Thai from union,' *Bangkok Post*, March 16, 1998.
50. 'The inner circle,' *Far Eastern Economic Review*, May 14, 1998.
51. *Mr. & Ms.*, July 5–11, 1985.

Chapter 15: Asian Eclipse and Beyond

1. This account is taken from Malcolm Smith, *A Physician at the Court of Siam* (1946).
2. 'World Bank tries to explain Indonesian economic crisis,' *Asian Wall Street Journal*, July 20, 1998.
3. 'Now for the hard part,' *Far Eastern Economic Review*, September 25, 1997.

Bibliography

Interviews, media and wire reports, stock exchange records, and information directly supplied by companies themselves have formed the principal information sources for this book.

Newspapers and journals that have been consulted and referred to in the text are:

Age (Australia). *Asia Inc.* (Hong Kong), *Asiamoney* (Hong Kong), *Asian Business* (Hong Kong), *Asian Wall Street Journal* (Hong Kong), *Asiaweek* (Hong Kong), *Australian* (Australia), *Australian Financial Review* (Australia), *Bangkok Post* (Thailand), *Borneo Bulletin* (Brunei), *Business Day* (Thailand), *Business Review Weekly* (Australia), *Business Times* (Singapore), *Daily Telegraph* (United Kingdom), *Economic and Business Review Indonesia* (Indonesia), *Eksekutif* (Indonesia), *Euromoney* (United Kingdom), *Far Eastern Economic Review* (Hong Kong), *Financial Times* (United Kingdom), *Forbes* (United States), *Fortune* (United States), *Indonesian Observer* (Indonesia), *Inside Indonesia* (Australia), *International Herald Tribune* (United States), *Jakarta Post* (Indonesia), *Korea Times* (South Korea), *Los Angeles Times* (United States), *Malaysian Business Times* (Malaysia), *Melbourne Age* (Australia), *Mr. & Ms.* (The Philippines), *New Straits Times* (Malaysia), *Nikkei Weekly* (Japan), *South China Morning Post* (Hong Kong), *South China Morning Post International Weekly* (Hong Kong), *Straits Times* (Singapore), *Sunday Telegraph* (United Kingdom), *Sunday Tribune* (Malaysia), *Swasembada* (Indonesia), *Sydney Morning Herald* (Australia), *The Economist* (United Kingdom), *The Edge* (Malaysia), *The Press* (New Zealand), *The Star* (Malaysia), *This is London* (United Kingdom), *Time* (United States), *Wall Street Journal* (United States), and the *Washington Post* (United States).

Other works are listed below:

Chapter 1
Bureaucrats, Bribery, and Bankruptcy
Achmadi, E. and Trommel, J. 'Indonesia's sound law and broken courts,' *Asian Wall Street Journal*, March 11, 1998.
Cheong, S., *Chinese Controlled Companies in the KLSE Industrial Counter* (Corporate Research Services, 1992).
East Asia Analytical Unit, *The Philippines. After the Crisis* (Department of Foreign Affairs and Trade, Australia, 1998).
Fang, T., *Chinese Business Negotiating Style: A Socio-Cultural Approach* (Linköping University, 1997).
Wood, P., *Principles of International Insolvency* (Sweet & Maxwell, 1995).

Chapter 2
Auditing Asia
Cameron, J., 'The useful death of traditional accounting,' *Asian Wall Street Journal*, April 22, 1998.
Wood, P., *Principles of International Insolvency* (Sweet & Maxwell, 1995).

Chapter 3
Asia's Corrupted Business Media
Backman, M., 'The economics of corruption,' *Asian Wall Street Journal*, September 3, 1996.

Institute of Social Analysis, *Logging Against the Natives of Sarawak*, 2nd ed. (INSAN, 1994).
Paisley, E., 'Buying up China with Oei Hong Leong,' *Institutional Investor*, January 1995.
Thornton Guide to Companies in Thailand (Thornton Publishing, 1996).

Chapter 4
Merchants of Menace? Conglomerates Asian-style
East Asia Analytical Unit, *Overseas Chinese Business Networks in Asia* (Department of Foreign Affairs and Trade, Australia, 1995).
Sender, H., 'Inside the overseas Chinese network,' *Institutional Investor*, August 1991.

Chapter 5
Asia's Conglomerates and their Banks
Bresnan, J., *Managing Indonesia: The Modern Political Economy* (Columbia University Press, 1993).
Economist Intelligence Unit, *Philippine Alert*, February 1998.
Hu, F., 'Should China grow chaebol?,' *Asian Wall Street Journal*, December 18, 1997.
Lien, Y.C., *From Chinese Villager to Singapore Tycoon: My Life Story* (with Louis Kraar) (Times, 1992).
Pusat Data Business Indonesia, *Conglomeration Indonesia*, 3rd ed., vol. 2 (1997).
Schwarz, A., *A Nation in Waiting: Indonesia in the 1990s* (Allen & Unwin, 1994).
Seagrave, S., *Lords of the Rim: The Invisible Empire of the Overseas Chinese* (Bantam, 1995).

Chapter 6
Lambs to the Slaughter: Investing in Asia's Stock Markets
Backman, M., 'The Salim Group,' in *IEBM Handbook of International Business* (International Thomson Business Press, 1998).
Federal Flour Mills Bhd, *Annual Report 1996*, Kuala Lumpur.
Institute for Economic and Financial Research, *Indonesian Capital Market Directory 1997* (Jakarta, 1997).
Perlis Plantations Bhd, *Annual Report 1996*, Kuala Lumpur.
Sato, Y., 'The Salim Group in Indonesia: The development and behaviour of the largest conglomerate in Southeast Asia,' *The Developing Economies*, December 1993.
Shangri-La Asia Limited, 'Proposed connected transactions involving the acquisition of SLIM International Limited and General Mandate,' September 3, 1997.
Shangri-La Asia Ltd, *Annual Report 1996*, Hong Kong.

Chapter 7
Polygamy and Family Squabbles
Bangkok Metropolitan Bank PCL, *Annual Report 1996*, Bangkok.
Chan, K.B. and Chiang, C. *Stepping Out: The Making of Chinese Entrepreneurs* (Prentice Hall, 1994).
Chin, E., *Gilding the Phoenix: The Straits Chinese and their Jewellery* (The National Museum Singapore, 1991).
Huang, E. and Jeffrey, L. *Hong Kong: Portraits of Power* (Weidenfeld & Nicolson, 1995).
Scotts Holdings Ltd, *Annual Report 1996*, Singapore.
Sender, H., 'Inside the overseas Chinese network,' *Institutional Investor*, August 1991.
Thornton Guide to the Companies of Singapore & Malaysia (Thornton Publishing, 1996).
Tripathi, S., 'Blood battle,' *Asia Inc.*, June 1996.
Yeap, J.K., *Far from Rangoon* (Lee Teng Lay Pte Ltd, 1994).

Chapter 9
What's Wrong with Japan?
Choy, J., 'Credit union takeovers take over financial system debate,' *Japan Economic Institute Report*, April 7, 1995.
East Asia Analytical Unit, *A New Japan? Change in Asia's Megamarket* (Department of Foreign Affairs and Trade, Australia, 1997).

East Asia Analytical Unit, *Asia's Global Powers: Japan and China* (Department of Foreign Affairs and Trade, Australia, 1996).

Fruin, W.M., *The Japanese Enterprise System* (Clarendon Press, 1994).

Fukuyama, F., *Trust: The Social Virtues and the Creation of Prosperity* (The Free Press, 1995).

Hills, B., *Japan Behind the Lines* (Hodder & Stoughton, 1996).

Johnson, C., *Japan: Who Governs?* (W.W. Norton & Company, 1995).

Nanto, D., 'Japan's industrial groups: The *keiretsu*,' Congressional Research Service, November 5, 1990.

Nanto, D., 'Japan's *keiretsu*: Industrial groups as trade barriers,' Congressional Research Service, January 30, 1994.

Rafferty, K., *Inside Japan's Power Houses* (Weidenfeld & Nicolson, 1995).

Tabb, W., *The Postwar Japanese System* (Oxford University Press, 1995).

Taka, I., 'Business Ethics in Japan,' *mimeo*, 1997, The International School of Economics and Business Administration, Reitaku University.

Chapter 10
China: Rising Star or Black Hole?

East Asia Analytical Unit, *China Embraces the Market* (Department of Foreign Affairs and Trade, Australia, 1997).

Faber, M., 'Who profited from the intervention?,' *Asian Wall Street Journal*, September 7, 1998.

Lo, C., 'China can dodge a financial crisis,' *Asian Wall Street Journal*, December 29, 1997.

Rawski, T.G., 'Is China next?,' *Asian Wall Street Journal*, January 23, 1998.

World Bank, *China's Management of Enterprise Assets: The State as Shareholder*, June 1997.

Chapter 11
Asia's Overseas Chinese

Backman, M., 'Blame Indonesia's Chinese,' The 5th Column, *Far Eastern Economic Review*, March 5, 1998.

East Asia Analytical Unit, *Overseas Chinese Business Networks in Asia* (Department of Foreign Affairs and Trade, Australia, 1995).

Gamba, C., 'Chinese associations in Singapore,' *Journal of the Malaysian Branch of the Royal Asiatic Society*, December 1966.

Hiscock, G., *Asia's Wealth Club* (Nicholas Brealey Publishing, 1997).

Institute for Economic and Financial Research, *Indonesian Capital Market Directory 1997* (Jakarta).

Kraar, L., 'The wealth and the power of the overseas Chinese,' *Fortune*, March 1971.

Kunio, Y., *The Rise of Ersatz Capitalism in South-East Asia* (Oxford University Press, 1988).

Pan, L., *Sons of the Yellow Emperor* (Mandarin, 1990).

Pusat Data Business Indonesia, *Conglomeration Indonesia*, 3rd ed. (Jakarta, 1997).

Sato, Y., 'The Salim Group in Indonesia: The development and behaviour of the largest conglomerate in Southeast Asia,' *The Developing Economies*, December 1993.

Singapore Chinese Chamber of Commerce and Industry, *Directory of Members of the 47th Council*, March 1993–March 1995.

Yamaguchi, M., 'The Emerging Chinese Business Sphere,' *Nomura Asian Perspectives*, 11(2), July 1993.

Chapter 12
Royal Business

Antah Holdings Bhd, *Annual Report 1996*, Kuala Lumpur.

Dhana Siam Finance and Securities PLC, *Annual Report 1996*, Bangkok.

Guide to the Companies of Thailand (Thornton Publishing, 1996).

Gunn, G., 'Rentier capitalism in Negara Brunei Darussalam,' in Hewison, K. *et al.*, *Southeast Asia in the 1990s* (Allen & Unwin, 1993).

Hewison, K., 'The financial bourgeoisie in Thailand,' *Journal of Contemporary Asia*, vol. 11, 1981.

Hiscock, G., *Asia's Wealth Club* (Nicholas Brealey Publishing, 1997).
Siam Cement Group, *Annual Report 1996*, Bangkok.
Weaver, M., 'Our far-flung correspondents: In the Sultan's palace,' *The New Yorker*, October 7, 1991.

Chapter 13
President of the Country; Chairman of the Board
Backman, M., 'Make way for Habibie, Inc.,' *Asian Wall Street Journal*, February 17, 1998.
Backman, M., 'What now for Suharto, Inc.?,' *Asian Wall Street Journal*, May 26, 1998.
Bresnan, J., *Managing Indonesia: The Modern Political Economy* (Columbia University Press, 1993).
Schwarz, A., *A Nation in Waiting: Indonesia in the 1990s* (Allen & Unwin, 1994).

Chapter 14
Other Politicians; Other Businesses
Backman, M., 'The legacy of "Dr. M",' *Asian Wall Street Journal*, October 15, 1998.
Backman, M., 'Mahathir is no Suharto,' *Asian Wall Street Journal*, October 16–17, 1998.
Cheong, S., *Bumiputera Entrepreneurs in the KLSE* (Corporate Research Services, 1996).
Cragg, C., *The New Taipans* (Century, 1995).
East Asia Analytical Unit, *Overseas Chinese Business Networks in Asia* (Department of Foreign Affairs and Trade, Australia, Canberra, 1995).
Goldtron Holdings Ltd, *Annual Report 1996*, Hong Kong.
Gomez, E.T., *Political Business: Corporate Involvement of Malaysian Political Parties* (James Cook University of North Queensland, 1994).
Hewison, K., 'The financial bourgeoisie in Thailand,' *Journal of Contemporary Asia*, vol. 11, 1981.
Pasuk Phongpaichat and Chris Baker, *Thailand's Boom!* (Silkworm Books, 1996).

Chapter 15
Asian Eclipse and Beyond
Smith, M., *A Physician at the Court of Siam* (Oxford University Press, 1982).

Index